FOUNDATION
Accounting

tutorial

NVQ LEVEL
ACCOUNTING

David Cox
Michael Fardon

WALMLEY
Tel: 0121

are up to 28 days.
urned by the due
Library, via the in
es. Items in deman
se use a bookma

JUL 2016
Res

EP 2016

D0727493

OSBORNE

© David Cox, Michael Fardon 2000

All rights reserved. No part of this publication may be reproduced, stored in a retrieval system, or transmitted in any form or by any means, electronic, mechanical, photo-copying, recording or otherwise, without the prior consent of the copyright owners, or in accordance with the provisions of the Copyright, Designs and Patents Act 1988, or under the terms of any licence permitting limited copying issued by the Copyright Licensing Agency, 90 Tottenham Court Road, London W1P 9HE.

Published by Osborne Books Limited
Unit 1B Everoak Estate
Bromyard Road
Worcester WR2 5HN
Tel 01905 748071
Email books@osbornebooks.co.uk
Website www.osbornebooks.co.uk

Cover and page design by Hedgehog

Printed by the Bath Press, Bath

British Library Cataloguing in Publication Data
A catalogue record for this book is available from the British Library

ISBN 1 872962 19 X

CONTENTS

ACKNOWLEDGEMENTS

The authors wish to thank the following for their help with the reading and production of the book: Janet Brammer, Jean Cox, Catherine Fardon, Jon Moore and Roger Petheram.

Thanks are also due to the Association of Accounting Technicians for their generous help and advice to our authors and editors during the preparation of this text. Thanks also go to Barclays Bank, The Royal Bank of Scotland and Marks & Spencer plc for permission to use illustrations reproduced within the text. The publisher is grateful to the Inland Revenue for the provision of tax forms, which are Crown Copyright and are reproduced here with the permission of Her Majesty's Stationery Office.

THE AUTHORS

David Cox has more than twenty years' experience teaching accountancy students over a wide range of levels. Formerly with the Management and Professional Studies Department at Worcester College of Technology, he now lectures on a freelance basis and carries out educational consultancy work in accountancy studies. He is author and joint author of a number of textbooks in the areas of accounting, finance and banking.

Michael Fardon has extensive teaching experience of a wide range of banking, business and accountancy courses at Worcester College of Technology. He now specialises in writing business and financial texts and is General Editor at Osborne Books. He is also an educational consultant and has worked extensively in the areas of Key Skills and GNVQ curriculum development.

INTRODUCTION

Osborne tutorials

Foundation Accounting Tutorial has been written to provide a study resource for students taking courses based on the revised Year 2000 NVQ Level 2 Accounting standards such as the AAT Foundation and ACCA equivalent. *Foundation Accounting Tutorial* covers the first four NVQ units in a single volume and has been written in consultation with AAT.

The chapters of *Foundation Accounting Tutorial* contain:

- a clear text with worked examples and case studies
- a chapter summary and key terms to help with revision
- a wide range of student activities

Foundation Accounting Tutorial provides the student with the theoretical background to the subject while at the same time including plenty of opportunity to put theory into practice. Our aim has been to introduce the right amount of material at the right level, and not to overload the student with unnecessary detail. The text is useful for classroom use and also for distance learning students. It is with the latter type of student in mind that the answers to the student activities have been included at the back of the book.

Osborne workbooks

Foundation Accounting Tutorial has been written to be used alongside the *Foundation Accounting Workbook,* which contains

- extended student activities
- simulations
- Central Assessment practice material

The answers to these tasks and Assessments are included in a separate *Tutor Pack* which also includes a range of photocopiable documents.

If you would like a workbook, please telephone Osborne Books on 01905 748071 for details of mail ordering or contact the Osborne on-line shop (see below) which has a downloadable mail order form.

surfing with www.osbornebooks.co.uk

The Osborne Books website is constantly developing its range of facilities for tutors and students. Popular features include the free resource page and the on-line shop. Log on and try us!

COVERAGE OF NVQ SPECIFICATIONS

UNIT 1 RECORDING INCOME AND RECEIPTS

Element 1.1
Process Documents Relating to Goods and Services Supplied

performance criteria		chapter
i	Invoices and credit notes are prepared in accordance with organisational requirements and checked against source documents	2
ii	Calculations on invoices and credit notes are checked for accuracy	2
iii	Invoices and credit notes are correctly authorised and coded before being sent to customers	2
iv	Invoices and credit notes are entered into primary records according to organisational procedures	3
v	Entries are coded and recorded in the appropriate ledger	3
vi	Statements of account are prepared and sent to debtors	2
vii	Communications with customers regarding accounts are handled politely and effectively using the relevant source documents	2,14

Element 1.2 Receive and Record Receipts

performance criteria		
i	Receipts are checked against relevant supporting information	4
ii	Receipts are entered in appropriate accounting records	6
iii	Paying-in documents are correctly prepared and reconciled to relevant records	5
iv	Unusual features are identified and either resolved or referred to the appropriate person	4

UNIT 2 MAKING AND RECORDING PAYMENTS

Element 2.1
Process Documents Relating to Goods and Services Received

performance criteria		chapter
i	Suppliers' invoices and credit notes are checked against delivery notes, ordering documentation and evidence that goods or services have been received	7
ii	Totals and balances are correctly calculated and checked on suppliers' invoices	7
iii	Available discounts are identified and deducted	7
iv	Documents are correctly entered as primary records according to organisational procedures	8
v	Entries are coded and recorded in the appropriate ledger	8
vi	Discrepancies are identified and either resolved or referred to the appropriate person if outside own authority	7
vii	Communications with suppliers regarding accounts are handled politely and effectively	7,14

Element 2.2 Prepare Authorised Payments

performance criteria		
i	Payments are correctly calculated from relevant documentation	9,10,12
ii	Payments are scheduled and authorised by the appropriate person	9,10,12
iii	Queries are referred to the appropriate person	9,10,12
iv	Security and confidentiality are maintained according to organisational requirements	9,10,12

Element 2.3 Make and Record Payments

performance criteria		
i	The appropriate payment method is used in accordance with organisational procedures	9,10
ii	Payments are made in accordance with organisational processes and timescales	9,10
iii	Payments are entered into accounting records according to organisational procedures	10,11,13
iv	Queries are referred to the appropriate person	9,10
v	Security and confidentiality are maintained according to organisational requirements	9,10,11

UNIT 3

PREPARING LEDGER BALANCES AND AN INITIAL TRIAL BALANCE

Element 3.1 Balance Bank Transactions

performance criteria	chapter
i Details from the relevant primary documentation are recorded in the cash book	16
ii Totals and balances of receipts and payments are correctly calculated	16
iii Individual items on the bank statement and in the cash book are compared for accuracy	16
iv Discrepancies are identified and referred to the appropriate person	16

Element 3.2 Prepare Ledger Balances and Control Accounts

performance criteria	
i Relevant accounts are totalled	17
ii Control accounts are reconciled with the totals of the balance in the subsidiary ledger, where appropriate	17
iii Authorised adjustments are correctly processed and documented	17,18
iv Discrepancies arising from the reconciliation of control accounts are either resolved or referred to the appropriate person	17
v Documentation is stored securely and in line with the organisation's confidentiality requirements	17,18

Element 3.3 Draft an Initial Trial Balance

performance criteria	
i Information required for the initial trial balance is identified and obtained from the relevant sources	16,19
ii Relevant people are asked for advice when the necessary information is not available	16,19
iii The draft initial trial balance is prepared in line with the organisation's policies and procedures	16,19
iv Discrepancies are identified in the balancing process and referred to the appropriate person	16,19

UNIT 4 SUPPLYING INFORMATION FOR MANAGEMENT CONTROL

Element 4.1 Code and Extract Information

performance criteria		chapter
i	Appropriate cost centres and elements of costs are recognised	20
ii	Income and expenditure details are extracted from the relevant sources	20
iii	Income and expenditure are coded correctly	20
iv	Any problems in obtaining the necessary information are referred to the appropriate person	20
v	Errors are identified and reported to the appropriate person	20

Element 4.2 Provide Comparisons on Costs and Income

performance criteria		
i	Information requirements are clarified with the appropriate person	21
ii	Information extracted from a particular source is compared with actual results	21
iii	Discrepancies are identified	21
iv	Comparisons are provided to the appropriate person in the required format	21
v	Organisational requirements for confidentiality are strictly followed	21

Note
For the 'Knowledge and Understanding' requirements of the course, please refer to the index for individual subjects, eg contract, double-entry, and so on.

1 INTRODUCTION TO ACCOUNTING

this chapter covers . . .

Before studying the financial transactions and documents involved in buying, selling and making payments it is important to obtain an overall picture of the accounting system in which they operate. Every organisation is different, and no single accounting system will be exactly the same as another. This chapter provides a brief introduction to the different types of business organisation, the types of transactions they will carry out and the different ways in which they set up their accounting systems. The chapter also explains the ways in which many businesses are now using computer accounting systems.

Set out below are the NVQ competences covered by this chapter. As you will see they involve the 'Knowledge and Understanding' content of the course.

NVQ PERFORMANCE CRITERIA COVERED

KNOWLEDGE AND UNDERSTANDING – THE BUSINESS ENVIRONMENT

● *types of business transaction and documents involved*

KNOWLEDGE AND UNDERSTANDING – ACCOUNTING METHODS

● *double entry book-keeping*

● *methods of coding data*

● *operation of manual and computerised accounting systems*

● *relationship between the accounting system and the ledger*

KNOWLEDGE AND UNDERSTANDING – THE ORGANISATION

● *relevant understanding of the organisation's accounting systems and administrative systems and procedures*

● *the nature of the organisation's business transactions*

BUSINESS ORGANISATIONS

There are three main types of business organisation:

sole trader

A sole trader is an individual trading in his/her own name, or under a trading name.

The majority of businesses are sole traders. A sole trader is likely to be a 'jack of all trades'; he or she will be in charge of buying and selling goods and services, hiring and firing of staff and will often, unless an outside book-keeper is employed, 'keep the books' – ie maintain the accounts. This is important because if the sole trader becomes bankrupt – ie s/he owes more than s/he has – the sole trader's personal belongings may have to be sold to pay off the business debts.

partnership

A partnership is a group of individuals trading in business, aiming to make a profit.

The partnership is clearly a step up from the sole trader: more people are involved in the business and so more expertise and money will be available. Examples of partnerships (normally from 2 to 20 people) include solicitors, accountants, dentists and small building firms. Like sole traders, partners in a partnership are fully liable for business debts. If the business becomes bankrupt, so do all the partners. The need for maintaining the accounts therefore becomes very important. Often one of the partners will take responsibility for the financial management of the business. As with a sole trader, a book-keeper may also be employed.

limited company

A limited company is a separate legal body, owned by shareholders and managed by directors.

The largest business organisations are usually limited companies. A limited company is quite different from a sole trader and a partnership in that it exists as a business in its own right. It exists separately from its owners, the shareholders, who will not be called upon to pay up if the company goes into liquidation (goes 'bust'). The shareholders have what is known as *limited liability*: all they can lose is the money they have invested in the company. The need for the keeping of accounting records by limited companies is strictly regulated in law. Many limited companies will have an Accounts Department which will carry out all the accounting functions.

ORGANISATIONAL STRUCTURES AND ACCOUNTING

We have just seen that in a small sole trader business the owner is likely to carry out all the 'bookwork' as well as all the other functions of running the business. This is why small business owners work such long hours and also why they are motivated by their work – it is so varied. The diagram below shows the organisational structure of the functions of a typical sole trader. The structure is known as a 'flat' structure.

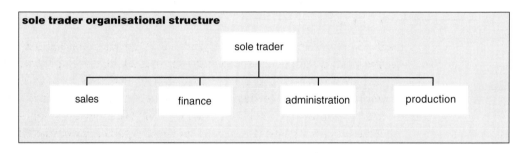

The organisational structure of a larger business such as a limited company is far more complex and 'taller', and as you will see from the diagram below, involves many more staff. Accounting jobs in a larger organisation may therefore be less varied but will allow greater specialisation. Nevertheless, as we will see in the Case Study on the next page, the transactions carried out are essentially the same: buying, selling, settling expenses, paying wages.

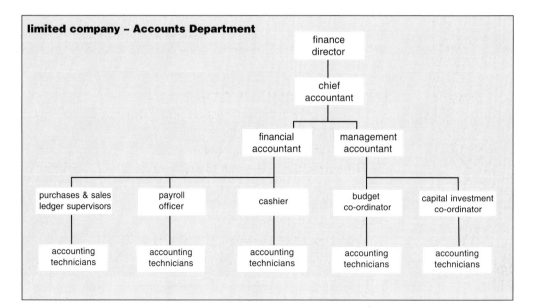

ACCOUNTING TRANSACTIONS

All businesses carry out transactions which need to be recorded in some form of manual or computerised accounting system. The most common transactions include:

- selling goods and services
- making purchases and paying expenses
- paying money into the bank and making payments from the bank account
- paying wages

If you consider all the activities undertaken during a working day, you will see that there are many different transactions taking place, all of which need recording accurately. Read through the following Case Studies which present two businesses: Stan Taylor Plumbing – a small 'one-person' business (which employs two assistants) and Osborne Electronics Limited – a larger limited company business which supplies computers and business machines and employs eight people.

CASE STUDY

STAN TAYLOR PLUMBING

sale of goods and services
- installation of lavatory for Fred Lush, £250 paid in cash, receipt given by Stan
- repair of burst pipe at City Architect's office, invoice for £95.50 issued to City Council, payment to be made in 30 days' time (normally a cheque will be posted to Stan)

purchases and payment of expenses
- settle account with builders merchant, a £1,750 cheque issued by Stan for items bought over the last six weeks
- buy new van, pay £12,000 by cheque
- buy diesel fuel for van, pay £18.50 by cheque

visit to the bank
- pay in cheques totalling £1,753.95
- cash a cheque, £250, for wages for employees
- query charges on the bank statement

pay wages
- complete documentation, including wage slips, and pay employees £250

OSBORNE ELECTRONICS LIMITED

sale of goods and services

- sale of fax machine to Merton Textiles, for £750, cheque received with order
- installation of photocopier for Mereford Tourist Office, cost £2,450, invoice issued to Tourist Office, payment to be made in 30 days' time (normally a cheque will be posted to Osborne)

purchases and payment of expenses

- pay for colour laser printer for use in the office, a £2,750 cheque is issued by Osborne Electronics
- settle account with Nippon Importers for computer software, a £5,675 cheque issued
- issue cheque for £3,500 for insurance premium due

visit to the National Bank plc

- pay in cheques totalling £10,645.50, money received from customers
- cash a cheque, £2,500, for the week's wages

pay wages

- complete documentation, make up pay packets, totalling £2,500

RECORDING FINANCIAL TRANSACTIONS

Although the two businesses in the Case Study are very different in size and in what they do, the types of transactions fall into distinct categories:

- *Cash transactions* – transactions which involve immediate payment, eg Fred Lush's loo and the sale of a fax machine to Merton Textiles. Note that 'cash' payment means 'immediate' payment and can include payment by cheque as well as payment using banknotes.
- *Credit transactions* – transactions which involve payment at a date later than the original transaction, eg the City Architect's burst pipe and the installation of the photocopier for Mereford Tourist Office.

The following transactions can be for cash or for credit:

- *Capital transactions* – the purchase (or sale) of items which are permanently used by the business, eg Stan's van and Osborne's colour laser printer.
- *Revenue transactions* – items of income or expense which occur on a day-to-day basis, eg Stan's diesel bill, Osborne's insurance premiums.

As you will see from the very varied items in the Case Study, recording financial transactions is a complex business. You have to keep track of:

- who owes you what, and when the payment is due
- amounts that you owe, and when the payment is due

You have to record what you pay into the bank and what you draw out. You need to record the amounts paid in wages to each employee. We will not at this stage explore in any detail how these transactions are recorded – such areas will be covered later in the book – but it is worth noting that if these transactions are not recorded accurately, the owner of the business and other interested parties such as the bank manager and the tax authorities will not know how the business is progressing!

ACCOUNTING SYSTEMS

The accounting system of a business is the system for recording information from documents (such as invoices and receipts) into the accounting records, checking that the information has been recorded correctly, and then presenting the information in a way which enables the owner(s) of the business and other interested people to review its progress.

Most businesses use an accounting system based on the double-entry book-keeping system, whereby each financial transaction is recorded in the accounts *twice*. Some small businesses will use a single-entry system, where each transaction is entered once only in a cash book, which records receipts and payments of money. Accounting records are usually kept in one of two forms: handwritten (manual) records or on a computer system.

handwritten accounts – the integrated ledger

This is the traditional method of keeping 'the books', particularly for the smaller business. It is relatively straightforward and cheap to operate. The main record is the *ledger* – a book into which each business transaction is entered by hand into individual accounts. This collection of accounts is known as the *integrated ledger*.

double-entry book-keeping and coding

Double-entry book-keeping involves making two entries in the accounts for each transaction: for instance, if you sell some goods and receive a cheque, you will make an entry in the sales account to record the sale, and an entry in the bank account to record the receipt of a cheque.

If you are operating a manual accounting system you will make the two entries by hand, if you are operating a computer accounting system you will make one entry on the keyboard, but indicate to the machine where the other entry is to be made, by means of a numerical code. Accurate coding is important in the efficient operation of any accounting system.

accounts

The sources for the entries you make are the financial documents. The ledger into which you make the entries is divided into separate accounts, eg a separate account for sales, purchases, each type of business expense, each customer, each supplier, and so on. Each account is given a specific name, and a number code for reference purposes. In a computer system, the accounts are held as data files on a disk, and each account becomes a computer record with its own reference number code.

division of the integrated ledger

Because of the number of accounts involved, the integrated ledger is divided into different ledgers, both in manual systems and also in computer systems:

- *sales ledger* – records of sales made to customers, and payments received at a later date (ie not cash sales) – each record shows the amount owed by a particular customer (debtor)

- *purchases ledger* – records of purchases from suppliers, and payments made at a later date (ie not cash purchases) – each record shows the amount owed to a particular supplier (creditor)

- *cash book* – a record of cash and bank transactions (a cash book is the main accounting record for the single-entry system mentioned earlier)

- *general (or nominal) ledger* – records all other transactions of the business, such as assets (things owned), expenses (the overheads of the business, eg wages, rent paid), drawings (the amount taken out of the business by the owner), loans to the business (eg by a bank), and the owner's capital (the amount invested in the business by the owner) – this is the *main ledger*, which also includes the cash book

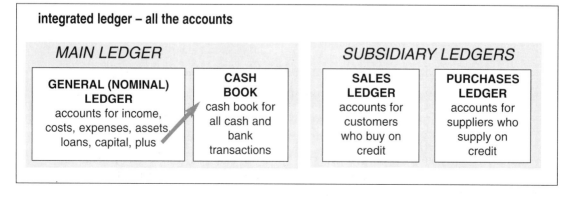

integrated ledger – all the accounts

MAIN LEDGER		SUBSIDIARY LEDGERS	
GENERAL (NOMINAL) LEDGER accounts for income, costs, expenses, assets, loans, capital, plus	**CASH BOOK** cash book for all cash and bank transactions	**SALES LEDGER** accounts for customers who buy on credit	**PURCHASES LEDGER** accounts for suppliers who supply on credit

trial balance

Double-entry book-keeping, because it involves making two entries for each transaction, is open to error. What if the book-keeper writes £45 in one account and £54 in another? The trial balance effectively checks the entries made over a given period of time and will pick up most errors. The trial balance sets out the balances of all the double-entry accounts, ie the totals of the accounts for a certain period. As well as being an arithmetic check, it is used to help in the preparation of financial statements – the final accounts of the business.

financial statements (final accounts)

The financial statements (final accounts) of a business comprise the profit and loss statement and the balance sheet.

WHAT THE PROFIT AND LOSS STATEMENT SHEET SHOWS

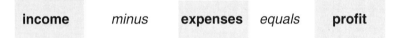

income   *minus*   **expenses**   *equals*   **profit**

The profit and loss statement of a business shows the day-to-day ('revenue') income a business has received over a given period for goods sold or services provided. It also sets out the expenses incurred – the cost of producing the product, and the overheads (eg wages, administration, rent, and so on). The difference between income and expenses is the profit of the business. If expenses are greater than income, then a loss has been made. The profit (or loss) belongs to the owner(s) of the business. The figures for sales, purchases, and expenses are taken from the double-entry system.

WHAT THE BALANCE SHEET SHOWS

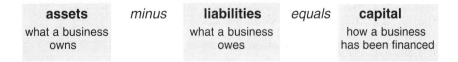

| **assets** | *minus* | **liabilities** | *equals* | **capital** |
| what a business owns | | what a business owes | | how a business has been financed |

The balance sheet of a business gives a 'snapshot' of the business at a particular date – eg the end of the accounting period of the business. It is prepared from the accounting records and shows:

assets	what the business owns – eg premises, vehicles, computers, stock of goods for resale, debtors (money owed by customers), money in the bank
liabilities	what the business owes – eg bank loans, creditors (money owed to suppliers)
capital	where the money to finance the business has come from – eg the owner's investment, profits made by the business

The equation shown on the previous page –

assets minus liabilities equals capital

is known as the 'accounting equation.' Now study the diagram below which summarises the way the accounting system operates from documents through to profit and loss statement and balance sheet.

prime documents

processing of documents relating to purchases, sales, payments and receipts

accounting records

recording financial transactions in the accounting system using primary accounting records (eg day books) and the double-entry book-keeping system

trial balance

the extraction of figures from all the double-entry accounts to check their arithmetical accuracy in the form of a list, known as the trial balance

financial statements

production from the double-entry accounts of:

• profit and loss statement

• balance sheet

together known as the 'final accounts'

COMPUTER ACCOUNTING SYSTEMS

facilities

A typical computer accounting program will offer a number of facilities:

- on-screen input and printout of sales invoices
- updating of customer accounts in the sales ledger
- recording of suppliers' invoices
- automatic updating of supplier accounts in the purchases ledger
- recording of bank receipts
- making payments to suppliers and for expenses
- automatic updating of the general (main) ledger
- automatic adjustment of stock records

Payroll can also be computerised – often on a separate program.

management reports

A computer accounting program can provide instant reports for management, for example:

- an aged debtors' summary – who owes you what and when
- trial balance, profit and loss statement and balance sheet
- stock valuation
- VAT Return
- payroll analysis

advantages of a computer accounting program

- it saves time
- it saves money
- it is accurate
- it provides management with a clear and up-to-date picture of what is happening

types of accounting program

The type of computer accounting program used by a business will depend on the size and needs of that business. Commercially available packages range from the simple 'cash trader' program, which assumes that the business keeps only a cash book, to the full ledger system, based on double-entry principles, used by larger businesses.

'Cash trader' programs are for the business which needs to keep track of money received and money spent, and to analyse expenditure; they are only really suitable for small businesses which deal on a cash-only basis. As this book deals with double-entry book-keeping and trading on credit terms we will deal exclusively with the ledger system of computer accounting.

computer accounting – ledger system

The 'Ledger', as we have seen, is a term used to describe the way the accounts of the business are grouped into different sections:

- **sales ledger**, containing the accounts of debtors (customers)
- **purchases ledger**, containing the accounts of creditors (suppliers)
- **cash books**, containing the main cash book and the petty cash book
- **nominal ledger** (also called **general ledger**) is the **main ledger** containing the remaining accounts, eg expenses (including purchases), income (including sales), assets, loans, stock, VAT

A diagram explaining these ledgers is shown on the opposite page. The interface of a ledger computer accounting system is designed to be user-friendly in software such as Windows. Look at the toolbar of the opening screen of a Sage Windows accounting system shown below and then read the notes printed underneath. Note that a toolbar is a series of icons (pictures) showing what the program can do; the icons can be 'clicked on' to access those activities.

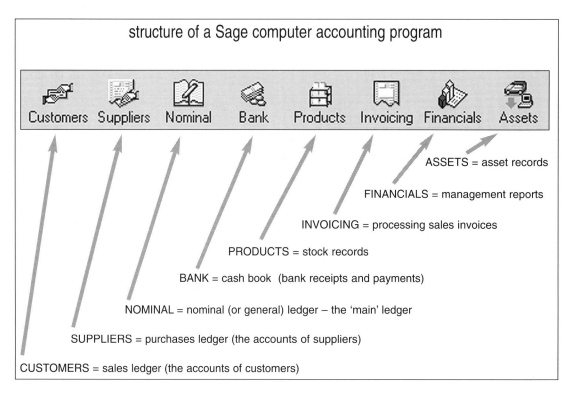

structure of a Sage computer accounting program

Customers Suppliers Nominal Bank Products Invoicing Financials Assets

ASSETS = asset records

FINANCIALS = management reports

INVOICING = processing sales invoices

PRODUCTS = stock records

BANK = cash book (bank receipts and payments)

NOMINAL = nominal (or general) ledger – the 'main' ledger

SUPPLIERS = purchases ledger (the accounts of suppliers)

CUSTOMERS = sales ledger (the accounts of customers)

computerised ledgers – an integrated system

A computerised ledger system is fully integrated. This means that when a business transaction is input on the computer it is recorded in a number of different records at the same time. For example, when a sales invoice for goods that you are selling is entered on the screen and the ledgers are 'updated' an integrated program will:

- record the amount of the invoice in the customer's account in the sales ledger
- record the amount of the invoice in the sales account in the nominal ledger
- reduce the stock of goods held in the stock records

The diagram below shows how the ledgers link with the nominal ledger which, in this case, is also linked to a payroll processing program. (Note: for the sake of simplicity we have ignored VAT here).

On the following pages we look at some of the screens of a Sage system.

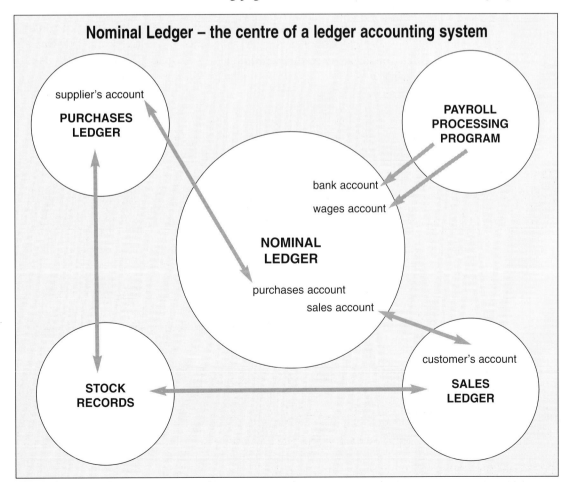

Nominal Ledger – the centre of a ledger accounting system

supplier's account

PURCHASES LEDGER

PAYROLL PROCESSING PROGRAM

bank account

wages account

NOMINAL LEDGER

purchases account

sales account

customer's account

SALES LEDGER

STOCK RECORDS

CUSTOMERS – SALES LEDGER

'Customers' on the toolbar represents the sales ledger – the accounts of customers to whom the business sells its products.

The toolbar of 'Customers' is shown below.

As you can see, there are a number of icons representing facilities available in 'Customers':

● **Record** brings up the screen which enables you to add, view and edit customer names and addresses. A typical record screen is shown below.

Details	Defaults	Sales	Graphs	Activity	Memo

A/C	2502 [Q] New Account		☐ Account on Hold
Name	The Trading Post	Delivery Address	

Street1	45 New Street
Street2	I
Town	Mereford
County	
Post Code	MR1 2JF

Contact Name	Henry Ford
Telephone	01908 562389
Fax	01908 562907

V.A.T. Reg. No	010293763	Customer Balance	0.00

● **Activity** shows you the transactions – invoices, credit notes, payments – which have taken place on individual customer accounts.

● **Aged** produces an aged debtors' summary, a list of customer account balances showing which accounts have been outstanding for 30 days, 60 days, 90 days or more. This is very useful in credit control (chasing up money that the business is owed).

● **Invoices** and **Credits** enable you to post to customer accounts invoices or credit notes that you have prepared by hand and which have not been generated by the computer accounting program. It is therefore not used for producing documents which can be printed out.

- If the computer is on-line, **Phone** enables the computer to dial automatically any customer you select from the screen.
- **Labels**, **Letters**, **Statements** and **Reports** enable you to print these documents for any customers that you select.

SUPPLIERS – PURCHASES LEDGER

'Suppliers' on the toolbar represents the purchases ledger – the accounts of suppliers from whom the business buys its materials and stock.

The toolbar of 'Suppliers' is shown below.

You will see that the icons on the Suppliers toolbar are exactly the same as the items on the 'Customers' toolbar and provide similar facilities. The supplier record screen is shown below.

NOMINAL LEDGER

The Nominal icon on the opening toolbar represents the Nominal Ledger. Click on it and the Nominal Ledger toolbar will appear.

Remember that the Nominal Ledger contains many of the commonly used accounts, eg bank, sales, purchases, expense accounts, assets, loans, capital, VAT.

- **Record**, as with 'Customers' and 'Suppliers,' contains details of the accounts held. Most computer accounting programs will be supplied with the nominal accounts that you will need already installed and ready for use; these are known as the 'default accounts' and can be used or changed as you wish.
- **Activity** provides details of the transactions on the individual accounts.
- **Journals** allows you to make 'one-off' entries between nominal accounts (see Chapter 18 for the double-entry equivalent in a manual accounting system).

- **Prepay** and **Accruals** allow the accounts to be adjusted for prepaid bills (prepayments) or bills paid in arrears (accruals) so that the expense appears in the profit and loss statement for the correct period.

- **Accounts** provides you with a 'Chart of Accounts' which places the nominal accounts in the correct part of the Ledger so that reports such as the profit and loss statement can be printed out with the accounts in the right section. When you set up the computer accounting system for the first time, the nominal accounts are normally already set up in the right place. Look at the illustration of the 'Chart of Accounts' below.

- **Reports** available in the Nominal Ledger include budget and performance reports.

Edit Chart of Accounts

Title

Default Layout of Accounts

Category Type

Category Type	Description
Sales	Sales
Purchases	Purchases
Direct Expenses	Direct Expenses
Overheads	Overheads
Fixed Assets	Fixed Assets
Current Assets	Current Assets
Current Liabilities	Current Liabilities
Capital & Reserves	Capital & Reserves

Category Account

Sales	Low	High
PRODUCT SALES	4000	4099
EXPORT SALES	4100	4199
SALES OF ASSETS	4200	4299
OTHER SALES	4900	4999

BANK

Bank

The Bank icon on the opening toolbar enables you to process payments in and out of the bank account. It also enables you to carry out some of the regular accounting procedures involving the bank.

Record Reconcile Payment Supplier Receipt Customer Transfer Recurring Statement Reports

- **Record** enables you to set up new bank accounts and edit existing ones
- **Supplier** should be selected when you are making a payment for an outstanding invoice on an account in the purchases ledger

- **Customer** should be selected when you are receiving payment onto the bank account from one of your customers in the sales ledger
- **Payment** and **receipt** are used to record payments you make and money received which do not involve invoices or which are cash (ie non-credit) transactions.

Note that when you input these payment and receipt transactions you are asked by the computer to enter a nominal account **code** which will analyse the payment for you, eg code 7211 when you pay a gas bill, 4900 when you receive interest on the bank account. The screen below shows a typical bank payment being made, in this case payment on Stationery Account 7500.

Bank Payments									

| Bank | Bank current account | | | | | Tax Rate | | 17.50 | |
| N/C Name | Stationery | | | | | Batch Total | | 53.46 | |

Bank	Date	Ref	N/C	Dept	Details	Net	Tc	Tax	
1200	17/12/1998	234234	7500	3	Copy paper	45.50	T1	7.96	

		45.50			7.96

PRODUCTS

The Products facility enables you to see what you have in stock and what has been sold.

The Products toolbar is shown below.

Each stock item is given a specific stock code and can be given a category number. This forms part of the coding system which you will use with when you prepare and check invoices.

INVOICING

Invoicing

Invoicing will allow you to enter invoice details on the computer screen and then to print out the invoices. Most businesses process invoices (and other documents) in batches: they will input a group (batch) of invoices and then print them out together in one run, ready for checking. The Invoicing toolbar is shown below.

| Product | Service | Credit | SrvCredit | Print | Update | Reports |

The toolbar shows that you can produce a Product invoice for an item sold which has a specific product code. If you are invoicing something which has no product code, for example a service or a 'one-off' item you use a Service invoice.

The invoicing function Credit also allows you to produce credit notes for items such as returns. The function SrvCredit allows you to produce credit notes for service invoices, eg a refund for an overcharged service provided.

An example of an invoice input screen is shown below; the printed invoice from this screen is illustrated on the next page.

| Invoice Details | Order Details | Footer Details | Payment Details |

R Patel & Co
Phoenix Business Park
Southampton Road
Salisbury
Wilts
SN1 9LX

Invoice No.	27398
Invoice Date	17/12/1998
Order No.	SA 234
A/C Ref	997

Product Code	Description	Qty	Net	V.A.T.
EDB	Enigma 35 (black)	20.00	119.00	20.83

Item 2 of 2

Totals	119.00	20.83
Carriage	0.00	0.00
Gross		139.83

Enigma Limited

34 Packhorse Road
Mereford MR2 7YH
Tel 01908 433927 Fax 01908 433812 email edgar@goblin.co.uk
UAT Reg 727 7262 01

INVOICE

R Patel & Co
Phoenix Business Park
Southampton Road
Salisbury
Wilts
SN1 9LX

invoice no.	27398
invoice date	17/12/1998
order no.	SA234
account ref.	997

quantity	description	discount %	net amount	VAT amount
20	Enigma 35 (black)	0.00	119.00	20.83

Payment 30 days net

Total net	119.00
Total tax	20.83
Carriage	00.00
Invoice total	139.83

PAYROLL PROCESSING

links with the main accounting system

If you refer back to the diagram on page 13 you will see that there is a payroll processing function which is linked into the Nominal (main) Ledger. Payroll software programs are available from suppliers such as Sage and are commonly used by businesses which also run computer accounting programs. Payroll programs are normally separate programs which link with accounts in the Nominal Ledger such as bank, wages, Inland Revenue and pension contribution accounts. Payroll software programs can also run completely independently if the business has no computerised Nominal Ledger.

facilities of a payroll processing program

Programs such as Sage Payroll run on Windows and provide a user-friendly interface. They enable the business to:

- calculate the gross pay (pay before deductions) for each employee
- calculate all the deductions due to the Inland Revenue
- process pension payments
- calculate the net pay (pay after deductions) for each employee
- print payslips and cheques, and prepare details of BACS transfers
- process all the paperwork needed for returns and payments of income tax and National Insurance made to the Inland Revenue

Processing payroll manually is a time-consuming and expensive task, involving lengthy calculations and form-filling. Once a computerised system is set up it will save a business both time and money.

data needed for a payroll processing program

The data needed by a computer payroll processing package is straightforward, but it must be accurate. It includes:

- employee records (see the screen on the top of the next page)
- up-to-date income tax and National Insurance rates

Each time the payroll is run, details are entered on-screen (see the bottom of the next page) for:

- employee hours, overtime and other extra payments
- deductions such as pensions

Personal	Employment	Banking

Reference	6	N.I. Number	AB763491B
Title	Miss Initials A	Works No.	6
Surname	Brown		
Forenames	Angela	Sex	Female
Address	66 Grassfield Crescent Mereford	Marital Status	Single
		Date of Birth	29/06/1981
Postcode	MR4 2JX Director □	Telephone	

On Hold □

Payroll processing package – employee record screen

Payments	Deductions	Attachments	Process

Payment Name	Tax	Hours	Rate	Amount
Casual	Pre	20.0000	6.0000	120.00

Total Gross Pay
120.00

PAYE
0.00

NIC
6.93

Net Pay
113.07

Total Payments 120.00

Payroll processing package – payroll deduction screen

ACCOUNTING SYSTEMS – CHECKING AND AUDITING

checking manual and computer data

Complete accuracy is essential in accounting. Mistakes in money amounts can result in suppliers being paid too much, the record of the bank balance in the cash book being wrong and, very importantly, employees' wages being wrong! An efficient business will therefore institute checking procedures for all calculations and listings of figures. Checking is equally important if a computer accounting system is used. Computers are very accurate, but only as accurate as the input data: the 'garbage in, garbage out' principle applies!

The checking may be carried out by employees at the same level of seniority, or it may be carried out by a supervisor. This type of checking will form part of the day-to-day procedures of the business, and will often be shown by the initials of the checker and date of checking.

auditors

Another form of checking is *auditing* this is carried out by *auditors* – people who do not normally carry out the job in question, and may not even be employees of the business. Auditors are normally employed by larger limited companies and similar-sized organisations, eg local authorities, because they are required to do so by law. Smaller businesses such as sole traders, partnerships and smaller limited companies do not have this legal obligation and so they rarely use auditors.

There are two types of auditor:

- internal auditors
- external auditors

Internal auditors are employees of the business being audited. They are concerned with the internal checking and control procedures of the business: for example control of cash, signing of cheques, authorising of purchases. In a limited company the internal auditors normally report directly to the Finance Director.

External auditors are independent of the business which is being checked (audited). External audit is still the 'bread and butter' business of many firms of accountants. The most common form of external audit is the audit of larger limited companies which is required by the Companies Acts. The auditors, when they have completed the audit, have by law to sign a declaration stating that the accounts represent a 'true and fair view' of the state of the company. The external auditors report to the shareholders (owners) of the limited company, and are appointed by them.

CHAPTER SUMMARY

- There are three main types of business organisation: sole trader, partnership and limited company.

- Larger businesses tend to have more complex structures than small businesses – the accounting jobs will be carried out by a greater number of specialised staff.

- All types of business carry out the same basic types of financial transaction – buying, selling, banking, paying wages; all these transactions need to be accurately recorded and coded.

- Accounting systems within a business may be handwritten (manual) or computerised; they may be single entry (for the smaller business) or, more commonly, double-entry – which involves two entries being made for each transaction.

- Financial transactions are recorded in separate 'accounts' which are grouped in 'ledgers'; this system is true of both handwritten and computerised accounts. The accuracy of the system is checked in a listing of balances known as the 'trial balance'.

- The accounting system is used to produce the financial statements of the business – the profit and loss statement and the balance sheet.

- Computer accounting systems have many advantages including speed of operation and accuracy. The main accounting advantage is that they are normally integrated – one entry on the keyboard will automatically change accounting records in different parts of the system.

- The accuracy of the accounting records should be checked regularly by the accounting staff. In the case of larger businesses it may also be checked by internal and external auditors.

KEY TERMS

sole trader	an individual trading on his or her own
partnership	a group of individuals trading in business
limited company	a separate legal body, owned by shareholders
cash transactions	transactions which involve immediate payment
credit transactions	transactions which involve payment at a later date
capital transactions	purchase (or sale) of items which are in permanent use by the business
revenue transactions	items of income or expense which occur on a day-to-day basis
double-entry book-keeping	an accounting system which involves two entries being made in the accounts for every transaction

KEY TERMS (continued)

coding	an identifying reference number or letter code given to accounting transactions, eg an account number, a supplier reference
ledger	a sub-division of the accounting system (strictly speaking a 'ledger' is a book, but the term is still used in computer accounting systems)
trial balance	a listing of the accounts in the accounting system, used to check the accuracy of that system
profit and loss statement	a financial statement showing the profit or loss made by the business in a given period
balance sheet	a financial statement showing what a business owns and owes
assets	items the business owns
liabilities	items the business owes
capital	where the money used to finance the business comes from
accounting equation	assets minus liabilities equals capital
integrated system	the feature of a computer accounting system which enables it to change records in different ledgers from the input of a single transaction
auditor	a person who independently checks the accuracy of the accounting records

STUDENT ACTIVITIES

1.1   A business which is owned by shareholders is known as:

(a)   a sole trader business

(b)   a partnership

(c)   a limited company

(d)   a limited partnership

Answer (a) or (b) or (c) or (d)

1.2   In each of the following cases, state whether the transaction is a **capital** transaction or a **revenue** transaction:

(a)   payment of wages by a bus company

(b)   purchase of a car by an advertising company

(c)   purchase of a car for a customer by a Ford dealer

(d)   sale of a table by a furniture store

(e)   sale of office furniture by a Ford dealer moving premises

1.3   State whether the following are **cash** transactions or **credit** transactions:

(a)   an office buys stationery and settles immediately by cash

(b)   an office buys stationery and settles immediately by cheque

(c)   an office buys stationery and pays thirty days later on an invoice

(d)   a petrol station sells petrol and is paid by cheque

(e)   a business sells goods and is paid thirty days later in cash

1.4   A person starting a new business is not clear about the meaning of the word 'ledger'. What exactly does it mean?

1.5   Write out the accounting equation. Explain the items which make up the two sides of the equation. What would happen to the capital of the business if the assets increased and the liabilities stayed the same (eg if a company revalued its premises)?

1.6   List the advantages and any disadvantages of installing and using a computer accounting system.

1.7   Explain in two short paragraphs:

(a)   why it is important to check financial transactions

(b)   what auditors do

1.8   The three examples set out below are mistakes that can and do happen in business. Read them through and state in each case what the consequences of each error might be.

(a)   The overtime sheet given to the accounting assistant who calculates the wages has not been checked. Jo Isback's fifteen hours of overtime have not been recorded on it.

(b)   Because of a computer input error a customer has been billed for 1,000 computer disks instead of 100 computer disks.

(c)   The bank has deducted £5,000 from the business bank account by mistake and has not noticed the error.

2 DOCUMENTS FOR GOODS AND SERVICES SUPPLIED

this chapter covers . . .

This chapter examines the procedures involved when a business sells goods or services on credit. The essential point here is that the business wants to get its money on time and it wants to get the right amount. It can achieve these aims through the efficient use and monitoring of business documents. The chapter covers the areas of:

- the use of business documents – quotations, purchase order, invoice, delivery note, returns note, credit note, statement

- the calculation of document totals and discounts

- the calculation of Value Added Tax (VAT)

- the coding of documents

- the checking and authorisation of documents

NVQ PERFORMANCE CRITERIA COVERED

unit 1: RECORDING INCOME AND RECEIPTS

element 1

process documents relating to goods and services supplied

- invoices and credit notes are prepared in accordance with organisational requirements and checked against source documents

- calculations on invoices and credit notes are checked for accuracy

- invoices and credit notes are correctly authorised and coded before being sent to customers

- statements of account are prepared and sent to debtors

- communications with customers regarding accounts are handled politely and effectively using the relevant source documents – (see also Chapter 14)

FINANCIAL DOCUMENTS

When a business sells goods or services it will use a number of different documents (mentioned in the diagram below). A single sales transaction of course involves both seller *and* buyer. In this chapter we look at the situation from the point of view of the *seller* of the goods or services. The transaction from the point of view of the buyer is dealt with in Chapter 9. Documents which are often used in the *selling* process include:

- the price *quotation* which the seller may be asked to provide
- the *purchase order* which the seller receives from the buyer
- the *delivery note* which goes with the goods from the seller to the buyer
- the *invoice* which lists the goods and tells the buyer what is owed
- the *credit note* which is sent to the buyer if any refund is due
- a *returns note* which is sent with any goods that are being returned
- the *statement* sent by the seller to remind the buyer what is owed

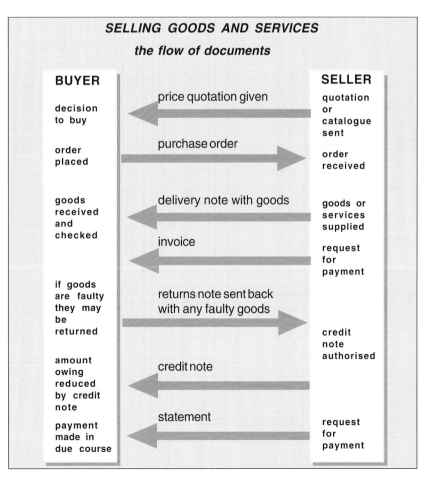

the flow of documents

Before you read the Case Study, examine the diagram set out on the previous page. Down the columns representing the buyer and the seller are various activities which lead to transactions which in turn generate documents.

CASE STUDY

COOL SOCKS – A SALES TRANSACTION

situation

Cool Socks Limited manufactures fashion socks in a variety of colours. It supplies a number of different customers, including Trends, a fashion store in Broadfield. In this Case Study, Trends places an order for 100 pairs of socks with Cool Socks. The socks are delivered, but some are found to be faulty, so some of the socks have to be returned. The Case Study looks in detail at the documents involved.

THE PRICE QUOTATION

Before placing the order the buyer at Trends will need to find out the price of the socks. This can be done by consulting Cool Socks' catalogue, or by means of a written or telephoned enquiry, or, if Cool Socks has a web page, by an on-line enquiry. Cool Socks *may* provide a written quotation for the socks if they are requested to do so, although this procedure is more common with higher value orders. A written quotation might look like this:

─────── QUOTATION ───────
COOL SOCKS LIMITED
Unit 45 Elgar Estate, Broadfield, BR7 4ER
Tel 01908 765314 Fax 01908 765951 Email toni@cool.u-net.com
VAT REG GB 0745 4672 76

Trends 4 Friar Street Broadfield BR1 3RF	date	19 09 2001

Thank you for your enquiry of 17 September 2001. We are pleased to quote as follows:

100 pairs Toebar socks (blue)@ £2.36 a pair, excluding VAT.

M Arnold

Sales Department

CASE STUDY

PURCHASE ORDER – THE SOCKS ARE ORDERED

The buyer at Trends, once she has accepted the quoted price will post or fax the authorised purchase order shown below. The order will have been typed out in the office, or produced on a computer accounting program.

Note the following details:

- each purchase order has a specific reference number – this is useful for filing and quoting on later documents such as invoices and statements; this reference number is an example of *coding* in accounting

- the catalogue number of the goods required is stated in the product code column – this number can be obtained from the supplier's catalogue – this number is a further example of coding

- the quantity of the goods required is stated in the quantity column – socks are obviously supplied in pairs!

- the description of the goods is set out in full

- the price does not need to be stated, although some purchase orders will include a price

- the purchase order is signed and dated by the person in charge of purchasing – without this authorisation the supplier is unlikely to supply the goods (the order will probably be returned!)

- if Trends had a separate warehouse for storage of its clothes the purchase order will state the address of the warehouse so that the goods could be sent there; in this case the socks will be delivered direct to the shop

- Cool Socks may respond to the purchase order with an *acknowledgement of order*

Trends	**PURCHASE ORDER**

4 Friar Street
Broadfield
BR1 3RF
Tel 01908 761234 Fax 01908 761987
VAT REG GB 0745 8383 56

Cool Socks Limited,	purchase order no	47609
Unit 45 Elgar Estate,	date	25 09 01
Broadfield,		
BR7 4ER		

product code	quantity	description
45B	100 pairs	Blue Toebar socks

AUTHORISED   signature......*D Signer*...date.........*25/09/01*.........

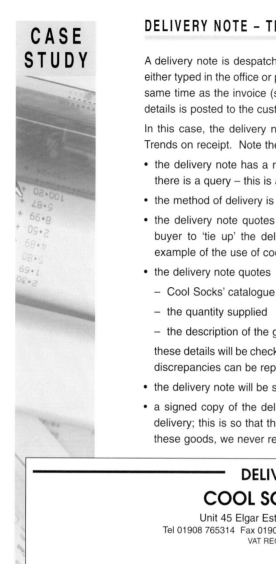

DELIVERY NOTE – THE SOCKS ARE DELIVERED

A delivery note is despatched with the goods when the order is ready. It is normally either typed in the office or printed out by a computer accounting program, often at the same time as the invoice (see next page). Sometimes an *advice note* with the same details is posted to the customer to advise that the goods have been sent.

In this case, the delivery note travels with the socks, and a copy will be signed by Trends on receipt. Note the following details:

- the delivery note has a numerical reference, useful for filing and later reference if there is a query – this is an example of coding
- the method of delivery is stated – here the delivery is by parcel carrier
- the delivery note quotes the purchase order number – 47609 – this enables the buyer to 'tie up' the delivery with the original purchase order – this is another example of the use of coding
- the delivery note quotes
  - Cool Socks' catalogue reference 45B
  - the quantity supplied
  - the description of the goods, but no price – it is not needed at this stage

  these details will be checked against the goods themselves straightaway so that any discrepancies can be reported without delay
- the delivery note will be signed and dated by the person receiving the goods
- a signed copy of the delivery note is normally retained by the carrier as proof of delivery; this is so that the buyer cannot say at a later date "We are not paying for these goods, we never received them!"

—— DELIVERY NOTE ——

COOL SOCKS LIMITED

Unit 45 Elgar Estate, Broadfield, BR7 4ER
Tel 01908 765314 Fax 01908 765951 Email toni@cool.u-net.com
VAT REG GB 0745 4672 76

Trends 4 Friar Street Broadfield BR1 3RF		delivery note no	68873
		delivery method	Lynx Parcels
		your order	47609
		date	02 10 01

product code	quantity	description
45B	100 pairs	Blue Toebar socks

Received

signature............*V Williams*............name (capitals).*V WILLIAMS*............date.*5/10/01*

CASE STUDY

INVOICE – THE SELLER REQUESTS PAYMENT

The invoice is the trading document which is sent by the seller to the buyer stating how much is owed by the buyer for a particular delivery of goods.

The invoice, like the delivery note, is prepared in the supplier's (seller's) office, and is either typed or produced on a computer printer using a computer accounting program. Invoices produced by different organisations will vary to some extent in terms of detail, but their basic layout will always be the same. The invoice prepared by Cool Socks Limited – illustrated on page 33 – is typical of a modern typed or computer printed document. An invoice will normally be printed as part of a multiple set of documents which might include the delivery note, possibly an advice note sent by post to the buyer, and always a copy invoice for the seller's own records. The copy invoice will normally be filed in numerical order (see 'references' below). If a computer accounting program is used, the invoice can, of course, be called up on screen, referenced by its invoice number.

Note the following details, and refer to the invoice on page 33.

addresses
The invoice shows the address:

- of the seller/supplier of the goods – Cool Socks Limited
- where the invoice should be sent – to Trends
- where the goods are to be sent – if it is different from the invoice address

references
There are a number of important references on the invoice:

- the numerical reference of the invoice itself – 787923
- the account number allocated to Trends by the seller – 3993 – possibly for use in the seller's computer accounting program
- the original reference number on the purchase order sent by Trends – 47609 – which will enable the shop to 'tie up' the invoice with the original order
- the VAT registration number (if the business is registered for VAT)

date
The date on the invoice is important because the payment date (here one month) is calculated from it. The invoice date is often described as the 'tax point' because it is the transaction date as far as VAT calculations are concerned, ie it is when the sale took place and the VAT was charged.

Note: VAT (Value Added Tax) is a tax on the supply of goods and services. At the time of writing the VAT rate is 17.5%.

CASE STUDY

the goods

As the invoice states the amount owing, it must specify accurately the goods supplied. The details – set out in columns in the body of the invoice – include:

- *product code* – this is the catalogue number which appeared on the original purchase order and on the delivery note
- *description* – the goods must be specified precisely
- *quantity* – this should agree with the quantity ordered
- *price* – this is the price of each unit shown in the next column
- *unit* is the way in which the unit is counted and charged for, eg
  - boxes of tights
  - single items, eg designer dresses
- *total* is the unit price multiplied by the number of units
- *discount %* is the percentage allowance (known as trade discount) given to customers who regularly deal with the supplier ie they receive a certain percentage (eg 10%) deducted from their bill; discounts are explained in more detail on page 36 – in this case no trade discount is given
- *net* is the amount due to the seller after deduction of trade discount, and before VAT is added on

totals and VAT

Further calculations are made in the box at the bottom of the invoice:

- *Goods Total* is the net amount due to the seller (the total of the net column)
- *Value Added Tax (VAT)*, here calculated as 17.5% of the total after deduction of any cash discount. VAT is added to produce the invoice final total
- Total is the VAT added to the Goods Total; it is the amount due to the seller

terms

The terms of payment are stated on the invoice. In this case these include:

- *Net monthly* – this means that full payment of the invoice should be made within a month of the invoice date
- *Carriage paid* means that the price of the goods includes delivery
- *E & OE* stands for 'errors and omissions excepted' which means that if there is a error or something left off the invoice by mistake, resulting in an incorrect final price, the supplier has the right to rectify the mistake and demand the correct amount

Other terms (not shown here) include:

- *COD* stands for 'cash on delivery' – payment is due when the goods are delivered
- *Cash Discount* – a further discount given when payment is made early, eg '2.5% cash discount for payment within 7 days'. See page 38 for further details
- *Ex-Works* – the price of the goods does not include delivery

INVOICE

COOL SOCKS LIMITED

Unit 45 Elgar Estate, Broadfield, BR7 4ER
Tel 01908 765314 Fax 01908 765951 Email toni@cool.u-net.com
VAT Reg GB 0745 4672 76

invoice to

Trends
4 Friar Street
Broadfield
BR1 3RF

invoice no	787923
account	3993
your reference	47609
date/tax point	02 10 01

deliver to

as above

product code	description	quantity	price	unit	total	discount %	net
45B	Blue toebar socks	100	2.36	pair	236.00	0.00	236.00

terms
Net monthly
Carriage paid
E & OE

goods total	236.00
VAT	41.30
TOTAL	277.30

**CASE
STUDY**

CREDIT NOTE – A REFUND IS DUE TO THE BUYER

A *credit note* is a 'refund' document. It reduces the amount owed by the buyer. The goods, remember, have not yet been paid for. The credit note is prepared by the supplier and sent to the buyer. For example:

• the goods may have been damaged, lost in transit or they may be faulty

• not all the goods have been sent – this is referred to as 'shortages'

• the unit price on the invoice may be too high

In this Case Study, when the staff of Trends unpack the socks in the stock room they find that ten pairs are faulty. They telephone Cool Socks to report the problem and Cool Socks authorise the return of the socks for credit. These socks will be sent back to Cool Socks with a returns note (see page 151) asking for credit – ie a reduction in the bill for the 10 faulty pairs. Cool Socks will have to issue the credit note for £27.73 shown below. Note the following details:

• the invoice number of the original consignment is quoted

• the reason for the issue of the credit note is stated at the bottom of the credit note – here 'damaged' goods

• the details are otherwise exactly the same as on an invoice

---

———— CREDIT NOTE ————
COOL SOCKS LIMITED
Unit 45 Elgar Estate, Broadfield, BR7 4ER
Tel 01908 765314 Fax 01908 765951 Email toni@cool.u-net.com
VAT REG GB 0745 4672 76

to

Trends 4 Friar Street Broadfield BR1 3RF	

credit note no	12157
account	3993
your reference	47609
our invoice	787923
date/tax point	10 10 01

product code	description	quantity	price	unit	total	discount %	net
45B	Blue Toebar socks	10	2.36	pair	23.60	0.00	23.60

Reason for credit
10 pairs of socks received damaged
(Your returns note no. R/N 2384)

GOODS TOTAL	23.60
VAT	4.13
TOTAL	27.73

STATEMENT – THE SELLER REQUESTS PAYMENT

A supplier will not normally expect a buyer to pay each individual invoice as soon as it is received: this could result in the buyer having to make a number of payments during the month. Instead, a *statement of account* is sent by the supplier to the buyer at the end of the month.

This statement, which can be typed out, or printed by the seller's computer accounting program, shows what is owed by the buyer to the seller. It contains details of:

- any balances (amounts owing) at the beginning of the month – these appear with the wording 'balance b/f' in the details column ('b/f' stands for 'brought forward')

- any payments received from the buyer

- invoices issued for goods supplied – the full amount due, including VAT

- refunds made on credit notes – including VAT

- the final amount due

The statement issued by Cool Socks to Trends for the period covering the sale and refund is shown below. Note that the balance of £150 owing at the beginning of the month has been paid off in full by a cheque on 2 October.

——————— **STATEMENT OF ACCOUNT** ———————
COOL SOCKS LIMITED
Unit 45 Elgar Estate, Broadfield, BR7 4ER
Tel 01908 765314 Fax 01908 765951 Email toni@cool.u-net.com
VAT REG GB 0745 4672 76

TO

Trends
4 Friar Street
Broadfield
BR1 3RF

account   3993

date   31 10 01

date	details	debit £	credit £	balance £
01 10 01	Balance b/f	150.00		150.00
02 10 01	Cheque received		150.00	00.00
02 10 01	Invoice 787923	277.30		277.30
10 10 01	Credit note 12157		27.73	249.57

AMOUNT NOW DUE	249.57

DISCOUNTS

The invoice in the Case Study (see page 33 and also the opposite page) shows a column for *trade discount*.

We also saw that the terms at the bottom of the invoice can allow for *cash discount*.

We will now explain these terms and show how the discount is calculated.

trade discount

It is common practice for suppliers to give businesses that order from them on a regular basis an agreed discount – a percentage reduction in the invoiced amount. This is known as *trade discount* because it applies to businesses 'in the trade' rather than to the general public. Discount may also be given by sellers to buyers who purchase in large quantities. Discount may also be offered as a 'carrot' to new buyers whose custom the seller is trying to attract.

In the example on the next page 10% discount has been given to Trends. Note how the discount percentage is shown in the discount column and the net amount is the amount after deduction of the discount.

The calculations on the invoice are as follows:

Step 1	Calculate the total price before discount
	100 x £2.36 = £236.00
Step 2	Calculate the trade discount
	£236.00 x 10% (ie 10/100) = £23.60
Step 3	Calculate the net price before VAT
	£236.00 - £23.60 = £212.40
Step 4	Calculate the VAT
	£212.40 x 17.5% (ie 17.5/100) = £37.17
Step 5	Calculate the total invoice price
	£212.40 + £37.17 = £249.57

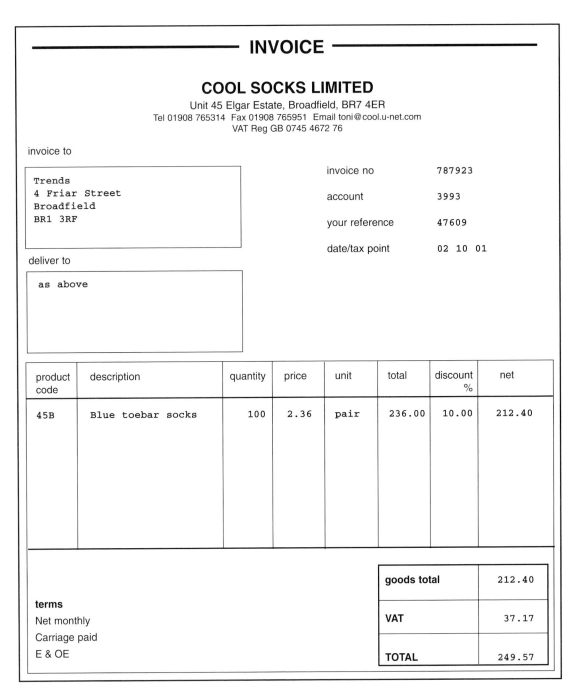

INVOICE

COOL SOCKS LIMITED

Unit 45 Elgar Estate, Broadfield, BR7 4ER
Tel 01908 765314 Fax 01908 765951 Email toni@cool.u-net.com
VAT Reg GB 0745 4672 76

invoice to

```
Trends
4 Friar Street
Broadfield
BR1 3RF
```

invoice no	787923
account	3993
your reference	47609
date/tax point	02 10 01

deliver to

```
as above
```

product code	description	quantity	price	unit	total	discount %	net
45B	Blue toebar socks	100	2.36	pair	236.00	10.00	212.40

terms
Net monthly
Carriage paid
E & OE

goods total	212.40
VAT	37.17
TOTAL	249.57

an invoice with 10% trade discount deducted

cash discount

Cash discount is a discount offered by the seller to the buyer to encourage the buyer to settle up straightaway or in a short space of time rather than waiting the thirty or more days specified on the invoice. For example, the terms on the bottom of the invoice may include the phrase:*"Cash discount of 2.5% for settlement within seven days"*. This means that the seller will allow 2.5% off the net invoice price (ie the price before VAT is added on) if the invoice is settled within seven days of the invoice date.

There are two important points to remember:

1 VAT charged on an invoice with cash discount offered is calculated *on the invoice amount <u>after deduction of cash discount.</u>*

2 The invoice total is the sum of this reduced amount of VAT and <u>*the goods total before deduction of cash discount.*</u>

If we take the Cool Socks invoice on the previous page, the calculations for a cash discount of 2.5% are as follows:

Step 1 Calculate the total price before trade discount (as before)
100 x £2.36 = £236.00

Step 2 Calculate the trade discount (as before)
£236.00 x 10% (ie 10/100) = £23.60

Step 3 Calculate the net price/Goods Total (as before)
£236.00 - £23.60 = £212.40

Step 4 NOW calculate the cash discount
£212.40 x 2.5% (ie 2.5/100) = £5.31

Step 5 Calculate the reduced goods total (this is not written on the invoice)
£212.40 - £5.31 = £207.09

Step 6 Calculate the VAT on this lower amount
£207.09 x 17.5% (ie 17.5/100) = £36.24

Step 7 Calculate the total invoice price (using the goods total before deduction of cash discount)
£212.40 + £36.24 = £248.64

INVOICE

COOL SOCKS LIMITED

Unit 45 Elgar Estate, Broadfield, BR7 4ER
Tel 01908 765314 Fax 01908 765951 Email toni@cool.u-net.com
VAT Reg GB 0745 4672 76

invoice to

| Trends |
| 4 Friar Street |
| Broadfield |
| BR1 3RF |

invoice no	787923
account	3993
your reference	47609
date/tax point	02 10 01

deliver to

as above

product code	description	quantity	price	unit	total	discount %	net
45B	Blue toebar socks	100	2.36	pair	236.00	10.00	212.40

terms

2.5% cash discount for settlement within 7 days, otherwise net monthly

Carriage paid

E & OE

goods total	212.40
VAT	36.24
TOTAL	248.64

an invoice with 10% trade discount deducted and 2.5% cash discount allowed for quick settlement

VALUE ADDED TAX (VAT)

VAT (Value Added Tax) is a government tax on the selling price charged to buyers at every level of sales, from the first supplier to the final consumer.

As we have seen on some of the business documents illustrated in this chapter, VAT is added to the purchase price of items sold. VAT is a tax on the consumer and, along with income tax, is an important source of revenue for the government.

registering for VAT

In Britain most businesses with a sales turnover (ie the total amount of sales in a given period) of more than a certain figure (increased from time-to-time by the government's budget) must be registered for VAT. The figure set in March 2000 was £52,000.

Once registered, a business is issued with a VAT registration number which must be quoted on all invoices and on other business documents. It charges VAT at the standard rate (currently 17.5 per cent) on all taxable supplies, ie whenever it sells goods, or supplies a service. From the supplier's viewpoint the tax so charged is known as *output tax*.

Businesses registered for VAT must pay to the VAT authorities (HM Customs and Excise Department):

*   the amount of VAT collected on sales (output tax)
*   less the amount of VAT charged to them (input tax) on all taxable supplies bought in

If the amount of input tax is larger than the output tax, the business claims a refund of the difference from HM Customs and Excise.

Every three months a form known as a VAT return (Form VAT 100) has to be completed, although some smaller businesses submit a VAT return on an annual basis. Payment of VAT due (if the business is not claiming a refund) is made with the VAT return.

zero-rated and exempt supplies

A number of items are zero-rated and no tax is charged when they are supplied: for example, food and children's clothing are zero-rated.

Some goods and services (such as postal services, loans of money, sales or lettings of land) are neither standard-rated nor zero-rated for VAT: instead they are exempt. The effect of this is that the supplier of such goods cannot charge VAT on outputs (as is the case with zero-rated goods) but cannot claim back all the tax which has been paid on inputs.

VAT – a tax on the final consumer

VAT is a tax which is paid by the final consumer of the goods. If we take, for example, a member of the public buying a computer for £705, the amount paid includes VAT of £105 (ie 17.5% of £600). The buyer stands the cost of the VAT, but the VAT is actually *paid* to HM Customs and Excise by all those involved in the manufacturing and selling process. This procedure is illustrated by the flow chart shown below. You will see that the right hand column shows the amount of VAT paid to HM Customs and Excise at each stage in the process.

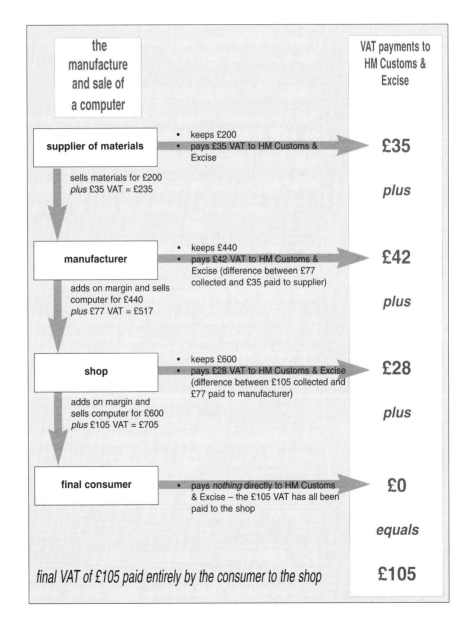

VAT records

Organisations must keep careful records of VAT paid and collected. This means filing documents such as invoices and credit notes for a minimum period of six years. HM Customs and Excise VAT inspectors visit businesses from time-to-time to ensure that:

- VAT is being charged and claimed correctly
- there are no VAT 'fiddles' taking place
- VAT records are being maintained correctly

If, for example, a business has been trading and not charging VAT, the VAT authorities can claim back payment of all the tax that should have been paid. Traders have been put out of business in this way because they have not been able to afford the VAT due.

some VAT calculations

You may be asked to carry out a variety of calculations involving VAT. Here are some of the more common ones.

what is the VAT to be charged?

If you need to work out the VAT on a given amount you apply the formula:

$$\text{amount} \times \frac{17.5}{100} \text{ (ie the VAT rate)} = \text{VAT payable}$$

VAT chargeable on £100 is therefore $£100 \times \frac{17.5}{100} = £17.50$

what is the VAT exclusive amount?

If you are given a total amount, for an example a shop till receipt which does not show the VAT amount, you may need to work out both the VAT content and also the amount before VAT is added (the 'VAT exclusive' amount). The formula for working out the amount before VAT is added is

$$\text{total amount including VAT} \times \frac{100}{117.5} = \text{amount excluding VAT}$$

The VAT exclusive amount in a receipt for £117.50 is therefore

$$£117.50 \times \frac{100}{117.50} = £100$$

A quick way to calculate the VAT exclusive amount on a calculator is to divide the total amount by 1.175.

VAT amounts – rounding down

When calculating VAT, the VAT amounts should always be rounded *down* to the nearest penny. VAT amounts should not be rounded up.

AUTHORISING INVOICES

credit limits

A credit limit of a customer is the maximum amount which the seller will allow the customer to owe at any one time.

Part of the accounting control system of a business is to set credit limits for its established customers and to establish limits for new customers. Each time therefore that an invoice is issued, a check should be made against the credit limit of that customer.

authorisation of invoices

Most invoices issued will be within the credit limit and processed with the authority of the person in charge of invoicing. What if the credit limit will be exceeded? No business is going to be foolish enough to refuse to supply a good customer. It may be that a cheque will soon come in from the buyer, or the amount involved is relatively small. In these cases the invoice will need authorisation from a more senior person in the accounts department. It is quite possible that a credit limit may have to be raised if a customer is buying more goods or services, and, of course, is paying invoices on time.

checking invoices

Few things are more annoying to a buyer than an incorrect invoice – the wrong goods, the wrong price, the wrong discount, and so on. It wastes the buyer's time and often leads to an adjusting credit note being issued. It is essential that the following details are checked by the seller before invoices are sent out:

- is the correct customer being invoiced? – there are often customers with similar names
- are the correct goods being sent? – the product coding on the purchase order must be checked carefully against the description – it is quite possible that the buyer has quoted an incorrect code!
- is the quantity correct?
- are the goods being sent to the correct place? – sometimes the delivery address can be different from the address normally held on file
- is the price right?
- is the discount allowed to the customer (if any) right? – do any special terms apply?
- are the calculations on the invoice correct? – this is especially relevant to invoices which are not produced on a computer

checking invoices – manual accounting

As you will see from the above list, the person processing the invoice will need to consult:

- the purchase order (this is very important)
- the seller's own record of any price quoted (this may be as simple as looking at a catalogue or stock list)
- the seller's file record of the buyer (which will normally give the credit limit and the discount allowed)
- a calculator!

checking and coding – computer accounting

Clearly, if the business uses a computer, many of these processes, particularly the calculations, will be automated. If a computer is used, *checking of coding* will be very important. There will be codes for

- the buyer (which will bring up the buyer's address on the invoice screen)
- the buyer's purchase order number (normally input in a 'reference' field on the invoice screen)
- the seller's product code (which is normally quoted in the catalogue and which will be input on the invoice screen to bring up the product details and price)

You will see from this that computerised invoicing is much easier than producing the documents manually. Accurate checking, however, is critically important.

the importance of customer communications

You will see from all these procedures that accounts staff need to communicate regularly with customers:

- providing information relating to prices, discounts and terms
- answering queries and dealing with problems
- coping with complaints
- politely chasing up overdue invoices
- putting the pressure on bad payers to avoid them becoming bad debts (if a customer cannot pay due invoices – perhaps because he or she has gone 'bust' – the seller loses the money, which becomes a *bad debt* which will reduce the seller's profits)

We will deal with the various forms of communication in detail in Chapter 14 which presents a number of situations commonly encountered in an accounts department and suggests practical solutions, giving examples of typical letters, memos and e-mails

CHAPTER SUMMARY

- When a business sells goods or services on credit it will deal with a number of business documents, including the quotation, purchase order, delivery note, invoice, credit note and statement (see key terms below).

- The seller of the goods or services will request payment by means of an invoice and then remind the buyer by means of a regular statement (normally monthly).

- Any refund due to the buyer will be acknowledged by means of a credit note.

- All documents and goods and services are normally coded (given a numerical code) both for reference purposes and also for input into the accounting systems of the seller and the buyer.

- All documents should be checked carefully both by the originator and by the recipient to make sure that the right goods or services have been supplied, and at the right price. It is essential that items such as discounts, VAT and totals are calculated correctly.

- All documents generated in the sales transaction are normally filed away for reference purposes.

- Some documents, eg the purchase order, will need to be authorised before issue – this is part of the control system of the accounting function.

KEY TERMS

purchase order	a document issued and authorised by the buyer of goods and services, sent to the seller, indicating the goods or services required
delivery note	a document sent by the seller with the goods
invoice	a document issued by the seller of goods or services indicating the amount owing and the required payment date
credit note	a document issued by the seller of the goods or services reducing the amount owed by the buyer
statement	a document issued by the seller to the buyer summarising invoices and credit notes issued and payments received
trade discount	a percentage reduction in the selling price given to the buyer because of the trading relationship
cash discount	a percentage reduction in the selling price given to the buyer if the buyer pays within a short space of time
Value Added Tax (VAT)	a government tax on spending, calculated on invoices and credit notes

STUDENT ACTIVITIES

2.1 What type of business document would normally be used when goods are sold on credit:

(a) to accompany goods from the seller to the buyer?

(b) to accompany faulty goods sent back by the buyer?

(c) as a formal notification of the amount owed?

(d) to remind the buyer of the amount owed to the seller?

(e) as a formal notification from the seller of a refund made to the buyer?

(f) to order the goods from the seller in the first place?

2.2 Compudisc sells computer floppy disks and has a special sales offer. A box of ten formatted disks normally sells at £8.00 (excluding VAT). Compudisc is offering to give a 20% discount for orders of ten boxes or more. It receives in the post one morning the following orders:

(a) 20 boxes ordered by Osborne Electronics Limited

(b) 50 boxes ordered by Helfield College

(c) 5 boxes ordered by Jim Masters

(d) 1000 boxes ordered by Trigger Trading Limited

Calculate in each case

- the total cost before discount

- the discount

- the cost after discount

- the VAT at the current rate

- the total cost

2.3 Recalculate the totals in Question 2.2 allowing for a cash discount of 2.5%.

2.4 Explain what is meant by the invoice terms 'net monthly' and 'E & OE' and 'carriage paid'.

2.5 Give three examples of coding on business documents. Why is coding important?

2.6 You work as one of three assistants in an accounts office. Your supervisor is off sick. You receive an urgent and large purchase order and find that the product code and goods description do not match up. The goods have to be despatched on the same day. What *exactly* is the problem and what would you do about it?

2.7 • Check the invoice extracts shown below.

• State what is wrong with them.

• Calculate the correct final totals.

Note: VAT is always rounded down to the nearest penny.

invoice (a)

description	quantity	price	total	discount %	net
Cotton shirts (red)	10	9.50	95.00	20	85.50

goods total		85.50
VAT @ 17.5%		14.96
TOTAL		100.45

invoice (b)

description	quantity	price	total	discount %	net
'Crazy Surfin' T-shirts (yellow)	50	5.00	225.00	10	202.50

goods total		202.50
VAT @ 17.5%		35.44
TOTAL		237.94

2.8 The following amounts include VAT. What is the VAT content and the amount before VAT is added in each case? Remember that VAT must be rounded down to the nearest penny.

(a) £47.00

(b) £40,670.98

(c) £39.98

(d) £94.00

(e) 47p

(f) £1.20

3 ACCOUNTING FOR CREDIT SALES AND SALES RETURNS

this chapter covers . . .

The previous chapter looked at the documents and procedures involved in selling on credit. In this chapter we examine the principles of the accounting system which is used to record the details of invoices and credit notes. We then apply these principles to credit sales (sales invoices) and sales returns (credit notes) and see how they are entered in the primary accounting records (sales day book and sales returns day book); the information is then transferred from the day books into the ledger accounts of the double-entry system.

NVQ PERFORMANCE CRITERIA COVERED

unit 1: RECORDING INCOME AND RECEIPTS
element 1
process documents relating to goods and services supplied

- invoices and credit notes are entered into primary records according to organisational procedures
- entries are coded and recorded in the appropriate ledger

THE ACCOUNTING SYSTEM

We have seen earlier in Chapter 1 (page 10) that the accounting system comprises a number of stages of recording and presenting financial transactions:

- prime documents
- primary accounting records (day books)
- double-entry book-keeping
- trial balance
- financial statements

In this chapter we look at the principles of recording documents relating to credit sales transactions in the primary accounting records and the entries to be made in the double-entry accounts. Later in the book we will see how a list of the balances of the double-entry accounts is used to form the trial balance (Chapter 16). Financial statements – the profit and loss statement and balance sheet – are the end result of the accounting system; they are covered at levels 3 and 4 of NVQ Accounting.

ACCOUNTING FOR CREDIT SALES TRANSACTIONS

This chapter focuses on credit sales transactions; the recording of transactions for cash sales will be covered when we study the receipts side of the cash book – Chapter 6.

In accounting, the term 'sales' has a specific meaning:

the sale of goods in which the business or organisation trades

Thus an office stationery shop will record as sales items such as photocopier paper, ring binders, etc; however, if the shop sells off its old cash till when it is replaced with a new one, this is not recorded as sales but, instead, is accounted for against the original cost of the till.

The accounting system starts its recording process from prime documents. The prime documents used to record different aspects of credit sales are:

- sales invoices
- credit notes issued

The diagram on the next page shows the order in which the accounting records are prepared for credit sales transactions. You will see that the steps for recording credit sales transactions in the accounting system are:

- start with a *prime document* (the source document for the accounting records)

- enter it in the appropriate *primary accounting record* (the first accounting book – or book of original entry – in which the prime document is recorded and summarised)

- transfer the information from the primary accounting record into the *double-entry accounts*

accounting for credit sales transactions

prime documents

- sales invoices
- credit notes issued

primary accounting records

- sales day book
- sales returns day book

double-entry accounts

- sales (debtors) ledger
- general (main) ledger
- cash book

We will now look in more detail at the mechanics of the primary accounting records and the double-entry system. We shall then apply the accounting system to the recording of credit sales and sales returns.

PRIMARY ACCOUNTING RECORDS

The primary accounting records comprise a number of *day books* which list money amounts and other details taken from prime documents.

The day books used for credit sales and and sales returns are:

- sales day book
- sales returns day book

These day books, as well as being called primary accounting records, are also known as the books of original ('prime') entry. This is because they are the first place in the accounting system where prime documents are recorded.

A sales day book is set out in the following way with sample entries shown (a sales returns day book uses the same layout):

Sales Day Book						**SDB 21**
Date	Customer	Invoice No	Folio	Gross	VAT*	Net
2001				£	£	£
3 Jan	Doyle & Co Ltd	901	SL 58	141.00	21.00	120.00
8 Jan	Sparkes & Sons Ltd	902	SL 127	188.00	28.00	160.00
13 Jan	T Young	903	SL 179	94.00	14.00	80.00
15 Jan	A-Z Supplies Ltd	904	SL 3	235.00	35.00	200.00
21 Jan	Sparkes & Sons Ltd	905	SL 127	141.00	21.00	120.00
31 Jan	Totals for month			799.00	119.00	680.00

* VAT = 17.5 per cent

Notes:

- The day book is prepared from prime documents – sales day book from sales invoices (or copies of sales invoices), and sales returns day book from credit notes (or copies) issued.
- The reference 'SDB 21' is used for cross-referencing to the book-keeping system: here it indicates that this is page 21 of the sales day book.
- The *folio* column is also used for cross-referencing purposes: 'SL' refers to Sales Ledger, followed by the account number.
- The *gross* column records the amount of each prime document, ie after VAT has been included.
- The day book is totalled at intervals – daily, weekly, or monthly (as here) – the total of the *net* column tells the business the amount of sales (as here), or sales returns for the period.
- The amounts from the day books are recorded in the book-keeping system.
- When control accounts (see Chapter 17) are in use, the total of the gross column is entered into the sales ledger (debtors) control account from both the sales day book and the sales returns day book.

day books and Value Added Tax

Many businesses and other organisations are registered for Value Added Tax (VAT). When a business is registered for VAT:

- VAT is charged on invoices issued to customers
- an allowance for VAT is made on credit notes issued
- VAT charged on invoices received from VAT-registered suppliers and allowed on credit notes issued is set off against VAT charged on invoices issued (any surplus which cannot be set off in this way can be reclaimed from HM Customs and Excise, the VAT authority)

When writing up day books from VAT invoices and credit notes:

- enter the total amount of the invoice or credit note in the gross column
- enter the VAT amount in the VAT column
- enter the total for goods or services before VAT in the net column

When a business is not registered for VAT, it cannot charge VAT on invoices issued and it cannot reclaim VAT charged on invoices received from suppliers. In such circumstances the total amount of the invoice is recorded in both the net and gross columns; a dash may be inserted in the VAT column. Likewise, VAT cannot be allowed on credit notes issued (nor recorded for credit notes received).

In this chapter we shall see how the VAT columns from the sales and sales returns day books are entered into the double-entry accounts. Chapter 8 shows how VAT on purchases and purchases returns is recorded in the accounts.

DOUBLE-ENTRY SYSTEM

The accounting system is organised on the basis of a number of *accounts* which record the money amounts of financial transactions: collectively these accounts are known as 'the ledger'.

Accounts are kept in the names of customers and of suppliers of the business, and also for other transactions such as the receipt and payment of money for various purposes. Accounts can be kept in the form of:

- handwritten records
- computer records

In a handwritten system, accounts are maintained either in a bound book or a series of separate sheets of paper or card – each account occupying a separate page. The business can set up its own manual system, or can buy one ready-made from a business supplies shop.

In a computerised system each account is held as data in a computer file. Whether a handwritten or computerised system is being used, the principles remain the same. For the moment we will concentrate on handwritten accounts.

A handwritten system can either use specially ruled accounting paper – known as ledger paper – which can be purchased from a business supplies shop, or a suitable layout can be ruled as follows:

Debit   **Name of Account, eg Sales Account**   Credit

Date	Details	£ p	Date	Details	£ p
↑ of trans- action	↑ name of other account	↑ amount of trans- action			

Note the following points about the layout of this account:

- the name of the account is written at the top (often followed by the account number)

- the account is divided into two identical halves, separated by a central double vertical line

- the left-hand side is called the 'debit' side ('debit' is abbreviated to 'Dr' – short for DebtoR)

- the right-hand side is called the 'credit' (or 'Cr') side

- the date, details and amount of the transaction are entered in the account

- in the 'details' column is entered the name of the other account (or primary accounting record) involved – this acts as a cross reference; as a further cross reference, a 'folio' column is often incorporated on each side of an account – to the left of the money amount columns

In practice, each account would occupy a whole page in a handwritten book-keeping system but, to save space when doing exercises, it is usual to put several accounts on a page. In future, in this book, the account layout will be simplified to give more clarity as follows (example transaction shown):

Dr   **Sales Account**   Cr

2001	£	2001	£
		31 Jan Sales Day Book SDB 21	680

This layout is often known in accounting jargon as a 'T' account; it is used to illustrate accounts because it separates in a simple way the two sides – debit and credit – of the account. An alternative style of account has three money columns: debit, credit and balance. This type of account is commonly used for bank statements, building society passbooks and computer accounting statements. Because the balance of the account is calculated after every transaction, it is known as a *running balance account* (see page 348).

debits and credits

The principle of double-entry book-keeping is that two entries are made, for every financial transaction, usually in different accounts:

• one account is *debited* with the money amount of the transaction, and

• one account is *credited* with the money amount of the transaction

The principle is often known as the *dual aspect* of book-keeping, ie each transaction has a dual effect on the accounts – one account gains, while another account gives value by recording a payment or a liability.

Debit entries are on the left-hand side of the appropriate account, while credit entries are on the right. The rules for debits and credits are:

• *debit entry* – the account which gains value, or records an asset, or an expense

• *credit entry* – the account which gives value, or records a liability, or an income item

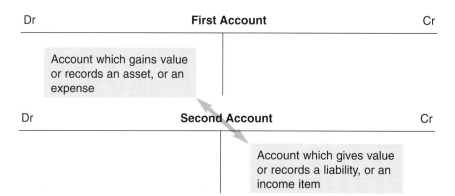

division of the ledger

Accounts, as mentioned above, are normally written on separate pages of a book known as 'the ledger'. In practice, several separate ledgers are kept: for credit sales transactions we shall be making use of the following ledgers:

• sales ledger, also known as the debtors ledger, containing the accounts of the firm's debtors (customers)

• cash book, containing the bank account and cash account records of the business

- general ledger (also known as the main or nominal ledger) containing sales account, sales returns account, Value Added Tax account, together with other accounts kept by the business.

The following diagram shows how ledgers and accounts are used in connection with sales:

SALES (DEBTORS) LEDGER	GENERAL (MAIN) LEDGER
separate accounts for each *debtor*, ie customers who owe money to the business	• *sales account* – to record sales invoices issued • *sales returns account* – to record credit notes issued • *Value Added Tax account* – to record the VAT amounts of credit sales and sales returns

Note that general ledger contains a number of other accounts in connection with purchases (see Chapter 8), expenses, receipts and payments, and the assets and liabilities of the business.

METHODS OF CODING IN ACCOUNTING SYSTEMS

As a business grows, methods of coding need to be used to trace transactions through the accounting system, ie:

- prime documents
- primary accounting records (day books)
- double-entry accounts
- trial balance

Uses of coding in the stages of the accounting system are:

prime documents

- each document, eg invoice, credit note, is numbered
- goods listed on invoices have reference numbers, eg catalogue number, which, if a computer accounting system is used, will enable the business to analyse sales by product

primary accounting records (day books)

- each page of the day books is numbered
- the number of the document, eg invoice, credit note is recorded
- the number of the debtors or creditors account is recorded in the folio column, eg 'SL' for sales ledger, followed by the account number (or short name – see below)

double-entry accounts

- the accounts system is divided into sections, the division of the ledger: sales ledger, purchases ledger (see Chapter 8), cash book (Chapters 6 and 11), and general ledger

- each account is numbered eg 'SL 58' (or some accounting systems use an abbreviated name, or short name, eg the account of Peterhead Trading Company might be coded as 'PETER')

- general (main) ledger accounts are numbered and are often arranged in a particular order, for example

0001 – 1299	Assets
2100 – 2399	Liabilities
3000 – 3099	Capital
4000 – 4999	Sales
5000 – 5299	Purchases
6000 – 8299	Expenses

ACCOUNTING SYSTEM FOR CREDIT SALES

The accounting system for credit sales fits together in the following way:

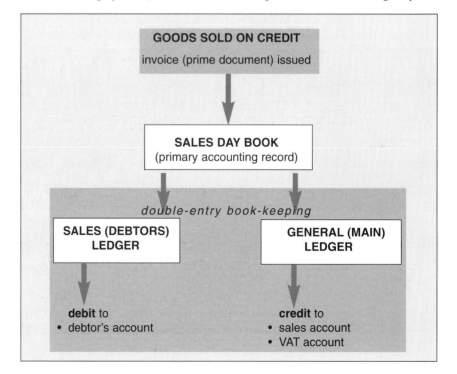

We shall now look in more detail at the sales day book and the double-entry accounts for credit sales. In the examples which follow we will assume that the business is registered for Value Added Tax and so:

- VAT is charged on invoices issued to customers
- VAT charged on invoices received from suppliers is either set off against VAT charged on invoices issued, or is reclaimed from HM Customs and Excise

The VAT rate used in the examples is 17.5%.

WRITING UP THE SALES DAY BOOK

The sales day book lists the credit sales made by a business. Following the issue of an invoice for each transaction, the sales day book is prepared from sales invoices (or copies of sales invoices). Please refer back to the example of a sales day book which was shown earlier in this chapter on page 51.

In order to write up the sales day book we take sales invoices or copy invoices – that have been checked and authorised – for the period and enter the details:

- date of invoice
- name of customer
- sales invoice number
- cross reference to the customer's account number in the sales ledger, eg 'SL 58'
- enter the gross amount of the invoice, being the final total
- enter the VAT amount shown on the invoice – don't be concerned with any adjustments to the VAT for the effect of any cash discounts (see page 38), simply record the VAT amount shown
- enter the net amount of the invoice (often described as 'goods or services total'), before VAT is added

DOUBLE-ENTRY BOOK-KEEPING FOR CREDIT SALES

After the sales day book has been written up and totalled, the information from it is transferred into the double-entry system. The accounts in the sales ledger and general ledger to record the transactions from the sales day book, seen earlier on page 51, are as follows:

SALES (DEBTORS) LEDGER

Dr	**A-Z Supplies Ltd** (account no 3)		Cr
2001		£	2001	£
15 Jan	Sales SDB 21	235	

Dr	**Doyle & Co Ltd** (account no 58)		Cr
2001		£	2001	£
3 Jan	Sales SDB 21	141	

Dr	**Sparkes & Sons Ltd** (account no 127)		Cr
2001		£	2001	£
8 Jan	Sales SDB 21	188	
21 Jan	Sales SDB 21	141	

Dr	**T Young** (account no 179)		Cr
2001		£	2001	£
13 Jan	Sales SDB 21	94	

GENERAL (MAIN) LEDGER

Dr	**Sales Account** (account no 4001)		Cr
2001		£	2001	£
			31 Jan Sales Day Book SDB 21	680

Dr	**Value Added Tax Account** (account no 2200)		Cr
2001		£	2001	£
			31 Jan Sales Day Book SDB 21	119

Note that from the sales day book:

• the amounts from the gross column *for each separate sale* have been debited to the accounts of the customers, ie the business has a debtor for the amounts shown

• the total of the VAT column, £119, has been credited to VAT account (which has given value)

• the total of the net column, £680, has been credited to sales account (which has given value)

- the sales day book incorporates a folio column which cross-references each transaction to the personal account of each debtor in the sales ledger (SL); this enables a particular transaction to be traced from prime document (invoice issued), through the primary accounting record (sales day book), to the debtor's ledger account
- each entry in the sales ledger and general ledger is cross-referenced back to the page number of the sales day book; here the reference is 'SDB 21'.

ACCOUNTING SYSTEM FOR SALES RETURNS

A credit note (see page 34) is the document issued by a business when it makes a refund to a customer who has bought goods on credit. A credit note reduces the amount owed by the debtor. *Sales returns* (or returns in) are when goods previously sold on credit are returned to the business by its customers.

The accounting procedures for sales returns involve:

- *prime documents* – credit notes issued to customers
- *primary accounting record* – sales returns day book
- *double-entry accounts* – sales ledger (accounts for each debtor) and general ledger (sales returns account, which records the totals of credit notes issued, and Value Added Tax account, which records the VAT amount of sales returns)

The accounting system for sales returns is summarised as follows:

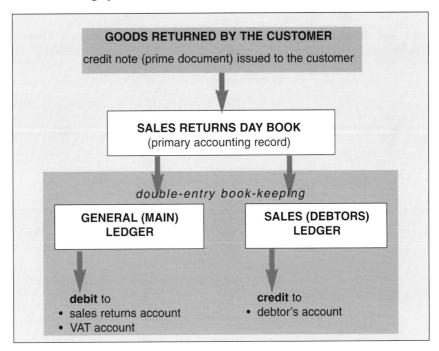

We shall now look in more detail at the sales returns day book and the double-entry accounts for sales returns. Note that the business is registered for Value Added Tax.

SALES RETURNS DAY BOOK

The sales returns day book uses virtually the same layout as the sales day book seen on page 51 of this chapter. It operates in a similar way, storing up information about sales returns until such time as a transfer is made into the double-entry accounts system. The prime documents for sales returns day book are credit notes (or copies of credit notes) issued to customers.

example transactions

2001

15 Jan   T Young returns goods, £40 + VAT, credit note no CN702 issued

27 Jan   A-Z Supplies Ltd returns goods, £120 + VAT, credit note no CN703 issued

The sales returns day book is written up as shown below:

Sales Returns Day Book						SRDB 5
Date	Customer	Credit Note No	Folio	Gross	VAT*	Net
2001				£	£	£
15 Jan	T Young	CN702	SL 179	47.00	7.00	40.00
27 Jan	A-Z Supplies Ltd	CN703	SL 3	141.00	21.00	120.00
31 Jan	Totals for month			188.00	28.00	160.00

* VAT = 17.5 per cent

Notes:

- The sales returns day book is prepared from credit notes (or copies of credit notes) issued to customers.
- The day book is totalled at appropriate intervals – weekly or monthly.
- The VAT-inclusive amounts from the gross column are credited to the debtors' personal accounts in the sales ledger.

- The total of the VAT column is transferred to the debit of the VAT account in the general ledger.
- The total of the net column tells the business the amount of sales returns for the period. This amount is transferred to the debit of sales returns account in the general ledger.
- The gross column records the amount of each credit note issued, ie after VAT has been included. When control accounts (see Chapter 17) are in use, the total of the gross column is entered into the sales ledger (debtors) control account.

DOUBLE-ENTRY BOOK-KEEPING FOR SALES RETURNS

After the sales returns day book has been written up and totalled, the information from it is transferred into the double-entry system. The accounts in the sales ledger and general ledger to record the transactions from the above sales returns day book (including any other transactions already recorded on these accounts) are:

SALES (DEBTORS) LEDGER

Dr			A-Z Supplies Ltd (account no 3)			Cr
2001		£	2001			£
15 Jan	Sales SDB 21	235	27 Jan	Sales Returns SRDB 5		141

Dr			T Young (account no 179)			Cr
2001		£	2001			£
12 Jan	Sales SDB 21	94	15 Jan	Sales Returns SRDB 5		47

GENERAL (MAIN) LEDGER

Dr			Sales Returns Account (account no 4010)			Cr
2001		£	2001			£
31 Jan	Sales Returns Day Book SRDB 5	160				

Dr			Value Added Tax Account (account no 2200)			Cr
2001		£	2001			£
31 Jan	Sales Returns Day Book SRDB 5	28	31 Jan	Sales Day Book SDB 21		119

THE USE OF ANALYSED SALES DAY BOOKS

As well as the layout of the day books we have seen in this chapter, a business can use analysed day books whenever it needs to analyse its sales and sales returns between

- different departments, eg a store with departments for furniture, carpets and curtains, hardware

- different categories of goods sold, eg paint, wallpaper, brushes, or services supplied

For example, a wholesaler of decorators' supplies may decide to write up its sales day book as shown below.

Sales Day Book									**SDB 48**
Date	Customer	Invoice No	Folio	Gross	VAT*	Net	Paint	Wallpaper	Brushes
2001				£	£	£	£	£	£
8 Aug	DIY Sales Limited	1478	SL 59	235.00	35.00	200.00	75.00	125.00	–
12 Aug	T Lane Decorators	1479	SL 108	141.00	21.00	120.00	–	100.00	20.00
15 Aug	Colour Painters Limited	1480	SL 38	329.00	49.00	280.00	150.00	100.00	30.00
22 Aug	Southern Decorators	1481	SL 211	188.00	28.00	160.00	100.00	60.00	–
31 Aug	Totals for month			893.00	133.00	760.00	325.00	385.00	50.00

* VAT = 17.5 per cent

Notes:

- The references in the folio column are to 'SL' (Sales Ledger), followed by the customer's account number.

- The analysis columns – here paint, wallpaper, brushes – show the amount of sales net of VAT (ie before VAT is added).

- The analysis columns analyse the net amount from sales invoices of products sold or services supplied.

In using analysed sales day books and sales returns day books, a business adapts the accounting records to suit its own particular requirements for information. There is not a standard way in which to present the primary accounting records – the needs of the user of the information are all important. By using analysed day books, the owner of the business can see how much has been sold by departments, or categories of goods and services.

BATCH CONTROL SYSTEMS

A variation on the use of day books is often used – particularly with computer accounting programs. With batched data entry a series of transactions for a day, week or month relating to, say, sales invoices is entered into the accounts in one 'run'. By batching, the computer operator concentrates on entering one type of transaction without the need to keep changing from one area of the computer program to another. Before entering a batch of transactions they are pre-listed on a separate batch control form such as that shown below for a batch of sales invoices:

Batch Control: sales invoices

Customer		Invoice		Gross	VAT*	Net
Account No	Name	Date	No	£	£	£
		2001				
SL 58	Doyle & Co Ltd	3 Jan	901	141.00	21.00	120.00
SL 127	Sparkes & Sons Ltd	8 Jan	902	188.00	28.00	160.00
SL 179	T Young	13 Jan	903	94.00	14.00	80.00
SL 3	A-Z Supplies Ltd	15 Jan	904	235.00	35.00	200.00
SL 127	Sparkes & Sons Ltd	21 Jan	905	141.00	21.00	120.00
Check list totals				799.00	119.00	680.00

Prepared by	*Gill Pate*	Date	*31 Jan 2001*
Checked by	*Karan Hopwood*	Date	*31 Jan 2001*
Posted by	*Ian Turner*	Date	*31 Jan 2001*

* VAT = 17.5 per cent

The sales invoice batch form is completed from invoices (or copy invoices) which have been prepared and checked. The transactions are then entered into the sales ledger section of the computer accounting program. The computer screen shows the total money amount of sales invoices and this is compared with the check list total from the sales invoice batch control form; if there is a discrepancy, the error must be located and corrected.

Note that businesses often use batch control forms in place of day books. Also, when sales ledger (debtors) control accounts (see Chapter 17) are in use, the totals from the batch control form are recorded in the control account.

**CASE
STUDY**

WYVERN TRADERS

To bring together the material covered in this chapter, we will look at a comprehensive Case Study which makes use of:

- **primary accounting records**
    - sales day book
    - sales returns day book
- **double-entry accounts**
    - sales (debtors) ledger
    - general (main) ledger

The Case Study also includes a diagram (see page 67) which summarises the procedures for recording credit sales and sales returns transactions in the accounting system.

situation

Wyvern Traders is a wholesaler of stationery and office equipment. The business is registered for VAT. The following are the credit sales and sales returns transactions for April 2001:

2001	
2 Apr	Sold goods to P Woodhouse, £200.00 + VAT, invoice no 2416
10 Apr	P Woodhouse returns goods, £60.00 + VAT, we issue credit note no CN12
14 Apr	Sold goods to Blackheath Limited, £80.00 + VAT, invoice no 2417
21 Apr	Blackheath Limited returns goods, £10.00 + VAT, we issue credit note no CN13
25 Apr	Sold goods to Butterworth Limited, £160.00 + VAT, invoice no 2418

The day books and double-entry accounts are illustrated on the next two pages: arrows indicate the transfers from the day books to the individual accounts. Note that some accounts have been represented on both pages in order to show, on the same page, the accounts relating to a particular day book: in practice a business would keep all the transactions together in one account.

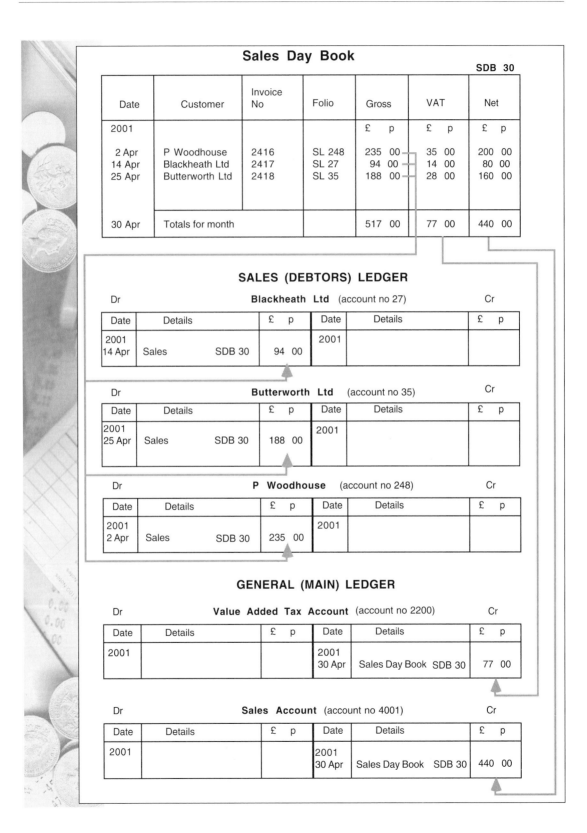

Sales Day Book

SDB 30

Date	Customer	Invoice No	Folio	Gross		VAT		Net	
2001				£	p	£	p	£	p
2 Apr	P Woodhouse	2416	SL 248	235	00	35	00	200	00
14 Apr	Blackheath Ltd	2417	SL 27	94	00	14	00	80	00
25 Apr	Butterworth Ltd	2418	SL 35	188	00	28	00	160	00
30 Apr	Totals for month			517	00	77	00	440	00

SALES (DEBTORS) LEDGER

Dr   **Blackheath Ltd** (account no 27)   Cr

Date	Details		£	p	Date	Details	£	p
2001					2001			
14 Apr	Sales	SDB 30	94	00				

Dr   **Butterworth Ltd** (account no 35)   Cr

Date	Details		£	p	Date	Details	£	p
2001					2001			
25 Apr	Sales	SDB 30	188	00				

Dr   **P Woodhouse** (account no 248)   Cr

Date	Details		£	p	Date	Details	£	p
2001					2001			
2 Apr	Sales	SDB 30	235	00				

GENERAL (MAIN) LEDGER

Dr   **Value Added Tax Account** (account no 2200)   Cr

Date	Details	£	p	Date	Details	£	p
2001				2001			
				30 Apr	Sales Day Book SDB 30	77	00

Dr   **Sales Account** (account no 4001)   Cr

Date	Details	£	p	Date	Details	£	p
2001				2001			
				30 Apr	Sales Day Book SDB 30	440	00

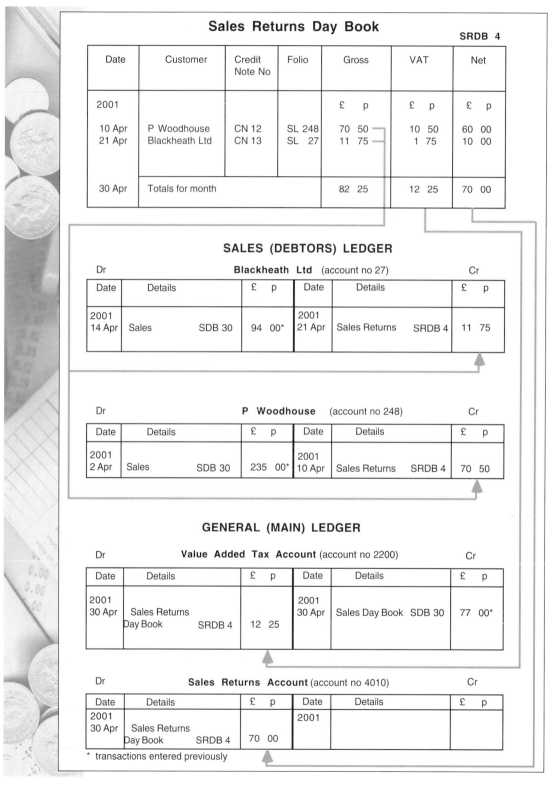

Sales Returns Day Book

SRDB 4

Date	Customer	Credit Note No	Folio	Gross		VAT		Net	
				£	p	£	p	£	p
2001									
10 Apr	P Woodhouse	CN 12	SL 248	70	50	10	50	60	00
21 Apr	Blackheath Ltd	CN 13	SL 27	11	75	1	75	10	00
30 Apr	Totals for month			82	25	12	25	70	00

SALES (DEBTORS) LEDGER

Dr   **Blackheath Ltd** (account no 27)   Cr

Date	Details		£	p	Date	Details		£	p
2001					2001				
14 Apr	Sales	SDB 30	94	00*	21 Apr	Sales Returns	SRDB 4	11	75

Dr   **P Woodhouse** (account no 248)   Cr

Date	Details		£	p	Date	Details		£	p
2001					2001				
2 Apr	Sales	SDB 30	235	00*	10 Apr	Sales Returns	SRDB 4	70	50

GENERAL (MAIN) LEDGER

Dr   **Value Added Tax Account** (account no 2200)   Cr

Date	Details		£	p	Date	Details		£	p
2001					2001				
30 Apr	Sales Returns Day Book	SRDB 4	12	25	30 Apr	Sales Day Book SDB 30		77	00*

Dr   **Sales Returns Account** (account no 4010)   Cr

Date	Details		£	p	Date	Details		£	p
2001					2001				
30 Apr	Sales Returns Day Book	SRDB 4	70	00					

* transactions entered previously

The diagram below summarises the material we have studied in this chapter. It shows the procedures for recording transactions in the accounting system for

- credit sales
- sales returns

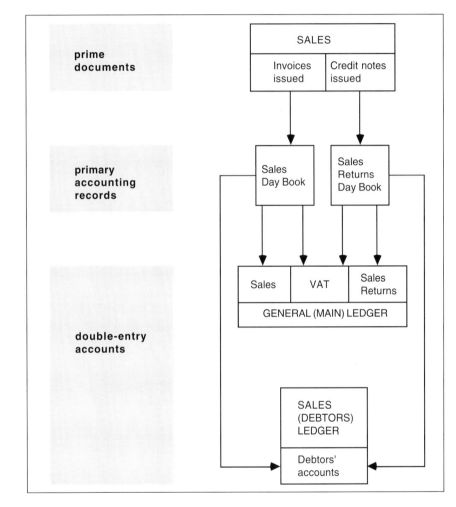

BALANCING ACCOUNTS

Where there is only one transaction recorded on an account, the amount of the transaction is the balance of the account, ie the total of the account to date. With several transactions recorded on an account it is necessary to work out the balance more formally from time-to-time. Such balancing of accounts is usually carried out at the end of each month, sometimes more often. We will look in more detail at balancing accounts and the use of balances in the trial balance in Chapter 16.

**CHAPTER
SUMMARY**

- The accounting system comprises a number of specific stages of recording and presenting financial transactions:
  - prime documents
  - primary accounting records (day books)
  - double-entry book-keeping
  - trial balance
  - financial statements

- The prime documents relating to credit sales are:
  - sales invoices
  - credit notes issued

- Sales day book is the primary accounting record for credit sales. It is prepared from sales invoices (or copy invoices) sent to customers.

- Sales returns day book is the primary accounting record for sales returns. It is prepared from credit notes (or copy credit notes) issued to customers.

- Analysed sales day books are used when a business wishes to analyse its sales between different departments or different categories of goods sold or services supplied.

- Recording credit sales in the double-entry system uses:
  - prime documents, sales invoices
  - primary accounting record, sales day book
  - double-entry accounts, sales ledger and general ledger

- Recording sales returns in the double-entry system uses:
  - prime documents, credit notes issued to customers
  - primary accounting record, sales returns day book
  - double-entry accounts, sales ledger and general ledger

KEY TERMS

prime documents	source documents for the accounting records
primary accounting records	the first accounting books in which transactions are recorded
books of original (prime) entry	another term for primary accounting records
folio	a form of cross-referencing used in the accounting system
ledger	collection of accounts; a sub-division of the accounting system
debit entry	records a gain in value, an asset, or an expense
credit entry	records the giving of value, a liability, or an income item
sales	the sale of goods in which the business or organisation trades
sales day book	primary accounting record prepared from sales invoices (or copy invoices)
sales returns	goods sold on credit which are returned by customers
credit note	the prime document for returned goods – issued by the business allowing credit to the customer
sales returns day book	primary accounting record prepared from credit notes (or copy credit notes) issued to customers
analysed sales day book	day book which incorporates analysis columns, for example between – different departments – different categories of goods sold, or services supplied
sales (debtors) ledger	subsidiary ledger which contains the accounts of the firm's debtors (customers)
general (main) ledger	division of the ledger which includes – sales account – sales returns account – Value Added Tax account

STUDENT ACTIVITIES

3.1   Which one of the following is a primary accounting record?

(a)   sales day book

(b)   sales account

(c)   account of T Smith, a debtor

(d)   profit and loss statement

Answer (a) or (b) or (c) or (d)

3.2   Which one of the following is in the right order?

(a)   sales invoice; sales day book; sales account; debtor's account

(b)   sales day book; debtor's account; sales account; sales invoice

(c)   sales day book; sales invoice; debtor's account; sales account

(d)   sales account; debtor's account; sales invoice; sales day book

Answer (a) or (b) or (c) or (d)

3.3   Explain in note format:

(a)   the principles of recording a credit sales transaction in the accounting system

(b)   the principles of recording a sales returns transaction in the accounting system

---

In the activities which follow, the rate of Value Added Tax is to be calculated at the current rate (17.5% at the time of writing). When calculating VAT amounts, you should ignore fractions of a penny, ie round down to a whole penny.

For Activities 3.4 and 3.5 use a cross-referencing system incorporating the following:

- *sales day book*   *– SDB 50*
  sales returns day book – SRDB 8

- *sales (debtors) ledger account numbers*
  A Cox   *– account no 32*
  Dines Stores   *– account no 48*
  E Grainger   *– account no 55*
  M Kershaw   *– account no 90*
  D Lloyd   *– account no 95*
  Malvern Stores   *– account no 110*
  Pershore Retailers   *– account no 145*
  P Wilson   *– account no 172*

- *general (main) ledger account numbers*
  sales account   *– account no 4001*
  sales returns account   – account no 4010
  Value Added Tax account– account no 2200

3.4 Wyvern Wholesalers sells office stationery to other businesses in the area. During April 2001 the following credit transactions took place:

2001

2 Apr	Sold goods to Malvern Stores £55 + VAT, invoice no 4578
4 Apr	Sold goods to Pershore Retailers £65 + VAT, invoice no 4579
7 Apr	Sold goods to E Grainger £28 + VAT, invoice no 4580
10 Apr	Sold goods to P Wilson £58 + VAT, invoice no 4581
11 Apr	Sold goods to M Kershaw £76 + VAT, invoice no 4582
14 Apr	Sold goods to D Lloyd £66 + VAT, invoice no 4583
18 Apr	Sold goods to A Cox £33 + VAT, invoice no 4584
22 Apr	Sold goods to Dines Stores £102 + VAT, invoice no 4585
24 Apr	Sold goods to Malvern Stores £47 + VAT, invoice no 4586
25 Apr	Sold goods to P Wilson £35 + VAT, invoice no 4587
29 Apr	Sold goods to A Cox £82 + VAT, invoice no 4588

You are to:

(a)   enter the above transactions in Wyvern Wholesaler's sales day book for April 2001

(b)   record the accounting entries in Wyvern Wholesaler's sales ledger and general ledger

3.5 The following details are the sales returns of Wyvern Wholesalers for April 2001. They are to be

(a)   entered in the sales returns day book for April 2001

(b)   recorded in the sales ledger and general ledger (use the ledgers already prepared in the answer to Activity 3.4)

2001

8 Apr	Pershore Retailers returns goods £20 + VAT, we issue credit note no CN572
10 Apr	E Grainger returns goods £28 + VAT, we issue credit note no CN573
16 Apr	D Lloyd returns goods £33 + VAT, we issue credit note no CN574
28 Apr	Malvern Stores returns goods £20 + VAT, we issue credit note no CN575
30 Apr	A Cox returns goods £40 + VAT, we issue credit note no CN576

4 RECEIVING AND RECORDING PAYMENTS

this chapter covers . . .

This chapter explains the different ways in which money is received by an organisation and then sets out the procedures it follows in recording those payments. It covers:

- receiving money in the form of cash, cheques and similar items, inter-bank transfers and payment by debit and credit card

- the legal meaning of cheque crossings and endorsements

- checking of the money against covering documentation where appropriate

- checking cash, giving change and issuing receipts

- recording incoming payments on remittance lists, cash books and cash registers

- dealing with problem payments – incorrect cheques, suspicious cards, situations where the money received does not tally with the accompanying documentation

NVQ PERFORMANCE CRITERIA COVERED

unit 1: RECORDING INCOME AND RECEIPTS

element 2

receive and record receipts

- receipts are checked against relevant supporting information

- unusual features are identified and either resolved or referred to the appropriate person

INCOMING PAYMENTS

Payments can be received by an organisation in a variety of ways:

- cash
- cheque
- credit card and debit card transactions (which can be manually or electronically processed)
- direct to the bank by inter-bank transfer: BACS and CHAPS

It depends on the nature and the size of the organisation how the payments are received and processed. In the retail sector, for example, a newsagent will depend to a great extent on cash transactions and the cash register, a large supermarket on the other hand will use electronic tills and accept cash, cheques, and credit and debit card payments.

CASH

Cash is still used for most small transactions, and we are still nowhere near the 'cashless society' which is often talked about.

As far as the organisation accepting payments in cash is concerned, the main disadvantage of cash is the security problem, and there is a risk of receiving forged notes.

receiving payment in cash

For a business receiving sums of money in the form of cash it is necessary for a member of staff to count the cash received and check it against the amount due. Notes should be checked for forgeries (held against the light or viewed on special machines). Change will need to be given when the exact amount is not tendered (given). For example:

Sale	£3.64
Amount tendered (given) by customer	£10.00
Change to be given	£6.36

The amount of change is the difference between the amount tendered and the amount of the sale. When a cash till is in use, modern types of till will indicate the amount of change to be given after the amount tendered has been entered through the keypad. You will know, from having bought items in shops, that many cashiers count out the change starting with the amount of the sale and working to the amount tendered.

Often when payment is made in cash, a receipt is given: this can take the form of a machine-produced receipt, such as is given in a shop, or a handwritten receipt. Look at these examples:

Everest Sports	retailer
15 High St Mereford	address
08 10 01 15.07	date and time of transaction
Salesperson Tina	salesperson
Tennis balls 5.99	goods purchased
Shin guards 8.99	goods purchased
TOTAL 14.98	total due
CASH 20.00	£20 (probably a £20 note) given by the customer
CHANGE 5.02	change given
Thank you for your custom	personal message to help public relations
Please retain this receipt in case of any query	advice to retain receipt in case of a problem with the goods
VAT REG 373 2888 11	VAT Registration number

a till receipt

ENIGMA MUSIC LIMITED	*receipt*	958

13 High Street, Mereford MR1 2TF
VAT Reg 343 7645 23

Customer ....*R V Williams*..date ....*3 Oct 2001*....

'Golden Oldies' by J Moore	£20.00
	£20.00
VAT @ 17.5%	£3.50
Total	£23.50

a hand-written receipt

tills and cash floats

At the end of the day it will be necessary to 'cash up' by balancing the amount of cash held. As most cash tills start each day with a float of cash (to enable change to be given, if necessary, to the first customers), the amount in the till at the end of the day will be:

cash float at start

plus sales made during the day (listed on the till roll)

equals amount of cash held at end of day

a modern electronic till

A cash float will be kept back for the following day, and the surplus will be transferred to the safe for paying into the bank next day. Alternatively, a bank paying-in slip (see the next chapter) might be made out, and the cash, together with the paying-in slip and any cheques received placed in a 'wallet' to be deposited in the bank's night safe (see the next chapter).

A typical calculation would be:

cash float at start	£150.00
plus sales made during the day (listed on the till roll)	£2608.50
equals amount of cash held at end of day	£2758.50
less cash float retained for next day	£150.00
amount transferred to safe or bank's night safe	£2608.50

If the cash in the till does not agree with the total on the till roll, the discrepancy needs investigation. Regular discrepancies for significant amounts, eg £5 or £10, will lead to urgent investigations – there could be pilfering taking place if the till is often short at the end of the day, or it could be caused by poor cashiering – giving the wrong change.

guidelines for cash handling

Those who handle cash in an organisation are responsible for its safekeeping. Cash is often a target for theft – and regrettably not only from people outside the organisation. General security guidelines for looking after cash received will vary according to the size and type of organisation:

- cash should be kept in a cash till or in a cash box which should be kept locked when not in use
- keys should be retained under the control of the cashier
- as little cash as is practically possible should be kept in tills
- cash should be paid into the bank as soon as possible

'topping up' the petty cash

The organisation may also operate a petty cash system for making small payments (see Chapter 12). The cash will be kept in a locked tin and will need to be 'topped up' from time-to-time to what is known as the 'imprest amount'. Care will have to be taken when transferring money from the main cash fund to the petty cash tin: security precautions should be observed and the transaction recorded.

CHEQUES

Cheques are issued by banks to their personal and business account customers. Building societies also issue cheques on current accounts – their customers are mainly personal. Payment by cheque is a common method of payment for all but the smallest amounts. A specimen cheque is shown below (there is more on how to write out a cheque in Chapter 9).

what is a cheque?

A cheque, as used in normal business practice, may be defined as

a written order to the bank (known as the 'drawee') signed by its customer (known as the 'drawer') to pay a specified amount to a specified person (known as the 'payee')

Some organisations – large retail stores, for example – have machines which print out their customers' cheques on the till. A large number of cheques, however, are still written by hand, and great care must be taken both when writing out cheques and also when receiving cheques in payment. The cheques must be examined to ensure that all the details and signatures are correct. The vast majority of cheques are 'crossed' – they have two parallel lines on the front of the cheque.

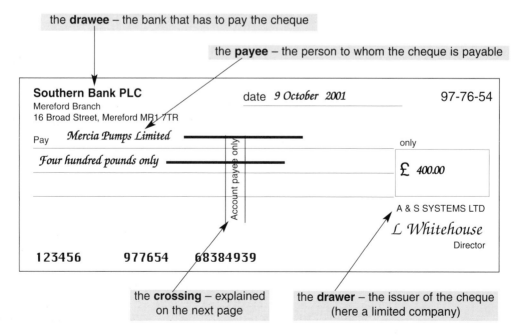

the **drawee** – the bank that has to pay the cheque

the **payee** – the person to whom the cheque is payable

the **crossing** – explained on the next page

the **drawer** – the issuer of the cheque (here a limited company)

the 'parties' and crossing on a cheque

examining the cheque

If you are receiving payment by cheque, whether it is direct from the customer over the counter or through the post on a remittance advice, there are a number of basic checks to carry out:

- is the cheque signed? – it is invalid if it is not
- is the payee's name correct? – it should be changed and initialled by the drawer (issuer) if it is not
- is the cheque in date? – a cheque becomes out of date ('stale') and invalid after six months; note that if the date is missing, it may be written in
- do the words and figures agree? – the cheque may be returned by the bank if they do not

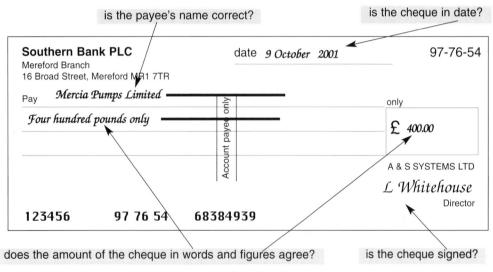

checking the cheque

If the organisation accepting payment by cheque is inefficient and does not carry out these precautions, the cheque concerned may be returned to the organisation's bank after it has been paid in, and the amount of the cheque deducted from the organisation's bank account. If the cheque is issued with a guarantee card, different conditions apply (see page 80).

crossings

Cheques may, as in the example shown above, be *crossed,* that is, they are printed with two parallel lines across the face of the cheque. Often there are words printed or written in the crossing. If a cheque is not crossed, it is an *open* cheque. *A crossed cheque may only be paid into a bank account*; it cannot be cashed (ie exchanged for cash) by the payee (the person to whom the cheque is made payable) unless the person writing out the cheque makes it payable to him/herself.

endorsements

Traditionally the payee of a cheque has been entitled to sign it on the back – *endorse* it – so that it can be passed on to another person who can pay it into his or her bank account and receive payment. This signature on the back – the *endorsement* – should read as follows:

Pay Ivor Brown
James Smith

Here James Smith, the payee, is endorsing the cheque over to Ivor Brown who will pay it into his bank account. He has written 'Pay Ivor Brown' above his signature. This might happen, for example, if James Smith did not have a bank account. He would endorse the cheque over to Ivor Brown who could then give him the cash for the cheque.

In recent years endorsements have become less common. Because of increasing fraud and changes in the law banks have started printing 'account payee' or 'account payee only' as a matter of course on most cheques, as is explained below and on the next page. . .

when endorsements are *not* possible

Endorsement and passing on of a cheque is *not* possible if

- the word 'only' appears after the payee's name on the front of the cheque
- the words 'account payee' or 'account payee only' appear in the crossing on the front of the cheque (see next page)

As these words are more and more frequently being printed on cheques, endorsements are becoming rare. As these cheques cannot be endorsed over to another person, they can only be paid into the payee's account.

types of crossing

If you are receiving cheques you will need to know the different types of crossing, as the type of crossing will affect whether or not the cheque can be paid into the organisation's bank account. These are the basic types of crossing:

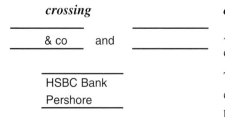

crossing	*effect*
& co and	A *general* crossing – no effect – the cheque can be paid into the bank
HSBC Bank Pershore	This crossing is known as a *special* crossing – the cheque can *only* be paid into HSBC Bank in Pershore

crossing	*effect*
not negotiable	This cheque *can* be endorsed and passed on to someone other than the payee – but in practice this is *not* recommended. It should be paid into the payee's account.
account payee	This cheque should only be paid into the account of the payee of the cheque. It should not be endorsed over to anyone else.

PAYMENT BY MULTIFUNCTION CARD

Banks nowadays issue 'multifunction cards' which combine a number of different services for their customers. These services include:

- giving cash from cash machines in the UK and abroad
- guaranteeing payment of customers' cheques up to a certain amount
- acting as debit cards – enabling customers to make payment without issuing a cheque

The Royal Bank of Scotland's multi-function Highline card combines five services in one card:

- **Switch debit card** – pay for goods and services without writing a cheque wherever you see the Switch symbol – and even get cash where you see the cashback sign
- **Cashline card** – access Britain's widest cash dispensing network – use your card not only in Royal Bank Cashline machines, but in cash machines belonging to any major bank or building society throughout Great Britain
- **Cheque guarantee card** – guarantee your cheques up to the limit shown on your card
- **Cirrus card** – access your money in local currency at thousands of cash dispensers worldwide – wherever you see the Cirrus symbol
- **Maestro debit card** – use your card to pay for goods and services worldwide – wherever you see the Maestro symbol

Businesses which accept payment from customers using these cards either over the counter, by telephone or through mail order must be familiar with the procedures for accepting payment.

The details shown on the left describe The Royal Bank of Scotland 'Highline' multifunction card. The symbols which are shown below relate to the functions of the card.

On the pages which follow we describe how businesses deal with:

- the cheque guarantee function
- the debit card function

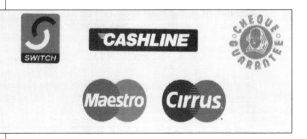

a card used to guarantee cheques

The rules for the use of a multifunction card used to guarantee a customer's cheques are normally set out in the agreement form signed when the card is issued. The following is an example of some of the conditions:

XYZ Bank plc guarantees in any single transaction the payment of one cheque taken from one of its own cheque books for up to £100 provided the cheque is not drawn on the account of a Limited Company, and

(1)   The cheque bears the same name and code number as this card.

(2)   It is signed, before the expiry of the card, in the United Kingdom of Great Britain and Northern Ireland, the Channel Islands or the Isle of Man in the presence of the payee by the person whose signature appears on this card.

(3)   The card number is written on the back of the cheque by the payee.

(4)   The card has not been altered or defaced.

receiving payment by cheque and guarantee card

If you have read the guarantee card conditions set out above you will appreciate that when you accept payment by cheque and cheque guarantee card you must take great care that all the conditions are met. If you do not, the purchaser's bank may not 'honour' (pay) the cheque, and your organisation stands to lose the money. Also, because of the large number of stolen and fraudulent cards in circulation, you must be on your guard against suspicious-looking cards and customers. The procedure is therefore as follows:

- examine the card to make sure it is not defaced – rub your finger along the signature strip, does it feel normal? – a stolen card may have been tampered with and a new signature added

- if the card is handed to you in a plastic wallet, take the card out, as it may be a forgery

- examine the card for

  - expiry date

  - amount of the guarantee

  - name agreeing with the name on the cheque

  - bank details agreeing with those on the cheque

- examine the cheque for

  - signature (this should agree with the signature on the card)

  - date

  - payee's name

  - amount in words and figures (they should agree)

- write the card number on the back of the cheque – an essential procedure, adding any other details which your organisation requires (some businesses use a rubber stamp on the back of the cheque to list the required details)

cheque card limits – a common mistake

Bank customers sometimes think that if the cost of the item being purchased is above the cheque guarantee limit, then a number of cheques may be issued and payment is guaranteed. This is not correct – the cheque card guarantee covers only *one cheque per transaction*.

DEBIT CARDS

Debit cards are issued to personal customers by banks and building societies to enable their customers to make payments from their bank accounts by Electronic Funds Transfer (see page 86). *No cheque is written out*. Debit cards are issued to selected customers of the bank; they enable a payment to be made from the person's bank account electronically. A debit card has the obvious advantages of being quicker to use and more convenient. Examples of debit cards are Barclays' Connect (see below) and Royal Bank of Scotland Highline cards.

From a seller's point of view, when a customer wishes to pay by debit card in person, the transaction is handled in a similar way to a credit card, (see next page) using either

- a manually completed sales voucher on an imprinter, or, more commonly
- an electronic swipe machine, either 'standalone' (used by smaller organisations) or connected to an electronic till (as in the big supermarkets)

CREDIT CARDS

Credit cards provide a means of obtaining goods and services immediately, but paying for them later. The commonest credit cards used in the UK use the names Visa and Mastercard. The card illustrated below is a Visa Barclaycard.

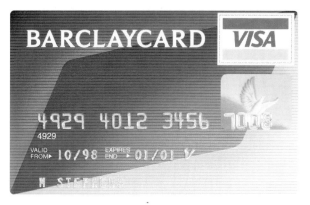

Credit cards are issued, upon application, to customers of banks, building societies, and retail groups. A credit limit is set on each cardholder's credit card account (which is entirely separate from his or her normal bank account). Goods and services can be obtained at shops and other outlets having computer terminals or the special machine (imprinter) for preparing sales vouchers to record the transaction. Credit cards can also be used for mail order and telephone order sales. Retailers pay to the credit card company a set percentage (up to 5%) of each transaction amount for the use of the credit card facility.

Each month a cardholder is sent a statement of the purchases made and can choose to pay off the balance of the account, or to pay part only (subject to a certain minimum amount), carrying forward the remaining balance to next month. Interest is charged on balances owing to the credit card company. An annual flat fee is sometimes charged to the cardholder for the use of the card.

ACCEPTING CARD PAYMENTS – 'OVER THE COUNTER' SALES

A business will have one of two methods of receiving payment by credit card or debit card by a customer who calls in person:

- a mechanical imprinter machine, which imprints the embossed details from the credit card onto the sales voucher
- a 'swipe' machine – as seen on electronic tills – which is able to read the details from a credit or debit card as it is passed through the card 'reader'

mechanical imprinter machine

The procedure is as follows:

- check that the card has not been defaced or tampered with – check the signature strip carefully
- check that the card has not expired
- imprint the sales voucher (see illustration below)
- complete the sales voucher with date, details of goods, and total money amount
- the customer signs the imprinted sales voucher, and the signature should be compared with that on the card
- the list of stolen cards is checked
- if the payment is above a certain amount – the *floor limit* (which varies according to the type of business) it will be necessary to telephone the credit card company to obtain an authorisation code allowing the transaction to go ahead (the authorisation code is recorded on the sales voucher)
- the top copy of the sales voucher is handed to the customer, and the other three copies are retained
- of the three copies of the sales voucher which are retained, the white copy is treated in the same way as a cheque, and is kept in the till and added to the cheques and cash received to give the total sales figure; the other two copies (yellow and blue) are kept in the event of a query in the future
- the white copy of the sales voucher kept in the till is then banked along with the cash and cheques

a credit card sales voucher

credit and debit card sales with a 'swipe' machine

A 'swipe' machine is so-called because the cashier accepting the payment 'swipes' it through an electronic reader on either a 'standalone' machine (used by smaller organisations) or connected to an electronic till (as in the big supermarkets – see the photograph on page 75).

A swipe machine can be used for both credit card and debit card transactions.

The cashier or clerk should:

- 'swipe' the card through the card reader – this 'captures' the details encoded in the magnetic stripe on the reverse of the card
- having captured the data, the system checks automatically that the card number is valid
- the amount of the transaction is keyed into the electronic till, and the system (if the till is on-line) checks the cardholder's credit limit or account balance and authorises the transaction
- a telephone call to the card company may be necessary to authorise the transaction if the till is not on-line
- the till prints a two-part receipt which includes space for the cardholder's signature
- the customer signs, and the signature is compared with that on the card
- the customer is handed the top-copy of the receipt, and the other copy is kept in the event of a query in the future
- the amount of the transaction is automatically debited
  - in the case of a credit card to the cardholder's credit card account
  - in the case of a debit card to the cardholder's bank account
- the amount of the transaction is automatically credited to the bank account of the business
- the business will receive a regular schedule of amounts automatically paid into the bank account (see illustration below); this will be checked with the bank statement when it is received

---

ALBION BANK CARD SERVICES **PAYMENT SUMMARY** 12 March 2001

Debit/credit card batches paid to account Hermes Trading Limited, Albion Bank, Mereford Account 1248934

Date	Type	Amount
05 03 01	Credit Card batch	1356.75
05 03 01	Switch transactions	56.75
07 03 01	Credit Card batch	1756.29
07 03 01	Switch transactions	128.00
09 03 01	Credit Card batch	5634.01
09 03 01	TOTAL FOR WEEK	8931.80

Charges to account.1248934: **Credit card charges** (2.5%) £218.68 **Debit card charges** £5.50

checks when accepting a card for a 'swipe' machine

There are a number of checks that should be made when accepting payment when operating a 'swipe' machine. These apply to debit cards and to credit cards. You should make sure that:

- the card has an appropriate logo, eg 'Switch' – you will probably have a list against which you can compare the logo
- the card has a magnetic stripe on the reverse
- the card has not expired
- the start date on the card is not in the future
- the card holder title is appropriate (eg a card issued to Miss Helen Jones is not used by a man!)
- the signature on the card is consistent and has not been tampered with
- the card has not been defaced or mutilated in any way
- any photograph on the card looks like the customer

credit and debit card mail order and telephone sales

Buying goods and services by credit card and debit card over the telephone or by mail order has become increasingly common. When accepting payment by this means, the organisation must exercise the same degree of care as a shop accepting an 'over the counter' transaction. Some organisations will complete the same type of sales voucher used for an 'over the counter' transaction and send the top copy to the customer as a receipt; some organisations will use a 'swipe' machine, and send a copy of the receipt to the customer. Organisations which have a large volume of transactions will not use vouchers but instead record the details of sales on a Mail Order Schedule, a form which will provide space for recording ten transactions or more.

When accepting payment by credit card by telephone or mail order, the following details must be obtained:

- the card number
- the expiry date of the card
- the issue number and/or start date of any debit card
- the name and initials of the cardholder as shown on the card
- the cardholder's address
- the cardholder's signature (mail order only)
- authorisation of amounts over the 'floor limit' must be carried out in the normal way

Internet sales are also booming – these are described on page 87.

floor limits and authorisations

As we have seen, it may be necessary from time-to-time for a business accepting a debit or credit card payment to seek authorisation for the transaction from the card merchant company (the company that deals with all the payments). Authorisation can be given over the telephone or in some cases electronically. Authorisation may be needed in a number of situations:

- when the amount of the transaction exceeds the Floor Limit (this limit is a figure set by the card merchant company)
- the terminal indicates that the card is not valid for some reason or other (it may be out of date)
- when the cashier is suspicious about the signature
- when the cashier is suspicious about the customer
- the terminal indicates that the cashier should contact the card merchant company (it may be a stolen card!)

These authorisations are important because if they are not carried out the business accepting payment may lose the money – it will not be a guaranteed payment. Many retail businesses give rewards to vigilant cashiers who recover a stolen card used by a suspicious customer – who normally runs out of the store when the cashier decides to ask for authorisation!

ELECTRONIC FUNDS TRANSFER AT POINT OF SALE (EFTPOS)

EFT stands for 'Electronic Funds Transfer'. Credit card and debit card transactions which go through a 'swipe' machine are processed by a system known as *Electronic Funds Transfer at Point Of Sale* (EFTPOS). This allows a retail outlet to debit the bank account or credit card account of the purchaser at the point of sale and, at the same time, to credit the retailer's bank account. Besides removing the need to carry a lot of cash, the system reduces the paperwork of writing out cheques or filling in card vouchers.

Details of the transaction are transmitted electronically by means of a computer link to a central computer either immediately, or, normally, at the end of the day.

The benefits of EFTPOS to a retail business are:

- greater efficiency, with less time taken by customers to make payment
- reduced queuing time
- less cash to handle (giving fewer security risks)
- guaranteed payment once acceptance has been made

INTERNET PAYMENT TRANSACTIONS

Businesses which have on-line facilities for selling their products from their websites carry out these sales on a 'remote control' basis. They do not deal with these customers personally. The customers order and pay for the goods on-line using a credit or debit card and all the the business has to do is to despatch the goods (eg an on-line shop) or provide the service (eg a holiday company). The money is credited directly to the bank account of the business.

The business will receive a schedule of the payments received which it can check against its bank statement.

The buying public is naturally concerned about the security of this system. Stories abound of people hacking into shop and bank websites and obtaining names and credit card numbers and then going on spending sprees. Businesses setting up on-line selling facilities have to ensure that the security of the system is as watertight as it can be. Software companies are constantly working to improve levels of security and methods of encoding data ('encryption') so that payment details – including card numbers – remain secret.

The mechanics of how the payment from an internet purchase reaches the bank of account of the seller is explained in detail on page 112.

PAYABLE ORDERS

Sometimes a business will receive documents similar to cheques as a means of payment. These *payable orders* include

- *Postal orders* – money orders purchased from the Post Office, often used by people who do not have bank accounts and who wish to send money through the post.

- *Bank drafts* – these are cheques issued by a *bank* and are as good as cash. They are bank cheques so they will not 'bounce' – the bank is both drawer (issuer) and drawee (the bank that pays). Drafts are often used by people wanting to pay large amounts, eg for a house or car purchase.

- *Building society cheques* – these work on the same principle as bank drafts, except that the drawer (issuer) is a building society and the drawee (the organisation who has to make payment) is a bank. Like bank drafts, they are considered to be as good as cash payments.

If you receive payment in the form of a postal order, bank draft or building society cheque, it can be paid into the bank account like a cheque.

CHECKING PAYMENTS AGAINST DOCUMENTATION

It is important that incoming payments received from customers are checked against any documentation that the supplier receives. This is to ensure that the correct amount is received and that no future disputes can arise – for example "We sent you £450, that's what it says on our advice" ... "No you didn't, you only sent us £405, that's what it shows on your account."

The most common type of document which advises the amount of a payment is a *remittance advice* (see page 179 for an explanation of this document).

Payments from customers can be received either through the post, or through the bank as inter-bank transfers. A remittance advice will be issued in both instances by the person paying.

postal payments

Any cheque received through the post should be checked carefully against the accompanying remittance advice, which can be

- a special form prepared by the person paying, setting out the amount of the cheque, the date and the item(s) the cheque is covering, or
- a tear-off slip sent with the statement of account by the seller; often the items being paid are ticked off by the buyer, but the amount of the cheque may not be written down

In both cases (and particularly the second) the organisation receiving payment *must* check that the total of the items being paid less any credit due equals the amount of the cheque. Failure to carry out this simple check could cause problems later on if there is a discrepancy. Any differences should be marked on the remittance advice which is then normally queried with the customer by telephone.

inter-bank transfers – BACS

An increasing number of payments are now made automatically from bank account to bank account, normally on the instructions of the payer, through the BACS system (BACS stands for Bankers Automated Clearing Services). As no cheque is issued, payment is made more quickly and more cheaply. The problem of how the seller is to *know* that payment is made is solved by the buyer sending a BACS advice – essentially a remittance advice for a BACS payment.

BACS payments are made in a number of situations:

- by customers who buy from a business regularly, settling up invoices
- by people paying standing orders (a regular payment) – the BACS payment is originated by the person sending the money

- by people paying direct debits – a regular payment from bank account to bank account where the payment is originated by the business receiving the money

The organisation receiving payment will have to check each advice carefully against the bank statement when it arrives to ensure that the correct amount has been received. In the case of the direct debit, the business receiving the money has also originated the transfer, so the bank statement will be checked against the payment schedule produced internally by the business.

Examples of remittance advices are shown below.

TO	**REMITTANCE ADVICE**	FROM	
Cool Socks Limited Unit 45 Elgar Estate, Broadfield, BR7 4ER		**Trends** **4 Friar Street** **Broadfield** **BR1 3RF** Tel 01908 761234 Fax 01908 761987 VAT REG GB 0745 8383 56	

date	your reference	our reference	payment amount
01 10 00 10 10 00	INVOICE 787923 CREDIT NOTE 12157	47609 47609	277.30 (27.73)
		CHEQUE TOTAL	249.57

remittance advice sent with a cheque payment

BACS REMITTANCE ADVICE

FROM: Trends
4 Friar Street
Broadfield BR1 3RF

TO
Cool Socks Limited
Unit 45 Elgar Estate, Broadfield, BR7 4ER

06 11 01

Your ref	Our ref		Amount
787923	47609	BACS TRANSFER	249.57
		TOTAL	249.57

THIS HAS BEEN PAID BY BACS CREDIT TRANSFER DIRECTLY INTO YOUR BANK ACCOUNT AT ALBION BANK NO 11451226 SORT CODE 90 47 17

remittance advice sent to advise of a BACS payment

RECORDING MONEY RECEIVED

The individual amounts of money received should be recorded by the organisation. The *way* in which they are recorded will depend on the way in which they are received. The fact that the amounts are recorded will help security by discouraging employees from being tempted to raid the till and steal money.

cash registers

Money received over a counter is likely to be recorded on a cash register tally roll or electronic till memory – the totals on the till roll or memory can then be checked with the actual money received, ready for paying into the bank. The security of cash registers is tightly controlled: they are operated by a security key and any transfer of change is recorded. The more modern cash registers (supermarket tills, for example) are linked to a central computer and automatically change the stock level records as items are sold.

remittance lists (postal items)

Cheques and other money received may be recorded manually on a *remittance list*. 'Remittance list' just means a list of what you have been sent. It can record items received through the post by a business, or it can be used at the counter of old-fashioned shops (eg old bookshops) instead of a cash register. A remittance list for items received through the post is likely to include columns for the date, sender, the nature of the 'remittance,' amount, and, as a security measure, the signature of the person opening the post.

date	sender	remittance	amount	signature
12.3.01	Travers Toys Ltd	cheque	234.50	G.Palmer
12.3.01	Grampian Traders	bank draft	10,500.00	G Palmer
12.3.01	Mrs D Dodds	cash	14.50	R Patel
12.3.01	Mercia Foods	cheque	450.00	G Palmer

example of a remittance list for items received through the post

remittance lists/cash received lists

A remittance list is also used to record payments received over the counter. It is an old-fashioned method, but it serves its purpose very well. The person at the till will record each sale as it occurs; the cash and cheques are likely to be kept in a locked cash box, as there is no cash register. The total of the remittance list (or *cash received list*) should be agreed with the takings at the end of each day.

The items can either be written on a separate piece of paper or they may be entered in a book. The example below shows the sales made by a second-hand bookshop during the course of day.

FOLIO BOOKS   takings for *22 January 2001*

Milton, Paradise Lost, 1793	*cash*	*£45.00*
Hardy, Mayor of Casterbridge, 1896	*cheque*	*£65.00*
Graham Greene, The End of the Affair	*cash*	*£1.75*
Punch selections	*cheque*	*£25.00*
T S Eliot, 4 Quartets	*cheque*	*£12.50*
Haynes, Worcester within the Walls	*cheque*	*£14.95*
Culpeper, Tudor Remedies	*cash*	*£4.95*
W English, Alvechurch - a History	*cheque*	*£9.95*
TOTAL CASH		*£51.70*
TOTAL CHEQUES		*£127.40*
Total Takings		*£179.10*

---

example of a remittance list for items received over the counter

cash book

The cash book is the central record of money amounts received and paid out by the organisation either in the form of cash, or as items passed through the bank account. All the receipts referred to in this chapter will eventually pass through the cash book. It will be dealt with in detail in Chapter 6.

CHAPTER SUMMARY

- Incoming payments can be received in a number of ways: cash, cheque, credit and debit card, inter-bank transfer from BACS and internet sales.

- Receipts are often issued for cash payments; either till receipts or handwritten receipts.

- Cash in a till will be counted up at the end of each day; the amount should equal the takings for the day plus any 'float' held in the till.

- Cheques should be examined carefully when taken in payment, either over the counter or through the post. Normally they are crossed, sometimes they can be endorsed over, although this practice is becoming less common.

- Cheques received over the counter are normally only accepted with a bank multi-function card which has a cheque guarantee. When this occurs, the card and the cheque should be carefully inspected together.

- Debit cards are commonly accepted as a means of payment in place of cash or cheques. They are processed either with a mechanical imprinter or alternatively with an electronic 'swipe' machine.

- Payment can also be accepted by credit card – here the seller has to generate a paper sales voucher, either with a mechanical imprinter or alternatively with an electronic 'swipe' machine. A credit card enables payment to be made to the credit card company by the buyer at a later date.

- If a business uses an electronic 'swipe' machine, the money will be transferred electronically from the customer's bank account or credit card account to the business bank account. This system is known as EFTPOS (Electronic Funds Transfer at Point Of Sale).

- Sales transaction over the Internet are processed under secure conditions and the money transferred automatically to the seller's bank account.

- When payments are evidenced by documentation such as a remittance advice, the payment should be checked against the documentation. Payment in this case can be by cheque or by inter-bank transfer.

- When money is received it should be recorded, both for security purposes and also as part of the operation of the accounting system. Forms of recording include the cash till roll, remittance lists and the cash book.

KEY TERMS

cash float	the amount of cash kept in a till at the end of the day to provide change when the till is next used
cheque	a written order to the bank, signed by its customer, instructing it to pay a specified amount to a specified person
drawer of a cheque	the person who signs the front of the cheque – the customer from whose account the money is to be paid

**KEY
TERMS
continued**

drawee of a cheque	the bank which has to make payment – its name and address normally appears at the top of the cheque
payee of a cheque	the person to whom the cheque is payable – normally specified on the first line of the cheque amount
cheque crossing	two parallel lines on the front of a cheque, with or without writing in them – they mean that the cheque has to be paid into a bank account
endorsement	a signature on the back of the cheque (normally the payee's) meaning that the cheque can be passed to someone else to pay into their account
'account payee' crossing	two parallel lines on the face of the cheque with the words 'account payee' between them – the cheque cannot be endorsed over – it must be paid into the account of the payee
bank guarantee card	a plastic card issued by a bank to its customer which will guarantee payment of its customer's cheque up to a certain limit
debit card	a plastic card which enables customers to make payment for purchases without having to write out a cheque – payment is made electronically from the bank account straightaway
credit card	a plastic card issued by a credit card company which enables customers to make purchases and pay for them at a later date
EFTPOS	EFTPOS stands for Electronic Funds Transfer at Point Of Sale – the electronic transfer of payments between the bank accounts of buyer and seller which is originated at a till
BACS	BACS stands for Bankers Automated Clearing Services, a body (owned by the banks) which organises computer payments between bank accounts
remittance advice	a document sent to the recipient of a payment, advising that a payment is being made
remittance list	also known as a 'cash received list' – a record of money amounts received, either through the post, or over the counter
cash book	the central record kept by a business of cash and bank transactions

STUDENT ACTIVITIES

4.1 You operate the cash till at the firm where you work. The following are the sales for one day:

		Amount of sale £	Notes and/or coin tendered
Customer	1	8.50	£10 note
	2	3.30	£10 note
	3	2.51	£5 note
	4	1.79	£5 note
	5	0.34	£1 coin
	6	6.22	£10 note
	7	12.76	£20 note
	8	1.42	two £1 coins
	9	6.54	£10 note
	10	3.08	£5 note

Calculate
(a) the amount of change to be given to each customer
(b) the notes and/or coins that will be given in change, using the minimum number possible

4.2 If the cash till in activity 1 had a float of £28.71 at the start of the day, how much cash should be held in the till after the sales from activity 1 had been made? Present your answer in the following form:

	£
cash float at start	28.71
plus sales made during the day	
equals amount of cash held at end of day	————

4.3 You work as a shop counter assistant at New Era Lighting. You make a number of sales during the day (use today's date) which require the completion of a handwritten receipt. Complete the receipts set out on the next page. Include VAT on all purchases at the current rate. All prices quoted here are catalogue prices and exclude VAT.

(a) 2 flexilamps @ £13.99, 2 60W candlelight bulbs @ 85p, to Mr George Ohm

NEW ERA LIGHTING   977

17 High Street Mereford MR1 2TF

VAT reg 141 7645 23

CASH RECEIPT

Customer...date............................

VAT	
TOTAL	

(b) 1 standard lamp @ £149.95, 1 3 amp plug @ 99p, to Mr Alex Bell

NEW ERA LIGHTING   978

17 High Street Mereford MR1 2TF

VAT reg 141 7645 23

CASH RECEIPT

Customer...date............................

VAT	
TOTAL	

(c) 2 external Georgian lamps @ £35.99, to Tom Edison

NEW ERA LIGHTING   979

17 High Street Mereford MR1 2TF

VAT reg 141 7645 23

CASH RECEIPT

Customer...date............................

VAT	
TOTAL	

4.4 Examine the cheque shown below and state who is

(a)   the drawer

(b)   the drawee

(c)   the payee

In each case, explain what the term means.

Southern Bank PLC Mereford Branch 16 Broad Street, Mereford MR1 7TR	date *9 October 2001*	97-76-54

Pay   *Electron Games Limited*   only

Three hundred pounds only   £ *300.00*

Account payee only

A & S SYSTEMS LTD

G Brown

762511   977654   68384939   Director

4.5 What difference does a crossing on a cheque make to the payee?

4.6 What do the following cheque crossings mean?:

(a)   _____

(b)   Barclays Bank, Hanover Square

(c)   & co

(d)   account payee

(e)   account payee only

(f)   not negotiable

4.7 Henry Enfield is the payee of a cheque which has the following crossing

_____

(a)   What *should* happen to the cheque if it is endorsed like this:

Pay Sandra Lobb
Henry Enfield

(b)   What *could* happen to the cheque if it is endorsed like this?

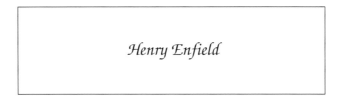

4.8   List three checks a cashier should make to a cheque when receiving it in the post for payment of an outstanding invoice.

4.9   List three checks a cashier should make when accepting a cheque over the counter when the cheque is supported by a bank guarantee card.

4.10   List three checks a cashier should make when accepting a credit card payment over the counter.

4.11   What should a cashier do if the amount of a purchase being made by a customer (£500) exceeds the cheque guarantee amount of £200 on the customer's card?
(a)   Refuse to allow the purchase to go ahead.
(b)   Ask for three cheques: £200, £200 and £100, all dated differently.
(c)   Ask the customer to use the credit card which the cashier has spotted in the customer's card wallet.
(d)   Request the customer to go and get a bank draft for £500.
Choose *one* answer.

4.12   If a credit card purchase exceeds the shop's floor limit, it should be refused. True or false?

4.13   The advantage to a shop of accepting payment by debit card is that
(a)   All cheques are automatically guaranteed.
(b)   There is no cheque.
(c)   The cheque is automatically debited to the customer' bank account.
(d)   The signature on the cheque is automatically verified.
Choose *one* answer.

4.14   EFT stands for:
(a)   Electronic Foreign Transfer
(b)   Electronic Financial Transaction
(c)   Electronic Funds Till
(d)   Electronic Funds Transfer
Choose *one* answer.

4.15   List three advantages to a shop of using EFTPOS.

4.16   (a)   Who is the drawer and the drawee of a bank draft?
(b)   Give examples of two transactions for which a bank draft would be suitable.

4.17   Give two examples of situations where a remittance list would be used.

5 PAYING INTO THE BANK

this chapter covers . . .

This chapter explains the relationship between banks and their customers and sets out the procedures for paying money into the bank. The chapter covers the areas of

- the legal relationship between the bank and its customers

- banking services available to customers

- the bank clearing system

- paying money into the bank using paying-in slips

- banking documents, including sales voucher summaries and statements

- security procedures used when handling cash

NVQ PERFORMANCE CRITERIA COVERED

unit 1: RECORDING INCOME AND RECEIPTS
element 2
receive and record receipts

- paying-in documents are correctly prepared and reconciled to relevant records

KNOWLEDGE AND UNDERSTANDING COVERAGE

- the use of banking documentation

- automated payments: CHAPS, BACS, Direct Debits, Standing Orders

- credit and debit cards

- methods of handling and storing money, including the security aspects

- banking and personal security procedures

BANKS AND CUSTOMERS

By way of introduction we will look briefly at the legal background to the bank and customer relationship, the main types of accounts offered by banks to their personal and business customers, and the bank clearing system.

a legal relationship

It is important to appreciate when studying and practising banking procedures that there is a distinct *legal relationship* between a bank and its customer. Normally this relationship does not give much cause for concern; it is only when something goes wrong – for example when a bank pays a cheque which its customer has stopped – that the legal relationship becomes particularly important.

bank and customer contract

In law there is said to be a *contract* between the customer and the bank. A contract may be defined as:

a legally binding agreement which is recognised in a court of law

You may wonder why a contract between a bank and a customer is important in business dealings. The answer is that the bank/customer contract means that the customer has certain rights and duties to perform, including keeping the bank account in credit (not overdrawn, unless by arrangement) and taking care when writing out cheques so that they cannot be altered by a fraudster.

If the customer fails in any of these duties and the bank loses a substantial amount of money, it has the right in law under the contract to take the customer to court to recover its money.

Similarly, the bank has certain rights and duties to perform under the contract, and if it fails to do so and the customer suffers a loss (money or reputation), the customer can take the bank to court. Examples of the bank's duties include:

- paying the customer's cheques when there is sufficient money in the account
- keeping details of the customer's account secret
- sending statements of account to the customer

Clearly a customer will not take a bank to court if a statement is not sent out! But it may do so if the bank by mistake fails to pay a business cheque issued to a supplier, and the supplier cuts off supplies to the business. This could bankrupt the customer and is a clear *breach of the contract* between the bank and the customer. For further details of the theory of contract see Chapter 15.

BANK/CUSTOMER RELATIONSHIPS

There are a number of different bank/customer relationships:

debtor and creditor

This terminology relates to whether or not the customer has any money in the bank. Remember that:

debtor = a person who owes money

creditor = a person to whom you owe money

Therefore:

customer has money in bank: *customer = creditor (is owed money)*
        bank = debtor (owes money)

customer is borrowing: *customer = debtor (owes money)*
        bank = creditor (is owed money)

This may seem complicated, but if you think it through, it is logical.

mortgagor and mortgagee

If the customer has a mortgage with the bank (a mortgage is a legal document which secures a loan), the customer is a *mortgagor* and the bank is a *mortgagee.*

bailor and bailee

If the customer deposits valuable items in the bank's safe, the customer is a *bailor* and the bank a *bailee.*

principal and agent

If the customer uses the bank to carry out a transaction, eg to arrange an insurance policy, to sell shares, then the customer is known as the *principal* and the bank the *agent.* Note that the word 'agent' is also used in 'travel agent' and 'estate agent' – businesses that arrange travel and property deals.

TYPES OF ACCOUNT

There are three main types of accounts offered by banks to its customers:

- current account
- deposit (savings) account
- loan accounts

current account

With this type of account a bank customer is issued with a cheque book and may make use of most of the services of the bank. Bank customers use a current account as a 'working account' into which receipts are paid and out of which are paid expenses by means of cheques and automated computer payments. Many current accounts now pay interest.

overdraft

Banks are often prepared to grant overdraft facilities to their current account customers on request. A business, for example, realizing that it will need overdraft facilities should contact the bank and seek agreement for an overdraft up to a certain limit for a specified time. Interest is charged on overdrawn balances and an arrangement/renewal fee is normally payable.

deposit account

A deposit account is used for savings by personal customers, or excess money held by a business, and interest is paid by the bank. Current account facilities such as cheque books, standing orders, direct debits, and overdrafts are not allowed on deposit accounts for business customers. Notice of withdrawal may need to be given to the bank. Other types of account may need a longer period of notice of withdrawal, perhaps one month or three months.

Many business customers have both a current and a deposit account. A business can use a deposit account as a temporary 'home' for surplus money. When the money is needed it can be transferred easily to the firm's current account.

loan accounts

Whereas an overdraft is a means of borrowing on an ordinary current account and will cover day-to-day running (revenue) expenses of the business, loan accounts are long-term loans for items of capital expenditure, eg machinery and new projects. Different banks will offer different types of loan account. Some typical examples include:

business loan

A loan for three to ten years to cover large items of expense such as new plant, premises expansion, a new project.

commercial mortgage

A loan for up to twenty five years to cover the purchase of property (the business equivalent of a 'home loan' mortgage to an individual).

CHEQUE CLEARING

Every working day each bank branch receives cheques paid in by customers. These cheques take a defined time to 'clear'. The term to 'clear' means that the cheque must have passed to the bank of the issuer of the cheque for payment before the money amount of the cheque – the amount paid in – can be used by the customer. The clearance times are normally:

- cheques paid in and issued by customers of the same branch – same day clearance

- cheques paid in by customers of other banks and branches – three working days' clearance

This means that if you are given a cheque by someone who has an account at your branch and you pay it in on Monday, you can draw against it, ie you can use the money on the account, on Monday, the same day. This assumes, of course, that the cheque is paid and does not 'bounce'. On the other hand, if you are given a cheque which is issued by someone who banks at another bank (or another branch of your bank), then if you pay it in on Monday, you will have to wait three working days, ie until Wednesday before the cheque is cleared, and you can use the money.

The reason for this delay is that the cheque will have to be sent to London for sorting. This long and expensive process, required by a law dating back to the nineteenth century, is illustrated on the next page. In this case Enigma Cafe, which banks at HSBC Bank in Malvern pays a cheque for £500 to their supplier, Broadheath Bakers, who then pay it into their bank, Barclays Bank in Worcester. The diagram follows the two hundred and fifty mile journey of the cheque. The two bank branches, incidentally, are seven miles apart.

special clearance

Sometimes you may need to know quickly whether or not a cheque will be paid, for example, if you sell goods for £5,000 to an unknown buyer. The banks offer a special clearance service, known as a Special Presentation, where for a fee (around £10) a bank will send a cheque to the issuer's branch by first class post, and then telephone the following day in the morning to establish whether or not the cheque will be paid.

returned cheques

You may be in the unfortunate position of having paid in a cheque and then discovering that the cheque has been returned to your bank *unpaid*, and the amount of the cheque deducted from your account. Your bank will normally send it back to you by post. You will receive it five days after paying it in.

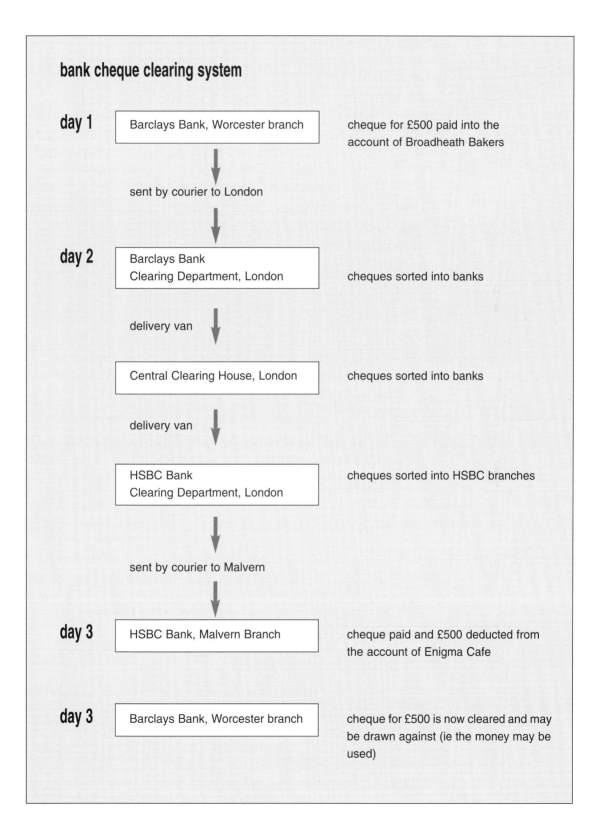

bank cheque clearing system

day 1 Barclays Bank, Worcester branch   cheque for £500 paid into the
                                                     account of Broadheath Bakers

sent by courier to London

day 2 Barclays Bank
           Clearing Department, London   cheques sorted into banks

delivery van

Central Clearing House, London   cheques sorted into banks

delivery van

HSBC Bank
Clearing Department, London   cheques sorted into HSBC branches

sent by courier to Malvern

day 3 HSBC Bank, Malvern Branch   cheque paid and £500 deducted from
                                                     the account of Enigma Cafe

day 3 Barclays Bank, Worcester branch   cheque for £500 is now cleared and may
                                                     be drawn against (ie the money may be
                                                     used)

It will have one of a number of answers written along the top:

- **refer to drawer** – the person who has given you the cheque (the drawer) has no money in the bank – you will have to contact him or her for an explanation! This answer is often abbreviated to "RD"

- **refer to drawer, please represent** – (abbreviated to "RDPR") – this means that there was not enough money in the account to meet the cheque, but that the cheque has been sent through the clearing again (represented) in the hope that it will be paid when it reaches the issuers bank (note that in this case the cheque will *not* be sent back to the payee)

- **payment countermanded by order of drawer** – the cheque has been stopped – you should contact the drawer to find out the reason

- **technical problems** such as a signature required, or words and figures differ, or out of date, will mean that you will have to contact the drawer for a new cheque (if the reason is out of date), or a signature, or an alteration (which will have to be signed by the drawer)

stopped cheques

We mentioned at the beginning of the chapter that it is the bank's duty in contract law to pay a customer's cheque as long as there is sufficient money in the account. A customer may order a bank not to pay a cheque; this is known as *stopping* a cheque. This often happens if a cheque is lost in the post and another cheque is issued in its place. The bank may make a charge for stopping a cheque, and will return the cheque marked "payment countermanded by order of drawer" if and when it is paid in and presented for payment.

PAYING-IN SLIPS

Business customers are issued with a *paying-in* book by the bank. These books will normally be pre-printed with the customer's name and account number together with details of the bank branch where the money will be paid in. Occasionally a blank paying-in slip will need to be completed, and that is the type illustrated on the next page. Details to be completed by the business paying in the money are:

- the name of the bank and branch where the account is held (normally pre-printed)

- the name of the account to be credited, together with the account number (normally pre-printed)

- a summary of the different categories of notes or coins being paid in, the amount of each category being entered on the slip

- amounts and details of cheques being paid in, usually entered on the reverse of the slip, with the total entered on the front
- the cash and cheques being paid in are totalled to give the amount being paid in
- the counterfoil is completed
- the person paying-in will sign the slip

A completed paying-in slip (with counterfoil) is illustrated below.

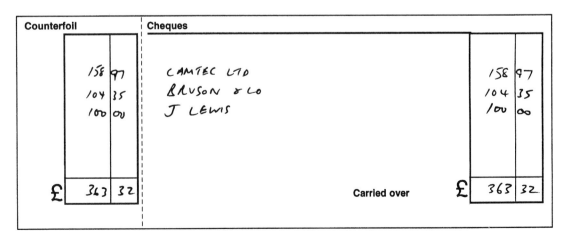

paying-in slip and counterfoil (front)

paying-in slip and counterfoil (back)

PROCEDURES FOR PAYING IN

the accounting process

Cash and cheques paid in at the bank will normally have been received by the business as cash sales and on remittance advices from debtors, and so form part of the accounting process. We will see how they are entered in the cash book in Chapter 6.

preparing the cash

The notes should be counted, checked and sorted so that they all face the same way, but should be kept separate. Defaced (damaged) notes, and notes from Scotland and Northern Ireland are normally accepted by banks.

Coins should normally be sorted and placed in bags as follows:

denomination	amount in bag
£2	£20
£1	£20
50p	£10
20p	£10
10p	£5
5p	£5
2p	£1
1p	£1

preparing the cheques

The cheques must first be examined carefully for any irregularities, such as

- **signatures** – has the drawer signed the cheque?
- **endorsements** – if the name on the payee line is not the same as the name of the account into which it is being paid, has it been suitably endorsed?
- **crossings** – if the cheque has the "account payee" wording in the crossing and your organisation is not the payee, it will not be possible to pay it in, even if it has been endorsed
- **date** – is it out of date (over six months old)? is it post-dated? – if so, it cannot be paid in
- **words and figures** – do they agree?

The details of the cheques – the amounts and the customer names – may then be listed on the back of the paying-in slip, as in the illustration on the previous page. If the volume of cheques paid in is very large, there will not be room on the paying-in slip, so the cheque details may be listed on a separate schedule. Some banks accept instead a calculator tally-roll listing the amounts, the number of cheques, and the total money amount transferred to the front of the paying-in slip. The important point is that the organisation paying in the cheques must keep a record of the cheque details in case of future queries, and in the unfortunate event of any of the cheques 'bouncing' – ie being returned unpaid.

paying in at the bank

At the bank the completed paying-in book is handed to the bank cashier together with the notes, coins, and cheques. The cashier counts the cash, ticks off the cheques and, if everything is correct, receipt stamps and initials the paying-in slip and counterfoil. The slip is retained by the bank for the amount to be credited to the account-holder, while the paying-in book is handed back, complete with the receipted counterfoil. A business paying-in book is sometimes larger than the paying-in slip illustrated, and sometimes there is a carbon copy behind the business paying-in slip which acts as a counterfoil.

security measures for cash handling – night safes

Care must be taken when taking large amounts of cash to the bank. If possible two staff members should visit the bank. If the amount is very large, for instance the takings from a department store, a security firm may be employed to carry the cash. If the cash is received by an organisation over the weekend or, late in the day, it may be placed in a special wallet and lodged in the bank's *night safe* – a small lockable door leading to a safe in the wall of the bank.

When a business pays in money to the bank, it will record the amount in its own records, called the cash book (see Chapter 6).

card voucher clearing – card merchant services

As we saw in the last chapter, the sales voucher is the basic document normally produced when a debit card and a credit card transaction are processed manually (see the illustration on page 83). The sales voucher may be produced as a result of an 'over the counter' sale or from a mail order or telephone sale. The details recorded on it will enable the card company to charge the amount to their customer's bank account (debit card transaction) or credit card account. The voucher like a cheque, is paid in at the bank and sent to the card company and 'cleared'.

Although there are a number of different card companies – Mastercard and Visa for example – the normal practice is for the organisation accepting payment to sign an agreement with a separate company – a card merchant – which will accept all vouchers from cards issued by different companies. For example, a customer of The Royal Bank of Scotland may sign an agreement with a company called Roynet (owned by The Royal Bank of Scotland) and accept payment by Mastercard and Visa and other nominated cards. The customer will pay in all credit card vouchers on the one paying slip and schedule (see below) at The Royal Bank of Scotland. The bank will pass them to Roynet, which will then process them by sending them to the issuing card company (Mastercard or Visa, for example). Roynet is only one of a number of 'card merchant' companies which will process credit card sales vouchers.

The customer paying in the vouchers is charged a set percentage fee – usually between 2% and 5% – of the total sales amount. Some debit card transactions, Switch for example, are charged at a flat amount 'item charge'.

preparing card sales vouchers for paying-in

The vouchers are paid in after completion of a three-part Retailer Summary, illustrated below and on the next page. In this case three sales vouchers are listed on the back of the summary.

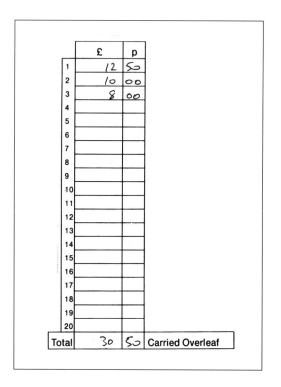

	£	p	
1	12	50	
2	10	00	
3	8	00	
4			
5			
6			
7			
8			
9			
10			
11			
12			
13			
14			
15			
16			
17			
18			
19			
20			
Total	30	50	Carried Overleaf

retailer sales voucher summary – back

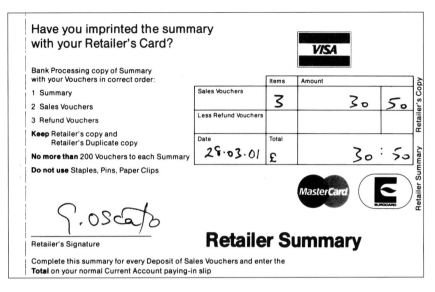

retailer sales voucher summary – front

The procedure for listing credit card sales vouchers on the retailer's summary is as follows:

- the summary is imprinted with details of the retailer using a plastic card – the Retailer's Card – supplied with the imprinter machine
- the amounts of the sales vouchers are listed on the reverse of the summary and totalled
- the total is carried forward to the front of the summary
- any refund vouchers are listed on the front of the summary
- the summary is dated, signed and totalled
- the summary is separated into its three copies – the top two are retained by the organisation and the bottom copy (the processing copy) is placed in front of the sales vouchers
- the processing copy and sales and any refund vouchers are placed in a transparent envelope and are paid into the bank on a paying-in slip, the total from the summary listed as a single item on the paying-in slip

Organisations which accept sales by mail and telephone may use schedules rather than sales vouchers for recording and listing the credit card transactions. The procedure for paying-in for these organisations is exactly the same, except that the totals of the schedule(s) are listed on the back of the Retailer Summary rather than the individual amounts of the sales vouchers as described above.

THE IMPORTANCE OF PAYING IN PROMPTLY

Organisations realise that if money is not banked promptly and safely, problems can arise.

theft

Cash is tempting to a thief, and it must be remembered that many instances of theft are carried out by employees of an organisation rather than by criminals with stockings over their heads. An organisation will therefore have a security policy, for example:

- cash and cheques being paid in will be kept under lock and key at the place of work, normally in a cash box, under the control of the cashier
- amounts received through the post or over the counter are recorded on remittance lists or on a cash register (or equivalent) as an additional security measure – money, once it is recorded, will be missed when stolen
- larger organisations will have a system of spot checking (internal audit) to identify any theft by employees
- arranging for cash and cheques to be taken to the bank by security firm (appropriate for large businesses)
- arranging for Friday and weekend takings of cash to be lodged in the bank's night safe
- making arrangements for payroll – the organisation will have to arrange the pick up of cash from the bank, using employees or a security firm

timescale – security and cashflow

Organisations will also have a policy for the prompt paying of money into the bank, for two main reasons – *security* and *cashflow.* Money kept on the premises is a security risk: the longer it remains there, the more likely it is that it will be stolen. Also, money not paid in is money that is not available for paying cheques and other items from the organisation's bank account: *cashflow* will be restricted. For example, it may be that the business is borrowing money on overdraft – it could save paying interest if money is banked promptly: a cheque for £50,000 lying around in the office for a week could cost the business over £50 in interest!

procedures

Because of these factors an organisation will draw up procedures for banking money. These will include the security measures mentioned above and also set timescales for paying in money, eg twice a week, one visit to coincide with the collection of the payroll cash (often a Friday). If you work in an accounts office, you will be familiar with these procedures.

confidentiality

If you work for an organisation, the importance of confidentiality will have been impressed on you. Confidentiality basically means not telling outsiders about the internal workings of your place of work. Important aspects of this include not talking to outsiders about your customers, not disclosing secret details of your products, and most importantly to this area of your studies, not disclosing your security arrangements for handling of money. Imagine the consequences of telling a group of friends in the pub that the firm's wages are collected from the bank every Friday at 10.00 in the morning.

AUTOMATED PAYMENTS INTO THE BANK

So far in this chapter we have looked at how a business pays into the bank manually, ie paying in on a paying-in slip. Many payments nowadays come into the bank account by computer transfer from other banks. The business will know about these payments because:

• it will receive notification either through the post or by e-mail

• the payments will appear on the bank statement (see page 114)

A business will enter details of cash and cheque payments in the accounts when the money is received. Payments received electronically must also be entered in the accounts when notification is received and checked in due course against the bank statement. The diagram below shows the variety of payments that can be received. The mechanics of *making* these payments are covered in Chapter 9.

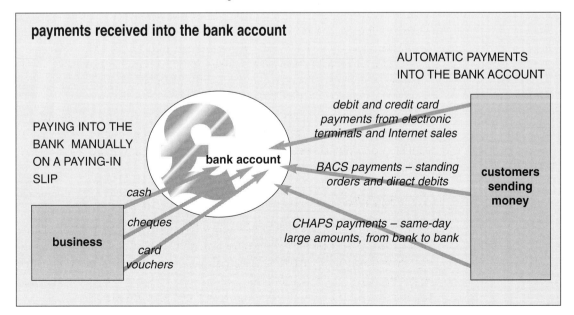

payments received into the bank account

PAYING INTO THE BANK MANUALLY ON A PAYING-IN SLIP

business

bank account

cash
cheques
card vouchers

AUTOMATIC PAYMENTS INTO THE BANK ACCOUNT

debit and credit card payments from electronic terminals and Internet sales

BACS payments – standing orders and direct debits

CHAPS payments – same-day large amounts, from bank to bank

customers sending money

PAYMENTS THROUGH THE INTERNET

the process

If a business has an Internet shopping facility, its customers order and pay for goods or services on-line using a credit or debit card and the money is credited direct to the bank account of the business. The business will receive a schedule of the payments received which it can check against its bank statement.

The diagram below shows the procedure adopted for this process. There is nothing significantly different about the way the system works – it is merely another way of providing a shopping outlet to customers with debit cards and credit cards.

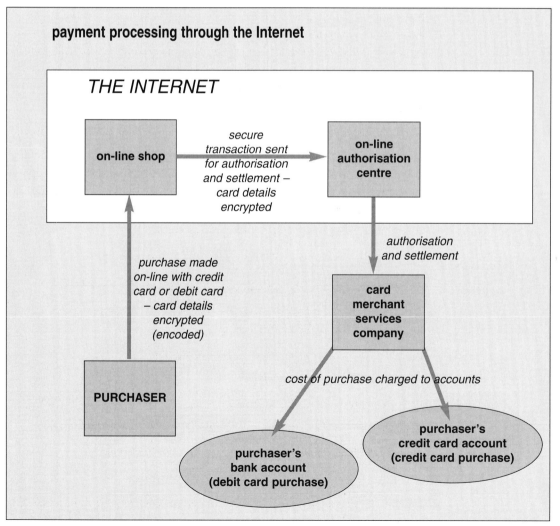

payment processing through the Internet

THE INTERNET

on-line shop

secure transaction sent for authorisation and settlement – card details encrypted

on-line authorisation centre

authorisation and settlement

purchase made on-line with credit card or debit card – card details encrypted (encoded)

card merchant services company

PURCHASER

cost of purchase charged to accounts

purchaser's bank account (debit card purchase)

purchaser's credit card account (credit card purchase)

As we noted in the last chapter, the buying public is concerned about the security of giving their names, addresses and card numbers on-line. Businesses setting up on-line selling facilities have to ensure that the security of the system is ensured by using software which encodes the data (data 'encryption') so that payment details remain secret.

This security is no different *in principle* from the security measures adopted by businesses which accept debit and credit card payments over the counter, ie to keep any records of customers and their card numbers under lock and key and not to throw copies of sales vouchers (with card numbers on) in the bin where they can be found by people commiting frauds.

BANK STATEMENTS

At regular intervals the bank sends out statements of account to its customers. A business current account with many items passing through it may have weekly statements, while a less active account or a deposit account may have monthly or even quarterly statements.

A bank statement is a summary showing:

- the balance at the beginning of the statement – 'balance brought forward'
- amounts paid into (credited to) the account
- amounts paid out of (debited to) the account – eg cheques issued, cheques returned 'unpaid', bank charges and standing orders and direct debits (automatic computer payments)

The balance of the account is shown after each transaction. A specimen bank statement is shown on the next page.

a note on debits, credits and bank accounts

You should be aware of the fact that the terms 'credit' and 'debit' mean different things to banks and their customers.

In the double-entry system of a business customer

> *debit = money received*
>
> *credit = money paid out*

Banks see things from the opposite angle. To their accounting system:

> *debit = money paid out from a customer's account*
>
> *credit = money paid into a customer's account*

In other words a credit to a bank account is the same as a debit in the books of a customer. Think about it!

Albion Bank plc

7 The Avenue, Broadfield, BR1 2AJ

		Account title	Trends
		Account number	11719512
		Statement	85

Date	Details	Payments	Receipts	Balance
2000				
1 Nov	Balance brought down			1,678.90 CR
9 Nov	Credit		1,427.85	3,106.75 CR
9 Nov	238628	249.57		2,857.18 CR
10 Nov	238629	50.00		2,807.18 CR
13 Nov	POS Switch		67.45	2,874.63 CR
16 Nov	Credit		100.00	2,974.63 CR
16 Nov	Albionet Card Services POS 2824242		500.00	3,474.63 CR
22 Nov	238630	783.90		2,690.73 CR
23 Nov	238626	127.00		2,563.73 CR
23 Nov	Albionet Netsales 43182639		1,006.70	3,570.43 CR
23 Nov	BACS ORLANDO 37646		162.30	3,732.73 CR
24 Nov	DD Westmid Gas	167.50		3,565.23 CR
27 Nov	238634	421.80		3,143.43 CR
27 Nov	DD RT Telecom	96.50		3,046.93 CR
30 Nov	Bank charges	87.50		2,959.43 CR

checking the bank statement for payments received

You will see from the specimen bank statement shown above that the balance of the account is followed each time by the abbreviation 'CR'. This means that the customer has a credit balance, ie has money in the bank. The abbreviation 'DR' would indicates a debit balance – an overdraft, ie the customer would owe the bank money and be a 'debtor' of the bank.

Note the following payments that have been received during the month:

- on 9 and 16 November the business has paid in on a paying-in slip
- on 13 November payment is received from debit card transactions
- on 16 November payment is received from credit card transactions
- on 23 November payment is received from Internet sales
- on 23 November payment is received via the BACS electronic transfer system – possibly a customer settling up an invoice

When a bank statement is received it should be checked and compared with the firm's record of bank receipts and payments – the cash book – (see Chapters 6 and 11).

- The legal relationship between a bank and its customer can take a number of forms: debtor and creditor, mortgagor and mortgagee, bailor and bailee, principal and agent.

- Banks offer a wide range of accounts: current accounts (including overdraft) deposit accounts and loan accounts.

- When a cheque is paid into a bank it normally takes three days to clear. When a cheque is cleared the person who has paid it in can draw on the money.

- A cheque can be returned unpaid ('bounce') for a number of reasons, eg 'refer to drawer' – which means there is no money in the drawer's bank account.

- Organisations pay money into their bank account on a paying-in slip which lists the cash and cheques paid in and totals the amounts.

- Cash and cheques must be checked and listed before they are paid in.

- Credit and debit card vouchers may also be paid into the bank account on a retailer summary form which lists all of the vouchers.

- Organisations should set up procedures to ensure that cash, cheques and card vouchers are kept safely on the premises and in transit to the bank.

- Money should be paid into the bank as soon as possible, both for security reasons and also to help the cashflow of the organisation.

- Automated payments – BACS, CHAPS and card payments processed electronically over-the-counter and through the Internet are also received into the bank account and will be advised to the business.

- Businesses should keep records of automatically processed card payments secure for security reasons – card numbers are valuable to thieves.

- Bank statements are sent regularly to customers and should be checked on receipt for manual and automatically processed payments received.

- To a bank, money paid in is a 'credit' and money paid out is a 'debit.'

KEY TERMS

contract	a legally binding agreement which is recognised in a court of law
mortgagor/mortgagee	when a mortgage is signed the borrower is the mortgagor and the bank the mortgagee
bailor/bailee	when a customer deposits items of value for safe keeping with a bank the customer is the bailor and the bank the bailee
principal/agent	when a customer asks the bank to carry out something on its behalf (eg arrange insurance) the customer is the principal and the bank the agent
cheque clearing	a system used by the banks to clear cheques paid in – the process takes three working days

KEY TERMS (continued)

paying-in slip	a paper slip listing cash and cheques paid into a bank
retailer summary	a form listing credit card sales vouchers paid into a bank account
night safe	a wallet or bag containing cash and cheques lodged with a bank (when it is closed) through an opening in the wall of the bank – used by shops banking their takings
card merchant	a company which handles all the payments by debit card and credit card received by a business over-the-counter or through the Internet
encryption	the encoding for security reasons of debit and credit card details sent over the Internet
BACS	Bankers Automated Clearing Services – used for sending computer payments from bank to bank
CHAPS	Clearing House Automated Payment System – used for sending same-day high value payments
bank statement	a document sent by the bank to its customer setting out transactions on the bank account

STUDENT ACTIVITIES

5.1 State two duties of a bank to its customer.

5.2 State two duties of a customer to the bank.

5.3 If a customer has an overdraft with a bank, the customer is a creditor of the bank. True or false?

5.4 If a customer has a credit balance with a bank, the customer is a debtor of the bank. True or false?

5.5 Write out and complete the following sentences:

(a) When a customer signs a mortgage to the bank, the customer is a .... and the bank is a ....

(a) When a customer deposits items of value with a bank, the bank is a .... and the customer is a ....

(c) A bank that arranges an insurance policy for a customer is known as an................................

5.6 What type of bank account would be appropriate in the following circumstances?

(a) A business needs finance for the purchase of a new machine (capital expenditure).

(b) A business needs finance for day-to-day expenses (revenue expenditure).

(c) A business needs an account which will pay interest on a large sum of money.

5.7   A business receives a large cheque from a customer for a purchase, but wants to make sure that the cheque will be paid before releasing the goods. The business bank account is at Midland Bank, Holborn Circus and the cheque bears the name of Barclays Bank, Finsbury Circus. How long will it take to obtain clearance

(a)   through the normal bank clearing system?

(b)   by means of special clearance?

Would it make any difference if the cheque bore the name of Midland Bank, Holborn Circus?

5.8   The cheque in Activity 7 is unfortunately returned unpaid. The answer on the cheque is 'Refer to Drawer, please Represent'. What are the implications of this for the business? Would the situation be any different if the answer on the cheque had been 'Refer to Drawer'?

5.9   State two advantages to the customer of using a night safe.

5.10   State two reasons why cash should not be kept on the business premises for a long period of time.

5.11   State whether the following entries are debits or credits – from the viewpoint of the bank:

(a)   an amount paid into a bank account

(b)   an amount paid out of the bank account

5.12   The firm you work for is Eveshore Traders Ltd., which has a bank account at Barclays Bank, Eveshore (sort code no. 20-23-88). The account number is 90003174. You are required to prepare the paying-in slip (below) and counterfoil (see next page) as at today's date. The cheques are to be listed on the back of the paying-in slip. The items to be banked are:

Cash	Cheques
two £20 notes	£20.00 Maytree Enterprises
five £10 notes	£18.50 Bakewell Catering
eight £5 notes	£75.25 Henderson & Co
two £1 coins	£68.95 Musgrave Fine Art
six 50p coins	
four 10p coins	
two 2p coins	

Counterfoil	Cheques			
£			Carried over	£

5.13 The firm you work for is Buxton Fine Wines, which has a bank account at Western Bank, Grantminster (sort code no. 47-21-95). The account number is 87163729. You are required to prepare the Retailers Summary and paying-in slip for ten credit card sales vouchers and a refund voucher. The documents are shown below and on the next page. The items to be banked are:

Sales vouchers	£45.60	£56.85
	£10.00	£56.00
	£15.50	£45.00
	£25.99	£49.50
	£67.50	£25.00
Refund voucher	£13.50	

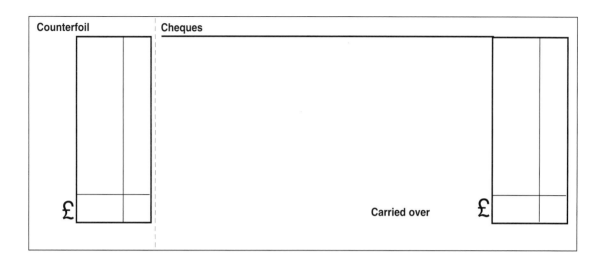

Date _____	Date _____	**bank giro credit**	£50 notes	
Credit _____	Cashier's stamp and initials		£20 notes	
£50 notes		Code no	£10 notes	
£20 notes		Bank _____	£5 notes	
£10 notes		Branch _____	£1	
£5 notes			50p	
£1			20p	
50p		Credit _____	10p,5p	
20p		Account No. _____	Bronze	
10p,5p			Total Cash	
Bronze		Number of cheques / Paid in by _____	Cheques etc	
Total Cash			£	
Cheques etc		Do not write below this line		
£				

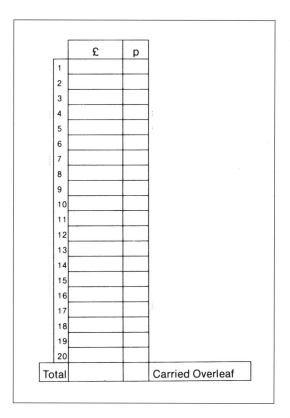

	£	p	
1			
2			
3			
4			
5			
6			
7			
8			
9			
10			
11			
12			
13			
14			
15			
16			
17			
18			
19			
20			
Total			Carried Overleaf

Have you imprinted the summary with your Retailer's Card?

VISA

Bank Processing copy of Summary with your Vouchers in correct order:

1 Summary

2 Sales Vouchers

3 Refund Vouchers

Keep Retailer's copy and Retailer's Duplicate copy

No more than 200 Vouchers to each Summary

Do not use Staples, Pins, Paper Clips

	Items	Amount		Retailer's Copy
Sales Vouchers				
Less Refund Vouchers				
Date	Total			
	£		:	

MasterCard

EUROCARD

Retailer Summary

_____
Retailer's Signature

Retailer Summary

Complete this summary for every Deposit of Sales Vouchers and enter the **Total** on your normal Current Account paying-in slip

6 CASH BOOK – RECORDING RECEIPTS

this chapter covers . . .

In this chapter we look at how the cash book records money received in the form of cash, cheques and other bank transfers.

The cash book is used to record the money side of book-keeping transactions and is part of the double-entry system.

This chapter focuses on the receipts (debit) side of the cash book; we will see also how the opposite credit entry is recorded in debtors' and other accounts.

NVQ PERFORMANCE CRITERIA COVERED

unit 1: RECORDING INCOME AND RECEIPTS

element 2

receive and record receipts

● *receipts are entered in appropriate accounting records*

THE CASH BOOK IN THE ACCOUNTING SYSTEM

For most businesses, accounting for cash – including both bank and cash transactions – takes place in the cash books which comprise:

- *cash book,* for receipts and payments in cash and through the bank (cheque, bank giro credit, and other bank transfers)
- *petty cash book* (see chapter 12), for low-value expense payments

The cash books combine the roles of primary accounting records and double-entry book-keeping. Cash books are:

- primary accounting records for cash and bank transactions
- double-entry accounts for cash and bank accounts

In this chapter we look at how the cash book is used to record receipts; the recording of payments made through the cash book is covered in Chapter 11; petty cash payments are dealt with in Chapter 12.

USES OF THE CASH BOOK

The cash book brings together the cash and bank transactions of a business. Thus it is used to record the money side of book-keeping transactions such as:

- cash transactions
  - all receipts in cash
  - most payments for cash, except for low-value expense payments (which are paid through petty cash book: see chapter 12)
- bank transactions
  - all receipts through the bank (including the payment of cash into the bank)
  - all payments through the bank (including the withdrawal of cash from the bank)

Note that receipts are dealt with in this chapter, whilst payments are considered in Chapter 11.

The cash book is usually controlled by a cashier who:

- records receipts and payments through the bank and in cash
- makes cash payments, and prepares cheques and other bank payment methods for signature by those authorised to sign
- pays cash and cheques received into the bank
- has control over the firm's cash, in a cash till or cash box

- issues cash to the petty cashier who operates the firm's petty cash book (see chapter 12)
- checks the accuracy of the cash and bank balances at regular intervals

It is important to note that transactions passing through the cash book must be supported by documentary evidence. In this way an audit trail is established which provides a link that can be checked and followed through the accounting system:

- prime document
- primary accounting record
- double-entry accounts

Such an audit trail is required both as a security feature within the business (to help to ensure that false and fraudulent transactions cannot be made), and also for taxation purposes – both for Value Added Tax and for the Inland Revenue.

The cashier has an important role to play within the accounting function of a business – most business activities will, at some point, involve cash or cheque transactions. Thus the cash book and the cashier are at the hub of the accounting system. In particular, the cashier is responsible for:

- issuing receipts for cash (and sometimes cheques) received
- making authorised payments in cash and by cheque against documents received (such as invoices and statements) showing the amounts due
- checking expenses claims (see Chapter 11) and seeking authorisation before making payment

With so many transactions passing through the cash book, accounting procedures must include:

- accuracy – in writing up the cash book, in cash handling, and in ensuring that payments are made only against correct documents and appropriate authorisation
- security – of cash and cheque books, correct authorisation of payments
- confidentiality – that all cash/bank transactions, including cash and bank balances, are kept confidential

If the cashier has any queries about any transactions, he or she should refer them to the accounts supervisor.

RECORDING RECEIPTS – LAYOUT OF THE CASH BOOK

In this chapter we focus on the debit side of the cash book, which is used for recording receipts. The credit side of the cash book – used for recording payments – is covered in Chapter 11.

A cash book can be set out in a variety of formats to suit the requirements of a particular business. However, a common format is the use of a columnar cash book incorporating several money columns. An example of the receipts side of a three-column cash book (with three money columns) is shown below:

Debit	Cash Book: Receipts					CBR
Date	Details	Folio	Discount allowed	Cash	Bank
			£	£	£

Notes:

- The receipts side of the cash book is the debit side (the payments side is the credit side – see Chapter 11); thus the cash book is part of the double-entry system.

- There are separate money columns for cash receipts and for bank receipts (eg cheques, bank giro credits, standing orders, direct debits received)

- A third money column is used to record cash discount allowed to customers (that is, an allowance offered to customers for quick settlement of the amount due, eg 2% cash discount for settlement within seven days).

- As the cash book is part of the double-entry system, each entry on the receipts side (the debit side) of the cash and bank columns must have an opposite entry on the credit side of another account elsewhere.

- The discount allowed column is not part of the double-entry system – it is used in the cash book as a listing device or memorandum column. We will see later in this chapter how amounts from this column are transferred into the double-entry system.

SEVERN TRADING COMPANY – CASH BOOK RECEIPTS

situation

The cashier at the firm for which you work, Severn Trading Company, is away on a training course this week. You are required, in her absence, to take over as cashier. The following receipts are to be entered into the firm's three column cash book:

2001
2 Apr   Balances at start of week: cash £300, bank £1,550
2 Apr   Cash sales £235 (including VAT of £35)
3 Apr   Received a cheque from S Wright, a debtor, for £98 – we have allowed her £2 cash discount
3 Apr   Received a bank giro credit from Peter Singh Limited, a debtor, for £205 (no cash discount)
4 Apr   J Jones settles her account of £80, by cheque, after deducting 5% cash discount
4 Apr   Cash sales £94 (including VAT of £14), a cheque received
5 Apr   Received £200 in cash which has been withdrawn from the bank for use in the business
6 Apr   Received a cheque for £45 from D Whiteman Limited in full settlement of the account of £48
6 Apr   Received a monthly standing order payment for £110 from Natasha Lloyd and Co, a debtor (no cash discount)

Note: all cheques are banked on the day of receipt

solution

The receipts side of the cash book records these transactions as shown below:

Debit		Cash Book: Receipts				CBR 24
Date	Details	Folio	Discount allowed	Cash	Bank
2001			£	£	£
2 Apr	Balances brought down			300	1,550
2 Apr	Sales	GL 4001/2200		235	
3 Apr	S Wright	SL 295	2		98
3 Apr	Peter Singh Limited (BGC)	SL 147			205
4 Apr	J Jones	SL 86	4		76
4 Apr	Sales	GL 4001/2200			94
5 Apr	Bank	C		200	
6 Apr	D Whiteman Limited	SL 278	3		45
6 Apr	Natasha Lloyd and Co (SO)	SL 121			110
			9	735	2,178

Notes:

- The cash book receipts page is numbered – here 'CBR 24'.

- The cash book forms a part of the double-entry book-keeping system. The receipts side of the cash book records the debit entry for cash and bank transactions – in the section which follows we shall see how the credit entry for each transaction is recorded in order to complete double-entry. (The discount allowed column is not part of double-entry – we will see how it is transferred into the accounts in the next section.)

- The balances brought down on 2 April are the amounts of cash held and the amount of money in the bank account as shown by the cash book at the beginning of the week. The cash book, like other accounts, is balanced at regular intervals – eg weekly or monthly – and we shall look at how it is balanced in Chapter 16

- The folio column has been completed to show in which division of the ledger and to which account number(s) the opposite book-keeping entry appears:

  GL = general ledger (or ML for main ledger)

  SL = sales ledger

  C   = contra entry, which means that the opposite entry for the receipt of cash from the bank is in the same account, ie it appears on the payments side of the cash book (see Chapter 11) in the bank column.

- Where receipts have been received direct into the bank account, for example here on 3 April by bank giro credit and on 6 April by standing order, the transactions have been indicated – this information will help when the firm's bank statement is received (see page 341).

- For cash sales, the amount of cash (or cheques) received and recorded in the cash book includes VAT; when recording the entries to be shown on the credit side of the accounts, we need to distinguish between the sales amount and VAT – see the section which follows. This is the reason why two general ledger account numbers are shown in the folio column against cash sales – the first number refers to sales account, the second to VAT account.

- The money columns of the cash book have been sub-totalled – this helps as we take information forward into other accounts within the double-entry system, and also when we balance the cash book (see Chapter 16).

COMPLETING DOUBLE-ENTRY TRANSACTIONS

We have seen how the debit side of the cash book is used to record receipts in the form of cash or through the bank account. In this section we look at how to complete the double-entry accounts for

- cash sales

- receipts from debtors

- contra entries

recording cash sales

By 'cash sales' we mean where a customer buys goods or services and pays immediately either in cash or by cheque (or other payment method through the banking system, eg debit card, credit card). The double-entry book-keeping entries are:

- payment received in cash
  - – *debit* cash column of the cash book
  - – *credit* sales account (or *credit* cash sales account – some businesses prefer to separate cash sales from credit sales)
  - – *credit* VAT account (with the amount of VAT)
- payment received by cheque (or other banking payment method)
  - – *debit* bank column of the cash book
  - – *credit* sales account (or *credit* cash sales account)
  - – *credit* VAT account

The credit entries from the Case Study for the cash sales transactions of 2 April and 4 April are recorded in the double-entry accounts as follows:

GENERAL (MAIN) LEDGER

Dr			**Sales Account** (account no 4001)			Cr
2001			£	2001		£
				2 Apr	Cash CBR 24	200
				4 Apr	Bank CBR 24	80

Dr			**Value Added Tax Account** (account no 2200)			Cr
2001			£	2001		£
				2 Apr	Cash CBR 24	35
				4 Apr	Bank CBR 24	14

recording receipts from debtors

When customers (debtors) pay for goods or services that have been sold to them on credit, the method of payment is:

- either by cheque, or other banking method such as bank giro credit, standing order
- or, less commonly, in cash

The double-entry book-keeping entries are:

- payment received by cheque (or other banking method)
  - *debit* bank column of the cash book
  - *credit* debtor's account
- payment received in cash
  - *debit* cash column of the cash book
  - *credit* debtor's account

Note that no entry is needed in VAT account as it will have been made when the credit sale was recorded in the accounting system (see Chapter 3).

Where cash discount allowed for prompt settlement has been taken by the debtor, ie cash discount has reduced the amount of the payment, entries must be made in the double-entry system for the cash discount as follows:

- *debit* discount allowed account (in the general ledger)
- *credit* debtor's account

The credit entries from the Case Study for the receipts from debtors are as follows (it is suggested that you 'tick back' each transaction).

Note: for illustrative purposes an amount for sales has been debited to each account (with the cross-reference to SDB 98).

SALES (DEBTORS) LEDGER

Dr				S Wright (account no 295)			Cr
2001			£	2001			£
15 Mar	Sales	SDB 98	100	3 Apr	Bank	CBR 24	98
				3 Apr	Discount Allowed GL 6501		2

Dr				Peter Singh Limited (account no 147)			Cr
2001			£	2001			£
15 Mar	Sales	SDB 98	400	3 Apr	Bank	CBR 24	205

Dr				J Jones (account no 86)			Cr
2001			£	2001			£
15 Mar	Sales	SDB 98	80	4 Apr	Bank	CBR 24	76
				4 Apr	Discount Allowed GL 6501		4

Dr	**D Whiteman Limited** (account no 278)			Cr
2001	£	2001		£
15 Mar Sales SDB 98	48	6 Apr Bank CBR 24		45
		6 Apr Discount Allowed GL 6501		3

Dr	**Natasha Lloyd and Co** (account no 121)		Cr
2001	£	2001	£
15 Mar Sales SDB 98	350	6 Apr Bank CBR 24	110

Notes:

- In the above accounts amounts for sales have been shown for illustrative purposes – see Chapter 3, which covers accounting for sales.

- In order to complete double-entry book-keeping, discount allowed amounts, which have been credited to the debtors' accounts, must also be debited to discount allowed account in the general ledger (the discount column in the cash book is not part of the double-entry system, but is a memorandum column only). The account is completed by entering the total of the discount column from the cash book, as follows:

GENERAL (MAIN) LEDGER

Dr	**Discount Allowed Account** (account no 6501)		Cr
2001	£	2001	£
6 Apr Cash Book CBR 24	9		

- Once the total of discount allowed has been taken from the cash book, the discount column 'starts again' (ie the amount of £9, above, for this week will not be included in next week's transfer).

- As an alternative to recording the total discount allowed for the week or month, separate amounts (for example, the three transactions here) could be shown in discount allowed account. The disadvantage of this is that, for a very busy business, there will be a lot of entries to make, which are a duplication of those already made in the cash book.

contra entries

A contra entry transaction – indicated by "C" in the folio column – means that the opposite double-entry transaction is in the same account. The two contra entries often seen in the cash book are:

- transfer to cash from bank (ie cash is withdrawn from the bank for use in the business)
    - *debit* cash column
    - *credit* bank column
- transfer to bank from cash (ie cash is paid into the bank)
    - *debit* bank column
    - *credit* cash column

The cash book in the Case Study shows a debit entry on 5 April described as 'bank': as the debit side entry is in the cash column, the contra entry will be on the credit side of the cash book and entered in the bank column (the detail will read 'cash'). Both transactions are for the same money amount and they tell the user of accounts that cash has been withdrawn from the bank and now forms part of the firm's cash float. We shall see how the credit entries are recorded in the cash book when we study the payments side in Chapter 11.

BATCH CONTROL SYSTEMS

Where businesses have a large number of receipts – from cash sales and/or from debtors – they often use batched data entry in order to enter such transactions into the accounts in one 'run'. As we have seen previously in Chapter 3, a batch of transactions for a day, week or month is pre-listed on a batch control form; the example shown below is for a batch of cheques received from debtors:

Batch Control: cheques received from debtors

Customer			Debit	Debit	Credit
Date	Account No	Name	Discount allowed	Bank	Sales ledger
2001			£	£	£
3 Apr	SL 295	S Wright	2.00	98.00	100.00
4 Apr	SL 86	J Jones	4.00	76.00	80.00
6 Apr	SL 278	D Whiteman Ltd	3.00	45.00	48.00
		Check list totals	9.00	219.00	228.00

Prepared by	*Neil Ford*	Date	*6 Apr 2001*
Checked by	*Barbara Smith*	Date	*6 Apr 2001*
Posted by	*Dan Ryan*	Date	*6 Apr 2001*

Note that receipts from customers by bank giro credit and by standing order have not been shown on the batch control form – only cheques received are listed. A business that has a lot of cash sales or receives large numbers of payments from customers by bank giro credit, standing order or other methods – such as credit and debit cards – will use batch control systems for each type of receipt. As always, in accounting, businesses adapt systems to suit their own circumstances.

Businesses that use control accounts (see Chapter 17) are able to record the totals from the cheques received batch control form in the sales ledger (debtors) control account.

THE CASH BOOK IN THE ACCOUNTING SYSTEM

The cash book performs two functions within the accounting system:

- it is a primary accounting record for cash/bank transactions
- it forms part of the double-entry system

For the receipts side of the cash book these functions are illustrated in the diagram which follows:

CASH AND BANK RECEIPTS

PRIME DOCUMENTS
- receipts issued
- bank paying-in slips
- bank giro credits received
- BACS payments received (standing orders and direct debits)
- debit and credit card vouchers received

**PRIMARY ACCOUNTING RECORD
AND DOUBLE-ENTRY BOOK-KEEPING**

DEBIT cash book receipts

DOUBLE-ENTRY BOOK-KEEPING

either
- sales (debtors) ledger
  CREDIT debtors' account (money received)

or
- general (main) ledger
  CREDIT other account, eg sales account (for cash sales), VAT account (for VAT on cash sales)

CASH BOOK INCORPORATING VAT

A cash book can be adapted to suit the needs of a business – already we have seen how a three-column cash book incorporates a memorandum column for cash discounts. Another common layout uses a fourth money column, for VAT, as shown in the Case Study which follows. The VAT column acts as a memorandum column and, at the end of the week or month, is transferred to VAT account.

CASE STUDY

CASH BOOK INCORPORATING VAT

situation

On Monday 4 June 2001, the cash book of Eveshore Growers showed balances of £86 in cash and £248 in the bank. Receipts for the week were:

4 June   Received a cheque for £470 from a debtor, Cisco Systems

4 June   Cash sales of £282, including Value Added Tax

5 June   Received a cheque for £230 from a debtor, P Leech, who was settling his account balance of £235 after deducting £5 cash discount

6 June   Cash sales of £423, including Value Added Tax, paid for by cheque

7 June   Transferred £100 to the bank from cash

The rate of Value Added Tax is 17.5%.
All cheques are banked on the day of receipt.

As cashier to Eveshore Growers, you are to:

• write up page 54 of the receipts side of the cash book for the week commencing 4 June 2001, using separate columns for discount, VAT, cash and bank

• sub-total the cash book at 7 June 2001

• explain how the totals for the discount and VAT columns will be entered in the general ledger of Eveshore Growers

solution

Debit			Cash Book: Receipts				CBR 54
Date	Details	Folio	Discount allowed	VAT	Cash	Bank	
2001			£	£	£	£	
4 Jun	Balances brought down				86	248	
4 Jun	Cisco Systems	SL				470	
4 Jun	Sales	GL		42	282		
5 Jun	P Leech	SL	5			230	
6 Jun	Sales	GL		63		423	
7 Jun	Cash	C				100	
			5	105	368	1,471	

Notes:

- The folio columns have been completed as follows (account numbers have not been shown)

  GL = general ledger (or ML for main ledger)

  SL = sales ledger

  C = contra (both parts of the transaction in the same book)

- For transactions involving sales ledger (eg Cisco Systems), no amount for VAT is shown in the VAT column. This is because VAT has been charged on invoices issued and was recorded in the VAT account (through the sales day book) when the sale was made.

- VAT on cash sales and other transactions is recorded in the VAT analysis column.

The discount and VAT columns:

- discount allowed column – the total of £5 will be debited to discount allowed account in the general ledger and credited to P Leech's account in the sales ledger

- VAT column – the total of £105 will be credited to VAT account in the general ledger (alternatively the individual amounts of £42 and £63 could be credited)

Note that, in cash book, the discount allowed and VAT columns 'start again' from zero after the totals have been transferred to the general ledger accounts.

ANALYSED CASH BOOK

Many businesses use an analysed cash book to provide more information. An analysed cash book divides receipts (and payments – see Chapter 11) between a number of categories.

Receipts could be divided between:

- the main sections of a business, such as (1) furniture, and (2) carpets, for a home furnishing shop

- (1) discount allowed, (2) Value Added Tax (where a business is registered for VAT), (3) cash sales, (4) sales ledger, ie receipts from debtors, (5) sundry receipts

A business will use whatever analysis columns suit it best: the cash book should be adapted to meet the needs of the business in the best possible way.

CASE STUDY

ANALYSED CASH BOOK

situation

Wyvern Auto Spares Limited sells car parts to local garages and to members of the public. The company is registered for Value Added Tax.

The business uses a cash book which analyses receipts as follows:

> **RECEIPTS**
> - discount allowed
> - VAT
> - cash sales
> - sales ledger
> - sundry receipts

The following receipts transactions are to be entered on page 31 of the receipts side of the cash book for the first week of December 2001:

3 Dec	Balances from previous week: cash £255, bank £875
3 Dec	Sales for cash £240 + VAT
4 Dec	A debtor, Main Street Garage, settles an invoice for £195, paying by cheque
4 Dec	Sales for cash £200 + VAT
5 Dec	Received £100 in cash which has been withdrawn from the bank for use in the business
6 Dec	A debtor, A45 Service Station, settles an invoice for £240, paying £235 by cheque and receiving £5 discount for prompt settlement
6 Dec	Sales £320 + VAT, received half in cash, and half by cheque
7 Dec	Sales for cash £200 + VAT

The rate of Value Added Tax is 17.5%. All cheques are banked on the day of receipt.

solution

Debit		Cash Book: Receipts							CBR 31
Date	Details	Folio	Cash	Bank	Discount allowed	VAT	Cash sales	Sales ledger	Sundry
2001			£	£	£	£	£	£	£
3 Dec	Balances brought down		255	875					
3 Dec	Sales	GL	282			42	240		
4 Dec	Main Street Garage	SL		195				195	
4 Dec	Sales	GL	235			35	200		
5 Dec	Bank	C	100						
6 Dec	A45 Service Station	SL		235	5			235	
6 Dec	Sales	GL	188	188		56	320		
7 Dec	Sales	GL	235			35	200		
			1,295	1,493	5	168	960	430	–

Notes:

- The receipts side of the analysed cash book analyses each receipt between a number of headings. A business will adapt the cash book and use whatever analysis columns suit it best for its receipts.

- References to the ledger sections only have been shown in the folio column.

- For transactions involving sales ledger, no amount for VAT is shown in the VAT columns. This is because VAT has been charged on invoices issued and was recorded in the VAT account (through the sales day book) when the sale was made.

- The columns are sub-totalled at the end of the week and the totals of the analysis columns are transferred to other accounts as follows:

  - discount allowed column total of £5 is debited to discount allowed account in the general ledger and credited to the account of A45 Service Station in the sales ledger

  - Value Added Tax column, the total of £168 is credited to VAT account in the general ledger

  - cash sales column, the total of £960 is credited to sales account (or cash sales account) in the general ledger

OTHER RECEIPTS

In addition to receipts from debtors and from cash sales, the debit side of the cash book is used to record other receipts of the business. These include:

- capital introduced by the owner(s)

- loans made to the business, such as a bank loan, or from a relative or friend

- income, such as rent received, commission received

We will look at further aspects of these transactions in more detail in Chapter 13 and see how they fit into the double-entry system. For the moment we will see how they are recorded in the double-entry system of cash book and ledger accounts:

- capital introduced

  - *debit* cash book

  - *credit* capital account

  The owner of the business pays in capital (or more capital) in the form of cash or a cheque.

- loans received

  - *debit* cash book

  - *credit* loan account, eg bank loan, loan from J Smith

  The amount of the loan is received in the cash book, by cheque or through the bank.

- income received
  - *debit* cash book
  - *credit* income account (using the appropriate account, eg rent received, commission received)

Business income, other than from sales, may be received in the form of cash, a cheque or through the bank.

example transactions

2001

18 Jun   The owner of the business pays in additional capital of £1,000, by cheque

19 Jun   Received a loan of £500, by cheque, from A Friend (no VAT)

20 Jun   Rent received from tenant, £150 in cash (no VAT)

The cash book (receipts) records these transactions as follows:

Debit		Cash Book: Receipts				CBR 10
Date	Details		Folio	Discount allowed	Cash	Bank
2001				£	£	£
18 Jun	Capital		GL			1,000
19 Jun	Loan: A Friend		GL			500
20 Jun	Rent received		GL		150	

The credit entries are shown in the general ledger (in which all of these accounts are contained) as follows:

GENERAL (MAIN) LEDGER

Dr		Capital Account		Cr
2001	£	2001		£
		18 Jun Bank CBR 10		1,000

Dr		Loan Account: A Friend		Cr
2001	£	2001		£
		19 Jun Bank CBR 10		500

Dr		Rent Received Account		Cr
2001	£	2001		£
		20 Jun Cash CBR 10		150

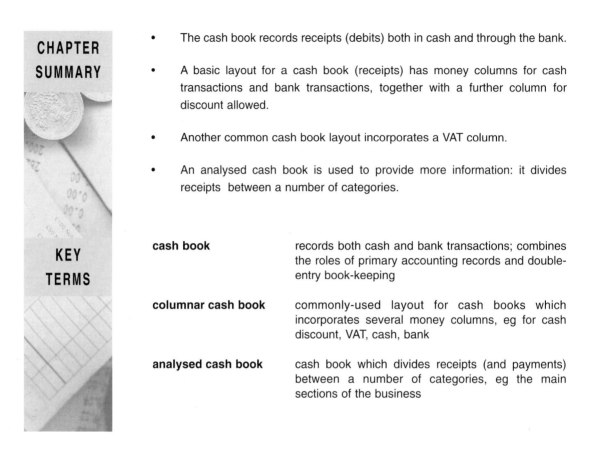

CHAPTER SUMMARY

- The cash book records receipts (debits) both in cash and through the bank.

- A basic layout for a cash book (receipts) has money columns for cash transactions and bank transactions, together with a further column for discount allowed.

- Another common cash book layout incorporates a VAT column.

- An analysed cash book is used to provide more information: it divides receipts between a number of categories.

KEY TERMS

cash book	records both cash and bank transactions; combines the roles of primary accounting records and double-entry book-keeping
columnar cash book	commonly-used layout for cash books which incorporates several money columns, eg for cash discount, VAT, cash, bank
analysed cash book	cash book which divides receipts (and payments) between a number of categories, eg the main sections of the business

STUDENT ACTIVITIES

6.1 The cash book is:

   (a)   a prime document

   (b)   a primary accounting record only

   (c)   part of double-entry book-keeping only

   (d)   combines primary accounting records and double-entry book-keeping

   Answer (a) or (b) or (c) or (d)

6.2 You work as the cashier for Wyvern Publishing, a company which publishes a wide range of travel and historical books. As cashier, your main responsibility is for the firm's cash book.

   Explain to a friend what your job involves and the qualities required of a cashier.

6.3 The following are the receipts transactions of Metro Trading Company for August 2001:

1 Aug	Balances from previous month: cash £276, bank £4,928
3 Aug	Received a cheque from a debtor, Wild & Sons Limited, £398
6 Aug	Sales for cash, £160 + VAT
13 Aug	Transferred £300 to the bank from cash
14 Aug	Received a cheque for £1,755 from A Lewis Limited in full settlement of their account of £1,775
16 Aug	Sales for cash, £240 + VAT
20 Aug	Received a cheque for £261 from Harvey & Sons Limited, a debtor
21 Aug	Received a loan of £750 from the bank (no VAT)
22 Aug	Sales £400 + VAT, received half in cash, and half by cheque
24 Aug	Rent received from tenant, £100 in cash (no VAT)
29 Aug	Received a cheque for £595 from Wild & Sons Limited in full settlement of their account of £610
30 Aug	Received £275 in cash which has been withdrawn from the bank for use in the business

The rate of Value Added Tax is 17.5%

All cheques are banked on the day of receipt

Account numbers are to be used – see below

You are to:

- Enter the above receipts on page 45 of the three column cash book of Metro Trading Company.

- Sub-total the money columns at 31 August.

- Show the entries to be made in the following accounts:

   sales (debtors) ledger

   Wild & Sons Limited (account no 843)

   A Lewis Limited (account no 531)

   Harvey & Sons Limited (account no 467)

   general (main) ledger

   discount allowed account (account no 6501)

   bank loan (account no 2210)

   rent received account (account no 4951)

   sales account (account no 4001)

   VAT account (account no 2200)

6.4 The following are the receipts transactions of Johnson Brothers for April 2001:

1 Apr	Balances from previous month: cash £85, bank £718
9 Apr	J Bowen, a debtor, settles an invoice for £90, paying £85 in cash and receiving £5 discount for prompt settlement
10 Apr	Cash sales £470 (including Value Added Tax) received by cheque
12 Apr	Rent received from tenant, £250 by cheque (no VAT)
17 Apr	Cash sales of £94 (including Value Added Tax) received by cheque
18 Apr	Received a cheque for £575 from J Burrows, a debtor, in full settlement of an invoice for £600
20 Apr	Cash sales of £188 (including Value Added Tax) received in cash
23 Apr	Received £200 in cash which has been withdrawn from the bank for use in the business
24 Apr	Received a cheque for £245 from Wilson Limited, a debtor, in full settlement of an invoice for £255

The rate of Value Added Tax is 17.5%

All cheques are banked on the day of receipt

Account numbers are to be used – see below

You are to:

- Enter the above receipts on page 88 of the cash book of Johnson Brothers, using columns for date, details, discount allowed, VAT, cash and bank.

- Sub-total the money columns at 30 April.

- Show the entries to be made in the following accounts:

    sales (debtors) ledger

    J Bowen (account no 117)

    J Burrows (account no 125)

    Wilson Limited (account no 855)

    general (main) ledger

    discount allowed account (account no 6501)

    rent received account (account no 4951)

    sales account (account no 4001)

    VAT account (account no 2200)

6.5 David Lewis runs a shop selling carpets to the public on cash terms and also to a few trade customers – such as carpet fitters – on credit terms. His business is registered for VAT.

He uses a cash book which analyses receipts between:

- discount allowed
- VAT
- sales
- sales (debtors) ledger
- sundry

The following transactions take place during the week commencing 14 May 2001 (all cheques are banked on the day of receipt):

14 May   Balances from previous week: cash £205.75, bank £825.30

14 May   Sales £534.62 (including VAT), cheque received

14 May   Rent received from tenant of flat above the shop, £255.50 by cheque (no VAT)

15 May   Sales £164.50 (including VAT), cash received

15 May   A debtor, T Jarvis, settles an invoice for £157.50, paying £155.00 by cheque, £2.50 discount being allowed for prompt settlement

16 May   David Lewis' brother, Terry, makes a loan to the business of £500.00 by cheque (no VAT)

16 May   Sales £752.00 (including VAT), cheque received

17 May   Sales £264.37 (including VAT), cash received

18 May   David Lewis pays in additional capital of £1,000.00 by cheque (no VAT)

18 May   A debtor, Wyvern District Council, settles an invoice for £565.45, paying £560.45 by cheque and receiving £5.00 discount for prompt settlement

The rate of Value Added Tax is 17.5%
All cheques are banked on the day of receipt
Account numbers are to be used – see below

You are to:

- Enter the above receipts on page 96 of the cash book of David Lewis (VAT amounts should be rounded down to the nearest penny).

- Sub-total the money columns at 18 May.

- Show the entries to be made in the following accounts:

  sales (debtors) ledger

  T Jarvis (account no 497)

  Wyvern District Council (account no 924)

  general (main) ledger

  capital account (account no 3005)

  discount allowed account (account no 6501)

  loan account: T Lewis (account no 2220)

  rent received account (account no 4951)

  sales account (account no 4001)

  VAT account (account no 2200)

7 DOCUMENTS FOR GOODS AND SERVICES RECEIVED

this chapter covers . . .

In Chapter 2 we looked at the selling of goods and services from the point of view of the supplier. This chapter examines the transactions from the point of view of the purchaser and describes the procedures and documents involved. The chapter covers the areas of:

- the use of business documents – purchase order, invoice, delivery note, goods received note, returns note, credit note, statement, remittance advice

- the checking of the supplier's documents against the purchaser's documents

- the calculation of document totals, including discounts and VAT

- the coding and filing of documents

- the checking and authorisation of documents and dealing with discrepancies

NVQ PERFORMANCE CRITERIA COVERED

unit 2: MAKING AND RECORDING PAYMENTS

element 1

process documents relating to goods and services received

- *suppliers' invoices and credit notes are checked against delivery notes, ordering documentation and evidence that goods or services have been received*

- *totals and balances are correctly calculated and checked on suppliers' invoices*

- *available discounts are identified and deducted*

- *discrepancies are identified and either resolved or referred to the appropriate person if outside own authority*

- *communications with suppliers regarding accounts are handled politely and effectively (see also Chapter 14)*

BUSINESS DOCUMENTS – THE PURCHASER'S POINT OF VIEW

When a business *sells* goods and services its main concern is that it provides what has been ordered and that it gets paid on time. When a business, on the other hand, *orders* goods and services it will want to ensure that:

- the correct goods and services are provided

- they are provided on time

- they are charged at the right price

Businesses vary in the way they achieve this. The normal procedure is for the purchaser to accumulate on file – normally stapled together – a series of documents which will be checked against each other as they are produced or come into the office, eg copy purchase order, delivery note, invoice, a copy of any returns note, any credit note, statement, and so on. These will often be kept in a 'pending invoices' file until payment is finally made, when they will go into a 'paid invoices' file. The diagram below shows this flow of documents.

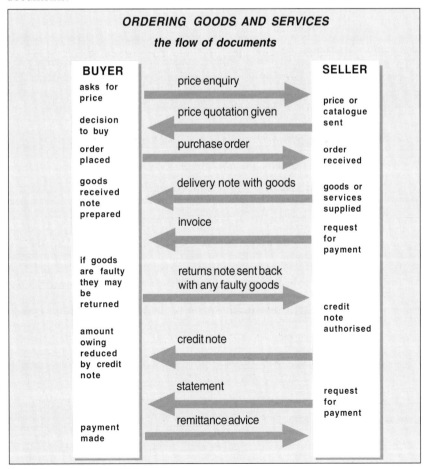

ORDERING GOODS AND SERVICES
the flow of documents

BUYER		SELLER
asks for price	price enquiry →	price or catalogue sent
decision to buy	← price quotation given	
order placed	purchase order →	order received
goods received note prepared	← delivery note with goods	goods or services supplied
	← invoice	request for payment
if goods are faulty they may be returned	returns note sent back with any faulty goods →	credit note authorised
amount owing reduced by credit note	← credit note	
	← statement	request for payment
payment made	remittance advice →	

ORDERING PROCEDURES

the traditional method

The diagram on the previous page shows the traditional method of ordering goods and services: a paper purchase order is issued, the goods (or services) are delivered (or provided) and an invoice is sent which is eventually paid by cheque. There are of course, many variations on this procedure, particularly with the introduction of e-commerce where buying and selling and settlement takes place on-line.

In this book and in your studies the emphasis is on the traditional method of ordering and paying because the principles of this method underlie all the other methods. You should however be aware of the other methods as you may encounter some of them in your day-to-day work.

other ordering methods – paper based

Businesses can order goods and services in a variety of other ways:

- filling in a catalogue order form and posting off a cheque with the order
- telephoning a company which is selling to you for the first time to ask them to issue you with a 'pro-forma invoice' for the goods or service you need; when you receive this invoice document, you will send it back with a cheque and the goods or service will be supplied by return
- faxing off a catalogue order form and quoting the company credit card details
- telephoning a catalogue order and quoting the company credit card details

other ordering methods – electronically based

Businesses are increasing turning to the Internet shop sites for purchases of goods and services, eg computers. Ordering goods or services from an Internet site is very straightforward: all you need to do is to get on-line, place your order on one of the virtual 'shopping malls' and quote the company credit card details.

Electronic ordering has produced terms which need some explanation:

- EDI (Electronic Data Interchange)
- e-commerce

EDI – electronic data interchange

This a method of connecting businesses by computer link so that documents such as purchase orders and invoices can be electronically generated and payments made electronically when they are due. The EDI system should *not* be confused with the Internet, which is basically an uncontrolled electronic free-for-all. EDI has been running for many years, the electronic links are private and secure; the system is expensive to set up. A number of supermarkets have adopted EDI: the supermarket is the 'hub' of the system and its suppliers are on 'spokes'. Look at the diagram below.

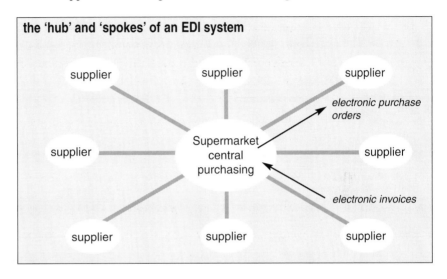

e-commerce

E-commerce is a loose term which is short for 'electronic commerce'. It covers selling and buying on the Internet, both business-to-business and business-to-customer. We have already seen in Chapter 5 how Internet sales receipts are tracked onto the bank account. The screen extract here shows this book for sale on the on-line shop at www.osbornebooks.co.uk

In the rest of this chapter we will look at the traditional method of ordering goods and services which is most likely to feature in your Assessments.

AUTHORISATION OF PURCHASE ORDERS

A purchaser, once the price of the product(s) has been agreed, normally issues a *purchase order*. It is essential that this purchase order is *authorised* by the appropriate person. This authority is shown on the document in the form of a signature and date. Some businesses will insist that more senior staff in the buying department sign larger orders. A business keeps a copy of every purchase order it issues and often files them in numerical order (each order has a numerical code). The purchase order from the Case Study in the last chapter is shown here.

It should be noted that a business may not *always* issue a purchase order: if the order is small, or if the buyer knows the seller well, the order may be made by telephone.

Trends		**PURCHASE ORDER**
4 Friar Street		
Broadfield		
BR1 3RF		
Tel 01908 761234 Fax 01908 761987		
VAT REG GB 0745 8383 56		

Cool Socks Limited,	purchase order no	47609
Unit 45 Elgar Estate,	date	25 09 01
Broadfield,		
BR7 4ER		

product code	quantity	description
45B	100 pairs	Blue Toebar socks

AUTHORISED   signature.......*D Signer*...date........*25/09/01*

CHECKS AND CONTROLS: PURCHASES

When an organisation purchases goods, it is important that the accounting system includes checks and controls to ensure that:

- the correct goods have been received in an acceptable condition
- the correct terms and price have been applied
- the goods are paid for once only (paying for goods twice does occur!)

The three main documents involved in the checking process are the *purchase order* (a copy of which will be kept by the purchaser), the *delivery note* and the *invoice,* received from the seller.

You should note that some organisations use an internal document known as a *goods received note* on which the buyer records the receipt of the goods and the details set out on the delivery note or advice note sent by the supplier. Most businesses, however, rely on the delivery note as a record of the goods received, and we will concentrate on this document here.

CHECKING INVOICE, DELIVERY NOTE AND PURCHASE ORDER

The checking process involves two separate procedures carried out in the Accounts Department:

- checking the three documents – the invoice, delivery note and copy purchase order – with each other
- checking the calculations on the invoice

We will deal with these in separate stages, starting with the checking of the three documents:

check 1 – goods received and delivery note

When the goods are received they should be checked against the delivery note – the quantities should be counted and the condition of the goods checked. Any discrepancies or damage should be notified immediately to the supplier, usually on a *discrepancy note*, so that replacements can be sent or the buyer credited with the value of the missing or damaged goods (ie the bill reduced by the issue of a credit note).

check 2 – delivery note and purchase order

The delivery note should then be checked in the Accounts Department against a copy of the original purchase order. The illustration on the next page shows the details that should be checked:

- catalogue number (ie the supplier's catalogue) – has the right type of goods been delivered?
- quantity – has the right number been delivered?
- specifications – are the goods delivered to the same specifications as those ordered
- purchase order reference number – do the goods relate to the purchase order being examined?

If all is in order, the delivery note will be filed with the copy purchase order under the purchase order reference number, ready for checking against the invoice when it arrives.

check 3 – invoice, delivery note and purchase order

When the invoice arrives from the supplier, it should be checked against the delivery note and the purchase order (which should be filed together). The specific points to look at are:

- *invoice and delivery note*
  Are the details of the goods on the invoice and delivery note the same? The product code, description and quantity of the goods should agree.

• *invoice and purchase order*

Has the correct price been charged? The unit price quoted by the supplier or obtained from the supplier's catalogue will be stated on the purchase order, and should agree with the unit price stated on the invoice. If there is a difference, it should be queried with the supplier.

student task

Look at the invoice below and the purchase order and delivery note on the next page. They all relate to the same transaction. Can you spot any discrepancies? The answers are set out at the bottom of the page.

INVOICE

Stourford Office Supplies

Unit 12, Avon Industrial Estate, Stourford, SF5 6TD
Tel 01807 765434 Fax 01807 765123 Email stourford@stourford.co.uk
VAT Reg GB 0745 4001 76

invoice to

Martley Machine Rental Limited 67 Broadgreen Road Martley MR6 7TR

deliver to

as above

invoice no	652771
account	MAR435
your reference	47780
date/tax point	30 03 01

product code	description	quantity	price	unit	total	discount %	net
3564748	80gsm white Supalaser	15	3.50	ream	52.00	0.00	52.00

terms		
Net monthly Carriage paid E & OE	**goods total**	52.00
	VAT	9.01
	TOTAL	42.99

The purchase order and delivery note agree, but the invoice has a number of discrepancies:

• the order reference differs (47700 and 47780)
• the product code differs (3564749 and 3564748)
• the product description differs (100 gsm and 80 gsm)
• the price differs (£4.00 and £3.50 per ream)

Martley Machine Rental

67 Broadgreen Road
Martley
MR6 7TR
Tel 01908 546321 Fax 01908 546335
VAT REG GB 0745 8383 56

PURCHASE ORDER

| Stourford Office Supplies
Unit 12
Avon Industrial Estate
Stourford SF5 6TD | purchase order no | 47700 |
| | date | 13 03 01 |

product code	quantity	description	
3564749	15 reams	100gsm white Supalaser paper	@ £4.00 per ream

AUTHORISED   signature.......... *C Farmer* ....date... *13 March 01*

| catalogue number | quantity | order specifications | purchase order reference number |

—— DELIVERY NOTE ——

Stourford Office Supplies

Unit 12, Avon Industrial Estate, Stourford, SF5 6TD
Tel 01807 765434 Fax 01807 765123 Email stourford@stourford.co.uk
VAT Reg GB 0745 4001 76

Martley Machine Rental Ltd 67 Broadgreen Road Martley MR6 7TR	delivery note no	26754
	delivery method	Puma Express
	your order	47700
	date	26 03 01

product code	quantity	description
3564749	15 reams	100gsm white Supalaser paper

Received
signature............... *G Hughes* ....print name (capitals).... *G. HUGHES* ....date. *30/03/01*

details to check on the purchase order and delivery note

CHECKING THE CALCULATIONS ON THE INVOICE

Another important step is for the Accounts Department to check the calculations on the invoice. If any one of these calculations is incorrect, the final total will be wrong, and the invoice will have to be queried with the supplier, so accurate checking is essential. The checks to be made are:

quantity x unit price   The quantity of the items multiplied by the unit price must be correct. The result – the total price or *price extension* – is used for the calculation of any trade discount applicable.

trade discount   Any trade discount – an allowance given to approved customers – must be deducted from the total price worked out. Trade discount is calculated as a percentage of the total price, eg a trade discount of 20% on a total price of £150 is calculated

£150 x $\dfrac{20}{100}$ = £30

The net price charged (before VAT) is therefore

£150 – £30 = £120 = net total

cash discount   Any cash discount – an allowance sometimes given for immediate payment – is deducted from the net total before VAT is calculated. Cash discount, when it is offered, is usually included as one of the terms at the bottom of the invoice. It is not normally, however, deducted from the invoice total, so it will be up to the buyer to settle early and to adjust the invoice total down.

VAT   Value Added Tax is currently charged at the rate of 17.5%. To calculate VAT, the total after the deduction of any cash discount is treated as follows

Total x $\dfrac{17.5}{100}$ = VAT amount

If you are using a calculator, all you need to do is to multiply the total by 0.175 to give the VAT, which is then added to the total.

Remember that any fractions of a penny are ignored. For example if the total price is £55.75, the VAT will be

£55.75 x 0.175 = £9.75625

£9.75625 then loses the last three digits – the fraction of a penny – to become £9.75.

For the purpose of your studies you must assume that the calculations on all invoices must be checked. In practice, invoicing programs perform the calculations automatically, and in principle should be correct.

Now check the calculations on the invoice on page 146. You should be able to detect a large number of errors:

- quantity x unit price should be £52.50, not £52.00
- the VAT is wrongly calculated £52.00 x 0.175 = £9.10, not £9.01 (it would be £9.18 on £52.50)
- the VAT has been deducted instead of added: the total should be £52.50 + £9.18 = £61.68

AUTHORISING THE INVOICE FOR PAYMENT

In most organisations checked invoices are passed to the person in the Accounts Department who deals with making payments to suppliers. First, however, an invoice will have to be *authorised* for payment. It will then, as long as no credit notes are due, be paid after the statement arrives and the date for payment is reached. Clearly only correct invoices can be passed forward for payment. Invoices with errors will need to be queried with the supplier.

When an invoice is checked and found to be correct, the person carrying out the check will usually mark the document and authorise it for payment. This authorisation can take a number of forms:

- the checker can initial and date the invoice, and tick it or write 'pay' as an authorisation
- the organisation may have a special rubber stamp which can be used in the authorisation process (see next page)

This procedure of authorisation obviously helps the efficiency of the organisation:

- only authorised invoices will be passed forward in the Accounts Department for entry into the purchases day book and double-entry accounts (see Chapter 8); each invoice will be attached to the copy purchase order and will eventually be paid when the due date comes
- the checker's initials will be there in case of any future query on the invoice, eg an undetected error

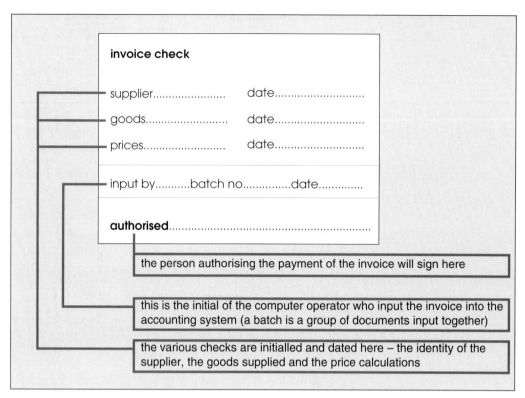

authorisation stamp placed on an invoice received for checking

GOODS RECEIVED NOTES (GRNS)

As mentioned earlier in the chapter some purchasers use a document known as a *goods received note* (GRN). This is essentially a checklist on which is recorded the name of the supplier and details of the goods ordered. As the goods are received and are checked in, the GRN is ticked and initialled to indicate that the right quantity and description of goods have been received. The GRN forms part of the payment authorisation process: only when a completed and correct GRN is approved by the Accounts Department can the relevant invoice be paid. As you will see, the GRN fulfils the same checking function as the entries on the invoice authorisation stamp shown above.

Shown on the next page is the goods received note relating to the Case Study in the last chapter in which the shop 'Trends' ordered some fashion socks from Cool Socks Limited. Note that the receipt of the 100 pairs of socks has been recorded, and also the fact that 10 pairs are damaged.

Trends   **GOODS RECEIVED NOTE**

Supplier

| Cool Socks Limited, Unit 45 Elgar Estate, Broadfield, BR7 4ER | GRN no | 1871 |
| | date | 05 10 01 |

quantity	description	order number
100 pairs	Blue Toebar socks	47609

| **carrier** | Lynx Parcels | consignment no   8479347 |

| **received by** | *V Williams* | checked by   *R Patel* |

condition of goods (please tick and comment)	good condition	**copies to**
	damaged ✓ (10 pairs)	Buyer ✓
	shortages	Accounts ✓
		Stockroom ✓

RETURNS

As you can see from the goods received note above, a purchaser will sometimes have to return faulty or incorrect goods and request a credit note from the seller to reduce the amount owed. Note that a purchaser should *never* for this reason change figures on an invoice – this would cause havoc with the accounting records! When the goods are sent back – the socks in the Case Study – they will be accompanied by a *returns note*.

When the goods are received back by the seller and checked, a *credit note* will be issued to reduce the amount owing. This is illustrated on the next page.

Trends   **RETURNS NOTE**

4 Friar Street
Broadfield
BR1 3RF
Tel 01908 761234 Fax 01908 761987
VAT REG GB 0745 8383 56

| Cool Socks Limited, Unit 45 Elgar Estate, Broadfield, BR7 4ER | returns note no | 2384 |
| | date | 08 10 01 |

product code	quantity	description
45B	10 pairs	Blue Toebar socks

REASON FOR RETURN: *faulty goods, credit requested*

SIGNATURE   *R SINGH*   DATE   *08 10 01*

```
———————————————— CREDIT NOTE ————————————————
                    COOL SOCKS LIMITED
                 Unit 45 Elgar Estate, Broadfield, BR7 4ER
           Tel 01908 765314  Fax 01908 765951  Email toni@cool.u-net.com
                        VAT REG GB 0745 4672 76
```

to		
Trends	credit note no	12157
4 Friar Street	account	3993
Broadfield	your reference	47609
BR1 3RF	our invoice	787923
	date/tax point	10 10 01

product code	description	quantity	price	unit	total	discount %	net
45B	Blue Toebar socks	10	2.36	pair	23.60	0.00	23.60

Reason for credit
10 pairs of socks received damaged
(Your returns note no. R/N 2384)

GOODS TOTAL	23.60
VAT	4.13
TOTAL	27.73

CHECKING THE CREDIT NOTE

When the credit note is received by the purchaser it will have to be checked carefully to make sure that the quantity of goods, the price, discount and VAT are correctly calculated. If it is correct, the document will be entered into the purchases returns daybook and double-entry accounts (see Chapter 8) and then filed with (stapled to) the appropriate copy purchase order, delivery note, invoice and copy returns note, awaiting the arrival of the statement.

PAYING SUPPLIERS' INVOICES

There are two common ways of setting up a system for paying invoices:

1 Many businesses pay on receipt of a statement, not on receipt of the invoice. As most statements tend to go out at the end of the month, paying of invoices often then becomes a monthly routine. In this case payments due can be put on diary for a set day of the month, eg the 27th.

2 Some businesses will pay invoices after the maximum number of days allowed – normally 30 days. In this case a diary system will be set up and the checked/authorised invoices filed in payment date order.

MAKING PAYMENT – REMITTANCE ADVICES

Although making payments is covered in full in Chapter 9, it should be mentioned here that the cycle of documents is completed by the issue of a remittance advice by the supplier when payments is made.

Payment can either be made by *cheque* or by *electronic transfer* through the bank using a system known as BACS (Bankers Automated Clearing Services).

Illustrated below are remittance advices for both types of payment.

TO	**REMITTANCE ADVICE**	FROM
Cool Socks Limited Unit 45 Elgar Estate, Broadfield, BR7 4ER		**Trends** **4 Friar Street** **Broadfield** **BR1 3RF**
Account 3993	6 November 2001	Tel 01908 761234 Fax 01908 761987 VAT REG GB 0745 8383 56

date	your reference	our reference	payment amount
01 10 01 10 10 01	INVOICE 787923 CREDIT NOTE 12157	47609 47609	277.30 (27.73)
		CHEQUE TOTAL	249.57

remittance advice sent with a cheque payment

BACS REMITTANCE ADVICE

FROM: Trends
4 Friar Street
Broadfield
BR1 3RF

TO: Cool Socks Limited
Unit 45 Elgar Estate,
Broadfield, BR7 4ER

05 11 01

Your ref	Our ref		Amount
787923	47609	BACS TRANSFER	249.57
		Total	249.57

THIS HAS BEEN PAID BY BACS CREDIT TRANSFER DIRECTLY INTO YOUR BANK ACCOUNT ALBION BANK NO 11451226 SORT CODE 90 47 17

remittance advice sent to advise of a BACS payment

CHAPTER SUMMARY

- Traditionally, a business placing an order will request the goods or services by means of a paper document – a purchase order. There then follows a 'flow' of paper documents, concluding with payment.

- Although electronic methods of ordering through e-commerce and EDI have become more common, the same traditional principles apply; it is just that the documents are on-screen rather than paper-based.

- A business purchasing goods or services will need to ensure that the right goods have been supplied, at the right price, before payment is made.

- When the goods arrive they should be checked against the delivery note which accompanies the goods. The delivery note is then checked against the purchase order and attached to it.

- Some businesses will prepare a goods received note to check off the goods when they arrive and to record any subsequent returns.

- When the invoice arrives it will be checked against the purchase order and delivery note and attached to the documents.

- The calculations and terms on the invoice will be checked carefully, particularly if it is not a computerised invoice.

- If any goods have to be returned they will be sent back with a returns note.

- Any credit notes issued to the purchaser (including any for returned goods) will have to be checked carefully on receipt.

- When the invoice and any relevant credit notes have been found to be correct the invoice can be authorised for payment.

- Authorised invoices are filed in a diary system until the appropriate payment date (normally after receipt of a statement).

- Payment is normally advised to the seller by means of a remittance advice.

KEY TERMS

EDI — Electronic Data Interchange is an electronic system of ordering goods and services using secure private computer links

e-commerce — buying and selling on the Internet – business to business and business to customer

purchase order — a document issued and authorised by the buyer of goods and services, sent to the seller, indicating the goods or services required

delivery note — a document listing and accompanying the goods sent to the purchaser

goods received note — a document sometimes used by purchasers to record receipt of stock and any returns made

invoice — a document issued by the seller of goods or services to the purchaser indicating the amount owing and the required payment date

returns note	a document sent with goods returned by the purchaser to the seller, requesting credit
credit note	a document issued by the seller of the goods or services reducing the amount owed by the buyer
statement	a document issued by the seller to the buyer summarising invoices and credit notes issued and payments received
remittance advice	a document sent by the purchaser to the seller advising the amount and date of payment of money due

STUDENT ACTIVITIES

7.1 What type of business document would normally be used when goods are bought on credit

(a) to order the goods from the seller?

(b) to accompany goods sent from the seller?

(c) to record the receipt and any return of goods at the buyer's premises?

(d) to advise the seller of the amount of money being paid on account?

(e) to advise the buyer in the first instance of the amount of money due on an order?

(f) to accompany faulty goods sent back by the buyer?

7.2 An unsigned purchase order is sent out to a supplier. What is likely to happen to it, and why?

7.3 Which documents would normally be checked by the buyer against the purchase order? Answer (a) or (b) or (c) or (d).

(a) the delivery note and the returns note

(b) the invoice and the returns note

(c) the goods received note and the remittance advice

(d) the delivery note and the invoice

7.4 What is the difference between a returns note and a credit note?

7.5 What would be the problem if the seller of goods accidentally forgot to include the normal trade discount on an invoice to a regular customer? What should the customer do?

7.6   Eduservice, an educational consultancy business, ordered some computer disks from Compusupply Limited on purchase order 53659 for courses it runs at Itec College in Broadfield. The goods were delivered to the Eduservice office at 45 The Ridings, Broadfield on 3 February.

You work in the Eduservice office as an administrative assistant. Part of your job is to deal with all the documents, including the accounting work.

You have today (5 February 2001) received an invoice from Compusupply. You are not happy with the service you are receiving from this company and are thinking of going elsewhere for a supplier.

Shown below and on the next page are:
*   a list of Compusupply customer discounts (for information purposes)
*   the original purchase order
*   the invoice you receive

You are to write a letter to Compusupply setting out the errors that have been made. Address the letter to the Sales Manager and sign it with your own name as an administrative assistant. The date is 5 February 2001.

Compusupply – Customer discounts and credit limits (extracts)

Customer	Discount (%)	Credit limit (£)
Donmar Estates	15	12,000
Dugdale, E	10	5,000
Easifit Ltd	15	10,000
Eduservice	15	12,500
Estima Designs	10	5,000

EDUSERVICE

45 The Ridings
Broadfield
BR2 3TR
Tel 01908 333691

PURCHASE ORDER

TO

Compusupply Limited
Unit 17 Elgar Estate,
Broadfield, BR7 4ER

purchase order no   53659

date   26 January 2001

product code	quantity	description
4573	10 disks	Zap 100MB Storage disks @ £95 per box of 10

Authorised   signature...... *J Wales* ....date *26.1.01* ....

INVOICE

COMPUSUPPLY LIMITED
Unit 17 Elgar Estate, Broadfield, BR7 4ER
Tel 01908 765756 Fax 01908 765777 Email rob@compusupply.u-net.com
VAT Reg GB 0745 4689 13

invoice to

Eduservice	invoice no 20424
45 The Ridings	account 242
Broadfield	your reference 53659
BR2 3TR	date/tax point 30.01.2001

deliver to

J Wales
Itec College
Fairacre
Broadfield BR5 7YT

product code	description	quantity	price	unit	total	discount %	net
4574	Zap 200MB Storage disk	10	125.00	box (10)	125.00	10	112.50

goods total	112.50
VAT	19.68
TOTAL	132.18

terms
Net monthly
Carriage paid
E & OE

ACCOUNTING FOR CREDIT PURCHASES AND PURCHASES RETURNS

this chapter covers . . .

In this chapter we apply the principles of the accounting system to credit purchases and purchases returns. We shall see how the prime documents for credit purchases (purchases invoices) and purchases returns (credit notes) are entered in the primary accounting records (purchases day book and purchases returns day book); the information is then transferred from the day books into the ledger accounts of the double-entry system.

NVQ PERFORMANCE CRITERIA COVERED

unit 2: MAKING AND RECORDING PAYMENTS

element 1

process documents relating to goods and services received

- *documents are correctly entered as primary records according to organisational procedures*

- *entries are coded and recorded in the appropriate ledger*

ACCOUNTING FOR CREDIT PURCHASES TRANSACTIONS

This chapter focuses on credit purchases transactions; the recording of transactions for *cash purchases* will be covered when we study the payments side of the cash book in Chapter 11.

In accounting, the term 'purchases' has a specific meaning:

the purchase of goods with the intention that they should be resold at a profit

Thus an office stationery shop will record as purchases those items – such as photocopier paper, ring binders – which it buys in with the intention of resale at a profit. Other items purchased in connection with the running of the business – eg buildings, shop fittings – are recorded not as purchases but, instead, are accounted for against the name of the item, ie buildings, shop fittings.

The accounting system for credit purchases starts its recording process from prime documents – these comprise:

- purchases invoices
- credit notes received

The diagram which follows shows the order in which the accounting records are prepared for credit purchases transactions.

accounting for credit purchases transactions

prime documents

- purchases invoices
- credit notes received

primary accounting records

- purchases day book
- purchases returns day book

double-entry accounts

- purchases (creditors) ledger
- general (main) ledger
- cash book

We will now look in more detail at the use of the primary accounting records and the double-entry system for credit purchases. These are very similar to the system already used for credit sales in Chapter 3 and you may wish to refer to the sections of Chapter 3 which cover primary accounting records (pages 50 - 52), the double-entry system (pages 52 - 55), and methods of coding in accounting systems (pages 55 - 56).

ACCOUNTING SYSTEM FOR PURCHASES

The accounting system for credit purchases fits together in the following way:

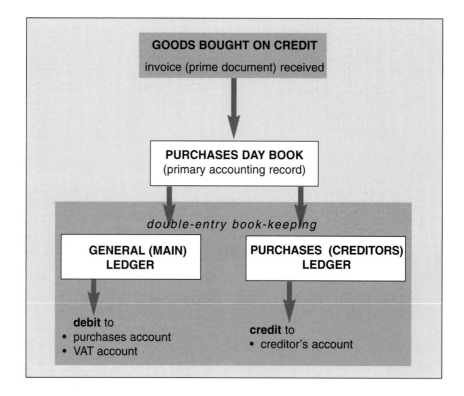

We shall now look in more detail at the purchases day book and the double-entry accounts for credit purchases. In the examples which follow we will assume that the business is registered for Value Added Tax. The rate of VAT used in the example is 17.5%.

PURCHASES DAY BOOK

The purchases day book is a collection point for accounting information on the credit purchases of a business and is set out in the following way (with sample entries shown):

Purchases Day Book						PDB 57
Date	Supplier	Invoice No	Folio	Gross	VAT*	Net
2001				£	£	£
2 Jan	P Bond Ltd	1234	PL 125	94.00	14.00	80.00
10 Jan	D Webster	A373	PL 730	141.00	21.00	120.00
16 Jan	P Bond Ltd	1247	PL 125	47.00	7.00	40.00
20 Jan	Sanders & Sons	5691	PL 495	188.00	28.00	160.00
31 Jan	Totals for month			470.00	70.00	400.00

* VAT = 17.5 per cent

Notes:

- The purchases day book is prepared from purchases invoices received from suppliers.
- The reference 'PDB 57' is used for cross-referencing to the book-keeping system: here it indicates that this is page 57 of the purchases day book.
- The *folio* column is also used for cross-referencing purposes: 'PL' refers to Purchases Ledger, followed by the account number.
- The *gross* column records the amount of each invoice, ie after VAT has been included.
- The day book is totalled at appropriate intervals – daily, weekly or monthly – and the total of the *net* column will tell the business the amount of credit purchases for the period.
- When control accounts (see Chapter 17) are in use, the total of the gross column from the purchases day book is entered into the purchases ledger (creditors) control account.

Thus, to write up the purchases day book, we take the purchases invoices – that have been checked and authorised (see page 145) – for the period and enter the details:

- date of invoice

- name of supplier

- purchase invoice number

- cross-reference to the supplier's account number in the purchases ledger, eg 'PL 125'

- enter the gross amount of the invoice, being the final total

- enter the VAT amount shown on the invoice – don't be concerned with any adjustments to the VAT for the effect of any cash discounts, simply record the VAT amount shown

- enter the net amount of the invoice (often described as 'goods or services total'), before VAT is added

DOUBLE-ENTRY BOOK-KEEPING FOR CREDIT PURCHASES

After the purchases day book has been written up and totalled, the information from it is transferred into the double-entry system. The accounts in the purchases ledger and general ledger to record the transactions from the purchases day book seen earlier are as follows:

PURCHASES (CREDITORS) LEDGER

Dr		**P Bond Limited** (account no 125)		Cr
2001	£	2001		£
		2 Jan	Purchases PDB 57	94
		16 Jan	Purchases PDB 57	47

Dr		**Sanders & Sons** (account no 495)		Cr
2001	£	2001		£
		20 Jan	Purchases PDB 57	188

Dr		**D Webster** (account no 730)		Cr
2001	£	2001		£
		10 Jan	Purchases PDB 57	141

GENERAL (MAIN) LEDGER

Dr   **Purchases Account** (account no 5001)   Cr

2001	£	2001	£
31 Jan Purchases Day Book PDB 57	400		

Dr   **Value Added Tax Account** (account no 2200)   Cr

2001	£	2001	£
31 Jan Purchases Day Book PDB 57	70		

Note that from the purchases day book:

- the amounts from the gross column *for each separate purchase* have been credited to the accounts of the suppliers, ie the business owes to each creditor the amounts shown
- the total of the VAT column, £70, has been debited to VAT account (which has gained value)
- the total of the net column, £400, has been debited to purchases account (ie the account which has gained value)
- the folio column in the day book gives a cross-reference to the creditors' accounts in the purchases ledger (PL)
- each entry in the purchases ledger and general ledger is cross-referenced back to the page number of the purchases day book; here the reference is to 'PDB 57'.

ACCOUNTING SYSTEM FOR PURCHASES RETURNS

Purchases returns (or returns out) are when goods previously bought on credit are returned by the business to its suppliers. A credit note (see page 152) is requested and, when received, it is entered in the accounting system to reduce the amount owing to the creditor.

The accounting procedures for purchases returns involve:

- *prime documents* – credit notes received from suppliers
- *primary accounting record* – purchases returns day book
- *double-entry accounts* – purchases ledger (accounts for each creditor) and general ledger (purchases returns account, which records the total of credit notes received, and Value Added Tax account, which records the VAT amount of purchases returns)

The accounting system for purchases returns is summarised as follows:

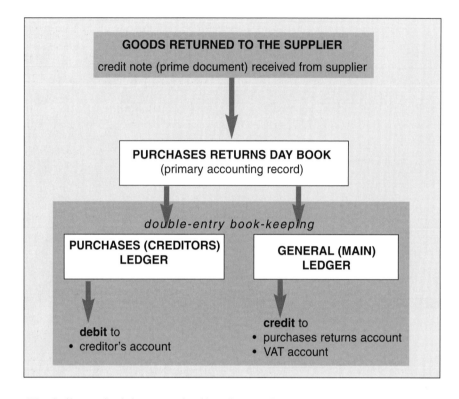

We shall now look in more detail at the purchases returns day book and the double-entry accounts for purchases returns. Note that the business is registered for Value Added Tax.

PURCHASES RETURNS DAY BOOK

The purchases returns day book uses virtually the same layout as the purchases day book seen earlier in this chapter. It operates in a similar way, storing up information about purchases returns until such time as a transfer is made into the double-entry accounts system. The prime documents for purchases returns day book are credit notes received from suppliers.

example transactions

2001

20 Jan   Returned goods, £40 + VAT to D Webster, credit note no 123 received

27 Jan   Returned goods, £80 + VAT to Sanders & Sons, credit note no 406 received

The purchases returns day book is written up as follows:

Purchases Returns Day Book						PRDB 3
Date	Supplier	Credit Note No	Folio	Gross	VAT*	Net
2001				£	£	£
20 Jan	D Webster	123	PL 730	47.00	7.00	40.00
27 Jan	Sanders & Sons	406	PL 495	94.00	14.00	80.00
31 Jan	Totals for month			141.00	21.00	120.00

* VAT = 17.5 per cent

Notes:

- The purchases returns day book is prepared from credit notes received from suppliers.
- The day book is totalled at appropriate intervals – weekly or monthly.
- The VAT-inclusive amounts from the gross column are debited to the creditors' personal accounts in the purchases ledger.
- The total of the VAT column is transferred to the credit of the VAT account in the general ledger.
- The total of the net column tells the business the amount of purchases returns for the period. This amount is transferred to the credit of purchases returns account in the general ledger.
- The gross column records the amount of each credit note received, ie after VAT has been included. When control accounts (see Chapter 17) are in use, the total of the gross column is entered into the purchases ledger (creditors) control account.

DOUBLE-ENTRY BOOK-KEEPING FOR PURCHASES RETURNS

After the purchases returns day book has been written up and totalled, the information from it is transferred into the double-entry system. The accounts in the purchases ledger and general ledger to record the transactions from the above purchases returns day book (including any other transactions already recorded on these accounts) are:

PURCHASES (CREDITORS) LEDGER

Dr		**Sanders & Sons** (account no 495)		Cr
2001		£	2001	£
27 Jan	Purchases Returns PRDB 3	94	20 Jan Purchases PDB 57	188

Dr		**D Webster** (account no 730)		Cr
2001		£	2001	£
20 Jan	Purchases Returns PRDB 3	47	10 Jan Purchases PDB 57	141

GENERAL (MAIN) LEDGER

Dr		**Purchases Returns Account** (account no 5010)		Cr
2001		£	2001	£
			31 Jan Purchases Returns Day Book PRDB 3	120

Dr		**Value Added Tax Account** (account no 2200)		Cr
2001		£	2001	£
31 Jan	Purchases Day Book PDB 57	70	31 Jan Purchases Returns Day Book PRDB 3	21

THE USE OF ANALYSED PURCHASES DAY BOOKS

Businesses use analysed day books whenever they wish to analyse purchases and purchases returns between different categories of purchases:

- goods for resale, perhaps split between types of goods, eg in a clothes shop between ladies wear and mens wear
- other items of expenditure, eg bills for expenses, such as telephone, electricity etc

An example of an analysed purchases day book is shown below.

Purchases Day Book									PDB 86
Date	Supplier	Invoice No	Folio	Gross	VAT*	Net	Ladies wear	Mens wear	Other expenses
2001				£	£	£	£	£	£
2 Sep	Fashions Limited	1478	PL 87	129.25	19.25	110.00	50.00	60.00	–
4 Sep	Eastern Telephones	2479	PL 61	175.66	26.16	149.50	–	–	149.50
8 Sep	Mercian Models	9799	PL 102	301.74	44.94	256.80	256.80	–	–
12 Sep	Media Advertising	2010	PL 92	528.75	78.75	450.00	–	–	450.00
15 Sep	Style Limited	4621	PL 379	432.87	64.47	368.40	218.20	150.20	–
19 Sep	Wyvern Motors	7447	PL 423	149.81	22.31	127.50	–	–	127.50
26 Sep	Denim Traders	3830	PL 45	322.36	48.01	274.35	65.50	208.85	–
30 Sep	Totals for month			2,040.44	303.89	1,736.55	590.50	419.05	727.00

* VAT = 17.5 per cent

Analysed purchases day books and purchases returns day books can be adapted to suit the particular needs of a business. Thus there is not a standard way in which to present the primary accounting records – the needs of the user are all important. By using analysed day books, the owner of the business can see how much has been bought for each of the different categories of purchases.

Notes:

- The references in the folio column are to the 'PL' (Purchase Ledger) and supplier's account number
- The analysis columns – here ladies wear, mens wear and other expenses – show the amount of purchases net of VAT (ie before VAT is added)
- The analysis columns analyse the net amount – by category of expenditure – from purchases invoices

BATCH CONTROL SYSTEMS

As we have seen with sales ledger (page 63), many firms use batch control systems in place of day books. Batched data entry for purchases enables a computer operator to enter a series of, say, purchases invoices without the need to keep changing from one area of the computer program to another. The pre-list is prepared on a batch control form such as that shown below for a batch of purchases invoices:

Batch Control: purchases invoices

Supplier		Invoice		Gross	VAT*	Net
Account No	Name	Date	No	£	£	£
		2001				
PL 125	P Bond Ltd	2 Jan	1234	94.00	14.00	80.00
PL 730	D Webster	10 Jan	A373	141.00	21.00	120.00
PL 125	P Bond Ltd	16 Jan	1247	47.00	7.00	40.00
PL 495	Sanders & Sons	20 Jan	5691	188.00	28.00	160.00
		Check list totals		470.00	70.00	400.00

Prepared by	*Keith Moore*	Date	*31 Jan 2001*
Checked by	*Karen Abrahall*	Date	*31 Jan 2001*
Posted by	*Clare McGougan*	Date	*31 Jan 2001*

* VAT = 17.5 per cent

The purchases invoice batch form is completed from invoices which have been received and checked. The transactions are then entered into the purchases ledger section of the computer accounting program. The computer screen shows the total money amount of purchases invoices and this is compared with the check list total from the purchases invoices batch control form; if there is a discrepancy, the error must be located and corrected.

Where a business uses control accounts (see Chapter 17), the gross total from the batch control form for purchases invoices is recorded in the purchases ledger (creditors) control account.

CASE STUDY

WYVERN TRADERS

To bring together the material covered in this chapter, we will look at a comprehensive Case Study which makes use of

- **primary accounting records**
  - purchases day book
  - purchases returns day book
- **double-entry accounts**
  - purchases (creditors) ledger
  - general (main) ledger

The Case Study also includes a diagram (page 172) which summarises the procedures for recording credit purchases and purchases returns transactions in the accounting system.

situation

Wyvern Traders is a wholesaler of stationery and office equipment. The business is registered for VAT. The following are the credit purchases and purchases returns transactions for April 2001:

2001	
1 Apr	Bought goods from Midland Supplies, £120.00 + VAT, their invoice no 12486
9 Apr	Returned goods to Midland Supplies, £20.00 + VAT, credit note no 104 received
14 Apr	Bought goods from National Stationery, £60.00 +VAT, their invoice no A184
28 Apr	Bought goods from Swan Equipment, £160.00 + VAT, their invoice no P102
30 Apr	Returned goods to Swan Equipment, £40.00 + VAT, credit note no X102 received

The day books and double-entry accounts are illustrated on the next two pages: arrows indicate the transfers from the day books to the individual accounts. Note that some accounts have been repeated on both pages in order to show, on the same page, the accounts relating to a particular day book: in practice a business would keep all the transactions together in one account.

The diagram on page 172 summarises the material we have studied in this chapters. It shows the procedures for recording transactions in the accounting system for

- credit purchases
- purchases returns

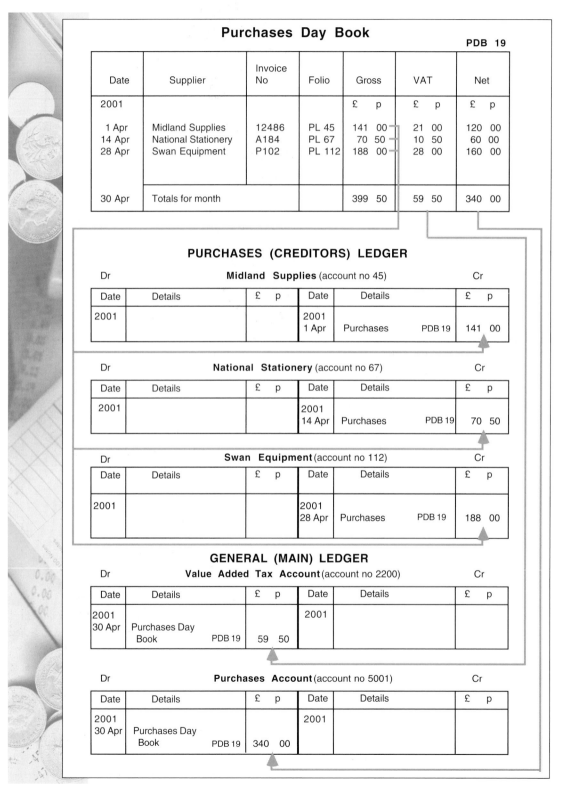

Purchases Day Book

PDB 19

Date	Supplier	Invoice No	Folio	Gross		VAT		Net	
2001				£	p	£	p	£	p
1 Apr	Midland Supplies	12486	PL 45	141	00	21	00	120	00
14 Apr	National Stationery	A184	PL 67	70	50	10	50	60	00
28 Apr	Swan Equipment	P102	PL 112	188	00	28	00	160	00
30 Apr	Totals for month			399	50	59	50	340	00

PURCHASES (CREDITORS) LEDGER

Dr   **Midland Supplies** (account no 45)   Cr

Date	Details	£	p	Date	Details		£	p
2001				2001				
				1 Apr	Purchases	PDB 19	141	00

Dr   **National Stationery** (account no 67)   Cr

Date	Details	£	p	Date	Details		£	p
2001				2001				
				14 Apr	Purchases	PDB 19	70	50

Dr   **Swan Equipment** (account no 112)   Cr

Date	Details	£	p	Date	Details		£	p
2001				2001				
				28 Apr	Purchases	PDB 19	188	00

GENERAL (MAIN) LEDGER

Dr   **Value Added Tax Account** (account no 2200)   Cr

Date	Details		£	p	Date	Details	£	p
2001					2001			
30 Apr	Purchases Day Book	PDB 19	59	50				

Dr   **Purchases Account** (account no 5001)   Cr

Date	Details		£	p	Date	Details	£	p
2001					2001			
30 Apr	Purchases Day Book	PDB 19	340	00				

Purchases Returns Day Book

PRDB 7

Date	Supplier	Credit Note No	Folio	Gross	VAT	Net
2001				£ p	£ p	£ p
9 Apr	Midland Supplies	104	PL 45	23 50	3 50	20 00
30 Apr	Swan Equipment	X102	PL 112	47 00	7 00	40 00
30 Apr	Totals for month			70 50	10 50	60 00

PURCHASES (CREDITORS) LEDGER

Dr   **Midland Supplies** (account no 45)   Cr

Date	Details	£ p	Date	Details	£ p
2001			2001		
9 Apr	Purchases Returns PRDB 7	23 50	1 Apr	Purchases PDB 19	141 00*

Dr   **Swan Equipment** (account no 112)   Cr

Date	Details	£ p	Date	Details	£ p
2001			2001		
30 Apr	Purchases Returns PRDB 7	47 00	28 Apr	Purchases PDB 19	188 00*

GENERAL (MAIN) LEDGER

Dr   **Value Added Tax Account** (account no 2200)   Cr

Date	Details	£ p	Date	Details	£ p
2001			2001		
30 Apr	Purchases Day Book PDB19	59 50*	30 Apr	Purchases Returns Day Book PRDB 7	10 50

Dr   **Purchases Returns Account** (account no 112)   Cr

Date	Details	£ p	Date	Details	£ p
2001			2001		
			30 Apr	Purchases Returns Day Book PRDB 7	60 00

* transactions entered previously

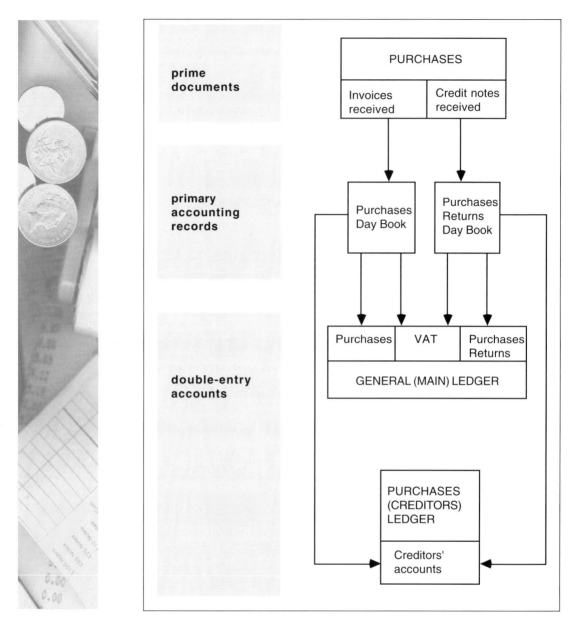

BALANCING ACCOUNTS

Where there is more than one transaction on an account, it is necessary to balance the account at regular intervals – often monthly, sometimes more often.

We will look in more detail at balancing accounts in Chapter 16, where we will also see how the balances are used in the preparation of a trial balance.

CHAPTER SUMMARY

- The prime documents relating to credit purchases are:
  - purchases invoices
  - credit notes received

- Purchases day book is the primary accounting record for credit purchases. It is prepared from purchases invoices received from suppliers.

- Purchases returns day book is the primary accounting record for purchases returns. It is prepared from credit notes received from suppliers.

- Analysed purchases day books are used when a business wishes to analyse its purchases between different categories of expenditure.

- Recording credit purchases in the double-entry system uses:
  - prime documents, purchases invoices
  - primary accounting record, purchases day book
  - double-entry accounts, purchases ledger and general ledger

- Recording purchases returns in the double-entry system uses:
  - prime documents, credit notes received from suppliers
  - primary accounting record, purchases returns day book
  - double-entry accounts, purchases ledger and general ledger

KEY TERMS

purchases	the purchase of goods with the intention that they should be resold at a profit
purchases day book	primary accounting record prepared from purchases invoices
purchases returns	goods purchased on credit which are returned to the supplier
purchases returns day book	primary accounting record prepared from credit notes received from suppliers
analysed purchases day book	day book which incorporates analysis columns between different categories of expenditure
purchases (creditors) ledger	subsidiary ledger which contains the accounts of the firm's creditors (suppliers)

8.1 Which one of the following is in the right order?

(a) purchases returns day book; credit note issued; purchases returns account; creditor's account

(b) purchases returns account; creditor's account; purchases returns day book; credit note issued

(c) purchases returns day book; purchases returns account; creditor's account; credit note issued

(d) credit note issued; purchases returns day book; purchases returns account; creditor's account

Answer (a) or (b) or (c) or (d)

8.2 Explain in note format:

(a) the principles of recording a credit purchases transaction in the accounting system

(b) the principles of recording a purchases returns transaction in the accounting system

---

In the Activities which follow, the rate of Value Added Tax is to be calculated at the current rate (17.5% at the time of writing). When calculating VAT amounts, you should ignore fractions of a penny, ie round down to a whole penny.

For Activities 8.3 and 8.4 use a cross-referencing system incorporating the following:

- *purchases day book* – PDB 36

  purchases returns day book – PRDB 11

- *purchases (creditors) ledger account numbers*
  - AMC Enterprises – account no 520
  - S Green – account no 574
  - I Johnstone – account no 604
  - Mercia Manufacturing – account no 627
  - L Murphy – account no 659
  - Severn Supplies – account no 721

- *general (main) ledger accounts*
  - purchases account – account no 5001
  - purchases returns account – account no 5010
  - Value Added Tax account – account no 2200

8.3 During April 2001, Wyvern Wholesalers had the following credit transactions:

2001

2 Apr	Bought goods from Severn Supplies £250 + VAT, invoice no 6789
4 Apr	Bought goods from I Johnstone £210 + VAT, invoice no A241
10 Apr	Bought goods from L Murphy £185 + VAT, invoice no 2456
15 Apr	Bought goods from Mercia Manufacturing £180 + VAT, invoice no X457
18 Apr	Bought goods from AMC Enterprises £345 + VAT, invoice no AMC 456
24 Apr	Bought goods from S Green £395 + VAT, invoice no 2846

You are to:

(a)   enter the above transactions in Wyvern Wholesaler's purchases day book for April 2001

(b)   record the accounting entries in Wyvern Wholesaler's purchases ledger and general ledger

8.4 The following are the purchases returns of Wyvern Wholesalers for April 2001. They are to be:

(a)   entered in the purchases returns day book for April 2001

(b)   recorded in the purchases ledger and general ledger (use the ledgers already prepared in the answer to Activity 8.3)

2001

7 Apr	Returned goods to Severn Supplies £50 + VAT, credit note no CN225 received
14 Apr	Returned goods to L Murphy £80 + VAT, credit note no X456 received
21 Apr	Returned goods to AMC Enterprises £125 + VAT, credit note no C3921 received
29 Apr	Returned goods to S Green £68 + VAT, credit note no CN/SG247 received

8.5 Jason Smythe owns a business selling furniture and carpets. During April 2001 he received the following invoices from his suppliers:

2001

2 Apr	Invoice no 2790 for furniture from T Table Limited for £1,247.50 + VAT
7 Apr	Invoice no 8461 for carpets from Eastern Imports for £796.80 + VAT
10 Apr	Invoice no A2431 for carpets from Minster Carpets Limited for £1,875.24 + VAT
14 Apr	Invoice no 27998 for furniture from Pegasus Limited for £498.13 + VAT
16 Apr	Invoice no 98421 for carpets from United Carpets Limited for £476.22 + VAT
21 Apr	Invoice no 47921 for furniture from Gerrard Furniture for £831.49 + VAT
23 Apr	Invoice no 2934 for furniture from T Table Limited for £648.90 + VAT
28 Apr	Invoice no 8991 for carpets from Eastern Imports for £1,297.31 + VAT

You are to:

(a)   enter the above transactions into page 21 of the *analysed* purchases day book including columns for VAT, net, furniture, and carpets

(b)   total the day book at 30 April 2001

Notes:

•   folio entries are *not* required.

•   entries in the purchases (creditors) ledger and general (main) ledger are *not* required

9 MAKING PAYMENTS

this chapter covers . . .

This chapter explains the different ways in which payments are prepared and made by an organisation; it sets out the procedures followed to make sure that all payments are authorised and that confidentiality is maintained. The chapter covers the areas of:

- making payments by cheque

- making payments by inter-bank transfer: giro credits, CHAPS and BACS (computer) payments such as standing orders, direct debits and autopay systems

Two other forms of making payment are covered by separate chapters:

- payroll payments and accounting records are explained in Chapter 10

- petty cash payments and accounting records are explained in Chapter 12

The recording of payments in the accounting records is covered in Chapter 11.

NVQ PERFORMANCE CRITERIA COVERED

unit 2: MAKING AND RECORDING PAYMENTS

element 2: prepare authorised payments

- payments are correctly calculated from relevant documentation

- payments are scheduled and authorised by the appropriate person

- queries are referred to the appropriate person

- security and confidentiality are maintained according to organisational requirements

element 3: make and record payments

- the appropriate payment method is used in accordance with organisational procedures

- payments are made in accordance with organisational processes and timescales

- queries are referred to the appropriate person

- security and confidentiality are maintained according to organisational requirements

OUTGOING PAYMENTS

If you work for an organisation, you will readily appreciate that there are different types of payments involved; some will involve the issue of cheques or cash, some will involve paying money from the organisation's bank account direct to the recipient's bank account, other will involve paying wages and salaries. Here are some typical examples of these different forms of payment:

issue of cheques

- paying suppliers by cheque for goods and services against invoices and statements
- paying for 'one-off' items of expenditure, for example a computer system
- paying bills (eg telephone, gas, electricity) by cheque and bank giro credit
- making small 'one-off' cash purchases

paying through the bank account

- paying wages
- paying regular suppliers for goods and services
- paying bills, for example business rates

PAYING TRADE SUPPLIERS

internal procedures

Each business or organisation will have its own policies and regulations laid down to ensure that payments to suppliers of goods and services are only made when the goods and services have been received as ordered. A supplier of goods and services is therefore paid when

- the documents relating to the transaction – the purchase order, delivery note (or goods received note) and invoice have been checked against each other (they are normally filed together)
- any credit due, eg for returned goods, has been received in the form of a credit note
- all discounts, whether *cash discount* (for early payment) or *trade discount* (a set percentage reduction) have been identified and allowed for
- the payment has received the necessary authorisation – often in the form of a supervisor's initials on the invoice, or a rubber stamp

timescales – when to pay?

Each business or organisation will also have its own policies and regulations dictating *when* payment is to be made.

payment on invoice

Some businesses or organisations will pay strictly according to the *due date of the invoice*. Each invoice (and all the accompanying documentation), when it is received will be marked with the due date of payment – eg 30 days after the invoice issue date – and placed in a diary system. With this system a business may make individual payments to different suppliers on any number of days of the month. The system is best suited to small businesses which do not have too many payments to make.

payment on statement

Another widely adopted system is for suppliers to be paid monthly *on the basis of the monthly statement* issued rather than in response to individual invoices. A statement received at, say, the end of March will show all the outstanding invoices; if an organisation normally pays invoices after thirty days, it will pay all the February invoices and any dated earlier than February on receipt of the statement. It will ignore any March invoices, which will be paid at the end of April. With this system all payments are made on the same day, normally at the end of the month. This system is easy to manage, particularly if the payments are computerised (see below) as only one 'payment run' is needed each month to originate either computer-printed cheques or BACS (inter-bank) payments.

payment schedule and remittance advices

We have already seen that the remittance advice tells the supplier what is being paid, either

- by *cheque,* in which case the remittance advice accompanies the payment, or
- by *BACS* (inter-bank computer payment), in which case the remittance advice is sent separately by post or by e-mail

If your job is to make payments and prepare remittance advices, you will probably have a *schedule* of payments to work from, with the payment amount already decided upon and authorised by a supervisor.

paying by cheque

If you are paying a supplier you should attach the cheque to the remittance advice. This may be a tear-off slip attached to the supplier's statement of account, or it may be a standard form used within your organisation. An example of the latter is illustrated on the next page and an example of a cheque on page 180. You should note that the following details are shown:

- the date of the payment
- the amount of the cheque
- the details – ie the reference number ('your reference') and date – of the invoice(s) being paid
- the details (reference number and date) of any credit notes deducted
- the purchaser's order number ('our reference')
- the account number of the buyer (from the sales ledger of the seller)

In addition the remittance advice may show further details such as the cheque number and the amount of any cash discount deducted for early settlement (there is none in the illustration).

TO	REMITTANCE ADVICE	FROM
Cool Socks Limited Unit 45 Elgar Estate, Broadfield, BR7 4ER		**Trends** **4 Friar Street** **Broadfield** **BR1 3RF** Tel 01908 761234 Fax 01908 761987 VAT REG GB 0745 8383 56

Account 3993		6 November 2001	

date	your reference	our reference	payment amount
01 10 01	INVOICE 787923	47609	277.30
10 10 01	CREDIT NOTE 12157	47609	(27.73)
		CHEQUE TOTAL	249.57

a remittance advice accompanying a cheque payment

payment of suppliers by BACS

The use of BACS, the inter-bank computer payment system, will be dealt with in detail later in the chapter. All BACS payments must be communicated to the supplier by means of a posted remittance advice, otherwise the supplier will not know that payment has been made until the bank statement is received, and even then it may be difficult to identify the origin of the payment. If the supplier does not know payment has been received, he or she may start chasing up the debt, which could prove embarrassing!

A BACS remittance advice is illustrated on page 153.

ISSUING OF CHEQUES

Cheques may be either completed manually, or printed out on a computer printer.

When writing out (using ink, not pencil) or typing out the cheque you should take care to complete the

- correct date

- name of the payee (person receiving the money)

- amount in words

- amount in figures (which should be the same!)

- authorised signature (it may be your signature, it may be that of a supervisor or manager)

- counterfoil (date, amount, payee)

No room should be left on the cheque for possible fraudulent additions or alterations; any blank spaces should be ruled through. If any errors are made when you are writing out the cheque, they should be corrected and an authorised signature placed close to the alteration in order to tell the bank that it is an approved correction.

tear off cheque here

counterfoil   *cheque*

Computer cheque printing is increasingly used by organisations which use computer accounting programs with a purchase ledger facility. The computer will automatically indicate payments that are due and, subject to authorisation, print out the remittance advice and cheque together, ready for posting. Clearly the computer involved must be closely controlled – and probably password protected – in order to prevent unauthorised access and fraudulent payments.

PAYING FOR 'ONE-OFF' ITEMS – CHEQUE REQUISITION FORMS

So far we have looked at the payment of trade suppliers who supply on a regular basis for the normal activities of an organisation, eg merchants who supply potatoes for crisps manufacturers. The procedure for the issue of cheques in this case is reasonably straightforward. There will be times, however, when a cheque is needed for a 'one-off' purpose, for example:

- purchase of an item of equipment, authorised by the organisation

- reimbursement of 'out-of-pocket' expenses incurred by an employee

- payment of a pro-forma invoice (a pro-forma invoice is a request for payment to be made before the supply of the goods or services – contrast this with a normal invoice when payment follows supply)

The normal procedure in these cases is the completion of a cheque requisition form by the person who needs the cheque, as shown below.

Mercia Pumps Limited
CHEQUE REQUISITION FORM

Required by ..`Tom Paget`... Department..`Marketing`.......

CHEQUE DETAILS

date for cheque...`30 March 2001`...

payable to ...`Media Promotions Limited`...

amount £ .....`360.00`...

despatch to (if applicable)...`Media Promotions Limited, 145 High Street,`.......
`Mereford, MR1 3TF`
....

....
reason....`Advert in trade journal`.........................nominal code...`7556`.......

DOCUMENTATION

invoice attached/to follow....`invoice 24516`...

receipt attached/to follow..

other..

AUTHORISATION ...*Andrew Wimbush, Marketing Director*.........date...*30 March 2001*.........

a cheque requisition form

Note the following details on the cheque requisition form:

- the cheque has been ordered by Tom Paget, but is to be sent direct to Media Promotions Limited
- the requisition is authorised by Andrew Wimbush, the Marketing Director
- the invoice is attached
- the nominal ledger code is included – this is the category of expense for which an account is maintained in the computer accounting system of the business – 7556 is the computer account number for 'advertising account'; if the business did not have a computer accounting system the name of the nominal account in the main ledger – 'advertising' – would be entered

CONTROL AND AUTHORISATION OF PAYMENTS

spending limits

In order to avoid fraud or unchecked spending within an organisation, all payments must be controlled and authorised. We have seen that incoming invoices must normally be stamped, and signed or initialled by an authorised person before being passed for payment. This is part of an overall system whereby no payment can be made without the necessary authority. The system will vary from organisation to organisation, but the following elements will be usually be found:

- the larger the payment, the more senior the person who needs to authorise it; often each level of management has a money limit imposed – for example a new vehicle costing £25,000 will be authorised at senior management level, a supplier's invoice for £250 will be paid at supervisory level
- when an item of expenditure is authorised, the person giving their authority will sign or initial and date the supporting document, eg an invoice, a cheque requisition form

cheque signatures

While an organisation will have an internal system of signing for and authorising expenditure, it will also have a written agreement with the bank – a bank mandate – which will set out who can sign cheques. A limited company or partnership may, for example, allow one director or partner to sign cheques up to £5,000, but will require two to sign cheques in excess of £5,000. It is common to have a number of different signatories to allow for partners and directors going on holiday, going sick and being otherwise unavailable for signing cheques.

cash payments and wages

Most organisations will keep a cash float – petty cash – to allow for small everyday items of expenditure such as taxi fares and coffee for customer reception. The operation of the petty cash system is strictly controlled and documented, and will be dealt with in Chapter 12. Organisations are also likely to use cash, cheques and/or BACS for the payment of wages; this will be dealt with in the next chapter.

BANK GIRO CREDITS

We have already seen in Chapter 5 how money can be paid into a bank account by means of a bank paying-in slip or bank giro credit. So far we have looked at an organisation which pays in at its own branch, and receives the money in the account on the same day. The banking system also allows for a *bank giro credit* – also known as a credit transfer – to be paid in at one branch and sent through a three day clearing system (like the cheque clearing system) to another bank or branch. This bank giro credit can, of course, be made out to a person or organisation other than the organisation making the payment. Please note that the word giro should not be confused with the payment system of the Girobank, which has nothing to do with the bank credit clearing system. This bank credit clearing system is used widely for

- paying wages
- paying bills (electricity, gas, telephone)
- settling credit card accounts

procedure for paying by bank giro credit

You may well be familiar as a personal bank customer with paying a bill by bank giro credit; the procedure for an organisation is exactly the same. The person or organisation making payment (or payments) prepares a cheque for the total amount to be paid (payment in cash would be very unusual for an organisation) and completes a bank giro credit, or a number of credits if more than one bank account is to receive payment. If more than one credit is to be completed – for example if wages are being paid – it is usual to list and total the credits on a separate schedule for the benefit of the bank.

If you are using a blank giro credit (illustrated on the next page) the details that need to be completed are:

- the name of the bank where the beneficiary's account is held (the beneficiary is the person receiving the money)
- the bank branch and sort code where the beneficiary's account is held. Note: the sort code is a system of numbering each bank branch. (The sort code of a bank branch appears in the top right hand corner of a cheque.)

- the name and account number of the beneficiary
- the sender's name and reference
- the amount of the payment
- the date
- the counterfoil

You may find that because of the danger of fraud, banks are increasingly unwilling to allow the issue of blank giro credits. A typical fraud is an employee paying company money into a holiday account he or she has opened at another bank! The answer to this problem is to have giro credits preprinted (as in the example at the bottom of the page).

Date _____	Date _____	**bank giro credit** 🔵	£50 notes		
Credit _____	Cashier's stamp and initials		£20 notes		
£50 notes		Code no _____	£10 notes		
£20 notes		Bank _____	£5 notes		
£10 notes		Branch _____	£1		
£5 notes			50p		
£1			20p		
50p		Credit _____	10p,5p		
20p		Account No. _____	Bronze		
10p,5p			Total Cash		
Bronze	Number of cheques	Paid in by _____	Cheques etc		
Total Cash					
Cheques etc		Do not write below this line	£		
£					

If you are using a pre-printed giro credit (to pay a bill, for example), all you need to do is complete the amount, date and name of person paying the water rates bill:

WYVERN WATER		Bank Giro Credit 🔵		
Credit account number	Amount due (no fee payable at PO counter)	By transfer from Alliance & Leicester Giro account number		
443 8906	£ 297.54			
	CHEQUE ACCEPTABLE AT PO COUNTER			
		Cash		
9826 9053 9100 2952 1890 647		Cheques	297	54
43-89-06		£	297·54	
Please do not write or mark below this line or fold this counterfoil				
02952189064418		000297542		

sending bank giros credits in bulk

Businesses will often need to settle up with creditors or pay wages by bank giro credit *in bulk*, ie they will issue a number of credits against a single cheque. In this case the credits (sometimes known as 'dispersal credits') are listed and totalled on a schedule. Look at the example shown below. The details for this schedule are likely to have been taken from a manually or computer-produced payments list within the business. It is important to ensure that the payments are authorised before listing them on the schedule.

bank giro credit schedule

to Northern Bank PLC

Branch *Mereford*   Customer account name *Osborne Electronics Limited*

Please distribute the credits listed below. Our cheque for £ *800.00* is enclosed.

signed *O. Hardy*   Director.   Date *28-9-01*

code	bank and branch	account	amount £
40-47-17	HSBC Worcester	R Tyst Associates A/c No. 10987652	209.50
20-37-39	Barclays Evestone	H Mullins Limited A/c No 98920482	190.50
16-04-66	Royal Bank of Scotland Borchester	M Proudfoot Enterprises A/c No. 11653421	312.60
20-31-01	Barclays Helliswell	John Deville Ltd A/c No 97652410	87.40

Northern Bank PLC
Mereford Branch
28 High Street, Mereford MR1 8FD

date *28 September 2001*   22-01-59   *800.00*

Pay *Northern Bank PLC*

Eight hundred pounds only   only

Account payee only

£ *800.00*

OSBORNE ELECTRONICS LIMITED

T. Osborne   O. Hardy

Director   Director

403167   22 01 59   37637148

BACS PAYMENTS

Bankers Automated Clearing Services (BACS) is a computer transfer payment system owned by the banks. It is widely used for regular payments such as insurance premiums, settlement of trade debts, wages and salaries BACS is a cheap and efficient means of payment because, instead of a piece of paper having to be prepared and despatched, the transfer is set up on a computer file and transferred between the banks' computers – the payment goes direct from account to account.

The payment cycle is three working days. If a business wants its suppliers or employees to have their money on account on Friday, the money must leave the employer's account on Wednesday. The payment instructions will need to be received by the end of Wednesday, so the accounts department will need to observe this deadline.

STANDING ORDER

The business that needs to make regular payments, eg a loan repayment, completes a written authority (a mandate – see below) instructing the bank what payments to make, to whom, and when. The bank then sets up the instructions on its computer, and the payments are made automatically by computer link on the due dates.

STANDING ORDER MANDATE

To ———————————————— Bank

Address ————————————————————————————

PLEASE PAY TO

Bank ———————————— Branch ———————————— Sort code [   ]

Beneficiary   Account number [   ]

The sum of £ [   ]   Amount in words ————————————————

Date of first payment ——————————   Frequency of payment ——————————

Until ————————————   Reference ————————————

Account to be debited [   ]   Account number [   ]

SIGNATURE(S) ....

If it is a business which is setting up the standing order, it is important that the mandate form is signed by a person (or persons) authorised to do so – it will often be the person(s) authorised to sign cheques.

BACS 'autopay' systems

Businesses often need to make regular payments of variable amounts, for example:

- paying wages on pay day
- making payments to established suppliers at the end of each month

The banks have established a BACS system whereby they set up standing orders to these regular beneficiaries. This is the BACS equivalent of the bulk giro credit 'dispersal' system shown on page 185.

setting up an 'autopay' system

To set up an 'autopay' system the bank needs written instructions from the customer before the amounts can be deducted from the account. What it does, in effect, is to set up a series of standing orders.

The details needed by the bank are:

- the name of the 'beneficiary' – the organisation or person that is to receive the money, eg supplier, employee, insurance company, hire purchase company, etc
- the details of the beneficiary's bank:
  - bank branch
  - sort code number
  - bank account number
- a unique reference number for each beneficiary which is used each time payment is to be made

operating an 'autopay' system

At the end of each month, for example, the accounts department will draw up a list of the suppliers to be paid and a payroll schedule (see the next chapter). Clearly these details will need careful checking and authorisation before instructions are given to the bank. All the business has to do each time payment is to be made is to complete and give to the bank a bank schedule setting out the date, beneficiaries, reference numbers and amounts. The bank will then input these details direct into its computer system, and payments will be made automatically via the BACS system on the due date.

Read through the Case Study shown on the next page.

CASE STUDY

PAYING SUPPLIERS BY 'AUTOPAY'

City Traders is a shop based in Mereford. In an attempt to cut administrative costs the Accounts Department has decided to pay suppliers through the BACS system. The bank has suggested its Auto Credit System. City Traders has supplied the banking details (sort code and account number) of its suppliers in advance for the bank to put in its own computer. The monthly payment details are then written by City Traders on the bank schedule shown below and sent into the bank by Wednesday 26 September. The suppliers will be paid on Friday 28 September.

Northern Bank PLC
AutoPay Schedule

Bank branch... Mereford ....

Originator name. City Traders ....reference... O7246 ....

Date.. 25-9-01 ....

Branch	Account no	Name	Payee no	Amount
45-45-62	10386394	Trendsetters	234	250.00
56-67-23	22347342	Cool Delivery Co	344	129.76
40-47-07	42472411	Jamesons Ltd	634	450.67
76-87-44	56944491	John Proctor	123	409.79
33-00-77	23442413	Red Skin Company	264	305.78
59-99-01	46244703	Tatters Ltd	197	560.85
		PAYMENT TOTAL		2106.85

Please make the above payments to reach the payees on .... 28-9-01 ....(date)

Please debit account no...... 87620261 ....with the sum of £... 2106.85 ....

authorised signature...... *J.Craig* ....

DIRECT DEBIT

The direct debit system is useful for organisations such as insurance companies that receive a large number of variable payments:

- direct debits can be used for either fixed and variable amounts and/or where the time intervals between payments vary
- it is the receiver (beneficiary) of the payment who prepares the computer instructions that request the payer's bank account for payment through the banking system; a direct debit is like a standing order operating backwards

paper-based direct debit instructions

The traditional procedure for setting up a direct debit was for the customer making payment to complete and sign a written authority (mandate) prepared by the beneficiary (the person getting the money, eg an insurance company); this was then returned to the beneficiary (eg the insurance company). The payment details were then posted off to the beneficiary's bank so that the computer instructions could be set up. The original form was then returned to the payer's bank. An example of a direct debit mandate is shown below.

———————— direct debit instruction ————————

DIRECT Debit

Tradesure Insurance Company
PO Box 134, Helliford, HL9 6TY

Originator's Identification Number 914208

03924540234

Reference (to be completed by Tradesure Insurance) ....

Please complete the details <u>and return this form to Tradesure Insurance</u>

name and address of bank/building society

instructions to bank/building society

- I instruct you to pay direct debits from my account at the request of Tradesure Insurance Company
- The amounts are variable and may be debited on various dates
- I understand that Tradesure Insurance Company may change the amounts and dates only after giving me prior notice
- I will inform the bank/building society if I wish to cancel this instruction
- I understand that if any direct debit is paid which breaks the terms of this instruction, the bank/building society will make a refund.

account name

account number   sort code

signature(s)   date

---

problems with paper-based direct debits

As you can see, setting up a paper-based direct debit was a protracted and expensive process, open to error and delay. As a consequence the decision was taken by BACS to allow the direct debit payment instructions to be sent electronically by a system known as AUDDIS (Automated Direct Debit Instruction Service).

AUDDIS – the paperless direct debit

A customer wanting to set up a direct debit through AUDDIS (Automated Direct Debit Instruction Service) does not have to sign anything. The instructions (including bank account number, account name and bank sort code) can be provided by the customer over the telephone or on-line over the Internet (see screen details below).

This is useful, for example, if a business wants to arrange finance for an item purchased and needs to set up repayments straightaway. A business subscribing to a service can also give similar repayment instructions – nothing need be in writing.

The organisation setting up the 'paperless' direct debit can then enter the details (the amounts, dates, paying bank) into its computer system and send them electronically to the bank making the payments.

an Internet screen for accepting AUDDIS instructions

COMPANY CREDIT CARDS, BANK DRAFTS AND CHAPS

If you work in an Accounts Office you may from time-to-time encounter other ways of making payment:

company credit cards

We have already examined the use of credit cards for making payments. Some organisations, particularly those which employ travelling sales representatives, may set up a company credit card scheme. This convenient and useful scheme allows nominated company representatives to have credit cards for paying for incidental expenses related to the company's business. A travelling salesperson may use one for paying for rail tickets, accommodation and food. The credit card bill is settled by the company which is then able to monitor the expenses incurred by its employees.

bank drafts

An organisation may have to make a large purchase – for example new vehicles – and be asked to pay by bank draft. A bank draft is a bank cheque, a guaranteed means of payment which is as good as cash, but without the security risks. In legal terms the bank is both drawer (issuer) and drawee (issuing bank) of the cheque.

The draft is in effect 'purchased' from the bank by the organisation. If you need to order a bank draft, you will need to fill in a form provided by the bank, giving details of the amount and the payee. A fee is payable for this service.

CHAPS

The CHAPS (Clearing House Automated Payments System) payment system is for high value payment sent by the banks through their computer networks. It is used extensively by solicitors when they are arranging the purchase and sale of property for their clients. Businesses will use it for high value, same day, transfers. Once transmitted by a bank, a payment cannot be recalled. If you are asked to set up a CHAPS payment you will need to fill in a bank form giving details of the bank and account where the money is to be sent, the account from which the money is to be taken, and the amount. Remember to check the amount carefully, because if you make a mistake, the money cannot be recalled!

A similar system, known as SWIFT, exists for making payments abroad through the banks' computer network. The banks provide forms for setting up these payments which are sometimes known as IMT's (International Money Transfers).

CHAPTER SUMMARY

- Outgoing payments made by an organisation include payments to suppliers, payment of bills, cash payments, 'one-off' items and wages.

- Before paying a supplier an organisation must see that all procedures and timescales are observed.

- Businesses often pay suppliers at the end of the month, they pay on receipt of the statement rather than in response to individual invoices.

- When making payment by cheque or by BACS a business will normally send the supplier a remittance advice.

- Care must be taken when issuing cheques to ensure that the details are correct and that no room is left on the cheque for fraudulent alterations.

- If an employee needs a cheque for a 'one-off' payment, he or she will need to have a cheque requisition form completed and authorised.

- The issue of cheques should be strictly controlled through a system of signing 'limits'; normally the larger the amount, the more senior the signatory and the greater number of signatures.

- Payments may be made through the inter-bank transfer system either in paper form or through computer links.

- Bank giro credits, which take three working days to reach their destination account, can either be completed from a blank form, or, in the case of bills, are partly preprinted.

- If a business needs to send a number of giro credits through the bank credit clearing system, it can complete a bank giro listing schedule provided by the bank and pay in the giro credits against a cheque for the total amount.

- Bank computer-based payments are made through Bankers Automated Clearing Services (BACS). These also take three working days to clear.

- A standing order is authorised by the customer in writing and instructs the bank to make regular BACS payments to the beneficiary.

- If a business needs to send a number of BACS payments on a regular basis but with differing amounts each time – eg when paying regular suppliers – it can ask the bank to set up an 'autopay' system. All it needs to do each month is to complete a bank schedule listing the amounts due and the accounts they have to be sent to.

- A direct debit is authorised by the customer in writing, over the telephone or the Internet and instructs the bank to allow the beneficiary to take sums of money through the BACS from the customer's bank account.

- Other methods of payment include:
  - company credit cards for use by employees for expenses
  - bank drafts (bank cheques which are 'as good as cash')
  - CHAPS (computer inter-bank same day payments, usually for large amounts)

remittance advice	a document sent by the buyer to the supplier to advise the details of payment being made
cheque requisition form	an internal form which is completed and authorised when a cheque needs to be issued, normally for a 'one-off' payment
bank giro credit	a paper slip (completed by the person making payment) which passes through the bank clearing system to the supplier's bank
BACS	the BACS system (Bankers Automated Clearing Services) passes payments through the banking system by computer transfer
beneficiary	the person or organisation who gets the money placed on his/her bank account
standing order	a BACS payment where the person paying the money sets up a regular series of payments through his or her bank
direct debit	A BACS payment where the person paying the money authorises the supplier's bank to take money from their bank account
AUDDIS	AUDDIS (Automated Direct Debit Instruction Service) allows the customer to authorise a direct debit by telephone or on-line and the beneficiary to send those instructions electronically to the payer's bank
autopay system	a system whereby periodic payments can be made to a number of suppliers through the BACS system – the payer completes a schedule setting out the amounts and beneficiaries and passes it to the bank
company credit card	a credit card – in the name of the company – issued to an employee and used for paying expenses
bank draft	a cheque issued by a bank (and drawn on the bank) purchased by a customer as a payment which is 'as good as cash'
CHAPS	a CHAPS payment (CHAPS = Clearing House Automated Payments System) is a high-value same-day inter-bank computer payment – often used for vehicle and property purchase payments

9.1   A BACS remittance advice is normally attached to the cheque sent in settlement of an account. True or false?

9.2   Why should a cheque not be completed in pencil?

9.3   A cheque requisition form is used for which *one* of the following purposes?

(a)   ordering a new cheque book

(b)   stopping a cheque

(c)   providing specimen signatures to the bank

(d)   requesting a cheque within an organisation

9.4   Explain why a partnership or limited company business has to sign a bank mandate.

9.5   (a)   What is the difference between a standing order and a direct debit?

State whether a standing order or a direct debit is the better method for the following payments, and why:

(b)   A repayment of a fixed loan: £125 per month for five years

(c)   A monthly insurance premium which is likely to increase over the years.

9.6   Name two commonly-used methods suitable for making high value 'one-off' payments:

(a)   a paper-based payment

(b)   a computer-based payment

9.7   Company credit cards are popular means of making payment.

(a)   State one advantage to the employee of the company credit card.

(b)   State one advantage to the employer of the company credit card.

For the remainder of the Activities in this chapter you are to take the role of an assistant in the Accounts Department of Nimrod Drainage Limited (a VAT-registered company).Part of your day's work is the preparation of remittance advices and cheques for payments to suppliers. You are not required to sign the cheques. The date is 30 April 2001.

9.8   Your supervisor, Ivor Cash, hands you a list of authorised invoices from Jaeger Building Supplies to pay this month. Calculate the amount of the cheque you will have to make out to send with the remittance advice. You do not need to complete any documents. The date is 30 April 2001.

invoice date	payment terms	invoice total (£)
30 March	30 days	125.89
2 April	30 days	14,658.95
3 April	2.5% cash discount for settlement within 7 days	345.50
9 April	30 days	125.00

9.9 Your Supervisor hands you a statement from Mercia Wholesalers, Unit 12 Riverside Industrial Park, Mereford MR2 7GH, with a note, indicating the following invoices to be paid, and a credit note to be set off against payment:

Invoice 8765 dated 12 March 2001, your order number 5517, £765.25

Invoice 8823 dated 2 April 2001, your order number 5792, £3,567.80

Credit note CN 3420 dated 25 April 2001 (your ref R/N 5168), £250.00

Complete the remittance advice and cheque set out below. Note that the total of the credit note should be shown in the money column in brackets, indicating that it is a deduction from the payment.

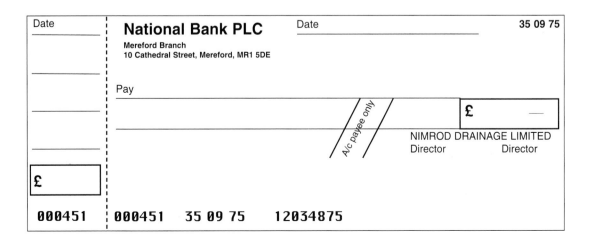

9.10 Your supervisor, Ivor Cash, has received a memorandum from the Human Resources Department stating that a new member of staff requires a refund for incidental expenses to be made direct to her bank account. The authorisation is in order, and the details are as follows:

Beneficiary   J Patel

Bank   HSBC, Stourford Branch, sort code 40 99 87, account 87875231

Payment   cheque

Amount   £78.50

You are to complete the bank giro credit shown below. The date is 30 April 2001.

Date _____	Date _____	**bank giro credit**		£50 notes		
Credit _____	Cashier's stamp and initials			£20 notes		
£50 notes		**Code no** _____		£10 notes		
£20 notes		**Bank** _____		£5 notes		
£10 notes		**Branch** _____		£1		
£5 notes				50p		
£1		Credit _____		20p		
50p		Account No. _____		10p,5p		
20p				Bronze		
10p,5p				Total Cash		
Bronze		Number of cheques Paid in by _____		Cheques etc		
Total Cash						
Cheques etc		Do not write below this line		**£**		
£						

9.11 You work at a clerical grade and cannot sign cheques or other payment instructions. The date is 30 April 2001. Your supervisor, Ivor Cash, hands you two documents (shown on the next page):

- a blank standing order form provided by the bank

- a direct debit instruction received from Tradesure Insurance Company

He is in rather a rush and asks you to process the two documents, and to return them to the appropriate address with a compliments slip. He also leaves you a piece of paper with written instructions:

> *Hire Purchase Payments*
> *12 monthly instalments of £350 to Broadbent Finance from 15 May 2001, under*
> *reference BE/6637.*
> *Bank details Barclays, Eveshore, 30 98 15, Account 72627161.*
> *Debit our Account 12034875*

You are to:

(a)   complete the forms as required (look at a Nimrod Drainage cheque for your banking details)

(b)   state to which address you will send them

(c)   comment on any other procedure which you may have to carry out before sending off the forms

STANDING ORDER MANDATE

To _____ Bank

Address _____

PLEASE PAY TO

Bank _____ Branch _____ Sort code [_____]

Beneficiary _____ Account number [_____]

The sum of [£ _____] Amount in words _____

Date of first payment _____ Frequency of payment _____

Until _____ Reference _____

Account to be debited [_____] Account number [_____]

SIGNATURE(S) ....

.... date.............................

---

direct debit instruction

Tradesure Insurance Company
PO Box 134, Helliford, HL9 6TY

Originator's Identification Number 914208

03924540234

Reference(tobecompletedbyTradesureInsurance)..

Please complete the details and return this form to Tradesure Insurance

name and address of bank/building society

instructions to bank/building society

- I instruct you to pay direct debits from my account at the request of Tradesure Insurance Company
- The amounts are variable and may be debited on various dates
- I understand that Tradesure Insurance Company may change the amounts and dates only after giving me prior notice
- I will inform the bank/building society if I wish to cancel this instruction
- I understand that if any direct debit is paid which breaks the terms of this instruction, the bank/building society will make a refund.

account name

account number   sort code   signature(s)   date

10 PAYROLL PAYMENTS

this chapter covers . . .

This chapter looks in detail at the completion of the documentation involved in preparing and authorising payroll payments. It also looks at the different ways in which payroll payments can be made. The chapter includes:

- an overview of the way in which wages and salaries are calculated

- an explanation of tax codes and the compulsory and voluntary deductions made from pay

- an explanation of the completion of payslips

- practical illustrations of the documentation used when making payroll payments

- examples of the double-entry accounting entries used when making payroll payments

NVQ PERFORMANCE CRITERIA COVERED

unit 2: MAKING AND RECORDING PAYMENTS

element 2: prepare authorised payments

- payments are correctly calculated from relevant documentation
- payments are scheduled and authorised by the appropriate person
- queries are referred to the appropriate person
- security and confidentiality are maintained according to organisational requirements

element 3: make and record payments

- the appropriate payment method is used in accordance with organisational procedures
- payments are made in accordance with organisational processes and timescales
- payments are entered into accounting records according to organisational procedures
- queries are referred to the appropriate person

WHAT IS PAYROLL?

payroll

Payroll is a system set up by an individual or an organisation employing people which:

- records the personal details of the employees
- records wages or salaries together with any other payments due to them
- arranges for the money to be paid
- calculates appropriate deductions to be made, eg income tax and National Insurance Contributions
- arranges for the deductions to be paid to the appropriate authority, eg income tax and National Insurance Contributions to the Inland Revenue

It goes without saying that a payroll system must be *accurate* and be kept *confidential.* Employees need to be paid the right amount and they need to be sure that the details of their pay are not circulated to all their colleagues.

manual and computer records

Payroll records may either be maintained manually (on paper) or on a computer-based system. There are a number of commercially available computer systems such as Sage. If a computer system is used it is essential that it has been approved by the Inland Revenue. You can normally assume that commercially available systems have been approved for use.

Any payroll system – manual or computer-based – must meet the needs of:

- the organisation's internal record keeping – its accounting system and employee records
- the employees – paying them promptly and accurately
- outside agencies to which returns have to be made, eg the Inland Revenue

Payroll records (and other business records) should be kept for a minimum of six years; some organisations keep them for longer periods. They should be filed in an organised way as they may be needed not only by the organisation but also by external auditors. They may also be the subject of inspection by the Inland Revenue.

the need for accuracy

The accuracy of the payroll records is essential. Staff must be paid for work done and external authorities such as the Inland Revenue must be paid the correct amount. Input of information into the payroll system (eg hours worked, rates of pay) must be carefully checked and authorised.

the need for security

The system must be organised to minimise the risk of information being corrupted or interfered with. Practical considerations include:

- information must not be processed without authorisation
- information must be checked, whether held manually or input into a computer system
- duties must be separated where possible – different people should carry out the various stages of payroll processing – if just one person did everything, carrying out fraud would become easier

When computers are used, care must be taken that data does not fall into the wrong hands. Practical precautions include:

- ensuring that the payroll program has been exited when the computer is unattended, eg lunchtimes, so that passers-by cannot see confidential data
- changing computer passwords regularly (and not writing them down where they can be seen!)

TYPES OF INCOME

salaries and wages – gross and net pay

An annual **salary** is agreed between employer and employee and a proportionate amount is either paid in weekly or monthly amounts.

Wages are normally paid weekly. A payment rate for each hour worked is agreed and the employee will be paid for the number of hours worked.

Gross pay is the total amount earned by an employee. It is the basic wage or salary plus any additional payments such as overtime and bonuses.

Net pay is the amount the employee receives after the employer has made tax deductions and voluntary deductions such as pensions (see page 203)

overtime

Overtime is any time worked beyond what is normal for the working day, or time worked on a day not normally worked. Overtime can be worked by salaried staff and also 'wages' staff.

shift allowances

Shift allowances are extra payments given to staff who work unsocial hours because of the demands of shift working. For example a production worker who works from 12 noon to 8pm may be paid an extra £1 per hour for 6pm to 8pm, or he/she may receive an fixed payment of, say, £10 a week.

bonus payments

A *bonus scheme* is an incentive to employees to reach and exceed set targets, or to save time. For example, an employer may fix the amount of work to be completed in a certain time; if the work target is exceeded, bonus payments will be paid. The bonus payment will be paid either individually to each employee based on his or her performance, or paid as an average bonus to every employee based on the amount by which the target has been exceeded. The bonus, often referred to as a 'productivity bonus', can be paid either as a specific amount of money or as a percentage of the basic pay.

commission

Commission payments are normally made to employees engaged in selling goods or services. A salesperson receives commission on the sales that are made during a specific period. The commission is usually paid as a percentage of the total sales made. Commission could be paid in addition to a basic salary, or instead of a salary.

output-related pay: piece rate payments

Piece rate payment is another form of incentive to employees to work more quickly. The employer will agree a rate of pay for each article produced or operation completed and the employees will be paid only for the work that they have completed. Normally, however, there is an agreement between employer and employees that a minimum wage will be paid regardless of the work completed. An agreement of this nature is to provide the employee with a wage when the employer cannot provide work.

authorisation process – records of attendance

An essential part of the payroll process is that all amounts due must be *authorised* before payment. In order to regularise the authorisation process it is important that all work done must be *documented* accurately and in line with the guidelines set down by the organisation. For staff paid on a time basis, a record of attendance must be kept. Employees' attendance records take a number of different forms which include the following:

- *time book* – a simple 'signing in' book into which is entered the time of arrival and departure and the signature of the employee
- *clock cards* – a card used in conjunction with a time 'clock' – the employee inserts his or her card when arriving and leaving from work
- *time sheets* – records used by employees who work away from the premises
- *'swipe card'* – a card which records the hours on a computer activated by the employee 'swiping' the card through a reader

When you are preparing payroll payment sheets you will need to ensure that the records of attendance – whatever form they may take – have been extracted accurately and suitably authorised.

TAX CREDITS

Another form of income which passes through the payroll process is not part of earnings but a form of State benefit known as a *tax credit*. There are two types of benefit which now appear in the 'wage packet' as tax credits:

- Working Families' Tax Credit (WFTC)
- Disabled Person's Tax Credit (DPTC)

This money which is paid to employees does not come out of the employer's pocket (that would hardly be fair!) but comes from a reduction in the amount of tax which the employer collects from employees and pays to the Inland Revenue. This is why it is called a 'tax credit.'

For example, if an employer pays out £450 in tax credits to employees in a month and owes the Inland Revenue £4,120 in income tax and National Insurance Contributions for that month, the employer will only be out of pocket by £4,120:

money paid by employer in tax credits to employees	£450
money due to Inland Revenue for tax collected	£4,120
less tax credit allowed	(£450)
net amount paid (the same as the tax bill)	£4,120

You will not have to calculate tax credits as part of your course, but you may well see it on documentation – for example on Sage computer payroll payslips – along with Statutory Sick Pay and Statutory Maternity Pay which employers are obliged by law to pay to employees.

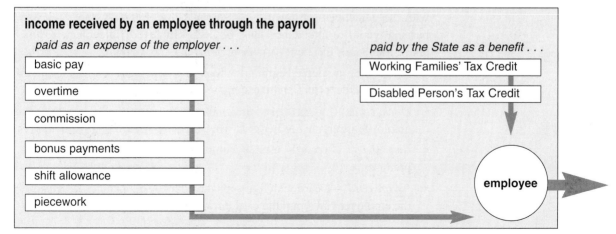

income received by an employee through the payroll

paid as an expense of the employer . . .   *paid by the State as a benefit . . .*

| basic pay |
| overtime |
| commission |
| bonus payments |
| shift allowance |
| piecework |

| Working Families' Tax Credit |
| Disabled Person's Tax Credit |

employee

DEDUCTIONS FROM PAY

There are a number of deductions an employer is likely to make from gross pay. Some are *compulsory* and some are *voluntary*.

compulsory deductions from gross pay

An employer must deduct two government taxes as and when they are due:

- income tax
- National Insurance Contributions

Income tax is collected by the Inland Revenue and is used to fund general government spending. *National Insurance Contributions* are collected by the Inland Revenue on behalf of the Department of Social Security and are used to fund state benefits.

Student Loan repayments may also be made from gross pay. If an employee used to be a student and took out a loan when studying, that loan will have to be repaid from earnings. When the student gets a job, the Inland Revenue will issue a notice to the employer with all the details.

voluntary deductions

An employer may deduct the following at the request of the employee:

- payments to charity by means of a Payroll Giving scheme – deducted *before* the tax calculations are made (not shown above)
- pensions (superannuation) scheme payments
- union fees (not shown above)
- SAYE (Save as You Earn) Sharesave Schemes for employees who wish to buy shares in the company that employs them

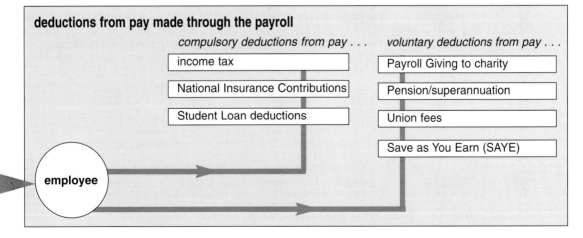

deductions from pay made through the payroll

compulsory deductions from pay . . .

income tax

National Insurance Contributions

Student Loan deductions

voluntary deductions from pay . . .

Payroll Giving to charity

Pension/superannuation

Union fees

Save as You Earn (SAYE)

employee

PAY AS YOU EARN – PAYE

what is PAYE?

Pay As You Earn, abbreviated and commonly referred to as *PAYE,* is the arrangement whereby an employer deducts income tax and National Insurance from an employee's gross pay on each pay day. This money is paid to the Inland Revenue by the employer who effectively *collects* the tax for the government. This is quite different from the regulations which apply to a self-employed person who has to settle up personally with the Inland Revenue, normally with a payment every six months.

the tax year

PAYE operates whether the employee is paid weekly, monthly or for any other time period. The income tax and National Insurance collected is normally paid to the Inland Revenue monthly, but can be paid quarterly if the amounts are low.

Tax calculations are based on amounts due on earnings during the course of a 'tax' year – which is *not* the same as a calendar year. The tax year runs from April 6 in one year to April 5 in the next year. The tax year April 6 2001 to April 5 2002, for example, is referred to as the '01/02' tax year.

The tax year is divided into numbered tax 'weeks' and 'months.' These are:

Week	Period	Month	Period
1	6 April to 12 April	1	6 April to 5 May
2	13 April to 19 April	2	6 May to 5 June
3	20 April to 26 April	3	6 June to 5 July
4	27 April to 3 May	4	6 July to 5 August
5	4 May to 10 May	5	6 August to 5 September
6	11 May to 17 May	6	6 September to 5 October
7	18 May to 24 May	7	6 October to 5 November
8	25 May to 31 May	8	6 November to 5 December
9	1 June to 7 June	9	6 December to 5 January
10	8 June to 14 June	10	6 January to 5 February
11	15 June to 21 June	11	6 February to 5 March
12	22 June to 28 June	12	6 March to 5 April
	and so on . . .		

cumulative pay and tax

Any pay day – whether the employee is paid weekly or monthly – will therefore fall in a given tax week or tax month. This is important to appreciate because tax calculations are carried out by reference to the appropriate tax week or month. Calculation of tax through the PAYE system is normally carried out in what is known as a *cumulative* way, ie an employer works out how much tax an employee has to pay using the totals of pay and tax deducted *since the start of the tax year* (April 6).

If the payroll is processed manually, sets of tax tables produced by the Inland Revenue, will be used. You do not need to study these for your course.

tax allowances

Income tax is a tax on the income received by an individual. 'Income' for tax purposes means wages and salaries, tips, bonuses, and benefits such as a company car.

Employees do not, fortunately, have to pay tax on all their income. In order to help the lower paid, the Government gives a *tax allowance* known as the *personal allowance*, an amount which can be earned during the tax year on which no tax is paid at all. This tax-free income is known as *Free Pay*.

The amount of the personal allowance varies, depending on factors such as whether employees are single or married, or over a certain age. Additional *tax allowances* are also available for items such as the purchase of special work clothing.

taxable income

Income which *is* liable to tax is known as *taxable income*. Taxable income is calculated by deducting the tax allowances (eg the personal allowance) from gross income. For any tax year therefore:

Taxable income = gross income minus the tax allowance

The basic personal allowance, for example, for the tax year 2000/2001 is £4,385. With this allowance only income above £4,385 will be taxed.

TAX CODES AND TAX RATES

calculation of the tax code

How does the employer know what allowances have been given to the employee and how much tax to deduct? The Inland Revenue gives each employee a *tax code*, a number which is used by the employer to calculate the taxable pay. The tax code incorporates all the tax allowances, including the personal allowance, and is quoted *less the final digit*. The tax code for someone with a basic personal allowance in the 00/01 year would be 438L, ie £4,385 less the final digit plus the letter 'L'.

income tax rates

The personal allowances and income tax rates used during a tax year are fixed in the government's previous *Budget*. The Budget – which also sets duties on various items including drink and cigarettes – is announced before the beginning of the tax year and receives wide coverage in the media.

There are three rates of income tax applicable to various 'slices' of taxable income.

The figures quoted here apply to the 2000/2001 tax year.

- *Starting Rate Tax*: 10%, charged on the first £1,520 of taxable income
- *Basic Rate Tax*: 22%, charged on the remaining taxable income up to £28,400, ie on the next £26,880
- *Higher Rate Tax*: 40%, charged on taxable income over £28,400

If, therefore, you are fortunate to receive more than £28,400 of taxable income, you pay income tax at 10% on the first £1,520 and 22% on £26,880 and 40% on the excess.

Take for example an accounts assistant earning £15,000 a year and a finance director earning £40,000. How much tax do they have to pay during the tax year, and at what rates?

Assume they both receive the basic personal allowance. The calculations are as follows:

	accounts assistant		finance director	
		nearest £		nearest £
Gross pay		15,000		40,000
Less personal allowance		4,385		4,385
Taxable pay		10,615		35,615
Income tax @ 10%	1,520 @ 10% =	152	1,520 @ 10% =	152
Income tax @ 22%	9,095 @ 22% =	2,000	26,880 @ 22% =	5,913
Income tax @ 40%		nil	7,215 @ 40% =	2,886
TOTAL INCOME TAX		2,152		8,951

NATIONAL INSURANCE

National Insurance Contributions are also deducted by the employer under the PAYE system. All employees, except those under 16 and those over 60 (females) and over 65 (males) are liable to pay National Insurance. In this explanation we refer to the Not Contracted Out Class 1 contributions which are deducted in most payroll systems.

National Insurance is payable *by both employer and employee* once an employee's earnings have reached a certain amount known as the *Earnings Threshold.* This is £76 a week for employees and £84 a week for employers in the 2000/01 tax year. The National Insurance payments – once these limits have been reached – are as follows:

employer   National Insurance at a fixed percentage rate (12.2%)on *all earnings* over the employer's Earnings Threshold

employee   National Insurance at a fixed percentage rate (10%) up to a maximum amount known as the *Upper Earnings Limit* (£535 a week in the 00/01 tax year).

Note from this that employees do *not* have to pay National Insurance on earnings over the Upper Earnings Limit

Employers, however, do have to pay National Insurance on these amounts. National Insurance can be a substantial cost to the employer. This is one reason why employers favour part-timers and temporary workers – if their earnings are below the Lower Earnings Limit, they do not have to pay National Insurance at all!

The diagram below illustrates the National Insurance Contributions paid by employer and employee in the case of an employee earning £700 a week, ie an amount greater than the Upper Earnings Limit.

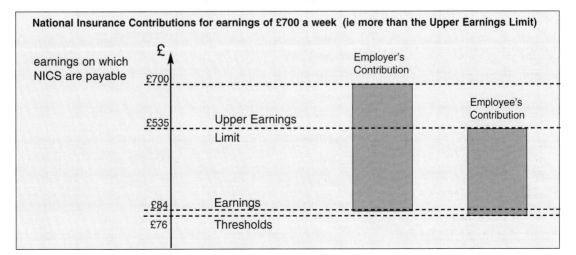

National Insurance Contributions for earnings of £700 a week (ie more than the Upper Earnings Limit)

THE PAYSLIP

Employees must by law be given a *payslip* showing gross pay and the deductions made to arrive at net pay. There is no set format for a payslip. Some organisations will write or type out the details on a printed form, other organisations may use a computer payroll program which will calculate all the figures and automatically print out the payslip. A typical payslip for an employee paid monthly is shown below.

OSBORNE ELECTRONICS		Pay Advice	June 2000
payments		**deductions**	
	£		£
Basic pay	918.75	Income tax	132.87
Overtime	100.00	National Insurance	70.80
Bonus	20.00	Pension	32.08
TOTAL GROSS PAY	1038.75	Student Loan deduction	0.00
		TOTAL DEDUCTIONS	235.75
Gross pay to date	3427.88		
		TOTAL NET PAY	803.00
Date	**Employee** **Code**	Income tax to date	467.00
30.06.00	J Smithers 438L	National insurance to date	244.00

details on the payslip

As noted above, there is no set format for a payslip. The details that will normally be found – if appropriate – are:

essential details

employer name

employee name

gross pay

statutory sick pay

statutory maternity pay

tax credits

deductions made, eg

- tax for the period

- tax and NI to date

- NI for the period

- Student Loan deductions

- employee's pension payment

net pay

optional details

tax code

payroll number

National Insurance number

method of payment

scheduling to deadlines

Weekly pay is normally paid on a Friday and monthly pay at or towards the end of the month. It is essential that timescales are observed for making sure that employees are paid promptly and provided with a payslip at the same time. The larger the organisation, very often the longer the lead time, particularly if the system is computerised. You may therefore sometimes find a delay in the payment of overtime – extra hours worked in January may be paid in February, particularly if the overtime has to be authorised first.

providing information to employees

Employees may query payslips if they are not happy with them. For example you may be asked:

"Please check my overtime; I am sure I did more hours than that."

"What has happened to my pay rise?"

You will see from this that many of the queries will have to be referred elsewhere – to the Human Resources Department in the case of a larger organisation, or to the boss in the case of a small business. Some queries you may be able to deal with yourself, others may need to be referred to a supervisor or manager. Remember always that the information will be highly confidential.

where do the figures come from? – payroll analysis

If your job is to prepare payslips, you will need to know where the figures come from. The income and deduction figures we have explained so far are brought together on a **payroll analysis**. If the business operates a manual payroll this will be a printed form which you will have to fill in with details of income and deductions taken from special Inland Revenue working sheets known as P11s. If you operate a computer payroll system, the computer does all the work for you, including the payslips. Study the form and payslip on the next two pages and see how the figures on the payslip are compiled.

payroll checking and authorisation

The payroll analysis and payslips will only be accurate as long as the information provided is correct, for example:

- the amount of gross pay – including any overtime, commission, or bonus
- the tax code applied
- the employee's identity (it has not been unknown for the right pay to go to the wrong person!)

It is essential therefore that all these payroll details are checked thoroughly and authorised before processing. Again, remember that the information you are dealing with is highly confidential.

CASE STUDY

OSBORNE ELECTRONICS – WEEKLY PAYROLL

OSBORNE ELECTRONICS — payroll analysis sheet — tax year ..../.......... — week/month.........

employee reference	employee name	Earnings				Deductions				Employer's National Insurance Contributions £	Employer's Pension Contributions £	Net Pay £
		Basic £	Overtime £	Bonus £	Total Gross Pay £	Income Tax £	National Insurance £	Pension Contributions £	Total Deductions £			
2345	W Rowberry	205.00	25.00	15.00	245.00	35.00	19.50	10.25	64.75	24.50	10.25	180.25
2346	M Richardson	205.00	10.00	15.00	230.00	32.50	18.00	10.25	60.75	23.05	10.25	169.25
2347	D Stanbury	205.00	25.00	15.00	245.00	35.00	19.50	-	54.50	24.50	-	190.50
2348	D Payne	205.00	25.00	15.00	245.00	35.00	19.50	-	54.50	24.50	-	190.50
2349	K Peters	205.00	10.00	15.00	230.00	32.50	18.00	10.25	60.75	23.05	10.25	169.25
2350	O Robinson	205.00	25.00	15.00	245.00	35.00	19.50	10.25	64.75	24.50	10.25	180.25
TOTALS		1230.00	120.00	90.00	1440.00	205.00	114.00	41.00	360.00	144.10	41.00	1080.00

CASE STUDY

situation

Osborne Electronics is a small manufacturing company which has six employees on a weekly payroll. Each Friday a payroll analysis sheet (see opposite page) is completed by the payroll clerk. The figures for this analysis are taken from the P11 deduction working sheet for each employee, except for the pension details which are kept in a separate file in the accounts office.

Before the payslips can be prepared, the payroll analysis has to be checked for accuracy and authorised by the Accounts Supervisor. The checks that have to be carried out are as follows:

gross pay the total of the columns (at the bottom of the form):

basic + overtime + bonus = total gross pay

This should equal the sum of the items in the total gross pay column.

total deductions the total of the columns (at the bottom of the form):

income tax + NI + pension = total deductions

This should equal the sum of the items in the total deductions column.

net pay the total of the columns (at the bottom of the form):

total gross pay − total deductions = net pay

This should equal the sum of the items in the net pay column.

When the payroll analysis has been checked and authorised, the payslips can be prepared, checked and authorised. The payslip for O Robinson is shown below. Note that the cumulative ('to date') figures are not included on the payroll analysis – they will be picked up from the P11 deduction working sheet.

OSBORNE ELECRONICS			Pay Advice	Week No ....
payments			**deductions**	
		£		£
Basic pay		205.00	Income tax	35.00
Overtime		25.00	National Insurance	19.50
Bonus		15.00	Pension	10.25
TOTAL GROSS PAY		245.00	Student Loan deduction	0.00
			TOTAL DEDUCTIONS	64.75
Gross pay to date		3500.00		
			TOTAL NET PAY	180.25
Date	**Employee**	**Code**	Income tax to date	450.00
..../.../.........	O Robinson	438L	National insurance to date	245.00

what else needs to be done?

All that now remains to be done is to pay the wages, pay the Inland Revenue the tax and NI collected, pay the pension company the money due and make the necessary entries in the accounting records of the business.

PAYING WAGES BY CASH

Calculating the net pay is the first part of the payroll process. The wages or salaries then have to be paid. There are a number of different ways of paying:

- by cash
- issuing a cheque
- direct to a bank account by bank giro credit
- direct to an account by electronic transfer (BACS)

We will deal with each of these in turn.

cash and the need for security

The traditional way of paying wages is by cash, and it is still popular despite the increasing number of people with bank accounts. An employer paying wages in cash can either sub-contract the work to a security firm which will make up the wage packets, or it can be completed by the company's own staff. Preparing wage packets involves collecting sufficient notes and coins from the bank to make up the exact amount for each pay packet. It is normal practice to telephone the bank in advance to tell them the exact denominations of notes and coins needed. Staff collecting this cash from the bank are a obvious target for armed robbery, so common security measures include using two people to collect the money, and for them to vary the route from the bank.

The cash is placed inside a wage packet marked with the name and pay reference or clock number of the employee. Details showing how the payment is made up and the deductions that have been made are provided to each employee. These details can be shown on a separate pay slip or written on the wage packet itself. The office in which this is carried out should be kept secure – for obvious reasons. Employees should sign for the cash wages when they are received.

The total number of notes and coins needed from the bank is worked out on a form known as a *cash analysis*. An important internal security check for the employer is to ensure that the total of the cash analysis is the same as the amount of the cheque given to the bank to cover the wages. A typical cash analysis is illustrated on the next page.

why pay cash wages?

There are a number of reasons why wages are still paid in cash:

- employees like cash in hand
- some employees may not have bank accounts

cash analysis for week ending.................

name	£50	£20	£10	£5	£2	£1	50p	20p	10p	5p	2p	1p	total
W Rowberry	1	2	1		2			2		1			104.45
D Stanbury	1	1	1		1	1	1	1	1				83.80
K Peters		2		1	1		1		2		1		47.72
O Robinson	2	2	1	1	1	1		2		1	1	1	158.46
M Richardson	1	1	2	1			1	1		1	1	1	95.78
NUMBER	5	8	5	3	5	2	3	6	3	3	2	2	
TOTAL (£.p)	250.00	160.00	50.00	15.00	10.00	2.00	1.50	1.20	0.30	0.15	0.04	0.02	490.21

a cash analysis

PAYMENT OF WAGES BY CHEQUE

Another traditional method of payment of wages and salaries is the issue of cheques. This avoids the complexities and security problems involved in the paying of cash wages.

The employee can either cash the cheque at the employer's bank, or, more commonly, pay it into a bank or building society account.

manual and computerised systems

If the employer uses a *manual* payroll system this will involve the person doing the payroll writing out individual cheques made payable to each employee for the net pay earned. This cheque will then be enclosed with the payslip in a sealed envelope.

If a *computerised* payroll system is used, it will commonly print out the payment cheque for each employee, together with the payslip (which may be physically attached to the cheque).

issue of pay cheques – manual payroll

A number of security and authorisation procedures will need to be followed:

- the cheques will need to be kept in a secure place
- the cheques will have to be written out carefully – the details (name, date, words and figures) will have to be checked carefully against the payroll analysis
- the cheques will have to be signed by the required number of authorised signatories (some cheques may be rubber stamped with signatures by authorised staff, or be passed through a 'cheque signing' machine)
- additional controls can include:
  - checking the cheque amounts against the payslips
  - adding up the cheque amounts on a tally-roll calculator and agreeing the total with the payroll analysis total for employees paid by cheque

Although the security risk is not as great as it is with handling cash wages, employers who pay employees by cheque will need to ensure that internal checks exist to prevent staff from fraudulently altering amounts on cheques.

A typical pay cheque is illustrated at the top of the opposite page. Note that:

- the words and figures agree
- lines are drawn after the payee's name and the amount in words – this is to deter fraud
- the cheque is signed by two authorised signatories – directors of the company

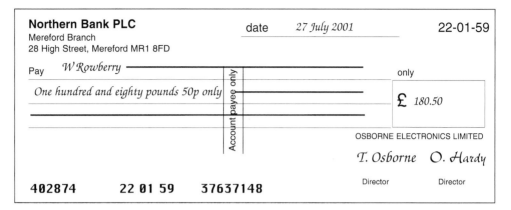

a typical pay cheque

PAYMENT BY BANK GIRO CREDIT

Salaried staff and many weekly-paid employees have their salaries and wages paid directly into their bank or building society account. This reduces the security problems of cash handling by both the employer and the employee. Payments direct to the bank account can be:

- paper based – bank giro credits, *or*
- electronic – BACS

When an employee is paid in this way the employer issues him or her with a payslip – normally in an envelope to preserve confidentiality – but there will obviously be no wage packet.

A bank giro credit (illustrated on the next page) is a piece of paper which is processed through the banking system. It takes three working days to get the money to its destination account, so the employer has to make sure that the bank giro credit is paid in on time.

procedure for processing bank giro credits

The procedure for the payment of the giro credits through the banking system is for the employer to:

- list and total the giro credits on a separate schedule (see page 217)
- to take the credits, schedule and a cheque for the total of all the credits to the bank

These are then processed through the banking system. It is quite common for the employer's computer to work out the net pay, and print out the credits and payslips for the employees. There is no limit to the number of credits that can be paid in: there can be hundreds or more, or as few as two for 'one off' situations such as new employees, as in the Case Study which follows.

OSBORNE ELECTRONICS – PAYING WAGES BY BANK GIRO CREDIT

Osborne Electronics Ltd pays its employees by cash, cheque, BACS and bank giro credit. In the last week of September 2001 two new employees have their wages paid by bank giro credit. Shown below are:

- the two bank giro credits

- the cheque which covers them (note that it is made payable to the bank where it is paid in – ie Northern Bank, Mereford)

- the schedule which lists the credits

Date 28-9-01	**bank giro credit**		
Cashier's stamp and initials		£50 notes	
	Code no 40 47 17	£20 notes	
	Bank HSBC	£10 notes	
	Branch Worcester	£5 notes	
		£1	
	N E Munney	50p	
Credit		20p	
Account No. 10987652		10p,5p	
		Bronze	
	Paid in by Osborne Electronics Ltd	Total Cash	
Number of cheques 1		Cheques etc	250 50
	Do not write below this line	£	250 50

Date 29-9-01	**bank giro credit**		
Cashier's stamp and initials		£50 notes	
	Code no 20 37 39	£20 notes	
	Bank Barclays	£10 notes	
	Branch Evestone	£5 notes	
		£1	
	B Roke	50p	
Credit		20p	
Account No. 98920482		10p,5p	
		Bronze	
	Paid in by Osborne Electronics Ltd	Total Cash	
Number of cheques 1		Cheques etc	275 50
	Do not write below this line	£	275 50

Northern Bank PLC
Mereford Branch
28 High Street, Mereford MR1 8FD

date *28 September 2001*

22-01-59

Pay *Northern Bank PLC* ——————————————————— only

Five hundred and twenty six pounds only

Account payee only

£ *526.00*

OSBORNE ELECTRONICS LIMITED

T. Osborne *O. Hardy*

Director   Director

403167   22 01 59   37637148

---

bank giro credit schedule

to Northern Bank PLC

Branch *Mereford*   Customer account name *Osborne Electronics Limited*

Please distribute the credits listed below. Our cheque for £ *526.00* is enclosed.

signed *O. Hardy*   Director.   Date *28-9-01*

code	bank and branch	account	amount £
40-47-17	HSBC Worcester	N E Munney A/c No. 10987652	250.50
20-37-39	Barclays Evestone	B Roke A/c No 98920482	275.50
		TOTAL	526.00

BACS PAYMENTS

We saw in the last chapter that the Bankers Automated Clearing Services (BACS) is a computer transfer payment system owned by the banks. It is widely used for regular payments such as

- insurance premiums
- settlement of trade debts
- wages and salaries

BACS is a cheap and efficient means of payment because, instead of a piece of paper having to be prepared and despatched, the transfer is set up on a computer file and transferred between the banks' computers – the payment goes direct from account to account.

Sometimes the organisation *receiving* the money will set up the computer data itself (direct debit), sometimes the organisation *sending* the money will set up the computer data, or will get the bank to set it up (standing order/ automated credit).

The payment cycle is three working days. If a business wants its employees to have their money on account on Friday, the money must leave the employer's account on Wednesday. The payment instructions will need to be received by the end of Wednesday, so the payroll department will need to observe this deadline.

payroll through BACS

Payment of wages and salaries through the BACS system can be made in two different ways:

1   The organisation paying the wages and salaries sets up the data on computer file *itself* and sends the data on disk or tape (or direct on-line via BACSTEL) to BACS – this is often the system used by large organisations which have thousands of wages and salary payments to make each week and month. With this system, the organisation's bank is not directly involved, except in that the transfer will pass from the organisation's account.

2   The organisation provides the data to its *bank* which then sets up the computer transfer. This 'automated credit' system requires the organisation to provide the name and banking details of the payees in advance so that the bank can set up the system. When each payroll date approaches the payment details are written on a schedule (see opposite page) and the bank then inputs them into its own computer. This 'automated credit' system is very useful for *smaller* organisations, not only for payroll but also for making payments to suppliers (see page 188).

CASE STUDY

WAGES BY BACS AUTOMATED CREDIT

City Insurance is an insurance broking firm, based in Mereford. In an attempt to cut administrative costs the Finance Manager has decided to pay employees through the BACS system. The bank has suggested its Auto Credit System. City Insurance has supplied the banking details (sort code and account number) of its employees in advance for the bank to put in its own computer. The weekly pay details are then written on the schedule shown below by City Insurance and sent into the bank on Wednesday 26 September. The employees will be paid on Friday 28 September.

Northern Bank PLC
Auto Credit System

Bank branch... Mereford

Originator name. City Insurance Co ....reference.. 07246

Date.. 24-9-01

Branch	Account no	Name	Payee no	Amount
45-45-62	10386394	Smithson H	347	250.00
56-67-23	22347342	Smith M	456	129.76
40-47-07	42472411	Olivier L	209	450.67
76-87-44	56944491	O'Casey S	492	409.79
33-00-77	23442413	French W	385	305.78
59-99-01	46244703	Jones R	546	560.85
		PAYMENT TOTAL		2106.85

Please make the above payments to reach the payees on .... 28-9-01 ....(date)

Please debit account no...... 37637927 ....with the sum of £... 2106.85 ....

authorised signature...... *S. Laurel* ....

procedures for the schedule

Note that:

- the employer has a reference – 07246 – which is quoted on all instructions

- each employee also a reference number, which is also quoted on all instructions

- the form is totalled to provide the amount which will be taken off the employer's bank account

- the form is signed by an authorised signatory within the organisation – the data cannot be processed without this signature

- it is common for a form of this type to be in two parts: the bank is given the top copy, and the bottom copy is retained by the organisation making payment

It is essential therefore that before the schedule is handed to the bank it is carefully checked for accuracy. The net pay amounts must tally with the figures on the payroll analysis and the authorised signature must be present.

BACS: CONFIDENTIALITY AND SECURITY

confidentiality

Payroll records should be kept confidential. If a person works on payroll and has access to colleagues' pay details, they will undoubtedly be very interesting, but on no account should they be revealed to anyone else, inside or outside the organisation. The only body which will require pay details is the Inland Revenue, as we will see in the next chapter.

security

We have already seen that cash and cheques must be kept securely in order to deter theft. Security measures must also be taken when computer payments are sent. Common frauds include:

- the sending of bogus BACS payments to an employee's account

- changing the totals of a large number of payments by a few pence in the hope that the changes will not be noticed – the total difference will then be diverted to an account to which the employee can gain access

These dangers can be overcome by exercising care and caution:

- the individual 'code' issued by BACS to an organisation – without which no payments can be made – should be restricted to a limited number of employees

- payment amounts on the BACS records should be carefully checked against the originals – in the Case Study the net pay amounts were checked against the payroll analysis

PAYMENTS TO THE INLAND REVENUE

Organisations operating PAYE collect income tax and National Insurance Contributions each time the payroll is run. This money must then be paid to the Inland Revenue. For most organisations this means a monthly payment sent within fourteen days of the end of the tax month, using a P30B payslip (bank giro credit). As the tax month ends on the 5th, this means that the money must by sent by the 19th. For example, the January income tax and National Insurance Contributions collected must be sent by 19 February. The payments will comprise:

- income tax collected from employees
- employees' and employer's National Insurance Contributions
- less any money reclaimable from the Inland Revenue (eg tax credits)

The data for these payments is first calculated for individual employees on the P11 deductions working sheet and is then transferred to a yellow summary sheet P32 and then transferred to the P30B giro credit for the appropriate month in the payslip booklet (this is a chequebook-sized book of bank giro credits used for paying the money to the Inland Revenue). The giro credit is normally paid into the bank with a covering cheque.

Now look at the diagram below which summarises the month-end procedure for a small business with three employees. Examples of the documents involved are shown on the next page.

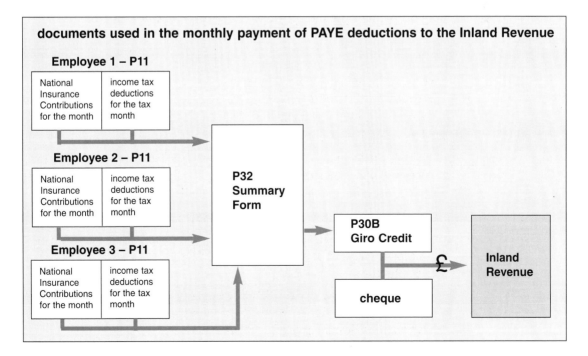

documents used in the monthly payment of PAYE deductions to the Inland Revenue

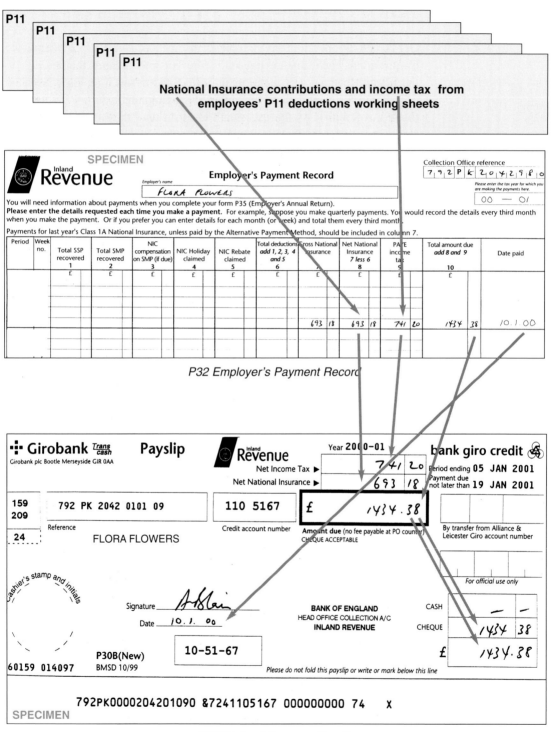

National Insurance contributions and income tax from employees' P11 deductions working sheets

P32 Employer's Payment Record

P30B Inland Revenue Payslip

PAYROLL AND THE DOUBLE-ENTRY ACCOUNTING SYSTEM

types of accounting system

Payroll accounting systems will either be paper-based, or computerised. Many 'off-the-shelf' computer accounting packages are now available, such as the widely-used Sage programs. You will doubtless be looking at computerised accounting elsewhere in your studies. In this chapter, however, we will use a paper-based system to illustrate the accounting entries generated by the operation of payroll so that you will understand the double-entry principles involved.

types of accounts used

Wages and salaries are a major *expense* for any organisation, but remember that the net pay received by employees is not the same as the *gross pay*, the expense to the employer. The wages and salaries expenses figure that appears in the trial balance of the organisation – the expenses that the employer will have to pay – will be the result of a number of adjustments:

- calculated in the payroll process
- entered in the double-entry accounts of the organisation

There is no 'hard-and-fast' rule which states what accounts have to be set up. The accounts used in this chapter are fairly typical, but you may well find that practice varies from organisation to organisation. The main accounts to be used will be

- in the cash book (for bank transactions)
- in the general (main) ledger (expenses)

The types of transaction which need entering in the accounts include:

- income tax collected by the employer under PAYE and paid to the Inland Revenue by the 19th of the month *after* the payroll has been processed

- employees' National Insurance Contributions collected by the employer under PAYE and paid to the Inland Revenue by the 19th of the month *after* the payroll has been processed

- employer's National Insurance Contributions paid to the Inland Revenue

- employees' pension contributions deducted from employees' pay and paid to pension funds

- pension contributions provided by the *employer* and paid to pension funds

The double-entry accounts commonly used include:

Bank this is in the cash book and records:

- payment of cash wages, wages cheques and BACS wages transfers – ie the *net pay* of employees
- payment of cheques to outside agencies, eg the monthly payment of deductions to the Inland Revenue and payments to pension funds

Wages & Salaries this is in the general ledger and records:

- employees' *gross pay*
- employer's National Insurance Contributions
- employer's pension contributions (if there are any)

- in short, it is the employer's *expense* account for paying employees

Inland Revenue this is in the general ledger and records amounts payable to the Inland Revenue (PAYE deductions)

Pension Fund this is in the nominal ledger and records amounts payable to external pension funds: the employer's and employees' contributions as appropriate (with some schemes the employer and employee make a contribution, with others it is just the employee that contributes)

A common practice is to put all the entries through a Wages and Salaries Control account.

wages and salaries control account

You may already have studied the *control accounts* used by businesses for purchases and sales. They are covered in Chapter 17 of this book.

A *control account* is a 'master' account which 'controls' a number of other subsidiary ledger accounts. It is used to record the total of transactions passing through the subsidiary accounts. The balance of the control account should always be equal to the total balances of the subsidiary accounts.

For example, the sales ledger *control account* will give the total of the debtors of an organisation and the purchases ledger *control account* will give the total of the creditors. This provides useful information for the management: they will be able to see how much the business is owed by its customers and the amount it owes to its suppliers.

A *wages and salaries control account* is also a master account: all the entries to the various accounts set up to deal with payroll transactions pass through the control account.

The diagram below shows the structure of the control account and subsidiary accounts. Note that the bank account is not shown here – it is involved in many of the transactions, as we will see in the Case Study which follows, but it is not strictly speaking 'subsidiary'.

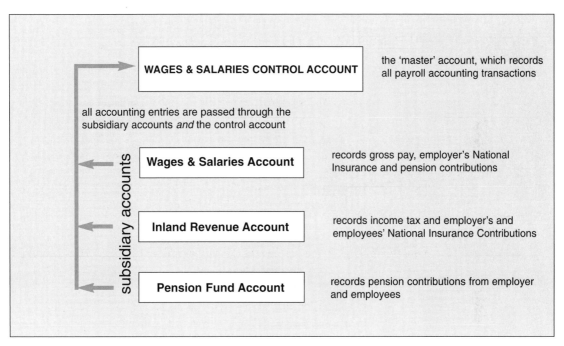

Wages & Salaries control account and subsidiary accounts

CASE STUDY

FLUFFIES: WAGES & SALARIES CONTROL ACCOUNT

Fluffies is a small knitwear business employing five staff. It operates a monthly payroll which is run on the last day of the month. Payroll figures for November 2001 are:

gross pay	£5,500
net pay received by employees	£3,875
income tax deducted by PAYE	£900
NIC (employees' contribution)	£450
NIC (employer's contribution)	£550
pension: paid by the employees by deduction from pay	£275
pension: employer's contribution	£275

What are the payments that are due, and to whom are they payable?

payments due to the Inland Revenue

Income tax deducted from employees' pay	£900
Employees' National Insurance Contributions	£450
Employer's National Insurance Contributions	£550
	£1,900

payments due to the pension fund, Allied Life PLC

Employees' contributions, deducted from pay	£275
Employer's contributions	£275
	£550

payments due to the employees

Gross pay	£5,500	
less		
Income tax	£900	
National Insurance	£450	
Pension contributions	£275	
Net pay due		£3,875

payments total

£6,325

These four amounts, shown here in the right-hand column, are recorded in the payroll records and have to be entered into the ledger accounts. This is done as follows:

Step 1

Transfer the total of the payments (here £6,325) to Wages & Salaries Account (this is the cost to the employer) and to Wages & Salaries Control Account

debit   Wages & Salaries Account
credit   Wages & Salaries Control Account

Dr			**Wages & Salaries Account**		Cr
2001		£	2001		£
30 Nov	Wages & salaries Control Account	6,325			

Dr	Wages & Salaries Control Account		Cr
2001	£	2001	£
		30 Nov Wages & salaries	6,325

You will see that this total agrees with the *total monthly payroll expense to the business*: gross pay (£5,500) *plus* employer's National Insurance (£550) *plus* employer's pension contribution (£275) *equals* £6,325.

Step 2

Make entries for the payment of wages (the net pay paid from the bank)

debit Wages & Salaries Control Account
credit Bank Account

Dr	Wages & Salaries Control Account		Cr
2001	£	2001	£
30 Nov Bank	3,875	30 Nov Wages & salaries	6,325

Dr	Bank Account		Cr
2001	£	2001	£
		30 Nov Wages & Salaries Control Account	3,875

Step 3

Transfer the amount due to the Inland Revenue to the Inland Revenue Account

debit Wages & Salaries Control Account
credit Inland Revenue Account (which will become a 'creditor' account until the amount is paid in December and 'clears' the account back to zero)

The 'amount due' is £1,900 and comprises income tax (£900) and National Insurance contributions (employer's [£550] and employees' [£450]).

Dr	Wages & Salaries Control Account		Cr
2001	£	2001	£
30 Nov Bank	3,875	30 Nov Wages & salaries	6,325
30 Nov Inland Revenue	1,900		

Dr			Inland Revenue Account		Cr
2001		£	2001		£
			30 Nov Wages & Salaries		
			Control Account		1,900

Step 4

Transfer the amount due to the pension fund, Allied Life PLC

The amount due is £550 (employer's contribution £275, employee's contribution £275)

debit   Wages & Salaries Control Account
credit Pension Fund Account (which will become a 'creditor' account until the
            amount is paid in December and 'clears' the account back to zero)

Dr		Wages & Salaries Control Account			Cr
2001		£	2001		£
30 Nov	Bank	3,875	30 Nov Wages & salaries		6,325
30 Nov	Inland Revenue	1,900			
30 Nov	Pension Fund	550			
		6,325			6,325

Dr			Pension Fund Account		Cr
2001		£	2001		£
			30 Nov Wages & Salaries		
			Control Account		550

conclusion

You will see from the double-entry book-keeping entries shown above that the Wages
& Salaries Control Account acts as a 'master' account for all the payroll accounting
transactions carried out each time the payroll is run. At the end of the process the
control account balance reverts to zero – you will see above that the total of both sides
after the pension fund transfer is £6,325 – ie the balance is nil.

The double-entry book-keeping also shows:

- *Wages & Salaries Account:* the cumulative cost during the year of paying the
  employees – this includes the gross pay, employer's National Insurance and any
  pension contributions paid by the employer; this is the figure that will appear in the
  organisation's profit statement – it is the expense borne by the employer

- in the *Inland Revenue Account* and *Pension Fund Account* any amounts owing – for
  example at the end of the month before payments are passed to these agencies –
  these will be *creditor* accounts

- Payroll records – which are highly confidential – must be maintained accurately and securely.

- Employees' income from the employer, which may be termed 'wages' or 'salary' can be made up of a number of elements: basic pay, overtime, shift allowance, bonus payments, commission, piece rate.

- The payroll is also used to pay certain forms of State benefit – Working Families' Tax Credit and Disabled Person's Tax Credit.

- Compulsory deductions from gross pay include income tax, National Insurance Contributions and any Student Loan repayments which are due to be made.

- Voluntary deductions from gross pay include Payroll Giving schemes, pensions (superannuation), Union fees, and Save as You Earn (SAYE) Sharesave schemes.

- The tax year runs from 6 April in one year until 5 April in the next and is divided into numbered tax weeks and tax months.

- Employees are given tax allowances – amounts of earnings which are free of tax. Taxable income is income on which tax has to be paid; it is gross income less the total tax allowance.

- The tax allowance of an employee is notified by the Inland Revenue by means of a tax code – the amount of the tax allowance less the final digit.

- Income tax is charged in three 'bands': Starting Rate, Basic Rate and Higher Rate tax. It is calculated and charged cumulatively – ie on the basis of how much tax is due by each employee since the beginning of the tax year.

- National Insurance is a tax on earnings paid by employers and employees – it is worked out on a percentage basis but is not cumulative, ie it is worked out each week or month and does not relate to the previous period.

- National Insurance is only payable once an employee's pay has reached a certain weekly or monthly money amount – the Earnings Threshold.

- All income items and deductions are shown on the employee's payslip together with 'year-to-date' figures.

- Each time the payroll is run the figures needed for the payslips and the payments that have to be made are drawn up on a payroll analysis form.

- Wages can be paid in cash, by cheque or by bank transfer (giro credit or BACS). The breakdown of notes and coins for cash wages is calculated on a cash analysis form.

- Payments of income tax and National Insurance Contributions to the Inland Revenue are made on a P30B bank giro credit form.

- Payroll transactions are recorded in the double-entry accounting records of the business – normally using a control account to record the total of transactions passing through the accounts involved in payroll.

gross pay	the total amount earned by an employee
net pay	the total amount earned by an employee less deductions, ie what the employee 'gets'
tax credit	a form of State benefit paid through the payroll and reclaimable by the employer
overtime	extra time worked by an employee, often at a higher rate of pay
shift allowance	an extra allowance paid for working a shift with unsocial hours
bonus payment	an extra 'bonus' payment normally calculated as a percentage of sales
commission	a payment which is calculated as a percentage of sales – a normal part of the payment package
piece rate payment	a payment which is based on the number of items processed by the employee
income tax	a tax, based on the level of an employee's income, collected by the Inland Revenue
National Insurance	(NI) – a tax based on an employee's earnings, collected by the Inland Revenue on behalf of the Department of Social Security
PAYE	Pay As You Earn is a cumulative tax collection system operated by employers on behalf of the Inland Revenue
tax allowance	an amount of income earned by an employee on which tax does not have to be paid
tax code	a numeric code (plus a letter) which enables the employer to calculate the amount of tax due – it is the tax allowance less the final digit
taxable income	the income earned by an employee which is subject to income tax (gross income minus the tax allowance)
payslip	a document given to the employee when the payroll is run, setting out income and deductions
payroll analysis sheet	summary or 'master' sheet showing all the figures produced when payroll is processed; also useful as a cross-checking device for accuracy of figures
cash analysis	a form setting out the details of notes and coin needed from the bank by an employer when paying wages in cash
P30B	a bank giro credit issued by the Inland Revenue – used for paying income tax and NI collected
control account	a double-entry account which acts as a 'master' account for other 'subsidiary' accounts

**STUDENT
ACTIVITIES**

10.1 What is the difference between
  (a)   gross pay and net pay
  (b)   overtime and shift allowance
  (c)   bonus payments and piece rate payments
  (d)   a time book and a time sheet
  (e)   a clock card and a swipe card

10.2 Calculate the *weekly* gross pay of the following employees:

	employee	annual salary
(a)	J Smith	£6,500
(b)	I Rose	£9,360
(c)	R Pellerini	£11,440
(d)	N Mutt	£6,760
(e)	R Singh	£7,800

10.3 Calculate the following employees' gross wages for the week, assuming that they are paid at an hourly rate of £6 for the first 40 hours and time-and-a-half for hours in excess of 40.

	Employee	Hours worked during week
(a)	Helen Marsh	35
(b)	Derek Hall	42
(c)	Eddie Bristow	48
(d)	Dilip Patel	50
(e)	Roger Draper	39

10.4 There are seven employees on your hospital payroll, each with a tax allowance of £4500. Their annual earnings are:

(a)	N Doskopi	£6,000
(b)	Ivor Payne	£11,000
(c)	N Trails	£14,000
(d)	L Bowe	£18,000
(e)	N Emmer	£27,000
(f)	Ray D Oligist	£40,000
(g)	Anne S Thettick	£60,000

Calculate the amount of income tax each employee will have to pay. Use the tax rates and tax bands used in this chapter (page 206) for Starting Rate Tax, Basic Rate Tax and Higher Rate Tax.

10.5 The payslip below shows a number of income items and deductions. Study it carefully.

OSBORNE ELECRONICS		Pay Advice	June 2000
payments		**deductions**	
	£		£
Basic pay	918.75	Income tax	132.87
Overtime	100.00	National Insurance	70.80
Bonus	20.00	Pension	32.08
TOTAL GROSS PAY	1038.75	Student Loan deduction	0.00
		TOTAL DEDUCTIONS	235.75
Gross pay to date	3427.88		
		TOTAL NET PAY	803.00

Date	Employee	Code	Income tax to date	467.00
30.06.00	J Smithers	438L	National insurance to date	244.00

(a) Write short explanatory notes on the income items (including any cumulative items).

(b) Write short explanatory notes on the deduction items (including any cumulative items). Identify in your notes the compulsory deductions and the voluntary deductions.

(c) What does the code 438L mean?

(d) What is the meaning of 'TOTAL GROSS PAY' and 'TOTAL NET PAY'?

(e) Why is there an entry for 'Student Loan deduction'? Why do you think the entry is zero?

(f) What item of payroll, which the employer will have to deal with, does *not* appear on the payslip?

10.6 Using the National Insurance Contribution rates quoted in this chapter (page 207), calculate the separate amounts payable by the employer *and* the employee for the following weekly-paid employees at a garage:

	employee	weekly pay (£)
(a)	Alf Romeo	50.00
(b)	Mike Rarr	79.00
(c)	Sue Barrew	100.00
(d)	S Tate-Carr	250.00
(e)	Portia Carrera	650.00

10.7 Using the Payroll Analysis sheet on page 210, draw up payslips for the first five employees. A blank payslip is shown on the next page.

All employees have a tax code of 438L. The week is week 17 of the tax year. You do not need to quote the employee reference number for the purposes of this exercise.

The P11 deduction working sheets show the following cumulative figures (these include week 17's figures shown on the payroll analysis form):

employee	gross pay to date	income tax to date	National Insurance to date
	£	£	£
W Rowberry	3,650.00	489.00	256.50
M Richardson	3,500.00	450.00	245.00
D Stanbury	3,120.00	410.00	203.50
D Payne	3,400.00	423.50	225.60
K Peters	3,510.00	490.00	260.50

OSBORNE ELECRONICS		**Pay Advice**	**Week**	
payments		**deductions**		
	£			£
Basic pay		Income tax		
Overtime		National Insurance		
Bonus		Pension		
TOTAL GROSS PAY		Student Loan deduction		
Gross pay to date		TOTAL DEDUCTIONS		
Employee	**Tax Code**	TOTAL NET PAY		
		Income tax to date		
		National insurance to date		

10.8 Refer again to the Payroll Analysis sheet on page 210. Also, look at the example P30B on page 222. You have been asked to complete a giro credit P30B for the four weeks ending week 17. The total figures for the three previous weeks are:

week	income tax	National Insurance (employee)	National Insurance (employer)
	£	£	£
14	205.50	115.00	125.00
15	227.00	120.50	132.00
16	210.75	118.50	128.00

What are the money amounts that you will enter on the P30B?

10.9 The six staff on the payroll of Osborne Electronics are paid in cash. The net pay of the staff for Week 8 is as follows:

W Rowberry	£211.56	M Richardson	£189.74
D Stanbury	£206.83	D Payne	£196.75
K Peters	£178.89	O Robinson	£183.69

You are to complete a cash analysis for the six employees. The format of the cash analysis can be found on page 213. The highest value notes and coins should be used, but no more than two £50 notes should be included in any pay packet.

10.10 What method of payment would you recommend for the payroll systems of the following businesses? Give reasons in each case.

(a) a fully computerised insurance company with 1,200 staff on its books

(b) a firm of solicitors with fifteen employees but no computers, apart from word processors

(c) a sole trader builder who employs two workers who do not have bank accounts

Your choice should be based on the cheapest and most convenient alternative. Choose from: cash wages, cheque payment, bank giro credit, automated credit (manually completed schedule for BACS input by the bank), direct BACS (tape/disk).

The following data will form the basis for multiple choice questions 10.11 to 10.13. In each case, choose one option from (a) to (d)

The payroll system of Home Fires Limited has recorded the following totals for the month of July:

gross pay	£350,780
income tax deducted by PAYE	£69,500
NIC (employees' contribution)	£31,450
NIC (employer's contribution)	£35,085
pension: paid by the employees by deduction from pay	£7,500
pension: employer's contribution	£7,500

10.11 The total payment to the Inland Revenue for the month will be

(a) £100,950

(b) £104,585

(c) £15,000

(d) £136,035

10.12 The total wages & salaries expense to the employer will be

(a) £350,780

(b) £462,865

(c) £393,365

(d) £308,195

10.13 The total net pay to employees will be

(a) £242,330

(b) £249,830

(c) £389,730

(d) £350,780

10.14 Pegasus Limited has recorded the following payroll totals for the month of October:

gross pay	£101,500
income tax deducted by PAYE	£20,500
NIC (employees' contribution)	£9,860
NIC (employer's contribution)	£10,150
pension: employer's contribution (non-contributory pension)	£7,500

(a)   Calculate the total payroll cost to the employer

(b)   Calculate the payment due to the Inland Revenue

(c)   Calculate the net pay due to employees

(d)   Draw up double entry accounts for Wages & Salaries, Inland Revenue, Pension Fund, Bank, and Wages & Salaries Control and enter the relevant entries. Assume a nil opening balance for each account. You do not need to balance the accounts.

10.15 Jasons Wool Shop has recorded the following payroll totals for the month of October:

gross pay	£50,000
income tax deducted by PAYE	£11,110
NIC (employees' contribution)	£4,985
NIC (employer's contribution)	£5,010
pension: paid by the employees by deduction from pay	£1,100
pension: employer's contribution	£1,100

(a)   Calculate the total payroll cost to the employer

(b)   Calculate the payment due to the Inland Revenue

(c)   Calculate the amount due to the Pension Fund

(d)   Calculate the net pay due to employees

(e)   Draw up double entry accounts for Wages & Salaries, Inland Revenue, Pension Fund, Bank, and Wages & Salaries Control and enter the relevant entries. Assume a nil opening balance for each account. You do not need to balance the accounts.

CASH BOOK – RECORDING PAYMENTS

this chapter covers . . .

In this chapter we look at how the cash book records payments in the form of cash, cheques and other bank transfers. As well as recording the money side of book-keeping transactions, the cash book is part of the double-entry system. This chapter focuses on the payments (credit) side of the cash book and we will see also how the opposite debit entry is recorded in creditors' and other accounts.

Also in this chapter we look at the authorisation and payment of expenses claims – a task which is often carried out by a firm's cashier.

NVQ PERFORMANCE CRITERIA COVERED

unit 2: MAKING AND RECORDING PAYMENTS

element 3

make and record payments

● *payments are entered into accounting records according to organisational procedures*

● *security and confidentiality are maintained according to organisational requirements*

USES OF THE CASH BOOK

The payments (credit) side of the cash book brings together:

- cash transactions – most payments for cash, except for low-value expense payments (which are paid through petty cash book – see next chapter)
- bank transactions – all payments through the bank (including the withdrawal of cash from the bank)

We have already seen in Chapter 6 (which dealt with the receipts side of the cash book) how the cash books – ie cash book and petty cash book – combine the roles of primary accounting records and double-entry book-keeping.

Cash books are:

- primary accounting records for cash and bank transactions
- double-entry accounts for cash and bank accounts

RECORDING PAYMENTS – LAYOUT OF THE CASH BOOK

The payments (credit) side of the cash book can be set out in a variety of formats to suit the requirements of a particular business. The columnar cash book is a common format which incorporates several money columns. An example of the payments side of a three-column cash book (with three money columns) is shown below:

Credit		**Cash Book: Payments**				**CBP**
Date	Details		Folio	Discount received	Cash	Bank
				£	£	£

This is an almost identical layout to that already seen in Chapter 6, page 123. The only differences are that:

- the payments side of the cash book is the credit side
- discount received column relates to cash discounts that have ben received by the firm in respect of prompt payments made to creditors

As the cash book is part of the double-entry system, each entry on the payments side (the credit side) of the cash and bank columns must have an opposite entry on the debit side of another account elsewhere. Note that the discount received column is not part of the double-entry system – it is used in the cash book as a listing device or memorandum column (we will see later in this chapter how amounts from this column are transferred into the double-entry system).

CASE STUDY

SEVERN TRADING COMPANY – CASH BOOK PAYMENTS

situation

The cashier at the firm for which you work, Severn Trading Company, is away on a course this week. You are required, in her absence, to take over as cashier. The following payments are to be entered into the firm's three column cash book:

2001

2 Apr   Paid E Lee & Son, a creditor, £160 by cheque no 101261

3 Apr   Paid Hayes Limited, a creditor, £200 by standing order

3 Apr   Paid S Crane, a creditor, £145 by cheque no 101262 – he has allowed £5 cash discount

4 Apr   Cash purchases £94 (including VAT of £14)

5 Apr   £200 withdrawn from the bank (cheque no 101263) in cash for use in the business

5 Apr   Cash purchases £282 (including VAT of £42), paid for by cheque no 101264

6 Apr   Paid cheque no 101265 for £70 to S Ford, a creditor, in full settlement of our account of £75

solution

Credit	Cash Book: Payments				CBP 24	
Date	Details		Folio	Discount received	Cash	Bank
				£	£	£
2001						
2 Apr	E Lee & Co	101261	PL 804			160
3 Apr	Hayes Limited	SO	PL 752			200
3 Apr	S Crane	101262	PL 610	5		145
4 Apr	Purchases		GL 5001/ 2200		94	
5 Apr	Cash		C			200
5 Apr	Purchases	101264	GL 5001/ 2200			282
6 Apr	S Ford	101265	PL 698	5		70
				10	94	1,057

Notes:

- The cash book payments page is numbered – here 'CBP 24'.

- The cash book forms a part of the double-entry book-keeping system. The payments side of the cash book records the credit entry for cash and bank transactions – in the section which follows we shall see how the debit entry for each transaction is recorded to complete double-entry. (The discount received column is not part of double-entry – we will see how it is transferred into the accounts in the next section.)

- The details column includes a note of the cheque number of each cheque drawn, together with standing orders and direct debits – this information will help when the firm's bank statement is received (see page 341).

- The folio column has been completed to show in which division of the ledger and to which account number(s) the opposite book-keeping entry appears:

  GL = general ledger (or ML for main ledger)

  PL = purchases ledger

  C = contra entry, which means that the opposite entry for the withdrawal of cash from the bank is in the same account, ie it appears on the receipts side of the cash book (see Chapter 6) in the cash column

- For cash purchases, the amount of cash (or cheques) paid and recorded in the cash book includes VAT; when recording the debit entries we need to distinguish between the purchases amount and VAT – see the section which follows. This is the reason why two general ledger account numbers are shown in the folio column against cash purchases – the first number refers to purchases account, the second to VAT account.

- The money columns of the cash book have been sub-totalled – this helps as we take information forward into other accounts within the double-entry system, and also when we balance the cash book (see Chapter 16).

COMPLETING DOUBLE-ENTRY TRANSACTIONS

The Case Study has shown us how the credit side of the cash book is used to record payments in the form of cash or through the bank account. In this section we look at how to complete double-entry accounts for

- cash purchases
- payments made to creditors
- contra entries

recording cash purchases

By 'cash purchases' we mean the purchase of goods (with the intention that they should be resold at a profit) from a supplier, with payment made immediately either in cash or by cheque (or other payment method through the banking system, eg debit card, credit card). The double-entry book-keeping entries are:

- payment made in cash
  - *debit* purchases account
  - *debit* VAT account (with the amount of VAT)
  - *credit* cash column of the cash book
- payment made by cheque (or other banking payment method)
  - *debit* purchases account
  - *debit* VAT account
  - *credit* bank column of the cash book

The debit entries from the Case Study for the cash purchases transactions of 4 April and 5 April are recorded in the double-entry accounts as follows:

GENERAL (MAIN) LEDGER

Dr		**Purchases Account** (account no 5001)			Cr
2001			£	2001	£
4 Apr	Bank	CBP 24	80		
5 Apr	Discount allowed	CBP 24	240		

Dr		**Value Added Tax Account** (account no 2200)			Cr
2001			£	2001	£
4 Apr	Cash	CBP 24	14		
5 Apr	Bank	CBP 24	42		

recording payments to creditors

When payment is made to creditors for goods that have been bought from them on credit, the method of payment is:

- either by cheque, or other banking method such as bank giro credit, standing order
- or, less commonly, in cash

The double-entry book-keeping entries are:

- payment made by cheque (or other banking method)
  - *debit* creditor's account
  - *credit* bank column of the cash book
- payment made in cash
  - *debit* creditor's account
  - *credit* cash column of the cash book

No entry is needed in VAT account when payment is made to creditors – the VAT entry will have been made when the credit purchase was recorded in the accounting system (see Chapter 8).

When cash discount for prompt settlement has been received from the creditor, ie cash discount has reduced the amount of the payment, entries must be made in the double-entry system as follows:

- *debit* creditor's account
- *credit* discount received account (in the general ledger)

The debit entries from the Case Study for the payments to creditors are as follows (it is suggested that you 'tick back' each transaction).

Note: for illustrative purposes an amount for purchases has been credited to each account (with the cross-reference to PDB 67).

PURCHASES (CREDITORS) LEDGER

Dr			E Lee & Co (account no 804)			Cr
2001			£	2001		£
2 Apr	Bank	CBP 24	160	20 Mar Purchases PDB 67		300

Dr			Hayes Limited (account no 752)			Cr
2001			£	2001		£
3 Apr	Bank	CBP 24	200	20 Mar Purchases PDB 67		540

Dr				**S Crane** (account no 610)			Cr
2001			£	2001			£
3 Apr	Bank	CBP 24	145	20 Mar Purchases	PDB 67		150
3 Apr	Discount						
	Received	GL 6502	5				

Dr				**S Ford** (account no 698)			Cr
2001			£	2001			£
6 Apr	Bank	CBP 24	70	20 Mar Purchases	PDB 67		75
6 Apr	Discount						
	Received	GL 6502	5				

Notes:

- Amounts for purchases have been shown in the above accounts for illustrative purposes – see Chapter 8, which covers accounting for purchases

- In order to complete double-entry book-keeping, discount received amounts, which have been debited to the creditors' accounts, must also be credited to discount received account in the general ledger (the discount column in the cash book is not part of the double-entry system, but is a memorandum column only). The account is completed by entering the total of the discount column from the cash book, as follows:

GENERAL (MAIN) LEDGER

Dr		**Discount Received Account** (account no 6502)			Cr
2001	£	2001			£
		6 Apr	Cash Book	CBP 24	10

- Once the total of discount received has been taken from the cash book, the discount column 'starts again' (ie the amount of £10, above, for this week will not be included in next week's transfer).

- An alternative to recording the total discount received for the week or month is to show the separate amounts (for example, the two transactions here) in discount received account. The disadvantage of this is that, in a busy book-keeping system, there will be a lot of entries to make, which are a duplication of those already made in the cash book.

contra entries

The transaction of 5 April described as 'cash' has a contra entry (ie opposite double-entry transaction) in the same account. The credit entry is recorded in the bank column; the opposite entry is recorded on the debit side of the cash book in the cash column. This indicates that a transfer has been made from bank to cash (ie cash has been withdrawn from the bank for use in the business).

The two contra entries often seen in the cash book are:

- transfer to cash from bank (ie cash is withdrawn from the bank for use in the business)
    - *debit* cash column
    - *credit* bank column
- transfer to bank from cash (ie cash is paid into the bank)
    - *debit* bank column
    - *credit* cash column

BATCH CONTROL SYSTEMS

Businesses that have a large number of payments to creditors will often use batched data entry in order to enter such transactions into the accounts in one 'run'. As we have seen previously in Chapter 8 (page 168), a batch of transactions for a day, week or month is pre-listed on a batch control form, for example:

Batch Control: cheques paid to creditors

	Supplier			Debit	Credit	Credit
Date	Account no	Name	Cheque no	Purchases ledger	Bank	Discount received
				£	£	£
2001						
2 Apr	PL 804	E Lee & Co	101261	160.00	160.00	–
3 Apr	PL 610	S Crane	101262	150.00	145.00	5.00
6 Apr	PL 698	S Ford	101265	75.00	70.00	5.00
			Check list totals	385.00	375.00	10.00

Prepared by	*Neil Ford*	Date	*6 Apr 2001*
Checked by	*Barbara Smith*	Date	*6 Apr 2001*
Posted by	*Dan Ryan*	Date	*6 Apr 2001*

Note that payments to suppliers by bank giro credit and by standing order have not been shown on the batch control form – only cheques paid are listed. Where a business has large numbers of payments – using methods such as bank giro credit, standing order, credit and debit cards – it can use batch control systems for each type of payment.

Businesses that use control accounts (see Chapter 17) are able to record the totals from the cheques paid batch control form in the purchases ledger (creditors) control account.

THE CASH BOOK IN THE ACCOUNTING SYSTEM

As noted earlier in this chapter (page 237), the cash book performs two functions within the accounting system:

- it is a primary accounting record for cash/bank transactions
- it forms part of the double-entry system

For the payments side of the cash book these functions are illustrated in the diagram which follows:

CASH AND BANK PAYMENTS

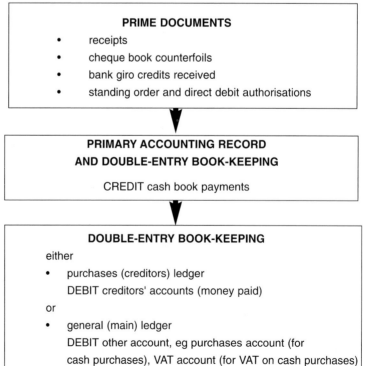

PRIME DOCUMENTS
- receipts
- cheque book counterfoils
- bank giro credits received
- standing order and direct debit authorisations

PRIMARY ACCOUNTING RECORD
AND DOUBLE-ENTRY BOOK-KEEPING

CREDIT cash book payments

DOUBLE-ENTRY BOOK-KEEPING
either
- purchases (creditors) ledger
  DEBIT creditors' accounts (money paid)
or
- general (main) ledger
  DEBIT other account, eg purchases account (for cash purchases), VAT account (for VAT on cash purchases)

CASH BOOK – ALTERNATIVE LAYOUTS

A cash book can be adapted to suit the needs of a business – earlier in this chapter we have seen how a three-column cash book incorporates a memorandum column for cash discounts. Two further layouts often used are:

- a cash book which incorporates a fourth money column for VAT
- an analysed cash book which divides both receipts (see Chapter 6) and payments between a number of categories; for example payments could be divided between
  - the main sections of a business, eg, for an audio/video shop, (1) compact discs, (2) video tapes, and (3) DVD discs
  - (1) cash discount received, (2) Value Added Tax, (3) cash purchases (4) purchases ledger payments, (5) sundry payments

Examples of these further cash book layouts are shown in the two Case Studies which follow: the first is for a cash book which incorporates a VAT column, the second is for an analysed cash book.

CASE STUDY

CASH BOOK INCORPORATING VAT

situation

The following payments transactions are to be recorded in the cash book of Eveshore Growers for the week commencing Monday, 4 June 2001:

4 Jun	Paid £235 by cheque to a creditor, Brooklyn Traders
4 Jun	Paid insurance premium of £130 by cheque (no Value Added Tax)
5 Jun	Paid for office stationery in cash £47, including Value Added Tax
5 Jun	Paid an invoice for £100 from A–Z Supplies, a creditor, by cheque after deducting £5 cash discount
6 Jun	Cash purchase of £188, including Value Added Tax, paid for by cheque
6 Jun	Paid wages of £305, partly by cheque for £105 and partly in cash £200
7 Jun	Transferred £100 from cash to the bank

The rate of Value Added Tax is 17.5%

As cashier to Eveshore Growers, you are to:

- write up page 54 of the payments side of the book for the week commencing 4 June 2001, using separate columns for discount, VAT, cash and bank
- sub-total the cash book at 7 June 2001
- explain how the totals for the discount and VAT columns will be entered in the general ledger of Eveshore Growers

solution

Credit			Cash Book: Payments				CBP 54
Date	Details	Folio	Discount received	VAT	Cash	Bank
2001			£	£	£	£
4 Jun	Brooklyn Traders	PL				235
4 Jun	Insurance	GL				130
5 Jun	Office stationery	GL		7	47	
5 Jun	A-Z Supplies	PL	5			95
6 Jun	Purchases	GL		28		188
6 Jun	Wages	GL			200	105
7 Jun	Bank	C			100	
			5	35	347	753

Notes:

• The folio columns have been completed as follows (account numbers have not been shown):

GL = general ledger (or ML for main ledger)

PL = purchases ledger

C = contra (both parts of the transaction in the same book)

• For transactions involving purchases ledger (eg Brooklyn Traders), no amount for VAT is shown in the VAT columns. This is because VAT has been charged on invoices received and was recorded in the VAT account (through the purchases day book) when the purchase was made.

• VAT on cash purchases, and other transactions, is recorded in the VAT analysis column.

The discount and VAT columns:

• discount received column – the total of £5 will be credited to discount received account in the general ledger and debited to the account of A-Z Supplies in the purchases ledger

• VAT column – the total of £35 will be debited to VAT account in the general ledger (alternatively the individual amounts of £7 and £28 could be debited)

Note that, in cash book, the discount received and VAT columns 'start again' from zero after the totals have been transferred to the general ledger accounts.

CASE STUDY

ANALYSED CASH BOOK

situation

Wyvern Auto Spares Limited buys car parts from manufacturers. The company is registered for VAT. The business uses a cash book which analyses payments as follows:

> **PAYMENTS**
> - discount received
> - VAT
> - cash purchases
> - purchases ledger
> - sundry payments

The following payments transactions are to be entered on page 31 of the payments side of the cash book for the first week of December 2001:

3 Dec	Purchases for cash, £120 + VAT
3 Dec	Paid £235 by cheque to a creditor, Wyvern Electronics
4 Dec	Paid rent on premises, £325 (no VAT) by cheque
4 Dec	Paid an invoice for £250 from Boxhall Supplies Limited (a creditor) by cheque for £240, £10 discount being received for prompt settlement
5 Dec	Transferred £100 from bank into cash
5 Dec	Paid for office stationery in cash, £40 + VAT
6 Dec	Paid for urgently needed spares in cash, £80 + VAT
6 Dec	Paid an invoice for £155 from Vord Supplies (a creditor) by cheque for £150, £5 discount being received for prompt settlement
7 Dec	Paid wages £385 in cash

The rate of Value Added Tax is 17.5%

solution

Credit					Cash Book: Payments				CBP 31
Date	Details	Folio	Cash	Bank	Discount received	VAT	Cash purchases	Purchases ledger	Sundry
2001			£	£	£	£	£	£	£
3 Dec	Purchases	GL	141			21	120		
3 Dec	Wyvern Electronics	PL		235				235	
4 Dec	Rent paid	GL		325					325
4 Dec	Boxhall Supplies Limited	PL		240	10			240	
5 Dec	Cash	C		100					
5 Dec	Office stationery	GL	47			7			40
6 Dec	Purchases	GL	94			14	80		
6 Dec	Vord Supplies	PL		150	5			150	
7 Dec	Wages	GL	385						385
			667	1,050	15	42	200	625	750

Notes:

- The payments side of the analysed cash book analyses each payment between a number of headings. A business will adapt the cash book and use whatever analysis columns suit it best for its payments.

- References to the ledger sections only have been shown in the folio column.

- For transactions involving purchases ledger, no amount for VAT is shown in the VAT columns. This is because VAT has been charged on invoices received and was recorded in the VAT account (through the purchases day book) when the purchase was made.

- The columns are sub-totalled at the end of the week and the totals of the analysis columns are transferred to other accounts as follows:

  - discount received column total of £15 is credited to discount received account in the general (main) ledger and debited to the accounts of Boxhall Supplies (£10), and Vord Supplies (£5)

  - Value Added Tax column, the total of £42 is debited to VAT account in the general ledger

  - cash purchases column total of £200 is debited to purchases account in the general ledger

OTHER PAYMENTS

As well as payments to creditors and for cash purchases, the credit side of the cash book is used to record other payments of the business. These include:

- drawings withdrawn from the business by the owner
- loan repayments made by the business to the loan provider
- expenses of running the business, such as wages, telephone
- purchase of fixed assets (items bought for use in the business on a semi-permanent basis, eg buildings, vehicles, office equipment)

Each of these will be considered in further detail in Chapter 13 where we will see where they fit into the double-entry system. For the moment we will see how they are recorded in the double-entry system of cash book and ledger accounts:

- **owner's drawings**

  - *debit* drawings account
  - *credit* cash book

  The owner of the business withdraws money from the business in the form of cash or a cheque.

- **loan repayments**
    - *debit* loan account
    - *credit* cash book

    The amount of the loan repayment is recorded in cash book.

- **business expenses**
    - *debit* expenses account (using the appropriate account, eg wages account, telephone expenses account)
    - *credit* cash book

    Business expenses are paid either in the form of cash or through the bank. Also note that low-value business expenses are often paid in cash through the petty cash book – see next chapter.

- **purchase of fixed assets**
    - *debit* fixed asset account (using the appropriate account, eg buildings account, vehicles account, office equipment account)
    - *credit* cash book

    The amount of the cost of fixed assets purchased is paid from cash book.

---

example transactions:

2001

18 Jun	The owner of the business withdrew £100 in cash for own use
19 Jun	Made a loan repayment of £750 by direct debit to MBC Bank (no VAT)
20 Jun	Paid telephone bill of £282 (including VAT) by cheque
21 Jun	Bought new computer for use in the office, £1,175 (including VAT) paid by cheque

---

The cash book (payments) records these transactions as follows:

Credit		Cash Book: Payments				CBP 10
Date	Details		Folio	Discount received	Cash	Bank
2001				£	£	£
18 Jun	Drawings		GL		100	
19 Jun	Loan: MBC Bank		GL			750
20 Jun	Telephone expenses		GL			282
21 Jun	Computer		GL			1,175

Note: alternative layouts of the cash book (payments) could be used; in particular, a layout incorporating the VAT column is especially useful on the payments side.

The debit entries are shown in the general ledger as follows:

GENERAL (MAIN) LEDGER

Dr		Drawings Account			Cr
2001			£	2001	£
18 Jun Cash	CBP 10		100		

Dr		Loan Account : MBC Bank			Cr
2001			£	2001	£
19 Jun Bank	CBP 10		750		

Dr		Telephone Expenses Account			Cr
2001			£	2001	£
20 Jun Bank	CBP 10		240		

Dr		Value Added Tax Account			Cr
2001			£	2001	£
20 Jun Bank	CBP 10		42		
21 Jun Bank	CBP 10		175		

Dr		Computer Account			Cr
2001			£	2001	£
21 Jun Bank	CBP 10		1,000		

PETTY CASH BOOK

Petty cash book is another type of cash book; it is used for low-value expenses payments made in cash. A particular benefit of the use of a petty cash book is that it takes a lot of small transactions away from the main cashier and reduces the number of transactions passing through the cash book.

We shall look in detail at petty cash book in the next chapter.

EXPENSES CLAIMS

A further duty of the cashier (or the petty cashier – see Chapter 12) is the checking of *expenses claims*.

Often an employee is required to pay for expenses incurred on behalf of the business or organisation, and then to claim back the amount already paid from the business. Typically, expenses which can be reclaimed include:

- Travel, eg rail, bus, air and taxi fares, mileage allowance where a private car, motorbike or cycle has been used. (Note that the costs of travel to and from work are not paid, except under special circumstances, eg the burglar alarm goes off in the middle of the night and the police request the presence of the keyholder).
- Hotel bills, including meals.
- Subsistence allowance – to cover the costs of working away from the normal place of employment, often paid at a daily rate.
- Other expenses, eg part of the employee's domestic telephone bill.

A business will establish the terms under which it will reimburse an employee. For example, travel claims might have to be at the cheapest form of travel, such as a bus, even if the employee uses his/her private car; first-class travel is likely to be available only to senior employees. Before refunding expenses, the business will usually require proof of the expense, eg a receipt, or the travel ticket.

claims procedure

At regular intervals – perhaps monthly – an employee will be required to submit an expenses claim (see next page). The procedure is likely to be:

- Employee completes and signs expenses claim form.
- Receipts for the expenses are attached to the expenses claim form.
- The form is passed to the employee's manager or section head for authorisation.
- The form is then sent to the accounts department where the amounts will be checked against the company's policies. The calculations on the form will also be checked. The various expenses will then be coded for the appropriate general ledger account, eg travel expenses, telephone expenses, etc. The book-keeping will be:

    – *debit* appropriate expense account (in the general ledger)

    – *credit* cash book payments (cash or bank column, as appropriate)
- The amount will either be paid direct to the employee in cash, by cheque or bank giro credit (small amounts can be paid out of petty cash – see Chapter 12), or the employee's pay will be credited and the amount paid at the next payroll run.

WYVERN TRADERS LIMITED

EXPENSES CLAIM FOR THE MONTH ENDING ....

Name:

Department:

Date	Item	Travelling £	Subsistence £	Entertaining £	Miscellaneous £	Total £	OFFICE USE ONLY	
							VAT £	Net £
Total								

Signed:

Date:

Authorised by:

Date:

expenses claim form

- The firm's general ledger expenses accounts will be debited with the cost. Where an expense includes VAT, a VAT-registered business will debit the appropriate expense account with the net amount of the expense, and debit the VAT to VAT account; in this way, the business claims back the VAT paid on the expense.

income tax and expenses

Most expenses are wholly incurred on behalf of the business or organisation. As such, their reimbursement does not form a part of the employee's salary, and is not subject to income tax. However, some expenses incurred are only partly used on behalf of the business, the other part is a benefit to the employee. Examples include the provision of a company car, or payment of the employee's telephone bill. The Inland Revenue lays down guidelines which, depending on the circumstances, state the employee's liability for income tax, together with the employee's and employer's liability for National Insurance Contributions.

CHAPTER SUMMARY

- The cash book records payments (credits) both in cash (except for low-value expense payments) through the bank.

- A basic layout for a cash book (payments) has money columns for cash transactions and bank transactions, together with a further column for discounts received.

- Another common cash book layout incorporates a VAT column.

- An analysed cash book is used to provide more information: it divides payments between a number of categories.

- The cashier may be responsible for checking expenses claims.

KEY TERMS

cash book	records both cash and bank transactions; combines the roles of primary accounting records and double-entry book-keeping
columnar cash book	commonly-used layout for cash books which incorporates several money columns, eg for cash discount, VAT, cash, bank
analysed cash book	cash book which divides payments (and receipts) between a number of categories, eg the main sections of the business
expenses claims	forms used by employees to claim back expenses paid by the employee but incurred on behalf of the business or organisation

STUDENT ACTIVITIES

11.1 The cash book records:

(a)   receipts and payments in cash only

(b)   receipts and payments through the bank only

(c)   all receipts and payments both in cash and through the bank

(d)   receipts and payments both in cash (except for low-value expense payments) and through the bank

Answer (a) or (b) or (c) or (d)

11.2 The following are the payments transactions of Metro Trading Company for August 2001:

2 Aug	Cash purchases paid for in cash, £80 + VAT
5 Aug	Paid T Hall Limited a cheque for £541 in full settlement of a debt of £565
8 Aug	Paid wages in cash, £254 (no VAT)
13 Aug	Transferred £300 from cash to the bank
17 Aug	Paid F Jarvis £457 by cheque
20 Aug	The owner of the business withdraws £200 in cash for own use
21 Aug	Paid rent by cheque, £275 (no VAT)
22 Aug	Paid wages in cash, £436 (no VAT)
24 Aug	Paid J Jones a cheque for £628 in full settlement of a debt of £661
28 Aug	Cash purchases paid for by cheque, £200 + VAT
28 Aug	Paid salaries by cheque, £2,043 (no VAT)
29 Aug	Paid telephone account by cheque, £282 (including VAT)
30 Aug	Bought office equipment, paying by cheque, £600 + VAT
31 Aug	Withdrew £275 in cash from the bank for use in the business

The rate of Value Added Tax is 17.5%.

Account numbers are to be used – see next page.

You are to:

•   Enter the above payments on page 45 of the three column cash book of Metro Trading Company.

•   Sub-total the money columns at 31 August.

•   Show the entries to be made in the following accounts:

purchases (creditors) ledger

T Hall Limited (account no 451)

F Jarvis (account no 510)

J Jones (account no 643)

general (main) ledger

discount received account (account no 6502)

drawings account (account no 7005)

office equipment account (account no 750)

purchases account (account no 5001)

rent paid account (account no 6950)

telephone expenses account (account no 6212)

VAT account (account no 2200)

wages and salaries account (account no 7750)

11.3   The following are the payments transactions of Johnson Brothers for April 2001:

2 Apr	Cash purchases of £47 (including VAT) paid in cash
3 Apr	Paid travelling expenses of £65 in cash (no VAT)
4 Apr	Paid the telephone bill of £235 (including VAT) by cheque
6 Apr	Loan repayment of £500 made to ABC Bank by direct debit (no VAT)
9 Apr	The owners of the business withdrew £600 by cheque for own use
13 Apr	Paid an invoice for £190 from M Hughes (a creditor) by cheque for £180, £10 being received for prompt settlement
16 Apr	Bought office stationery £80 + VAT, paying in cash
17 Apr	Cash purchases of £94 (including VAT) paid in cash
18 Apr	Bought office equipment, paying by cheque, £400 + VAT
23 Apr	Withdrew £200 in cash from the bank for use in the business
24 Apr	Paid a cheque for £245 to Wilson Limited, a creditor, in full settlement of an invoice for £255
25 Apr	Cash purchases of £120 + VAT, paid by cheque
27 Apr	Paid wages in cash, £350 (no VAT)
30 Apr	Paid a cheque for £560 to Lucinda Luz, a creditor, in full settlement of an invoice for £580

The rate of Value Added Tax is 17.5%

Account numbers are to be used – see next page.

You are to:

- Enter the above payments on page 88 of the cash book of Johnson Brothers, using columns for date, details, discount received, VAT, cash and bank.

- Sub-total the money columns at 30 April.

- Show the entries to be made in the following accounts:

purchases (creditors) ledger

M Hughes (account no 498)

Wilson Limited (account no 752)

Lucinda Luz (account no 601)

general (main) ledger

discount received account (account no 6502)

drawings account (account no 7005)

loan account: ABC Bank (account no 2250)

office equipment account (account no 750)

office stationery account (account no 6384)

purchases account (account no 5001)

telephone expenses account (account no 6212)

travelling expenses account (account no 6330)

VAT account (account no 2200)

wages and salaries account (account no 7750)

11.4 David Lewis runs a shop selling carpets. He buys his carpets direct from the manufacturers, who allow him credit terms. His business is registered for VAT.

He uses a cash book which analyses payments between:
- discount received
- VAT
- purchases
- purchases (creditors) ledger
- sundry

The following transactions take place during the week commencing 14 May 2001:

14 May   Cash purchases of £75.70 + VAT paid by cheque

14 May   Paid telephone bill of £238.90 (including VAT) by cheque

15 May   Loan repayment of £250.00 made to Wyvern Finance by direct debit (no VAT)

15 May   Paid shop rent by cheque, £255.50 (no VAT)

16 May   Cash purchases of £100.00 (including VAT) paid by cheque

16 May   Paid an invoice for £368.20 from Terry Carpets Limited (a creditor) by cheque for £363.55 and receiving £4.65 discount for prompt settlement

16 May   Paid for stationery in cash, £28.20 (including VAT)

17 May   David Lewis withdraws £100.00 in cash from the business for own use

17 May   Bought shop fittings £265.00 + VAT, paying by cheque

18 May   Paid an invoice for £295.80 from Longlife Carpets Limited (a creditor), paying £291.50 by cheque, £4.30 discount being received for prompt settlement

18 May   Paid wages, £314.20 in cash (no VAT)

18 May   Paid a cheque to Trade Supplies (a creditor) for £145.50 in full settlement of an invoice for £149.00

The rate of Value Added Tax is 17.5%

Account numbers are to be used – see below

You are to:

- Enter the above payments on page 96 of the analysed cash book of David Lewis (VAT amounts should be rounded down to the nearest penny).

- Sub-total the money columns at 18 May.

- Show the entries to be made in the following accounts:

  purchases (creditors) ledger

  Terry Carpets Limited (account no 721)

  Longlife Carpets Limited (account no 624)

  Trade Supplies (account no 784)

  general (main) ledger

  discount received account (account no 6502)

  drawings account (account no 7005)

  loan account: Wyvern Finance (account no 2270)

  purchases account (account no 5001)

  shop fittings account (account no 740)

  shop rent account (account no 6345)

  stationery account (account no 6382)

  telephone expenses account (account no 6212)

  VAT account (account no 2200)

  wages and salaries account (account no 7750)

12 PETTY CASH BOOK

this chapter covers . . .

A petty cash book is used to record low-value cash payments for various small purchases and expenses incurred by a business or other organisation.

An amount of cash is handed by the main cashier to a member of staff, the petty cashier, who:

- is responsible for security of the petty cash money
- makes cash payments against authorised petty cash vouchers
- records the payments made, and analyses them, in a petty cash book

NVQ PERFORMANCE CRITERIA COVERED

unit 2: MAKING AND RECORDING PAYMENTS

element 2

prepare authorised payments

- payments are correctly calculated from relevent documentation
- payments are scheduled and authorised by the appropriate person
- queries are referred to the appropriate person
- security and confidentiality are maintained according to organisational requirements

THE PETTY CASH PROCEDURE

The petty cash book is used to record low-value cash payments for purchases and expenses – such as small items of stationery, postages – items which it would not be appropriate to enter in the main cash book. Instead, an amount of cash is handed by the main cashier to a member of staff, the petty cashier, who is responsible for all aspects of the control of petty cash, principally:

- security of the petty cash money
- making cash payments against authorised petty cash vouchers
- recording the payments made, and analysing them, in a petty cash book

In order to operate the petty cash system, the petty cashier needs the following:

- a *petty cash book* in which to record and analyse transactions
- a lockable *cash box* in which to keep the money
- a stock of blank *petty cash vouchers* (see page 263) for claims on petty cash to be made
- a *lockable desk drawer* in which to keep these items

making a claim

As an employee you are most likely to encounter the petty cash system when making claims for money for small purchases you have made. Before studying the form-filling procedures in detail, read the summary of a typical petty cash transaction set out below:

your supervisor asks you to go and buy a box of computer disks from an office supplies shop

↓

you go to the shop and buy the computer disks; having paid for them, you retain the receipt (for £5.50) which you hand to the petty cashier on your return to the office

↓

the petty cashier authorises a petty cash voucher which contains details of the purchase

↓

the petty cashier gives you £5.50 in cash

↓

the petty cashier attaches the receipt to the petty cash voucher and enters the details in the petty cash book

WHAT ITEMS CAN BE PASSED THROUGH PETTY CASH BOOK?

Petty cash is used to make small cash payments for purchases and expenses incurred by the business. Examples of the type of payments made from petty cash include:

- stationery items
- small items of office supplies
- casual wages
- window cleaning
- bus, rail and taxi fares (incurred on behalf of the business)
- meals and drinks (incurred on behalf of the business)
- postages
- tips and donations

Petty cash should not be used to pay for private expenses of employees, eg tea, coffee, and milk, unless the business has agreed these in advance.

All payments made through petty cash must be supported by relevant documentation. Such documentation includes:

- receipt from a shop
- Post Office receipt for postage
- rail or bus ticket
- restaurant bill
- receipt from taxi company
- receipt from window cleaning firm

The petty cashier is usually able to authorise petty cash transactions up to a maximum value – for example, up to £25 for any one expense item is a common figure. Larger amounts can often be paid from petty cash provided the expense is authorised by the accounts supervisor.

CASE STUDY

PETTY CASH EXPENSES

situation

You work in the accounts office of Tyax Engineering Limited. One of your duties is that of petty cashier; you are able to authorise transactions up to £25. Which of the following expenses would you allow to be paid out of petty cash?

- envelopes for use in the office, £2.50
- postage on an urgent parcel of engineering parts, £3.75
- bus fare to work claimed by secretary £1.20
- car mileage to work of office manager called in late at night when the burglar alarm went off (false alarm!), £5.50

- tea and coffee for use in the office, £3.70
- office window cleaning, £2.80
- pot plant bought for reception area, £5.50
- computer disks, £35.00
- donation to local charity by the business, £5.00
- meal allowance paid to a member of staff required to work during the lunch hour, £3.50

Note: you may assume that all expenses are supported be relevent documentation, such as receipt from a shop, Post Office etc.

solution

For most expenses it is clear whether or not they can be drawn from petty cash. However, there are points to consider for some of the expenses.

Envelopes	pay from petty cash
Postage	pay from petty cash
Bus fare to work	this is a personal expense and cannot be drawn from petty cash
Car mileage	travel to work is a personal expense, as seen with the previous item; however, as this expense was a special journey in the middle of the night in order to resolve a business problem, it can be paid from petty cash
Tea and coffee	this is a personal expense of employees and cannot normally be paid out of petty cash; however, if the ingredients were used to make drinks for official visitors and customers, it can be paid from petty cash
Window cleaning	pay from petty cash
Pot plant	pay from petty cash (but plants for the general office cannot be bought with the company's money)
Computer disks	this is a business expense but, in view of the amount (above the authorised limit of the petty cashier) it should be referred to the supervisor or manager for authorisation
Donation	pay from petty cash, subject to authorisation by supervisor
Meal allowance	pay from petty cash, provided that it is company policy to make an allowance in these circumstances

notes to the case study

- If the petty cashier is unable to resolve whether or not an expense can be paid from petty cash, the item should be referred to the accounts supervisor for a decision.
- Before payments can be made for petty cash expenses, they must be:
  - within the authorisation limit of the petty cashier (for example, £25 maximum for any one expense item)

– supported by documentary evidence, such as a receipt or a rail/bus ticket

– authorised by the petty cashier, or referred to the appropriate supervisor or manager

• Some businesses allow amounts above the authorisation limit of the petty cashier to be paid from petty cash provided that the expense is authorised by the accounts supervisor.

THE IMPREST SYSTEM

Most petty cash books operate on the imprest system. With this method the petty cashier starts each week (or month) with a certain amount of money – the imprest amount. As payments are made during the week (or month) the amount of money will reduce and, at the end of the period, the cash will be made up by the main cashier to the imprest amount. For example:

Started week with imprest amount	£100.00
Total of petty cash amounts paid out during week	£80.50
Cash held at end of week	£19.50
Amount drawn from cashier to restore imprest amount	£80.50
Cash at start of next week, ie imprest amount	£100.00

If, at any time, the imprest amount proves to be insufficient, further amounts of cash can be drawn from the cashier. Also, from time-to-time, it may be necessary to increase the imprest amount so that regular shortfalls of petty cash are avoided.

Where a petty cash book is *not* kept on the imprest system, the petty cashier has a float of cash which is replenished by the main cashier whenever it runs low. Thus, unlike the imprest system where the cash float is replenished at regular intervals eg weekly or monthly, the float of the non-imprest system is 'topped up' only as and when required.

PETTY CASH VOUCHER

Payments out of petty cash are made only against correct documentation – usually a petty cash voucher (see below). Petty cash vouchers are completed as follows:

• details and amount of expenditure

• signature of the person making the claim and receiving the money

• signature of the person authorising the payment to be made – usually the petty cashier for amounts within the authorisation limit; larger amounts will be authorised by the accounts supervisor or manager

- additionally, most petty cash vouchers are numbered, so that they can be controlled, the number being entered in the petty cash book
- relevant documentation, such as a receipt from a shop or Post Office etc, should be attached to the petty cash voucher

petty cash voucher			Number *807*
		date	*12 May 2001*
description			amount
		£	p
C5 Envelopes		2	35
5 Floppy disks		4	70
		7	05
signature	*T Harris*		
authorised	*R Singh*		

Petty cash vouchers are the *prime documents* for the petty cash book.

LAYOUT OF A PETTY CASH BOOK

Petty cash book is usually set out as follows:

Receipts	Date	Details	Voucher No	Total Payment	Analysis columns				
					VAT	Postages	Stationery	Travel	Ledger
£				£	£	£	£	£	£

The layout shows that:

- receipts from the main cashier are entered in the column on the extreme left
- there are columns for the date and details of all receipts and payments

- there is a column for the petty cash voucher number
- the total payment (ie the amount paid out on each petty cash voucher) is in the next column
- then follow the analysis columns which analyse each transaction entered in the 'total payment' column (note that VAT may need to be calculated – see below)

A business or organisation will use whatever analysis columns are most suitable for it and, indeed, there may be more columns than shown in the example. It is important that expenses are analysed to the correct columns so that the contents show a true picture of petty cash expenditure.

PETTY CASH AND VAT

Value Added Tax is charged by VAT-registered businesses on their taxable supplies. Therefore, there will often be VAT included as part of the expense paid out of petty cash. However, not all expenses will have been subject to VAT. There are four possible circumstances:

- VAT has been charged at the standard rate
- VAT has not been charged because the supplier is not VAT-registered
- the zero rate of VAT applies, eg food and drink (but not meals which are standard-rated), books, newspapers, transport (but not taxis and hire cars)
- the supplies are exempt (eg financial services, postal services)

Often the indication of the supplier's VAT registration number on a receipt or invoice will tell you that VAT has been charged at the standard rate.

Where VAT has been charged, the amount of tax might be indicated separately on the receipt or invoice. However, for small money amounts it is quite usual for a total to be shown without indicating the amount of VAT. An example of a receipt which does not show the VAT content is illustrated below. The receipt is for a box of envelopes purchased from Wyvern Stationers. It shows:

- the name and address of the retailer

- the date and time of the transaction

- the VAT registration number of the retailer

- the price of the item – £4.70

- the amount of money given – a £10 note

- the amount of change given – £5.30

Wyvern Stationers	
25 High St Mereford	
08 10 01 16.07	
VAT Reg 454 7106 34	
Salesperson Rashid	
Stationery	4.70
TOTAL	4.70
CASH	10.00
CHANGE	5.30

What it does not show, however, is the VAT content of the purchase price – it only shows the price after the VAT has been added on.

How do you calculate purchase price before the VAT is added on?

The formula, with VAT at 17.5%, is:

price including VAT ÷ 1.175 = price before VAT is added on

in this case …

£4.70 ÷ 1.175 = £4.00 = price before VAT is added on

The VAT content is therefore

£4.70 less £4.00 = 70p

Here £0.70 will be entered in the VAT column in the petty cash book, £4.00 in the appropriate expense column, and the full £4.70 in the total payment column.

Remember when calculating VAT amounts that fractions of a penny are ignored, ie the tax is rounded *down* to a whole penny.

CASE STUDY

PETTY CASH BOOK

situation

You work in the accounts office of Wyvern Traders. One of your tasks is to keep the petty cash book, which is operated on the imprest system. There are a number of transactions which you have authorised (all transactions, unless otherwise indicated, include VAT at 17.5%) to be entered for the week on page 30 of the petty cash book:

2001

7 Apr	Started the week with an imprest amount of £50.00
7 Apr	Paid stationery £3.76 on voucher no 47
7 Apr	Paid taxi fare £2.82 on voucher no 48
8 Apr	Paid postages £0.75 (no VAT) on voucher no 49
9 Apr	Paid taxi fare £4.70 on voucher no 50
9 Apr	Paid J Jones, a creditor, £6.00 (no VAT shown in petty cash book – amount will be on VAT account already) on voucher no 51
10 Apr	Paid stationery £3.76 on voucher no 52
10 Apr	Paid postages £2.85 (no VAT) on voucher no 53
11 Apr	Paid taxi fare £6.11 on voucher no 54

solution

The petty cash book is written up as follows:

Receipts	Date	Details	Voucher No	Total Payment	Analysis columns				
					VAT	Postages	Stationery	Travel	Ledger
£	2001			£	£	£	£	£	£
50.00	7 Apr	Balance b/d							
	7 Apr	Stationery	47	3.76	0.56		3.20		
	7 Apr	Taxi fare	48	2.82	0.42			2.40	
	8 Apr	Postages	49	0.75		0.75			
	9 Apr	Taxi fare	50	4.70	0.70			4.00	
	9 Apr	J Jones	51	6.00					6.00
	10 Apr	Stationery	52	3.76	0.56		3.20		
	10 Apr	Postages	53	2.85		2.85			
	11 Apr	Taxi fare	54	6.11	0.91			5.20	
				30.75	3.15	3.60	6.40	11.60	6.00

Petty Cash Book — PCB 30

notes to the case study

Each page of the petty cash book is numbered – here 'PCB 30' – this helps with cross-referencing in the accounts system.

- For each petty cash item, the analysis columns add up to the amount shown in the 'total payment' column

- The totals of the analysis columns add up to the total payment

- The petty cashier will give the firm's book-keeper a posting sheet (see below) giving details of the total of each analysis column so that the amounts can be recorded in the double-entry accounts system

- Total payments are £30.75 and, as the petty cash book is kept on the imprest system, this is the amount of cash which will need to be drawn from the main cashier in order to restore the imprest

- We shall see in a later chapter (Chapter 16) how the petty cash book is balanced

PETTY CASH AND DOUBLE-ENTRY BOOK-KEEPING

At regular intervals – weekly or monthly – the petty cashier prepares a posting sheet which gives the firm's book-keeper details of the amounts from the analysis columns. The posting sheet for the transactions from the Case Study is as follows:

WYVERN TRADERS

Posting sheet: Petty Cash

account name	account number	debit	credit	reference
		£	£	
VAT	GL 2200	3.15		PCB 30
Postages	GL 6348	3.60		PCB 30
Stationery	GL 7290	6.40		PCB 30
Travel expenses	GL 7755	11.60		PCB 30
J Jones	PL 421	6.00		PCB 30
Cash control	GL 925		30.75	PCB 30
TOTAL		30.75	30.75	

Prepared by	*D. Ajose*	Date	*11 April 2001*	
Checked by	*M. Chan*	Date	*11 April 2001*	
Posted by	*M. Hopwood*	Date	*11 April 2001*	

The posting sheet shows:

- *debits* to expenses accounts (and VAT account) in the general ledger in respect of the total of each expenses column
- *debits* to creditors' accounts in the purchases ledger in respect of the ledger column amounts (eg J Jones in the Case Study)
- *credit* to cash control account, being the total amount of expenses paid from petty cash during the period; for petty cash books operated under the imprest system, this is the amount that will need to be withdrawn from the bank in order to restore the imprest amount (we will look at this aspect of petty cash books when we see how they are balanced in Chapter 16)

From the Case Study, above, and posting sheet, accounts will be written up as follows at the end of the week (11 April):

GENERAL (MAIN) LEDGER

Dr	**Value Added Tax Account** (account no 2200)			Cr
2001		£	2001	£
11 Apr	Petty cash book PCB 30	3.15		

Dr	**Postages Account** (account no 6348)		Cr
2001	£	2001	£
11 Apr Petty cash book PCB 30	3.60		

Dr	**Stationery Account** (account no 7290)		Cr
2001	£	2001	£
11 Apr Petty cash book PCB 30	6.40		

Dr	**Travel Expenses Account** (account no 7755)		Cr
2001	£	2001	£
11 Apr Petty cash book PCB 30	11.60		

Dr	**Cash Control Account*** (account no 925)		Cr
2001	£	2001	£
7 Apr Balance b/d	50.00	11 Apr Petty cash book PCB 30	30.75

PURCHASES (CREDITORS) LEDGER

Dr	**J Jones** (account no 421)		Cr
2001	£	2001	£
11 Apr Petty cash book PCB 30	6.00		

* We will look in more detail at the use of control accounts in Chapter 17. Here the control account shows the total of payments made by the petty cashier during the week. Note that cash control account is in the general (main) ledger while petty cash book forms a subsidiary ledger.

CHAPTER SUMMARY

- The petty cash book records payments for a variety of low-value business expenses.

- The person responsible for maintaining the petty cash book is the petty cashier, who is responsible for security.

- Payment can only be made from the petty cash book against correct documentation – usually a petty cash voucher, which must be signed by the person authorising payment.

- Where a business is registered for Value Added Tax, it must record VAT amounts paid on petty cash purchases in a separate column in the petty cash book.

- Cash control account is used as the general (main) ledger account, while the petty cash book forms a subsidiary ledger.

KEY TERMS

petty cash book	subsidiary accounting record used for low-value cash payments for business expenses
petty cashier	the person responsible for the petty cash system
imprest system	where the money held in the petty cash float is restored to the same amount for the beginning of each week or month
petty cash voucher	the prime document used to claim amounts from petty cash
cash control account	the general (main) ledger account which shows the total payments made by the petty cashier during the week or month

STUDENT ACTIVITIES

12.1 Most petty cash books operate on the imprest system. This means that:

(a)   the petty cashier draws money from the main cashier as and when required

(b)   the main cashier has to authorise each petty cash payment

(c)   a copy has to be kept of each petty cash voucher

(d)   the petty cashier starts each week or month with a fixed amount of money

Answer (a) or (b) or (c) or (d)

12.2 You work as an accounts clerk in the office of Temeside Printers Limited. One of your duties is that of petty cashier; you are able to authorise transactions up to £30 each. Which of the following expenses will you allow to be paid out of petty cash?

(a) postage on a parcel of printing sent to a customer, £3.85

(b) a rubber date stamp bought for use in the office, £4.60

(c) rail fare to work claimed by the office manager's secretary, £2.50

(d) donation to charity, £5.00

(e) tea and coffee for use by office staff, £5.50

(f) mileage allowance claimed by works foreman who had to visit a customer, £4.80

(g) meal allowance paid to assistant who had to work her lunch hour, £4.00

(h) window cleaning, £3.50

(i) purchase of shelving for the office, £55.00

(j) taxi fare claimed for delivering an urgent parcel of printing to a customer, £6.25

Note: you may assume that all expenses are supported by relevent documentation.

Explain any expenses that you will refer to the accounts supervisor.

12.3 As petty cashier, prepare the petty cash vouchers shown on the next page under today's date for signature by the person making the claim. You are able to authorise payments up to £10.00 each.

• £4.45 claimed by Jayne Smith for postage (no VAT) on an urgent parcel of spare parts sent to a customer, Evelode Supplies Limited.

• £2.35, including VAT, claimed by Tanya Howard for air mail envelopes bought for use in the office.

• £8.60, including VAT, claimed by Toni Wyatt for a taxi fare used on a business visit to a customer, Jasper Limited.

Number the vouchers, beginning with number 851

What documentation will you require to be attached to each voucher?

12.4 The business for which you work is registered for VAT. The following petty cash amounts include VAT at 17.5% and you are required to calculate the amount that will be shown in the VAT column and the appropriate expense column (remember that VAT amounts should be rounded down to the nearest penny):

(a) £9.40

(b) £4.70

(c) £2.35

(d) £2.45

(e) £5.60

(f) £3.47

(g) £8.75

(h) 94p

(i) 99p

(j) £9.41

petty cash voucher

No. 851

date

description		amount (£)
VAT		

signature ....

authorised ....

petty cash voucher

No. 852

date

description		amount (£)
VAT		

signature ....

authorised ....

petty cash voucher

No. 853

date

description		amount (£)
VAT		

signature ....

authorised ....

12.5 On returning from holiday, you are told to take charge of the petty cash book of Carr Trading. This is kept on the imprest system, the float being £75.00 at the beginning of each month. Analysis columns are used for VAT, travel, postages, stationery, meals, and miscellaneous.

There are a number of transactions for the month which you authorise (all transactions, unless otherwise indicated, include VAT at 17.5%). You are to enter the transactions for the month on page 42 of the petty cash book.

2001

1 Aug	Balance of cash £75.00
4 Aug	Voucher no 39: taxi fare £3.80
6 Aug	Voucher no 40: parcel postage £2.35 (no VAT)
7 Aug	Voucher no 41: pencils £1.26
11 Aug	Voucher no 42: travel expenses £5.46 (no VAT)
12 Aug	Voucher no 43: window cleaner £8.50 (no VAT)
14 Aug	Voucher no 44: large envelopes £2.45
18 Aug	Voucher no 45: donation to charity £5 (no VAT)
19 Aug	Voucher no 46: rail fare £5.60 (no VAT); meal allowance £5.00 (no VAT)
20 Aug	Voucher no 47: recorded delivery postage £0.75 (no VAT)
22 Aug	Voucher no 48: roll of packing tape £1.50
25 Aug	Voucher no 49: excess postage paid £0.55 (no VAT)
27 Aug	Voucher no 50: taxi fare £5.40

Total the analysis columns and prepare a posting sheet which shows the entries to be recorded in the general (main) ledger at the end of the month, on 31 August. Account numbers need not be shown.

12.6 Prepare a petty cash book for Tyax Systems Limited with analysis columns for VAT, postages, travel, meals, and sundry office expenses. Enter the following authorised transactions for the week on page 18 of the petty cash book. The voucher amounts include VAT at 17.5% unless indicated.

2001

2 June	Balance of cash £100.00
2 June	Postages £6.35 (no VAT), voucher no 123
3 June	Travel expenses £3.25 (no VAT), voucher no 124
3 June	Postages £1.28 (no VAT), voucher no 125

4 June   Envelopes £4.54, voucher no 126

4 June   Window cleaning £5.50, voucher no 127

5 June   Taxi fare £4.56, meals £10.85, voucher no 128

5 June   Postages £8.56 (no VAT), packing materials £3.25, voucher no 129

5 June   Taxi fare £4.50, meals £7.45, voucher no 130

6 June   Marker pens £2.55, envelopes £3.80, voucher no 131

Total the analysis columns and prepare a posting sheet which shows the entries to be recorded in the general (main) ledger at the end of the week, on 6 June. Account numbers need not be shown.

13 FURTHER ASPECTS OF DOUBLE-ENTRY ACCOUNTS

this chapter covers . . .

So far we have studied the principles of double-entry book-keeping and applied them to transactions for sales, purchases, returns, receipts and payments. In this chapter, we look in detail at a number of transactions (some of which we have seen briefly in earlier chapters):

- *capital*
- *fixed assets*
- *expenses*
- *income*
- *drawings*
- *loans*
- *stock*
- *bad debts written off*

Firstly though, we look in detail at the division of the ledger, and the types of accounts found in the book-keeping system.

NVQ PERFORMANCE CRITERIA COVERED

unit 2: MAKING AND RECORDING PAYMENTS

element 3

make and record payments

- *payments are entered into accounting records according to organisational procedures*

DIVISION OF THE LEDGER

In previous chapters we have already made use of the division of the ledger, whereby separate ledgers are kept, each containing different classes of account. The ledger of a business is usually divided into four sections:

- *sales ledger*, containing the accounts of the firm's debtors (customers)
- *purchases ledger*, containing the accounts of the firm's creditors (suppliers)
- *cash book*, containing bank and cash records of the receipts and payments of the business
- *general ledger*, (often known as main ledger) containing all other accounts

When computers are used for accounting, the physical ledger books do not exist. However, the principles of manual and computerised accounting are the same, and the term 'ledgers' is used in computer accounting systems. Accounting software is available for each of the ledgers mentioned above, usually combined into one integrated computer program. The four divisions of the ledger are illustrated in full on the next page.

TYPES OF ACCOUNT

Within a book-keeping system there are different types of accounts: a distinction is made between personal and impersonal accounts. Personal accounts are in the names of people or businesses, eg the accounts for debtors and creditors. Impersonal accounts are non-personal accounts; these are usually divided between real accounts, which represent things such as cash, bank balance, computers, motor vehicles, machinery, etc, and nominal accounts, which record income and expenses such as sales, purchases, wages, etc. The diagram below distinguishes between the different types of account.

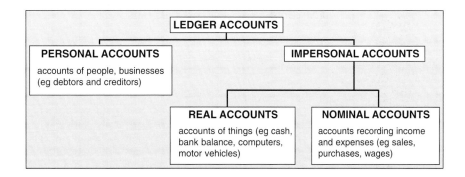

DIVISION OF THE LEDGER

sales (subsidiary) ledger

Sales ledger (or debtors ledger) contains the accounts of debtors, and records:
• sales made on credit to customers of the business
• sales returns by customers
• payments received from debtors
• cash discount allowed for prompt settlement
Sales ledger does not record cash sales.

Sales ledger contains an account for each debtor and records the transactions with that debtor. The total of the sales ledger account balances is the debtors figure which appears in the trial balance (see Chapter 16).

purchases (subsidiary) ledger

Purchases ledger (or creditors ledger) contains the accounts of creditors, and records:
• purchases made on credit from suppliers of the business
• purchases returns made by the business
• payments made to creditors
• cash discount received for prompt settlement
Purchases ledger does not record cash purchases.

Purchases ledger contains an account for each creditor and records the transactions with that creditor. The total of the purchases ledger account balances is the creditors figure which appears in the trial balance (see Chapter 16).

cash books

The cash books comprise:
• Cash Book
  – records all transactions for bank account and cash account
  – cash book is also often used for listing the amounts of cash discount received and allowed and for recording Value Added Tax

• Petty Cash Book
  – records low-value cash payments too small to be entered in the main cash book

general (main) ledger

The general (or main) ledger contains the other accounts of the business:
• Nominal Accounts
  – sales account (cash and credit sales)
  – purchases account (cash and credit purchases)
  – sales returns, purchases returns
  – expenses and income
  – loan
  – capital, drawings
  – Value Added Tax (where the business is VAT-registered)

• Real Accounts
  – fixed assets, eg premises, computers, motor vehicles
  – other assets, eg cash, bank balance, stock

In previous chapters we have used accounts to record transactions for purchases, sales, returns, receipts and payments. In order to complete our study of double-entry accounts at NVQ level 2 we will look in detail at a number of transactions (some of which have been seen briefly in earlier chapters):

- capital
- fixed assets
- expenses
- income
- drawings
- loans
- stock
- bad debts written off

Note that aspects of Value Added Tax (VAT) are considered later in the chapter (page 281-283).

CAPITAL ACCOUNT

Capital is the amount of money invested in the business by the owner (or owners). The amount is owed by the business to the owner, although it is unlikely to be repaid immediately as then the business would be unable to operate. A capital account is used to record the amount(s) paid into the business; the book-keeping entries are:

- **capital introduced**
    - *debit* cash book (bank or cash columns as appropriate)
    - *credit* capital account

The dual aspect (see page 54) of this transaction is that cash book (bank or cash columns) has gained value and has been debited; capital account records a liability (to the owner) and is credited. Remember that book-keeping entries look at transactions from the point of view of the business or organisation.

The introduction of capital into a business is often the very first transaction to be entered into the accounts.

Sometimes capital is introduced into the business in forms other than in cash or by cheque. For example, the owner might transfer property or other fixed assets (see below) into the business as capital; the book-keeping entries are:

- *debit* property account (or other account as appropriate)
- *credit* capital account

FIXED ASSETS

Fixed assets are items purchased by a business for use on a permanent or semi-permanent basis. Examples are buildings, machinery, motor vehicles and office equipment. All of these are bought by a business with the intention that they will be used for some time in the business. When a business buys fixed assets, the expenditure is referred to as capital expenditure (not to be confused with the owner's capital). Capital expenditure means that items have been bought for use in the business for some years to come. By contrast, revenue expenditure is where the items bought will be used by the business quite quickly. For example, the purchase of a car is capital expenditure, while the cost of fuel for the car is revenue expenditure.

When fixed assets are bought, a separate account for each type of fixed asset is used, eg buildings account, machinery account, motor vehicles account, etc. The book-keeping entries are:

* **purchase of a fixed asset**
  - *debit* fixed asset account (using the appropriate account)
  - *credit* cash book (bank or cash column, as appropriate)

Here the fixed asset account, which has gained value, is debited. The account which has given value – cash book (bank or cash column) – is credited.

Sometimes fixed assets are returned to the supplier because they do not work, or are unsuitable. When the returns transaction has been agreed with the supplier it will be recorded in the accounts as:

* **return of unsuitable fixed assets**
  - *debit* cash book* (bank or cash column, as appropriate)
  - *credit* fixed asset account (using the appropriate account)
  - *   assuming that a bank/cash payment is received for the return

As you will see, such a transaction is the opposite of the original purchase.

Often fixed assets are bought on credit terms (rather than immediate payment by cheque or in cash). The book-keeping entries are:

* **purchase of a fixed asset on credit**
  - *debit* fixed asset account
  - *credit* creditor's account

The creditor's account shows the amount the business owes, which will be subsequently paid by cheque or in cash.

EXPENSES

Businesses and other organisations pay various running expenses, such as rent, wages, electricity, telephone, vehicle running expenses, etc. These day-to-day expenses are referred to as *revenue expenditure*. A separate account is used in the accounting system for each main class of revenue expenditure, eg rent account, wages account, etc.

The book-keeping entries are:

- **payment of an expense**
    - *debit* expense account (using the appropriate account)
    - *credit* cash book (bank or cash column as appropriate)

Here the expense account is debited because the business has gained value – for example, with rent paid the business has had the use of the premises for a certain time. The account which gives value, cash book (bank or cash column), is credited.

Often with expenses, there may be a period of credit allowed. For example, the electricity bill may be received today stating that payment is to be made by the end of the month. The business will treat the electricity supplier as a creditor and makes the following accounting entries:

- *debit* electricity account
- *credit* creditor's account (in the name of the electricity supplier)

When payment is due it can then be made through the cash book as follows:

- *debit* creditor's account (electricity supplier)
- *credit* cash book

INCOME

From time-to-time a business or organisation may receive amounts of income apart from its normal sales income. Examples of such 'other income' include rent received, commission received, or fees received. These are recorded in separate accounts for each category of income, eg rent received account, commission received account. The book-keeping entries are:

- **receipt of income**
    - *debit* cash book (bank or cash column as appropriate)
    - *credit* income account (using the appropriate account)

The account which has gained value, cash book, is debited; the account which has given value, eg rent received, is credited.

OWNER'S DRAWINGS

Drawings is the term used when the owner takes money, in cash or by cheque (or sometimes goods), from the business for personal use. A drawings account is used to record such amounts; the book-keeping entries for withdrawal of money are:

- **owner's drawings**
  - *debit* drawings account
  - *credit* cash book (bank or cash column)

When the owner of the business takes some of the goods in which the business trades for his or her own use, the book-keeping entries are:

- *debit* drawings account
- *credit* purchases account

Note that where a business is VAT-registered, VAT must be accounted for on goods taken by the owner.

LOANS

When a business or organisation receives a loan, eg from a relative or the bank, it is the cash account or bank account which gains value, while a loan account (in the name of the lender) records the liability.

- **loan received**
  - *debit* cash book (bank or cash column)
  - *credit* loan account (in name of the lender)

Interest paid to the lender is recorded by means of an expenses account called loan interest paid account. Repayment of the loan, or part of the loan by instalments, is recorded in the accounts as:

- **loan repayment**
  - *debit* loan account
  - *credit* cash book (bank or cash column)

STOCK

We have seen in earlier chapters how businesses use separate purchases and sales accounts to record when the goods in which they trade are bought and sold. The reason for using separate accounts for purchases and sales is because there is usually a difference between the buying price and the selling price – the latter is higher and gives the business its profit. At least once a year, however, a business values the stock it has on the shelves of the shop, for example, or in the warehouse (the techniques of stock valuation are covered at NVQ level 3). As stock is an asset of a business, the valuation is debited to stock account (also known as stock control account – page 377); the credit transaction is to trading account (part of the profit and loss statement) where it is used to assist in the calculation of profit.

To summarise, stock account is used only when the stock of a business is valued – at least once a year at the end of the financial year. The book-keeping entries to record the valuation in the accounts are:

- **stock valuation**
  - – *debit* stock account
  - – *credit* trading account (part of the profit and loss statement)

Thus at the start of each financial year there will, for most businesses, be a debit balance on stock account representing the value of stock held.

BAD DEBTS WRITTEN OFF

A bad debt is a debt owing to a business or organisation which it considers will never be paid.

One of the problems of selling goods and services on credit terms is that, from time-to-time, some customers will not pay. As a consequence, the balances of such accounts have to be written off when they become uncollectable. This happens when all reasonable efforts to recover the amount owing have been exhausted, ie statements and letters have been sent to the debtor requesting payment, and legal action – where appropriate – or the threat of legal action has failed to obtain payment.

In writing off a debtor's account as bad, the business is bearing the cost of the amount due. The debtor's account is closed and the amount (or amounts, where a number of accounts are dealt with in this way) is debited to bad debts written off account. This account stores up the amounts of account balances written off during the year (in much the same way as an expense account).

The book-keeping transactions are:

- **bad debt written off**
  - – *debit* bad debts written off account
  - – *credit* debtor's account

VAT AND DOUBLE-ENTRY ACCOUNTS

When a business is registered for Value Added Tax it is able to claim back VAT paid on purchases of goods, fixed assets, and expenses. At the same time it must charge VAT whenever it supplies goods and services (except for zero-rated and exempt goods and services).

We have already seen in previous chapters how VAT is dealt with for purchases, sales and returns. When a business buys, for example, fixed assets it will enter the amount of VAT direct to the debit side of VAT account.

example transaction

On 16 April 2001, Acme Supplies Limited, a company which is registered for Value Added Tax, buys a new computer at a cost of £600 + VAT (at 17.5%) of £105, paying by cheque.

This is recorded in the double-entry accounts as:

Dr	Computer Account		Cr
2001	£	2001	£
16 Apr Bank	600		

Dr	Value Added Tax Account		Cr
2001	£	2001	£
16 Apr Bank	105		

Credit	Cash Book: Payments				CBP
Date	Details	Folio	Discount received	Cash	Bank
2001			£	£	£
16 Apr	Computer				705

The Value Added Tax account in the general ledger records:

Value Added Tax Account

Debits (input tax)	Credits (output tax)
VAT on purchases	VAT on sales and/or services
VAT on purchases of fixed assets (except cars)	VAT on the sale of fixed assets
VAT on expenses	VAT on other income
VAT on sales returns	VAT on purchases returns

Not all goods and services purchased can be assumed to include VAT: as well as zero-rated and exempt goods, the supplier might be a business which is not registered for VAT.

VAT relief on bad debts

A VAT-registered business can reclaim VAT originally charged on debts which are now being written off. However, in order to claim relief, *the debt must be more than six months overdue*, ie more than six months from the date the payment was originally due – a sale made on 30 day terms on 1 January would be due for payment on 31 January; if this sale is written off as a bad debt, VAT relief would be available after 31 July.

businesses not registered for VAT

Where businesses and other organisations are not registered for Value Added Tax, they cannot reclaim VAT paid on purchases, fixed assets and expenses, nor can they charge VAT when they supply goods and services.

Thus, for a non-registered business, expenses which include VAT are entered in the accounts at the full invoice value.

PRIME DOCUMENTS AND PRIMARY ACCOUNTING RECORDS

The types of transactions that we have looked at in this chapter follow the pattern that we have seen earlier:

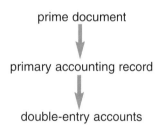

prime documents

For each of the transactions we have seen, there will be a prime document. These include:

- *purchase of fixed assets* – receipt or invoice from supplier
- *expenses* – receipt or invoice from supplier
- *income* – copy of receipt or invoice issued to a tenant for rent received, or a statement showing amount of commission earned

- *loans* – details of loan agreement, statement of interest paid, receipts for loan repayments
- *capital introduced* – copy of receipt for the money, or memorandum showing how much capital is being introduced
- *owner's drawings* – receipt signed by the owner, or note showing amount of withdrawal
- *stock* – stock-taking sheets and records
- *bad debt written off* – note or memorandum from accounts supervisor to write off debts

The type of prime document will vary from transaction to transaction. For external transactions (ie those involving outsiders) there will usually be some form of receipt, or invoice, or other document. For internal transactions (ie those taking place within the business, including with the owner), there will be more reliance on notes or memorandums.

primary accounting records: regular transactions

For routine day-to-day transactions which pass through the cash book, such as payment of expenses, the cash book forms *both* the primary accounting record *and* one of the double-entry accounts. Income transactions involving the cash book, if routine in nature, are dealt with in the same way, ie no separate primary accounting record is needed.

Where a period of credit is received from expenses suppliers, the bill is listed in an analysed purchases day book as the primary accounting record and the supplier is recorded in the accounts as a creditor. The purchases day book is easily adapted to give appropriate analysis as shown below with sample transactions.

Purchases Day Book							PDB 49
Date	Supplier	Invoice No	Folio	Gross	VAT	Purchases	Expenses
2001				£	£	£	£
14 May	Western Electricity	400791	PL 779	235.00	35.00		200.00
15 May	P Bond	1479	PL 125	94.00	14.00	80.00	

primary accounting records: non-regular transactions

For non-regular transactions – such as the introduction of capital to the business, purchase of fixed assets, raising a loan, valuation of stock, writing off bad debts – the primary accounting record is called the *journal*. Like the day books that we have seen in earlier chapters, the journal is used to list transactions before they are recorded in the double-entry accounts.

An example journal entry for the introduction of capital is as follows:

Date	Details	Folio	Dr	Cr
2001			£	£
1 Jul	Bank account	CBR	20,000	
	Capital account	GL		20,000
	Opening capital introduced			

Notes:

* journal entries are prepared from authorised prime documents (which are stored securely for possible future reference)
* the names of the accounts to be debited and credited in the book-keeping system are written in the details column; in a journal entry it is customary to show the debit transaction first
* the money amounts of the debit and credit entries are stated in the appropriate columns
* a journal entry always balances, ie the debit entry is equal to the credit entry
* it is usual to include a brief narrative explaining why the transaction is being carried out
* each journal entry is complete in itself and is ruled off to separate it from the next entry
* journal entries are dealt with in more detail in Chapter 18

CASE STUDY

DOUBLE-ENTRY ACCOUNTS – GALAXY MEDIA

situation

You are the book-keeper to Galaxy Media, which has just been started by its owner Henry Stardust. The business is an agency which supplies actors and actresses to advertising agencies. The business is registered for Value Added Tax

The transactions for the first month of trading, May 2001, are listed on the next page:

2001

1 May   Started in business with capital of £5,000, a cheque from Henry Stardust paid into the business bank account

7 May   Paid rent for the office, £500 (no VAT) by cheque

8 May   Bought office equipment for £2,000 + VAT, paying by cheque

10 May   Received a loan of £1,000 (no VAT) from Mike Way by cheque

15 May   Received commission of £200 + VAT in cash

17 May   Received electricity bill of £80 + VAT from Western Electric to be paid by 31 May

18 May   Withdrew £100 in cash for own use (drawings)

21 May   Returned some of the office equipment (unsuitable) for £400 + VAT, a refund cheque being received

30 May   Paid Western Electric the amount due

Show how the above transactions will be recorded in the double-entry accounts of Galaxy Media. Primary accounting records and account numbers need not be shown.

solution

The double-entry accounts for May 2001 will be entered as follows:

CASH BOOK

Debit	Cash Book: Receipts					CBR
Date	Details	Folio	Discount allowed	Cash	Bank	
2001			£	£	£	
1 May	Capital				5,000	
10 May	Loan: M Way				1,000	
15 May	Commission received			235		
21 May	Office equipment				470	

Credit	Cash Book: Payments					CBP
Date	Details	Folio	Discount received	Cash	Bank	
2001			£	£	£	
7 May	Rent paid				500	
8 May	Office equipment				2,350	
18 May	Drawings			100		
30 May	Western Electric				94	

GENERAL (MAIN) LEDGER

Dr	Capital Account		Cr
2001	£	2001	£
		1 May Bank	5,000

Dr	Rent Paid Account		Cr
2001	£	2001	£
7 May Bank	500		

Dr	Office Equipment Account		Cr
2001	£	2001	£
8 May Bank	2,000	21 May Bank	400

Dr	Value Added Tax Account		Cr
2001	£	2001	£
8 May Bank	350	15 May Cash	35
17 May Western Electric	14	21 May Bank	70

Dr	Loan Account: M Way		Cr
2001	£	2001	£
		10 May Bank	1,000

Dr	Commission Received Account		Cr
2001	£	2001	£
		15 May Cash	200

Dr	Electricity Account		Cr
2001	£	2001	£
17 May Western Electric	80		

Dr	Drawings Account		Cr
2001	£	2001	£
18 May Cash	100		

PURCHASES (CREDITORS) LEDGER

Dr	Western Electric		Cr
2001	£	2001	£
30 May Bank	94	17 May Electricity	80
		17 May VAT	14

Notes:

- Account numbers have not been used here for cross referencing
- The primary accounting record for each transaction is as follows:
  - capital introduced, primary accounting record is the *journal*
  - rent paid, primary accounting record is the *cash book*
  - purchase of office equipment, *journal*
  - loan received, *journal or cash book*
  - commission received, *cash book*
  - electricity bill, *analysed purchases day book*
  - drawings, *journal or cash book*
  - office equipment returned, *journal*
  - payment of electricity bill, *cash book*

Remember that:
- cash book is the primary accounting record for regular transactions
- journal is the primary accounting record for non-regular transactions
- analysed purchases day book is the primary accounting record for expenses where credit is received

A list of the double-entry accounting entries for the transactions shown in this Case Study is illustrated in the form of a posting sheet on page 291.

CASE STUDY

WRITING OFF A BAD DEBT – DON'S DINER

situation

You work as a sales ledger clerk in the accounts department of Severn Catering Supplies Limited. The company, which is VAT-registered, sells kitchen equipment to hotels and restaurants throughout the country. The company's terms of trade are for payment within 30 days of invoice date.

It is December 2001 and the accounts supervisor, Sue Robinson, has been reviewing the debtors' accounts in the sales ledger before the end of the financial year on 31 December. She has been looking at the following account:

Dr		**Don's Diner** (account no 258)	Cr
2001	£	2001	£
5 Jan Sales	47		

Monthly statements of account and 'chaser' letters have been sent to this debtor – the last letter was dated 28 September and was returned marked 'gone away, not known at this address'.

solution

The accounts supervisor has decided that it is time to write off the account of Don's Diner as a bad debt. The debt outstanding is £47 and it is not worthwhile taking legal action for such an amount. You are given the following memo which authorises you to go ahead with the write off:

MEMORANDUM

TO: Sales Ledger Accounts Clerk

FROM: Accounts Supervisor

DATE: 10 December 2001

SUBJECT: DON'S DINER

Please write off the balance of this account as a bad debt – we have done all we can to collect the amount. As we charged VAT on the original invoice, do not forget to reclaim VAT when writing off the balance.

Thanks

Sue

Sue Robinson

---

prime document

The memo acts as the authorised prime document for this accounting transaction.

primary accounting record

The primary accounting record for this non-regular transaction is the journal. The journal entry to write off the account of Don's Diner is as follows:

Date	Details	Folio	Dr	Cr
2001			£	£
15 Dec	Bad debts written off account	GL 7000	40	
	Value Added Tax account	GL 2200	7	
	Don's Diner	SL 258		47
	Bad debt written off as per			
	memo from accounts			
	supervisor dated 10 December 2001		47	47

Note: journal entries are dealt with in more detail in Chapter 18.

double-entry accounts

The account of Don's Diner is closed off as follows:

SALES (DEBTORS) LEDGER

Dr		**Don's Diner** (account no 258)	Cr
2001	£	2001	£
5 Jan Sales	47	10 Dec Bad debts written off	40
		10 Dec Value Added Tax	7
	47		47

The balance net of VAT, ie £40, is transferred to the debit of bad debts written off account, (together with any other accounts being written off). The VAT amount, ie £7, (VAT at 17.5%) is transferred to the debit of VAT account.

GENERAL (MAIN) LEDGER

Dr		**Bad Debts Written Off Account** (no 7000)	Cr
2001	£	2001	£
10 Dec Don's Diner	40		

Dr		**Value Added Tax Account** (no 2200)	Cr
2001	£	2001	£
10 Dec Don's Diner	7		

Thus the account of Don's Diner is now closed and no further goods will be supplied to this customer on credit terms. To summarise writing off a bad debt:

• *prime document* – memo or other authority from accounts supervisor

• *primary accounting record* – the journal

• *double-entry accounts* (for a VAT-registered business claiming VAT relief)

  – *debit* bad debts written off account with the amount of the bad debt, net of VAT

  – *debit* Value Added Tax account with the VAT part of the debt

  – *credit* debtor's account with the amount of the bad debt and the VAT relief

Remember that the debt must be more than six months overdue before VAT relief can be claimed.

THE USE OF POSTING SHEETS

In a large business or organisation, the various aspects of the accounting function will be allocated to a number of staff. For example, to look more closely at the recording and payment of credit purchases:

• one person may be involved in checking invoices received

• another person may prepare the purchases day book

- another may pass invoices or statements received for payment
- another may prepare remittance advices and cheques for sending to creditors
- another may keep the double-entry accounts up-to-date

These job allocations are given as an example only – as always, it is for the business to organise its accounting function to suit its needs. The essential point, though, is that in a larger business several people may be involved in just one area of record keeping, such as purchases, sales, etc. (In a small business, all of these tasks and more would, most likely, be carried out by just one person.)

One feature of a large business is that use may be made of a posting sheet. This lists transactions that are to be entered (or posted) into the double-entry accounts and will be prepared by a member of the accounts department. For example, a posting sheet for the transactions of Galaxy Media (see case Study, page 285) is prepared as follows:

Posting Sheet			
Account	**Folio**	**Debit** £	**Credit** £
Bank	CBR	5,000	
Capital	GL		5,000
Rent paid	GL	500	
Bank	CB		500
Office equipment	GL	2,000	
VAT	GL	350	
Bank	CBP		2,350
Bank	CBR	1,000	
Loan: M Way	GL		1,000
Cash	CBR	235	
Commission received	GL		200
VAT	GL		35
Electricity	GL	80	
VAT	GL	14	
Western Electric	PL		94
Drawings	GL	100	
Cash	CBP		100
Bank	CBR	470	
Office equipment	GL		400
VAT	GL		70
Western Electric	PL	94	
Bank	CBP		94
TOTALS		9,843	9,843

Prepared by	*J Jarris*	Date	*30 May 2001*
Checked by	*N Wilson*	Date	*30 May 2001*
Posted by	*S Ahmed*	Date	*30 May 2001*

Notes:

- The posting sheet can be designed in any format to suit the needs of the business.

- It can be used for one day's transactions, or for longer periods such as a week or a month – much depends on the number of transactions to be recorded.

- Essential information includes:
  - name of account
  - folio, usually together with the account number
  - amount of debit entry
  - amount of credit entry

- The posting sheet is totalled – this shows that the money amounts of debit entries are equal to credit entries.

- The name of the person preparing the posting sheet is stated with the date, together with the person checking it and the date.

- The name of the person posting the transactions to the firm's double-entry accounts, together with the date, is given.

CHAPTER SUMMARY

- Ledger accounts are classified between:
  - personal accounts
  - impersonal accounts (which are further classified between real accounts and nominal accounts)

- Entries in the cash book are:
  - debit money in
  - credit money out

- Other accounts are opened in the book-keeping system for:
  - capital
  - fixed assets
  - expenses
  - income
  - drawings
  - loans
  - stock
  - bad debts written off

- Posting sheets are used to list transactions to be entered in the double-entry accounts.

**KEY
TERMS**

personal accounts — accounts in the names of people or businesses, eg the accounts for debtors and creditors

impersonal accounts — non-personal accounts, usually divided between real accounts and nominal accounts

real accounts — accounts which represent things, such as cash, bank balance, computers, motor vehicles, machinery

nominal accounts — accounts which record income and expenses, such as sales, purchases, wages

capital account — records the amount of money invested in the business by the owner (or owners)

fixed assets — items purchased by a business for use on a permanent or semi-permanent basis, such as buildings, machinery, motor vehicles, office equipment – the *capital expenditure* of a business

expenses — the running expenses (or *revenue expenditure*) of a business, such as rent, wages, electricity, telephone, vehicle running expenses

drawings — amount of money taken by the owner in cash, or by cheque (or sometimes goods), from the business for personal use

stock account — an asset of the business, stock is valued usually at the end of the financial year and the amount is debited to stock account

bad debt — a debt owing to a business or organisation which it considers will never be paid

bad debts written off account — the account to which the amounts of account balances written off as bad are transferred

journal — primary accounting record for non-regular transactions

posting sheets — a list of transactions to be entered in the double-entry accounts

STUDENT ACTIVITIES

13.1 Sales ledger contains:

(a)   creditors' accounts

(b)   sales account

(c)   debtors' accounts

(d)   sales returns account

Answer (a) or (b) or (c) or (d)

13.2 Which one of the following is not a division of the ledger?

(a)   general ledger

(b)   sales account

(c)   sales ledger

(d)   cash book

Answer (a) or (b) or (c) or (d)

13.3 A friend has recently set up in business. To help him, you have written up the first month's double-entry accounts. Your friend asks you to reply to the following points:

- "I bought a computer, but you've shown it on the debit side. Surely it must go on the credit side? You must be wrong."

- "Why is the transaction for my capital on the credit side of capital account. I've paid in capital, so surely this is the account which has gained value?"

13.4 James Anderson set up in business on 1 February 2001 and registered for Value Added Tax. During the first month he has kept the cash book up-to-date as follows:

Debit	Cash Book: Receipts				CBR
Date	Details	Folio	Discount allowed	Cash	Bank
2001			£	£	£
1 Feb	Capital				7,500
14 Feb	Bank loan				2,500
20 Feb	Commission received*			141	

Credit	Cash Book: Payments				CBP
Date	Details	Folio	Discount received	Cash	Bank
2001			£	£	£
6 Feb	Computer*				2,350
7 Feb	Rent paid				500
12 Feb	Wages				425
23 Feb	Drawings				200
26 Feb	Wages				380
27 Feb	Van*				5,875

The items with asterisks (*) include Value Added Tax.

James Anderson has not got around to the other double-entry accounts.

You are to draw up the other accounts for James Anderson, and to make the appropriate entries.

Notes:

• Use the current rate of Value Added Tax (17.5% at the time of writing)

• Account numbers need not be used

• Separate primary accounting records need not be shown

13.5 The following are the business transactions of Tony Long, who is registered for Value Added Tax, for the month of May 2001:

1 May	Started a business with capital of £6,000 in the bank
4 May	Bought a machine* for £2,350, paying by cheque
7 May	Bought office equipment* for £2,820, paying by cheque
9 May	Paid rent £350, by cheque
13 May	Obtained a loan of £1,000 from a friend, Lucy Warner, and paid her cheque into the bank
15 May	Paid wages £250, by cheque
18 May	Commission received* £188, in cash
21 May	Drawings £85, in cash
29 May	Paid wages £135, by cheque

The items with asterisks (*) include Value Added Tax

You are to:

(a)   write up Tony Long's cash book receipts and cash book payments (with columns for cash and bank)

(b)   complete the double-entry book-keeping transactions

Notes:

• Use the current rate of Value Added Tax (17.5% at the time of writing)

• Account numbers need not be used

• Separate primary accounting records need not be shown

13.6   Enter the following transactions into the double-entry book-keeping accounts of Jean Lacey, who is registered for Value Added Tax. Include a cash book with columns for cash and bank.

1 Aug	Started in business with capital of £5,000 in the bank
3 Aug	Bought a computer for £1,800 + VAT, paying by cheque
7 Aug	Paid rent £100, by cheque
10 Aug	Received commission £200 + VAT, in cash
13 Aug	Bought office fittings £2,000 + VAT, paying by cheque
15 Aug	Received a loan £1,000, by cheque from a friend, Sally Orton
17 Aug	Drawings £100, in cash
20 Aug	Returned some of the office fittings (unsuitable) and received a refund cheque of £240 + VAT
24 Aug	Received commission £160 + VAT, by cheque
28 Aug	Made a loan repayment to Sally Orton of £150, by cheque

Notes:

• Use the current rate of Value Added Tax (17.5% at the time of writing)

• Account numbers need not be used

• Separate primary accounting records need not be shown

13.7   You work as a sales ledger clerk in the accounts department of Fleet Sales Limited, a VAT-registered company.

The sales (debtors) ledger includes the following account:

Dr		**Dailey Trading Company** (account no 754)		Cr
2001		£	2001	£
15 Jan	Sales	94		

Monthly statements of account and 'chaser' letters have been sent to this debtor – the last letter was dated 11 September 2001 and was returned marked 'gone away, not known at this address'.

Today, 29 November 2001, the accounts supervisor gives you the following memo:

MEMORANDUM

TO: Sales Ledger Accounts Clerk

FROM: Accounts Supervisor

DATE: 29 November 2001

SUBJECT: DAILEY TRADING COMPANY

Please write off the balance of this account as a bad debt – we have done all we can to collect the amount. As we charged VAT on the original invoice, do not forget to reclaim VAT when writing off the balance.

Thanks.

Lucinda

Lucinda Luz

You are to show:

- the journal entry made on 29 November
- the transactions on Dailey Trading Company's account in the sales (debtors) ledger
- the bad debts written off account in the general (main) ledger
- the VAT account in the general (main) ledger

Note: account numbers need not be used

14 COMMUNICATING WITH CUSTOMERS AND SUPPLIERS

this chapter covers . . .

This chapter explains the importance of polite and effective handling of communications between a business and customers and suppliers. It covers:

- the need for politeness – adopting the right mental attitude

- the need for effectiveness – choosing the right means of communication and expressing the facts accurately and in an appropriate way

- an illustration of the wide variety of business communication formats

- practical examples of how those formats are used

NVQ PERFORMANCE CRITERIA COVERED

unit 1: RECORDING INCOME AND RECEIPTS

element 1: process documents relating to goods and services supplied

- communications with customers regarding accounts are handled politely and effectively using the relevant source documents

unit 2: MAKING AND RECORDING PAYMENTS

element 1: process documents relating to goods and services received

- communications with suppliers regarding accounts are handled politely and effectively

COMMUNICATING WITH CUSTOMERS AND SUPPLIERS

Your course requires that you communicate with your customers (the people to whom you sell) and your suppliers (the people from whom you buy) **politely** and **effectively**.

In other words, you are pleasant and respectful in your communication and you transfer the necessary message accurately and within the correct timescale. These principles are often set out in an organisation's 'customer charter' scheme or will form part of a general 'quality' policy adopted by a business.

Politeness involves putting the other person first, no matter how stupid or arrogant that person might be – politeness is your mental attitude – it may come naturally, or it may not! **Effectivness** of communication, on the other hand, is less easy to achieve. It means:

- choosing the right means of communication
- getting your facts right
- being able to express those facts in the appropriate way

Effectiveness is a skill that has to be learned over a period of time.

Over the next few pages we will look at the different types of communication used internally in an organisation and externally with customers and suppliers. You will need to study these; they will feature not only in the Case Study at the end of the chapter, but also in the last two chapters of the book which deal with communicating management information. First however, we give some examples of situations relating to customers and suppliers which will require your communication skills.

customer communications

The types of situation which might arise include:

- answering a customer enquiry about an invoice – eg the terms
- sending a customer a copy of a document which had gone astray
- sending back a customer's cheque with a missing signature
- chasing up debts from an aged debtors analysis (a summary of amounts owed by customers)

supplier communications

The types of situation which might arise include:

- querying a discount on an invoice
- complaining about a credit note which has not been sent
- complaining about the delivery of incorrect goods

THE MEMORANDUM

format

The memorandum (plural memoranda) is a formal written note used for internal communication within an organisation. It may be typed or handwritten, and will often be produced in a number of copies which can be circulated as necessary. A memorandum may be sent by e-mail within an organisation.

A memorandum can be used for situations such as:

• giving instructions
• requesting information
• making suggestions
• recording of opinions
• confirming telephone conversations

A memorandum is normally pre-printed by the organisation with all the headings in place, and can be half page or full page in size.

elements of the memorandum

'to' and 'from'	the name and job title of the sender and the recipient are entered in full, and the formal phrases you find on letters, eg 'Dear......' and 'Yours ....' are not necessary
copies to	memoranda are sometimes sent to a number of people; the recipients will be indicated in this section of the document
subject	the subject matter of the memorandum must be stated concisely
text	the message of the memorandum should be clear and concise
signature	a memorandum can be signed, initialled, or even – as is often the case – left blank
enclosures	if material is circulated with the memorandum, the abbreviation 'enc' or 'encl' should be used

Study the two examples of memoranda illustrated on the next page. One relates to customers, the other to suppliers.

MEMORANDUM

To	John Stone, Finance Manager
From	Tim Blake, Sales Manager

Ref TB/AC/1098

Copies to n/a

Date 22 June 2001

Subject Bad payers

Please can you let me have an updated list of our customers who exceed their credit period and pay late.

I need to give this list to the sales reps so that they will not be tempted to extend credit any further to these customers.

a completed memorandum relating to customer accounts

MEMORANDUM

To	Tom Flint, Purchasing Manager
From	John Stone, Finance Manager

Ref JS/TT/2374

Copies to n/a

Date 22 June 2001

Subject Supplier discounts

Please can you let me have an up-to-date list of the trade discounts you have negotiated with all our suppliers. We have had one or two queries about these recently. Many thanks.

J.S.

a completed memorandum relating to supplier accounts

INTERNAL COMMUNICATIONS – THE NOTE

One of the most common forms of communication within an organisation is the *note*. This can be:

- an informal written note, passing on a message or an instruction

- a telephone message (some organisations use preprinted telephone message pads)

The important elements of a written note are

- the name of the person who is sending the note

- the name of the person who is to receive the note

- the time and date that the note is written

- a clearly stated message

- a clear indication of any action to be taken as a result of the message

Examine the examples set out below and see how they contain all these elements.

```
To Tim Blackstock,
Order Processing

Please remember to allow PDT
Ltd an extra 10% trade discount
on invoices this month.

John Tregennick, Sales
03.04.01   10.30
```

```
                 TELEPHONE MESSAGE
TO       Karin Schmidt, Accounts
FROM     H Khan, Sales
DATE     19 April 2001
TIME     12.30

Please ring Jim Stoat at RF
Electronics – he is complaining
that they have not received a
credit note for returned damaged
stock (order ref 823423).

Please treat urgently – he is
not very happy!

HK
```

THE FAX

The fax (short for 'facsimile') enables you to transmit electronically an exact copy of the details on a sheet of paper. This can either be done on a computer or on a fax machine. If you use a fax machine you feed the sheet into the machine, dial up the recipient on the inbuilt telephone pad and transmit the document down the line. The machine at the other end will print out an exact copy of the original document.

The fax can be used within an organisation or for external contact with a customer. You normally send a 'fax header' first sheet (see illustration below) and then feed in any further pages/documents as required.

The fax is very useful for sending copies of documents. A frequent excuse given by people who are slow at paying is "I can't pay because I don't seem to have the original invoice". This can be replied to with "No problem! We can fax you a copy. What is your fax number?" Look at the example below.

Osborne Electronics Limited

Unit 4 Everoak Estate, Bromyard Road
St Johns, Worcester WR2 5HN
tel 01905 748043 fax 01905 748911

facsimile transmission header

To: Jamie Milne, Accounts Office, Zippo Computers

Fax number: 01350 525504

Number of pages including this header: 2   Date: 18 October 2001

message

Invoice 24375

Further to our recent telephone conversation I am faxing you a copy of invoice 24375 which is now overdue.

I shall be grateful if you will arrange for the £4,678.50 owing to be paid to us as soon as possible.

R Pound

Credit Controller

THE E-MAIL

E-mail is the sending and receiving of electronic messages by means of computer. E-mails can be

- external – communications with customers through the Internet, or
- internal – through a network of computers in the business – an intranet

E-mails can be sent quickly and cheaply within the UK and overseas.

When someone wants to check an e-mail account, it is necessary to log in. A list of messages is displayed. The user can read them or delete them. When a message is read, it is easy to reply to it. The original message re-appears and comments can be added to the original. If a message is of interest to someone else, it can be forwarded. Computer files – eg spreadsheets – can also be sent by e-mail as 'attachments'.

When composing an e-mail, a screen such as the one illustrated below is used.

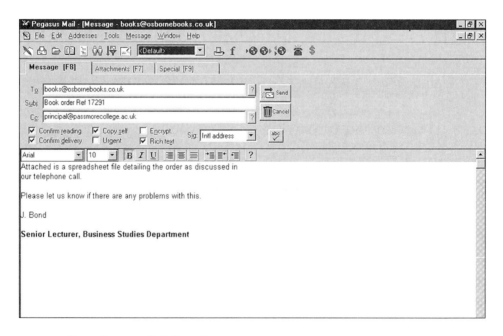

It can be seen that there is:

- space for the message
- a place to type in the e-mail address of where the e-mail has to go
- a box to summarise the content of the e-mail – useful so that the person reading a message list knows which ones are the most important
- a CC (carbon copy) box so that a copy of the e-mail can be sent to anyone else who needs to know about the message

THE 'HOUSE STYLE' LETTER

When you deal with business letters you will see that the appearance and format of each letter is in a uniform 'house' style, a style which identifies that business, and is common to all letters that it sends. The letter will normally be on standard printed stationery showing the name, address and details of the business, and will be set out with headings, paragraphs, signatures – the 'elements' of the letter – in a uniform way.

There are a number of different ways of setting out the text of a letter. The most of common of these – the 'fully blocked' style is illustrated and explained on the next two pages.

characteristics of a fully blocked letter

- the most commonly used style of letter

- all the lines start at the left margin

- the use of open punctuation, ie there is no punctuation, except in the main body of the letter, which uses normal punctuation

- paragraphs are divided by a space, and are not indented

- a fully blocked letter is easy to type as all the lines are set uniformly to the left margin

elements of the letter

The explanations which follow refer to the illustration of the letter on page 307.

printed letterhead — The name and address of the business is normally pre-printed, and must be up-to-date.

reference — The reference on the letter illustrated – DH/SB/69 – is a standard format

- DH (Derek Hunt), the writer
- SB (Sally Burgess), the secretary
- 69, the number of the file where Mr Smart's correspondence is kept

If you need to quote the reference of a letter to which you are replying, the references will be quoted as follows: Your ref TR/FG/45 Our ref DH/SB/69.

date	The date is typed in date (number), month (word), year (number) order.
recipient	The name and address of the person to whom the letter is sent. This section of the letter may be displayed in the window of a window envelope, so it is essential that it is accurate.
salutation	'Dear Sir. . . Dear Madam' if you know the person's name and title (ie Mr, Mrs, Miss, Ms) use it, but check that it is correct – a misspelt name or an incorrect title will ruin an otherwise competent letter.
heading	The heading sets out the subject matter of the letter – it will concentrate the reader's mind.
body	The body of the letter is an area where the message of the letter is set out. The text must be
	• laid out in short precise paragraphs and short clear sentences
	• start with a point of reference (eg referring to an invoice)
	• set out the message in a logical sequence
	• be written in plain English – but avoid 'slang' expressions and, equally, avoid 'posh' words
	• finish with a clear indication of the next step to be taken (eg please telephone, please arrange appointment, please buy our products, please pay our invoice)
complimentary close	The complimentary close (signing off phrase) must be consistent with the salutation:
	'Dear Sir/Dear Madam' followed by 'Yours faithfully'
	'Dear Mr Sutton/Dear Ms Jones' followed by 'Yours sincerely'.
name and job title	It is essential for the reader to know the name of the person who sent the letter, and that person's job title, because a reply will need to be addressed to a specific person.
enclosures	If there are enclosures with the letter, the abbreviation 'enc' or 'encl' is used at the bottom of the letter.

the 'house style' letter

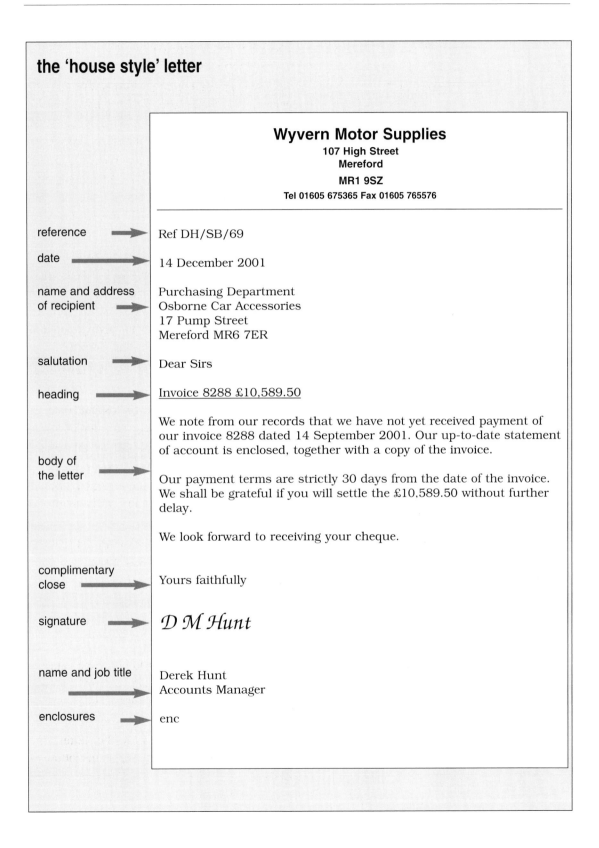

reference ➔ Ref DH/SB/69

date ➔ 14 December 2001

name and address of recipient ➔ Purchasing Department
Osborne Car Accessories
17 Pump Street
Mereford MR6 7ER

salutation ➔ Dear Sirs

heading ➔ Invoice 8288 £10,589.50

body of the letter ➔ We note from our records that we have not yet received payment of our invoice 8288 dated 14 September 2001. Our up-to-date statement of account is enclosed, together with a copy of the invoice.

Our payment terms are strictly 30 days from the date of the invoice. We shall be grateful if you will settle the £10,589.50 without further delay.

We look forward to receiving your cheque.

complimentary close ➔ Yours faithfully

signature ➔ *D M Hunt*

name and job title ➔ Derek Hunt
Accounts Manager

enclosures ➔ enc

Wyvern Motor Supplies
107 High Street
Mereford
MR1 9SZ
Tel 01605 675365 Fax 01605 765576

TYPES OF BUSINESS LETTER

Different types of business letter require different treatment. We will look at four situations and in each case give an examples of how the text of the letter might read:

- providing information
- chasing a debt
- making a complaint
- dealing with a complaint

a letter providing information

The body of a letter providing information in answer to enquiry will be structured in a number of stages:

1   Refer to the original enquiry, eg 'Further to your telephone enquiry/visit/letter' and give the enquiry a date ... 'of 1 April.'

2   Provide the information, either in the text, or by enclosing promotional literature, eg a catalogue.

3   Finish the text of the letter on a positive note or 'selling' note, eg 'Please let us know if we can be of further help' ... 'We look forward to your order' ... 'If you wish to order the goods, please contact Mr Eden in our Sales Department, telephone 01908 384983.'

Here is an extract from a letter following a telephone enquiry to a bathroom centre. Note that the text is not particularly lengthy, but is polite and to the point. It follows the three stages set out above.

```
Dear Mr Knott

Shower Enclosures

Thank you for your telephone enquiry of today.

I am now pleased to enclose a brochure and price
list for the Niagara range of shower enclosures.

If you require further information, please do not
hesitate to give me a call.

Yours sincerely

J Waterman

J Waterman
Sales Executive
```

a letter chasing a debt

This type of letter is used by an accounts department or by a sole trader chasing up overdue invoices. Often the letter will be a 'set' letter, already formatted on a word processor. There may be a number of set letters on file: a gentle reminder, a firm reminder, a threat of legal action and a formal demand.

Each letter is set out in a number of stages:

1   Details of the amount owing is clearly stated: the amount itself and the date of the original invoice(s). Sometimes a copy invoice(s) will be included in the letter to avoid the common problem of the customer claiming that the original invoice has been lost!

        Mention will often be made of the fact that statements of account have also been sent.

2   The terms of the invoice will be stated and the fact that the terms have not been complied with will be stressed.

3   Payment will be firmly requested – often a time limit will be stated.

4   Sometimes it may be necessary to threaten what will happen if the money is not received, eg 'If we do not receive settlement by this date we regret we will have no alternative but to place the matter in the hands of our solicitors.'

Here is an example of a chaser for a long overdue invoice.

---

30 April 2001

Dear Mr Khan

Invoice 23846 £1,250

We note from our records that invoice 23846 (copy enclosed) for £1,250, dated 8 January 2001, has not yet been settled.

The terms of this invoice were strictly 30 days and therefore it is well overdue.

We shall be grateful if you will kindly settle this amount by return of post.

Yours sincerely

N Wakefield

N Wakefield
Accounts Manager

a letter making a complaint

This type of letter sometimes has to be written: goods supplied may be faulty or the bank may have made a mistake. The important point about this type of letter is that it must be polite and factually accurate. You may feel extremely angry or upset about the situation, but this must not show in the letter.

The letter will follow set stages:

1   The details of the problem must be set out in full. If goods are involved, the order number must be quoted, if an invoice is wrong, the invoice number must be referred to, and so on. The actual problem must be set out in strictly factual form ... not 'the carrier you used was so hopeless that the parcel was mangled on arrival' but 'the goods (delivery note 3477) were received damaged.'

2   Explain how the problem has inconvenienced you – again in factual terms.

3   State what action you are looking for to remedy the situation.

Here is an example of a letter to a bank. The writer has found a number of errors on the business account bank statement.

Dear Sir

Account 12039834 Bank Statement 120

We have just received our bank statement dated 30 March 2001 and note the following errors:

Cheque 894439 for £350 was paid on 12 March. We stopped payment of this cheque on 9 March.

A standing order for £120 to the Martley Chamber of Commerce was paid on 2 March as well as on 2 February. This is an annual standing order due to be paid at the beginning of February each year.

I shall be grateful if you will look into these matters and refund the amounts to the bank account as soon as possible.

Yours faithfully

N Wakefield

N Wakefield
Accounts Manager

a letter making an apology to a customer

If you receive a letter of complaint you are likely to have to write a letter of apology. There are a number of points to bear in mind:

- get the facts right first – the person making the complaint may be in the wrong and may be distorting the truth!

- decide what is to be done to put the situation right – refer to a superior authority if necessary

- when writing the apology be polite, but do not overdo it – if you are over-apologetic the reader will lose all respect for you!

The letter will follow set stages:

1   Acknowledge receipt of the complaint.

2   Acknowledge the problem and apologise (but not too much). Do not go into long explanations of how the problem arose – the reader will not be interested.

3   Explain what you are going to do to put the matter right.

4   Conclude with a further brief apology.

Here is a letter a clothes supplier might write when a shop (its customer) has not been sent the correct colour T shirts.

Dear Mrs Lockwood

Purchase Order 1283892

Thank you for your fax of 12 March pointing out that we had supplied the wrong colour T shirts on your Purchase Order 1283892.

As we stated on the telephone, we expect delivery of the red T shirts into our warehouse on 16 March. We have therefore arranged for our carrier to deliver the red T shirts on 19 March and to collect the incorrect ones at the same time.

We apologise for the inconvenience this has caused you.

Yours sincerely

A Gaffe

Ann Gaffe
Sales Manager

Now read the Case Study on the next four pages. It illustrates the many ways in which a business communicates with customers and suppliers.

CASE STUDY

VALLEYMORE FOODS

situation

Valleymore Foods Limited produces a variety of foodstuffs – pies, deserts, ready-made meals – which are sold frozen to its customers, who include supermarkets, pubs and local shops.

You work in the Accounts Department of Valleymore Foods and spend some of your time answering customer queries, debt chasing and dealing with suppliers.

This Case Study illustrates some of the more common tasks you have to undertake.

situation 1: a customer overpays

You receive a telephone message on your voicemail from Sid Parks, owner of the 'The Pig and Whistle', a local pub which you supply with snack meals.

"Hello there. I have just received my monthly statement of account from you. The balance should be back down to zero, but in fact it is showing a credit balance. of £40. Does this mean that you owe me money? If so, can you let me have it? Perhaps you can let me know. Bye."

You look into the ledgers and find that Sid's last cheque to you was for £155 rather than the £115 owing on the account. He has overpaid by £40. You speak to your Customer Accounts Manager who agrees that you can issue him with a refund cheque. He asks you to write a covering letter for his signature.

Valleymore Foods Limited

Martley Road, St Gregorys, MR2 5GT

Tel 01908 675234 Fax 01908 675332 E-mail foods@valleymore.com

---

S Parks
The Pig and Whistle
The Green
Clitteridge
MR4 9YH

2 August 2001

Dear Mr Parks

Account 29847

Further to your recent telephone message left with us we have pleasure in enclosing our cheque for £40. This represents the balance of your account with us. The account had gone into credit because the last settlement cheque you issued was for £155 rather than the £115 owing.

Yours sincerely

Ivor Penny, Customer Accounts Manager

situation 2: an unsigned customer cheque

You receive a cheque through the post from a customer Totley Limited. Unfortunately the cheque is unsigned. Your Manager says that you will have to send it back to the customer with a request for the customer to sign it ...

Valleymore Foods Limited
Martley Road, St Gregorys, MR2 5GT
Tel 01908 675234 Fax 01908 675332 E-mail foods@valleymore.com

---

Accounts Department
Totley Limited
Unit 17 Deepend Estate
Bath
BA2 3BR

3 August 2001

Dear Sirs

Account 28761

I return your cheque 564132 for £12,349.50 which was received in our office today. Unfortunately the cheque has not been signed. I shall be grateful if you will arrange for it to be signed by the appropriate signatories and returned to us as soon as possible.

Yours faithfully

Ivor Penny, Customer Accounts Manager

---

situation 3: querying a supplier invoice

You receive an invoice from one of your suppliers. When you check it you notice that the trade discount of 20% which you normally receive is not deducted from the goods total of £400. You mention this to your Purchase Ledger Manager who says:

"I expect they have got a new member of staff on the job. I should e-mail them and ask for an amended invoice to be issued. Don't forget to work out the figures for them. They may get it wrong again!"

The text of your e-mail is as follows:

---

to address <hillside.coop@goblin.net>
subject Trade Discount
08.08.01.10.30.34

To Accounts Department
We note that on invoice 981237 we have not been given our customary trade discount of 20%. By our calculations, the net goods total should be £320 and not £400. Please can you issue us with an amended invoice.
Many thanks
Abe Shaw
Accounts Department (Purchases Ledger)

situation 4: a missing credit note

You receive an e-mail from Tredco Limited. The text reads:

"We have received your July statement today. It lists a credit note for £1,876.50 which we cannot trace. Please can you let us have a copy."

You refer it to your Purchases Ledger Manager who suggests you fax the document with a suitable fax header message...

Valleymore Foods Limited

Martley Road, St Gregorys, MR2 5GT
Tel 01908 675234 Fax 01908 675332 E-mail foods@valleymore.com

facsimile transmission header

To: Asaf Patel, Accounts Office, Tredco Limited

Fax number: 01350 525504

Number of pages including this header: 2   Date: 3 August 2001

message

Credit Note 8732

Further to your e-mail of 3 August I am faxing you a copy of credit note 8732 for £1,876.50.

Abe Shaw

Purchase Ledger
Accounts Department

situation 5: dealing with the aged debtors analysis

Every month you print out from the computer an aged debtors analysis which lists all your sales ledger customers, their balances, limits and the length of time invoices have been outstanding. It is an important document in the credit control process – it highlights customers who are not paying up on time.

Every month you have to send out standard chaser letters to late payers. Some letters are polite reminders, others are stronger in their terms.

An extract from this month's aged debtors analysis is shown at the top of the next page.

VALLEYMORE FOODS LIMITED		AGED DEBTORS ANALYSIS				JULY 2001	
Account	Turnover	Credit Limit	Balance	Current	30 days	60 days	Older
Thamesco Trading	370.00	1000.00	164.50	164.50	0.00	0.00	0.00
J Singh	320.00	750.00	376.00	376.00	0.00	0.00	0.00
Maxwell Foods	1730.00	2000.00	1632.75	799.00	333.75	500.00	0.00
Premier Chef Trading	2025.00	2000.00	1926.88	380.00	0.00	1046.88	500.00
H Dunlittle	425.00	750.00	499.38	499.38	0.00	0.00	0.00
TOTALS	4870.00		4599.51	2218.88	333.75	1546.88	500.00

Valleymore gives a standard 30 days credit to its sales ledger customers. You have been asked to send 'Letter A' (a polite reminder) to any customers who have not settled within 60 days and 'Letter B' (a firm reminder) to any customer who is exceeding 60 days. These letters are to be signed by Ann Dover, the Credit Controller.

The aged debtor analysis shows that Maxwell Foods are due Letter A and Premier Chef Trading are due Letter B. The letters are as follows …

Letter A (full version)

Valleymore Foods Limited

Martley Road, St Gregorys, MR2 5GT
Tel 01908 675234 Fax 01908 675332 E-mail foods@valleymore.com

The Manager, Accounts Department
Maxwell Foods Limited
Parsons Road
Farmborough
SY3 7YH

2 August 2001

Dear Sir

Account 29613

We note from our records that we have not yet received settlement of due invoices totalling £833.75. Our invoice terms are strictly 30 days and these items are now overdue.

We shall be grateful if you will kindly settle this amount by return of post.

Yours faithfully

Ann Dover
Credit Controller

Letter B (extract)

Valleymore Foods Limited

Martley Road, St Gregorys, MR2 5GT
Tel 01908 675234 Fax 01908 675332 E-mail foods@valleymore.com

Accounts Manager, Premier Chef Trading

Dear Sir

Account 28745

Further to our previous reminders we still have not received settlement of the overdue invoices on your account. We shall be grateful if you will kindly forward us your cheque for £1546.88. If this amount has not been received at this address within seven working days we will have no alternative but to place the matter in the hands of our solicitor.

Yours faithfully

Ann Dover
Credit Controller

- Businesses need to communicate regularly with their customers and suppliers.

- The communications should be both polite and effective – they should use the appropriate format and the appropriate wording and be sent within the appropriate timescale.

- There are a number of different forms of written communication which are used both within an organisation and also when dealing with outsiders.

- The memorandum is a formal written note used within an organisation; it may be typed, word processed or handwritten. Memoranda may also be sent by internal e-mail. Examples of its use include giving information, asking for information, giving instructions and recording.

- Informal written notes are also widely used for communicating information. It is important that they record the date and time of writing. They range from informal scribbled messages to the pre-printed telephone message.

- The fax can be used for internal or external communications. It is useful for sending copy documents and also for more informal communications.

- The e-mail is a fast and convenient form of communication both for external (Internet) use and internal (intranet) networks. Files can be sent by e-mail.

- The written letter, sent by post or by fax, is still a widely used form of business communication. Letters can be used for a variety of purposes in the context of accounting, including giving information, making a complaint, writing an apology and chasing debts.

memorandum	a formal written communication used internally within an organisation
fax	short for 'facsimile' – an electronic transmission of an exact image
e-mail	an electronic message sent from one computer to another
Internet	a world-wide network of interlinked computers
intranet	a linked network of computers within an organisation
attachment	a digital file (text or image, for example) which is sent with an e-mail
house style letter	a letter produced by a business in a style which has been adopted as standard by the business
aged debtors analysis	a regular report scheduling all the sales ledger customers, their balances, limits and length of time their invoices have been outstanding

STUDENT ACTIVITIES

In these exercises you may have to make up names, addresses and dates. Unless your tutor states otherwise, make these up as you think appropriate.

14.1 You receive a cheque through the post from a sales ledger customer. The words and figures are different. The words say 'five hundred and fifty pounds' and the figures '£500'. The amount should be £550. Write the text of a suitable letter to the customer.

14.2 You receive an invoice (No 3241) from one of your suppliers, Clifton Trading Company, clifton@cliftontrading.co.uk. You are normally given a 2.5% cash discount and a 20% trade discount, but these are not included on this invoice. Write the text of an e-mail pointing this out, as you want to settle the invoice as soon as possible to take advantage of the discount. The goods total before any discounts is £500.

14.3 One of your sales ledger customers, Adrian Duffe Associates, is well known in your Accounts Department as a bad payer. When telephoned recently about the non-payment of invoices, the assistant said "We don't seem to have received these invoices. Are you sure they are ours?" You check your records and find that the invoices were sent to Adrian Duffe Associates with the goods. How would you deal with this problem?

14.4 You are an Accounts Supervisor and you need to circulate to all the Sales Managers in the business a list of the customers who are more than 2 months behind in settling their accounts. These customers should be referred to the Accounts Manager before any further credit sales are made. You are to write a suitable memorandum, using your own name and today's date.

Note: you do not need to produce the list (which has been produced on your computer).

14.5 Draft a letter chasing up an overdue invoice. The letter is a 'gentle' reminder and follows previous statements of account. Complete the letter with details of a specimen invoice. The letter is for signature by you as Accounts Manager.

14.6 You have just received a bank statement from The National Bank, 10 High Street, Mereford, MR1 5FD, dated 31 December. You notice the following problems:

(a) A direct debit for £50 to Allied Insurance was paid on 15 December. On 1 December you had written to the bank cancelling the direct debit.

(b) On 31 December you were charged £125.65 in overdraft interest. According to your calculations the sum should have been approximately £75.

Draft a suitable letter to the Manager of the bank. The letter is for signature by you as Accounts Manager.

14.7 You are an Accounts Supervisor in the Accounts Department of Janus Fabrics. You receive the following e-mail message from your Customer Services Department on 1 April:

'Mrs Joan Pearce of Lizard Designs telephoned. She is furious. She placed an urgent customer order for 25 square metres of Roma velvet curtain fabric, colour burgundy, and has only received 15 square metres. I have sent a further 10 square metres today. Please write to her – she is a valued customer and needs to be kept happy.'

You check your records and find that on her purchase order (no 6234) the figure '25' could be read as '15' because the first digit is indistinct. Write her a suitable letter, using your own name and today's date. Her address is Lizard Designs, 13 Regency Passage, Mereford, MR2 6DA.

15 BUSINESSES AND THE LAW

this chapter covers . . .

This chapter explains how businesses are affected by the law – both by contract law and by statute law (Acts of Parliament). The chapter covers:

- the agreement in a contract – the offer and the acceptance

- the bargain in a contract – the need for both parties to provide something (known as 'consideration')

- the need for both sides to a contract to intend it to be legally binding

- breach of contract – what to do when things go wrong

- protection given in statute law when someone purchases goods or services

- the implications for businesses of the Data Protection Act

- the legal reasons for retaining documents

NVQ REQUIREMENTS

unit 1: RECORDING INCOME AND RECEIPTS

KNOWLEDGE AND UNDERSTANDING COVERAGE

- basic law relating to contract law, sale of goods act and document retention policies

unit 2: MAKING AND RECORDING PAYMENTS

KNOWLEDGE AND UNDERSTANDING COVERAGE

- basic law relating to contract law, sale of goods act and document retention policies

- basic law relating to data protection

Note: the legal requirements relating to cheques, cheque crossings and endorsements are covered in full on pages 76 to 79.

A CONTRACT DEFINED

Part of your course involves the understanding of the legal framework which enables buying and selling to take place and which states what can happen if there is a dispute. The agreement between the parties is known as a *contract.*

what is a contract?

a contract is a legally binding agreement enforceable in a court of law

Contracts, which may be in writing, or by word of mouth (oral), are agreements between two parties. Examples include:

- a written contract which you sign if you buy a house
- a written contract for a loan agreement if you borrow money
- a written contract of employment
- an oral contract if you buy goods in a shop
- an oral contract if you order goods over the telephone
- an oral contract if you hire a decorator to paint your house

In each case somebody does something for which some kind of payment is made. A contract is *an agreement with legal consequences* because if the work done is not satisfactory, or if the payment is not made, the wronged party can take the other person to court for *breach of contract.*

You may rightly wonder how all this affects you in the workplace. The answer is that the principles of contract affect any person carrying out normal business activities. For example if you quote an incorrect price to a customer, they may be able to hold your business to that price, under the terms of the contract of sale. If you fail to finish a job for a customer, they may be able to go to court to obtain a court order for your business to complete the work under the contract.

the three elements of contract

There are three elements which are common and essential to all contracts:

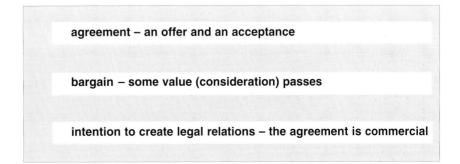

agreement – an offer and an acceptance

bargain – some value (consideration) passes

intention to create legal relations – the agreement is commercial

THE AGREEMENT – OFFER AND ACCEPTANCE

the offer

A firm and clear offer must be made either to a single party, a group, or to the world at large. In a famous legal case in 1893, a manufacturer of medicines (the Carbolic Smoke Ball Company) advertised a patented smoke ball and promised to pay a £100 reward to any person who contracted a specified illness having used the ball three times a day for two weeks. A Mrs Carlill used the ball for eight weeks and still contracted 'flu. She claimed her £100, the company refused, and she had to take the matter to the court which ruled that she should be granted her £100, as the offer of £100 had been to the "whole world" and needed no communicated acceptance from Mrs Carlill. It formed part of a valid contract which the company had to honour. Note that this is *not* the same situation as an *advertised price* which is not an offer but information which will enable a purchase – the contract – to be made (see below).

invitation to treat

An offer is quite different from an *invitation to treat* which is an invitation for a person to make an offer. Goods on supermarket shelves are an invitation for a customer to take them to the checkout where that customer can offer to purchase them at the price indicated at the checkout, which is where the contract takes place. That is the reason why shop tills indicate the price for each item, normally on an illuminated display; it is also the reason why a shop is not obliged to sell the goods at the price shown on the shelves.

---

practical example – invitation to treat

problem
Basil sees a holiday advertised in the local paper for £50. He telephones the travel company which tells him that the figure is a printing error – it should have been £500. Basil is angry and insists on booking his week in Menorca for £50. The problem is, does a contract exist on the basis of the £50 quoted?

answer
Basil has no rights here. There is no contract because the £50 quoted is only *an invitation to treat*, an invitation for Basil to make an agreement for booking the holiday. The company will clearly not agree to £50 for a week in Menorca!

termination of an offer

An offer may only be accepted while it is still open for acceptance. An offer may be terminated in the following circumstances:

- the time limit (if there is one) expires; if there is no time limit the offer lapses after a reasonable period of time
- the offeror – the person making the offer – may revoke (cancel) the offer
- an offer may be rejected by the making of a counter-offer; for instance, if you offer your car for sale for £1,500 and someone offers you £1,350, that is a counter-offer
- by acceptance or rejection of the offer

acceptance of an offer

Acceptance of an offer must be firm and unambiguous; it may be in spoken words, written form or even implied by action. Acceptance cannot be assumed from silence on the part of the person to whom the offer is made. For instance, if you say "I offer you my car for £1,500; if I have not heard from you within a week I will assume the deal is done", there is no acceptance. The offeree may go on holiday, or forget it even happened. Acceptance must also be *unconditional.* Any new term introduced – "I will agree to buy your car as long as the wing is resprayed" – amounts to a counter-offer (see above) and revokes the original offer.

---

practical example – conditional acceptance

problem
Basil works for Martley Garden Centre and has recently sent a quotation for a fountain to Mrs Waters: the cost will be £250.00 plus VAT and the fountain will have to be ordered from an outside supplier. Mrs Waters writes back saying she wants to accept the price, but the fountain must be delivered before the end of the month. Is there a valid contract between Mrs Waters and the garden centre?

answer
No. There is no contract because the acceptance has been conditional. *Acceptance must be unconditional.* Any new term introduced amounts to a counter-offer: "I will pay £250 plus VAT if the fountain is delivered by the end of the month."

The term "subject to contract", often seen on estate agents' boards, means that the terms of the offer to the offeree are agreeable, but have not been finally accepted. The two parties involved have agreed to draw up a formal contract for signature at a later date. There is no binding contract at this point.

communication of acceptance

The rules relating to communication of acceptance are largely dictated by what is required by the offer:

- the acceptance must normally be communicated to the person making the offer
- if the offer requires acceptance by a specific means (letter/fax/verbal message) then that means must be used

the postal rule

An acceptance by post is effective as long as the letter of acceptance is correctly addressed, correctly stamped and actually posted.

The time of acceptance is when the letter is posted (not when it is received). Given that letters may be delayed or lost in the post, this rule may seem unjust to the offeror! The postal rule only applies to an acceptance, it does not apply to a posted offer which must reach the offeree.

---

practical example – acceptance by post

problem
On 1 April Cotheridge Conifers telephones Basil at Martley Garden Centre to offer a job lot of 150 Leylandii trees at a knock-down price of £1.50 each. Basil needs time to think about this and says he will drop a line in the post. On 3 April he posts a reply to Cotheridge Conifers accepting the offer and placing an order for the trees. On 5 April the order is received. The question is, what is the date on which the contract was formed?

answer
3 April. The postal rule states that the date of posting of an acceptance of an offer is the effective date of the contract.

THE BARGAIN: CONSIDERATION

definition of consideration

A valid contract involves a bargain, a passing of value, known in law as consideration. If a business buys goods there is a two way process involved:

- the supplier promises to deliver the goods
- the buyer agrees to pay for them

The parties involved are:

- the promisor, the supplier that promises to supply the goods
- the promisee, the buyer who has to make payment

The consideration here is the payment, the price paid for the service provided. The principle is simple in itself, but there are a number of rules which relate to consideration.

consideration must be sufficient

Consideration must by law be sufficient. This means that:

- it must have value, although the value need not be adequate in some eyes; for example, you could sell this book for 5p; many would consider the amount to be inadequate, but the 5p still has value and is therefore consideration
- it must be sufficient, ie it must be in return for the promise; money due for some other reason or obligation is not sufficient consideration

consideration must move from the promisee

This legal phrase means, in effect, that the person who is promised goods or a service must themselves provide payment if the promise is to be enforceable as a contract. If you buy goods, you must make the payment. If someone else pays for you (an unlikely event!) you cannot take the supplier to court if the goods do not arrive.

consideration cannot be past

This legal phrase means that the consideration should not precede the promise. If you mend someone's car without any mention of payment, and the car owner the following week promises to give you £5, and subsequently refuses to pay you, there is no contract. The promise of payment followed the good turn done, consideration (the repair) was past as it had taken place the previous week.

practical example – consideration

problem
Basil promises to cut down some trees for a friend free of charge one weekend. Unfortunately Basil cuts down the wrong trees. His friend is very upset and says he will sue Basil. Can he? Is there a contract?

answer
No. There is no contract because there is no consideration – no money has been paid. Basil has made a mistake but he cannot be sued.

THE INTENTION TO CREATE LEGAL RELATIONS

A contract is an agreement involving consideration which the parties intend to be legally binding. In other words the parties entering a contract can reasonably expect the agreement to be enforced in a court of law if the necessity arises. The law assumes:

- commercial agreements are intended to be legally binding
- social and domestic arrangements are not intended to be legally binding

In short, if a person enters a contract to buy your car and then, without reason, refuses to pay for it, you can take him or her to court. If you ask a friend out for the evening, promising to take him or her out for a meal, and your friend doesn't turn up, you can not take court action. The sale of a car involves the intention to create legal relations, the invitation out does not.

BREACH OF CONTRACT

A contract normally contains certain terms which must be fulfilled as part of the agreement. If a person breaks one of those terms, that person is in *breach of contract*. For example, if a supplier undertakes to supply goods, it must send the goods on the due date, and in turn expects the goods to be paid for by a certain time. If the customer does not pay, he or she is in breach of contract and may be taken to court for damages (money compensation).

Contract terms may be classified as follows:

express terms	explicitly stated terms which are binding on both parties to the contract
conditions	fundamental terms of the contract which, if broken, will enable the injured party to reject the contract and to go to court to sue for damages
warranties	minor terms which if broken can be cause for an action for damages for loss suffered; the contract, however, remains in force
implied terms	terms which are not stated, but which are implied by trade custom or by law; for instance, goods sold should be of "satisfactory quality", in accordance with the Sale of Goods Act

In short:

- express terms are written into the contract; implied terms are not
- conditions are important terms, warranties are less important

> ## *practical example – breach of contract*
>
> **problem**
> Martley Garden Centre orders 1500 flower arrangements from a London wholesale supplier for delivery two days before Mothers Day. Unfortunately, because of a transport strike they arrive during the week following Mothers Day. Martley Garden Centre threatens to sue the supplier. Is the garden centre within its rights to do so?
>
> **answer**
> There is a clear breach of contract – the delivery date is a term of the contract and has not been met. Martley Garden Centre could sue.

SELLING AND STATUTE LAW

Statute law is law set down in an Act of Parliament.

There are a number of statutes which govern the way in which goods and services are sold, and they obviously affect the way in which businesses operate. The principal statutes are the Trades Descriptions Act, the Sale of Goods Act and the Unfair Contract Terms Act.

Trades Descriptions Act

The Trades Descriptions Act makes it a criminal offence:

* to make false statements about goods offered for sale
* to make misleading statements about services

Examples of offences therefore include:

* stating that a car for sale has clocked up 15,000 miles, when in fact the figure is 25,000 miles
* making a misleading statement about the price of goods, eg saying 'Now only £49.95, was £99.95' when it has only ever sold for £69.95
* making a misleading statement about a service, eg 'our dry cleaning is guaranteed to remove every stain' when it does not, or 'our apartments are within easy reach of the sea' when they are fifteen miles away

Sale of Goods Act

This Act states that you are entitled to expect any goods that you buy from a shop to be:

of 'satisfactory quality'
This means they must meet the standard that a 'reasonable' person would expect given the description and the price.

'fit for the purpose'

The goods must do what they are supposed to do, or what the shop claims they can do: an umbrella should keep the rain out, a watch should keep accurate time.

'as described'

The goods must be what they are claimed to be: a 'leather coat' must be made of leather, a 'stereo TV' must provide stereo sound.

If any of these three conditions is not met, the purchaser is entitled to a full or a part refund, depending on how soon the fault appears, how serious it is and how quickly the matter is taken up. Note also the following practical points:

- the buyer can accept a replacement, but can also insist on a refund if a replacement is not wanted
- the buyer does not have to accept a credit note for spending on other purchases
- a shop is not entitled to put up a notice saying "No Refunds!"

---

practical example – Sale of Goods Act

problem
Jason buys a watering can from Martley Garden Centre but finds that it leaks. He returns it to the Garden Centre, asking for a refund. The sales assistant refuses, pointing to a sign on the counter which states "No refunds given!" What is Jason's position?

answer
Jason *is* entitled to a refund. The Sale of Goods Act clearly states that goods must be of 'satisfactory quality'. The shop has no right to try and avoid statute law.

Unfair Contract Terms Act

Any organisation that tries to insist on *unfair* terms (eg in small print on the back of a sales contract) may be in breach of the Unfair Contract Terms Act. This would protect, for example, holidaymakers who are not put up in the hotel they booked because the small print stated that the holiday company had the right to move them to another resort. This would be seen as an 'unfair term' and would enable the holidaymaker to seek compensation. In short, a business cannot 'contract out' through the small print

DATA PROTECTION LEGISLATION

data

Businesses inevitably keep records of their customers and suppliers on file – either manually – a card index system, for example – or, more likely, on computer file. This is 'personal data'. In the normal course of business this poses no problem to the person whose details are kept on file. But what if those details are passed into the hands of a third party and those details are wrong? Think about the following examples:

- a credit reference agency gives a bad credit reference on Mrs A Jones who is applying to a shop for finance on some new furniture – in fact they have got their files mixed up and are reporting on a different Mrs A Jones who had been to court for non-payment of debt – as a consequence the first Mrs Jones is unlikely to get finance for her furniture

- Trader A is asked to give a trade reference on one of its customers, Trader B; Trader A gets his files muddled up and gives a poor reference which results in Trader B being refused credit by the business asking for the reference

Clearly these two 'individuals', a consumer and a trader, need protection for their personal data. This is provided by the Data Protection Act.

Data Protection Act

The Data Protection Act (1998) which came into force on 1 March 2000 establishes rules for the processing of personal data. It follows the guidelines of EC Directive 95/46/EC and brings the UK in line with European legal principles. The Act applies to:

- a filing system of records held on **computer** – eg a computer database of customer names, addresses, telephone numbers, sales details

- a **manual** set of accessible records – eg a card index file system of customer details

Data protection is regulated by the Data Protection Commission.

There are certain terms which are defined by the Act:

personal data	information which relates to an individual
data subject	the individual whose information is stored
data controller	the person in the organisation who is responsible for the processing of the data
recipient	the person who receives the data

the eight principles of 'good information handling'

All organisations which process personal data should register with the Data Protection Commission. Their 'data controllers' should follow the eight guiding principles set out in the Data Protection Act. These principles require that personal data is handled properly. They state that personal data must be:

1 fairly and lawfully processed

2 processed for limited purposes

3 adequate, relevant and not excessive

4 accurate

5 not kept for longer than is necessary

6 processed in line with the data subject's rights

7 kept securely

8 not transferred to countries outside the European Union unless it is adequately protected in those countries

right of access

People have the legal right to know what personal details about them is held by an organisation. They should apply in writing for a copy of the personal data held on file by the organisation; they may have to pay a fee.

implications for confidentiality

We have already seen throughout this book the need for confidentiality in business dealings. The Data Protection Act reinforces this duty. A business should not without permission reveal:

• information about one customer to another customer

• information about its employees

implications for storage and retention of data

We have already seen (page 199) that business records should be stored for at least six years. The Data Protection Act reinforces the requirement that personal data is kept securely and that it should be accurate. There are a number of legal reasons why financial data (which will include personal data) should be kept for this period of time:

• accounting records should be kept so that they can be inspected by the Inland Revenue if required (if there is a tax inspection)

• accounting records should be kept so that they can be inspected by HM Customs & Excise if required (if there is a VAT inspection)

• accounting records should be kept for at least six years in case they are needed as evidence in any legal action

**CHAPTER
SUMMARY**

- A contract is an agreement between two people ('parties') with legal consequences – if something goes wrong with the agreement, the matter can go to court if necessary.

- A contract contains three elements: an agreement made between two parties, a bargain struck involving each party giving up something of value, and an intention that the agreement is a legal one.

- A contract involves an offer being made and accepted. An offer may be made to an individual, a group of people or to everyone. For a contract to exist, an offer must be accepted clearly and without any conditions attached.

- The bargain in a contract – the passing of something of value – must involve both parties and must follow the contract.

- The intention behind a contract should be to form a legal agreement; arrangements such as 'doing someone a favour' do not form a contract.

- If one of the parties breaks the terms of a contract – eg does not pay, does not do the work required – the matter can be taken to court as a breach of contract, either for damages (money compensation) or to ensure the work is done.

- Statute law (laws passed in Parliament) protects buyers of goods and services. Examples include the Trades Descriptions Act and the Sale of Goods Act.

- The Data Protection Act (1998) ensures that data held by organisations on computer or in manual records is handled properly. There are eight principles set out in the Act. They state that personal data must be:
  1 fairly and lawfully processed
  2 processed for limited purposes
  3 adequate, relevant and not excessive
  4 accurate
  5 not kept for longer than is necessary
  6 processed in line with the data subject's rights
  7 kept securely
  8 not transferred to countries outside the European Union unless it is adequately protected in those countries

- Accounting data (and all other business records) should kept confidential and should be retained for at least six years in case of tax investigations or legal actions being taken.

contract	a legally binding agreement enforceable in a court of law
parties	the people directly involved in a contract
consideration	value which is passed between the parties to a contract, eg money, doing a job
invitation to treat	an invitation for someone to make an offer, eg priced goods on a shop shelf
subject to contract	the stage reached when the terms of an offer are said to be acceptable but the final agreement has not been finalised
postal rule	if an acceptance of an offer is made by post, the contract comes into being when the acceptance is correctly posted
breach of contract	the situation where one of the parties to a contract breaks one or more of the terms of the contract
damages	money compensation awarded in a court of law
personal data	information which relates to an individual held by an organisation on computer or manual file
data subject	the individual whose information is stored
data controller	the person in the organisation who is responsible for the processing of the data
recipient	the person who receives the data
right of access	the legal right of the individual to request a copy of the personal data held by an organisation

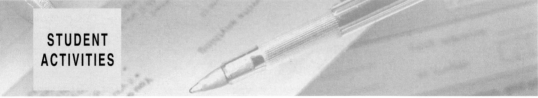

STUDENT
ACTIVITIES

15.1   Write down a sentence defining a contract – use your own words.

15.2   State the three elements of a contract, writing down a sentence describing each of the three elements.

15.3 State in each of the following situations whether a contract exists. In each case give reasons for your answer.

(a) You order goods over the phone and agree a price but do not issue a purchase order.

(b) You order goods by sending a signed purchase order by fax to the supplier who then despatches them.

(c) You do a job for someone free of charge and as a favour. She later gives you £10 but then complains that the job has not been done properly.

(d) You do a job for a friend and agree a price, but after you have done the job he refuses to pay you.

15.4 You go to a local DIY store and see a power drill on the shelves with a price sticker of £39.95. You think it is a good buy and take it to the till. The cashier says that the price is now £49.95; the lower price was for a special offer that has now expired. Is the cashier right to insist on charging the higher price or can you insist that the contract is based on the lower price being the offer price? Give *legal reasons* for your answer.

15.5 You fill in an order form for some stationery. The order form is contained in the catalogue sent to you by the supplier. At the bottom of the form you write in red "We are only placing this order on the basis that we will receive the goods by 4 April." The order form says "Allow 28 days for delivery." The date is 15 March. Is this a valid acceptance of the offer for sale made by the stationery company in its catalogue?

15.6 You telephone for a mail order catalogue on 15 March, complete the order form on 16 March and post the order form on 17 March. It is received by the mail order company on 19 March. On what date is the contract formed?

15.7 You buy a word processor from Zenith Office Supplies. Unfortunately the machine will not work – it appears to be damaged. You take it back to Zenith. The salesman says "Sorry - nothing we can do – you will have to get in touch with the manufacturer!" Is he right? What is the legal position?

15.8 You buy an office chair from Summit Office Furniture. It is advertised as having an adjustable back. When you get it back to your office, you find it does not. You telephone the supplier to complain and are told "Sorry we can't change it – you saw what it was like when you picked it up." Is the supplier right?

15.9 The Data Protection Act only covers personal data held on computer file. True or false?

15.10 State the eight principles set out in the Data Protection Act which ensure that personal data is handled properly.

15.11 Financial records should be retained by a business for

A a minimum of six months

B a minimum of twelve months

C a minimum of six years

D a maximum of six years

Answer A, B, C, or D.

BALANCING ACCOUNTS
AND THE TRIAL BALANCE

this chapter covers . . .

With the 'traditional' form of account (the 'T' account), it is necessary to calculate the balance of each account from time-to-time, according to the needs of the business, and at the end of each financial year. The balance of an account is the running total of that account to date, eg the amount of wages paid, the amount of sales made, the amount of money in the bank. In this chapter we shall see how this balancing of accounts is carried out.

We shall then use the balances from each account in order to check the double-entry book-keeping by extracting a trial balance, which is a list of the balances of ledger accounts.

In the chapter we also look at the importance of comparing cash book transactions with those recorded on the bank statement.

NVQ PERFORMANCE CRITERIA COVERED

unit 3: PREPARING LEDGER BALANCES AND AN INITIAL TRIAL BALANCE

element 1

balance bank transactions

- *details from the relevant primary documentation are recorded in the cash book*

- *totals and balances of receipts and payments are correctly calculated*

- *individual items on the bank statement and in the cash book are compared for accuracy*

- *discrepancies are identified and referred to the appropriate person*

element 3

draft an initial trial balance

- *information required for the initial trial balance is identified and obtained from the relevant sources*

- *relevant people are asked for advice when necessary information is not available*

- *the draft initial trial balance is prepared in line with the organisation's policies and procedures*

- *discrepancies are identified in the balancing and referred to the appropriate person*

BALANCING THE ACCOUNTS

At regular intervals, often at the end of each month, accounts are balanced in order to show the amounts, for example:

- owing to each creditor
- owing by each debtor
- of sales
- of purchases
- of sales returns (returns in)
- of purchases returns (returns out)
- of expenses incurred by the business
- of fixed assets, eg premises, machinery, etc owned by the business
- of capital and drawings of the owner of the business
- of other liabilities, eg loans

When accounts are produced using a computer accounting system, there is no need to balance each account – the balance is calculated automatically after each transaction. Such 'running balance accounts' are discussed on page 348.

METHOD OF BALANCING ACCOUNTS

Set out below is an example of a debtor's account which has been balanced at the month-end:

Dr			**Johnson and Company**			Cr
2001		£	2001			£
1 Sep	Balance b/d	250	10 Sep	Bank		240
4 Sep	Sales	520	10 Sep	Discount allowed		10
19 Sep	Sales	180	17 Sep	Sales returns		70
			30 Sep	Balance c/d		630
		950				950
1 Oct	Balance b/d	630				

The steps involved in balancing accounts are set out on the next page.

Step 1

The entries in the debit and credit money columns are totalled; these totals are not recorded in ink on the account at this stage, but can be recorded either as sub-totals in pencil on the account, or noted on a separate piece of paper. In the example above, the debit side totals £950, while the credit side is £320.

Step 2

The difference between the two totals is the balance of the account and this is entered on the account:

- on the side of the smaller total
- on the next available line
- with the date of balancing (often the last day of the month)
- with the description 'balance c/d', or 'balance carried down'

In the account of Johnson and Company above, the balance carried down is £950 – £320 = £630, entered in the credit column.

Step 3

Both sides of the account are now totalled, including the balance which has just been entered, and the totals (the same on both sides) are entered on the same line in the appropriate column, and bold-underlined or double-underlined. The underline indicates that the account has been balanced at this point using the figures above the total: the figures above the underline should not be added in to anything below the underline.

In the debtor's account on the previous page the totals on each side of the account are £950.

Step 4

As we are using double-entry book-keeping, there must be an opposite entry to the 'balance c/d' calculated in Step 2. The same money amount is entered on the other side of the account below the underlined totals entered in Step 3. We have now completed both the debit and credit entry. The date is usually recorded as the next day after 'balance c/d', ie often the first day of the following month, and the description can be 'balance b/d' or 'balance brought down'.

In the example above, the balance brought down on the bank account on 1 October 2001 is £630 debit; this means that, according to the accounting records, Johnson and Company owes £630, ie is a debtor of the business. (You will note that the first item on the debit side of the account is '1 Sep Balance b/d £250': this shows that the account was balanced in August, with the balance brought down to September.)

a practical point:

When balancing accounts, use a pen and not a pencil (except for Step 1). If any errors are made, cross them through neatly with a single line, and write the corrected version on the line below. Do not use correcting fluid: at best it conceals errors, at worst it conceals fraudulent transactions.

FURTHER EXAMPLES OF BALANCING ACCOUNTS

Dr			**Wages Account**		Cr
2001		£	2001		£
1 Apr	Balance b/d	4,500	30 Apr	Balance c/d	6,750
9 Apr	Bank	750			
16 Apr	Bank	800			
23 Apr	Bank	700			
		6,750			6,750
1 May	Balance b/d	6,750			

The above wages account has transactions on one side only, but is still balanced in the same way. This account shows that the total amount paid for wages in the financial year-to-date is £6,750.

Dr			**B Lewis Limited**		Cr
2001		£	2001		£
10 Apr	Purchases returns	30	1 Apr	Balance b/d	200
25 Apr	Bank	450	7 Apr	Purchases	280
		480			480

This account in the name of a creditor has a 'nil' balance after the transactions for April have taken place. The two sides of the account are totalled and, as both debit and credit side are the same amount, there is nothing further to do, apart from entering the bold- or double-underlined total.

Dr			**Office Equipment account**		Cr
2001		£	2001		£
14 Apr	Bank	2,000			

This account has just the one transaction and, in practice, there is no need to balance it. It should be clear that the account has a debit balance of £2,000, which is represented by the asset of office equipment.

Dr		Malvern Manufacturing Company		Cr
2001	£	2001		£
29 Apr Bank	250	18 Apr Purchases		250

This creditor's account has a 'nil' balance, with just one transaction on each side. All that is needed here is to bold- or double-underline the amount on both sides.

RECONCILIATION OF CREDITORS' STATEMENTS

Once creditors' accounts in the purchases ledger have been balanced, a task for the accounts department is to compare the balance with that shown on statements of account received from creditors. If the two – ie the balance of the account in the purchases ledger and balance shown on the statement of account – do not agree, it will be necessary to reconcile them. Such reconciliation can be summarised as follows:

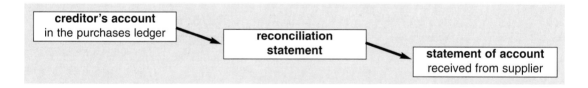

Assuming that there are no errors either in the creditor's account or on the statement of account, the discrepancies are caused by:

- items in transit, which have been invoiced by the supplier, but the invoice is not yet recorded by the buyer

- payments in the post or banking system, recorded by the buyer, but not yet received and recorded on the supplier's statement

- purchases returns, for which a credit note has been issued by the supplier, but is not yet recorded by the buyer

These three discrepancies are all caused by timing differences, ie the business document – invoice, payment, credit note – has not yet been recorded in the accounts of both buyer and seller. The reconciliation statement must take note of these.

CASE STUDY

RECONCILIATION OF A CREDITOR'S STATEMENT

situation

The following creditor's account appears in the purchases ledger of A Jarvis:

Dr		£			Cr £
2001			2001		
10 Jan	Bank	200	1 Jan	Balance b/d	200
30 Jan	Bank	150	13 Jan	Purchases	150
31 Jan	Balance c/d	125	24 Jan	Purchases	125
		475			475
			1 Feb	Balance b/d	125

T Smith

Note: The credit balance of £125 on T Smith's account, in the books of A Jarvis at 1February, indicates that Jarvis owes Smith £125.

The following statement of account is received from T Smith on 2 February:

Statement of Account: A Jarvis					
		Dr	Cr	Balance	
2001		£	£	£	
1 Jan	Balance b/d	200		200	Dr
9 Jan	Invoice no 374	150		350	Dr
14 Jan	Payment received		200	150	Dr
20 Jan	Invoice no 382	125		275	Dr
29 Jan	Invoice no 413	100		375	Dr
31 Jan	Credit note CN24		25	350	Dr

Note: The debit balance of £350 on the statement from T Smith indicates that, in Smith's books, A Jarvis owes £350.

How will the creditor's account balance be reconciled with that of the statement received by A Jarvis?

solution

Reconciliation of T Smith's statement of account as at 31 January 2001	
	£
Balance of account at 31 January 2001	125
Add: payment sent on 30 January, not yet appearing on statement	150
	275
Add: invoice no 413 sent by T Smith on 29 January, not yet received	100
	375
Less: credit note CN24 sent by T Smith on 31 January, not yet received	25
Balance of statement at 31 January 2001	350

As each of these items are timing differences, they will correct themselves within a few days as they are entered into the accounts of buyer and seller.

BALANCING THE CASH BOOK

The cash book is the ledger for cash and bank transactions and, like other accounts, needs to be balanced at regular intervals. As we have seen in earlier chapters, the debit (receipts) and credit (payments) sides of the cash book include columns for cash and bank transactions; other columns, such as discount allowed, discount received and Value Added Tax may also be incorporated.

The following are the receipts and payments pages from a sample cash book (which we have seen earlier in Chapters 6 and 11 respectively):

Debit		Cash Book: Receipts				CBR 24
Date	Details	Folio	Discount allowed	Cash	Bank	
			£	£	£	
2 Apr	Balances brought down			300	1,550	
2 Apr	Cash sales	GL 4001/ 2200		235		
3 Apr	S Wright	SL 295	2		98	
3 Apr	Peter Singh Limited (BGC)	SL 147			205	
4 Apr	J Jones	SL 86	4		76	
4 Apr	Cash sales	GL 4001/ 2200			94	
5 Apr	Bank	C		200		
6 Apr	D Whiteman Limited	SL 278	3		45	
6 Apr	Natasha Lloyd and Co (SO)	SL 121			110	
			9	735	2,178	

Credit			Cash Book: Payments			CBP 24
Date	Details		Folio	Discount received	Cash	Bank
2001				£	£	£
2 Apr	E Lee & Co	101261	PL 804			160
3 Apr	Hayes Limited	SO	PL 752			200
3 Apr	S Crane	101262	PL 610	5		145
4 Apr	Purchases		GL 5001/ 2200		94	
5 Apr	Cash	101263	C			200
5 Apr	Purchases	101264	GL 5001/ 2200			282
6 Apr	S Ford		PL 698	5		70
				10	94	1,057

In handwritten book-keeping systems the debit (receipts) side forms the left-hand page of cash book, while the credit (payments) side is detailed on the right-hand page. Thus the examples we have just seen can be put side-by-side and balanced after the weeks transactions as follows:

Dr							Cash Book					Cr
Date	Details	Folio	Discount allowed	Cash	Bank	Date	Details	Folio	Discount received	Cash	Bank	
2001			£	£	£	2001			£	£	£	
2 Apr	Balances b/d			300	1,550	2 Apr	E Lee & Co				160	
2 Apr	Cash sales			235		3 Apr	Hayes Ltd (SO)				200	
3 Apr	S Wright		2		98	3 Apr	S Crane		5		145	
3 Apr	Peter Singh Ltd (BGC)				205	4 Apr	Purchases			94		
4 Apr	J Jones		4		76	5 Apr	Cash	C			200	
4 Apr	Cash sales				94	5 Apr	Purchases				282	
5 Apr	Bank	C		200		6 Apr	S Ford		5		70	
6 Apr	D Whiteman Ltd		3		45							
6 Apr	Natasha Lloyd and Co (SO)				110							
			9	735	2,178				10	94	1,057	
						8 Apr	Balances c/d			641	1,121	
			9	735	2,178				10	735	2,178	
9 Apr	Balances b/d			641	1,121							

Note: in the above 'side-by-side' cash book, details from the folio columns and cheque numbers have not been shown (they are shown in the separate receipts and payments sections seen earlier).

The cash and bank columns are balanced using the sub-totals, as follows:

- for the cash columns compare the two subtotals, ie £735 and £94

- deduct the lower figure from the higher (payments from receipts) to give the balance of cash remaining (£735 – £94 = £641)

- the higher total is recorded at the bottom of both cash columns in a totals 'box' (£735)

- the balance of cash remaining (£641) is entered as a balancing item above the totals box (on the credit side), and is brought down underneath the total on the debit side as the opening balance for next week (£641)

- the two bank columns are dealt with in the same way (£2,178 – £1,057 = £1,121)

Notice that, in the cash book shown above, the cash and bank balances have been brought down on the debit side. It may happen that the balance at bank is brought down on the credit side: this occurs when payments exceed receipts, and indicates a bank overdraft. It is very important to appreciate that the bank columns of the cash book represent the firm's own records of bank transactions and the balance at bank – the bank statement may well show different figures (see the next page).

At the end of the month, each discount column is totalled separately – no attempt should be made to balance them. At this point, amounts recorded in the columns and the totals are not part of the double-entry system. However, the two totals are transferred to the double-entry system as follows:

- the total on the debit side (£9 in the example above) is debited to discount allowed account in the general ledger (see Chapter 6, page 128)

- the total on the credit side (£10 in the example) is credited to discount received account, also in the general ledger (see Chapter 11, page 242)

The opposite book-keeping entries will have been entered already in the debtors' and creditors' accounts respectively – see Chapters 6 and 11.

CHECKING THE CASH BOOK

As the cash book forms such an integral part of a firm's book-keeping system, it is essential that balances are calculated correctly at regular intervals, eg weekly or monthly – depending on the needs of the business. How can the cash book be checked for accuracy?

cash columns

To check the cash columns is easy. It is simply a matter of counting the cash in the cash till or box, and agreeing it with the balance shown by the cash book. In the example above there should be £641 in the firm's cash till at 8 April 2001. If the cash cannot be agreed in this way, the difference needs to be investigated urgently and any discrepancy referred to the accounts supervisor or other appropriate person.

bank columns

How are these to be checked? We could, perhaps, enquire at the bank and ask for the balance at the month-end, or we could arrange for a bank statement to be sent to us at the end of each month. However, the balance of the account at the bank may well not agree with that shown by the bank columns of the cash book.

The reasons why the cash book and bank statement may differ are because:

- there are timing differences caused by
  - unpresented cheques, ie the time delay between writing out (drawing) a cheque and recording it in the cash book, and the cheque being entered on the bank statement
  - outstanding lodgements, ie amounts paid into the bank, but not yet recorded on the bank statement
- the cash book has not been updated with items which appear on the bank statement and which should also appear in the cash book, eg bank charges

RECEIVING THE BANK STATEMENT

When the bank statement is received it must be compared with the cash book in order to identify any differences. These are:

- timing differences
- updating items for the cash book

timing differences

The two main timing differences between the bank columns of the cash book and the bank statement are:

- *unpresented cheques*, ie cheques drawn, not yet recorded on the bank statement
- *outstanding lodgements*, ie amounts paid into the bank, not yet recorded on the bank statement

The first of these – unpresented cheques – is caused because, when a cheque is written out, it is immediately entered on the payments side of the cash book, even though it may be some days before the cheque passes through the bank clearing system and is recorded on the bank statement. Therefore, for a few days at least, the cash book shows a lower balance than the bank statement in respect of this cheque. When the cheque is recorded on the bank statement, the difference will disappear. We have looked at only one cheque here, but a business will often be issuing many cheques each day, and the difference between the cash book balance and the bank statement balance may be considerable.

With the second timing difference – outstanding lodgements – the firm's cashier will record a receipt in the cash book as he or she prepares the bank paying-in slip. However, the receipt may not be recorded by the bank on the bank statement for a day or so, particularly if it is paid in late in the day (when the bank will put it into the next day's work), or if it is paid in at a bank branch other than the one at which the account is maintained. Until the receipt is recorded by the bank the cash book will show a higher bank account balance than the bank statement. Once the receipt is entered on the bank statement, the difference will disappear.

For these two timing differences the cash book must *not be altered* because, as we have seen, they will correct themselves on the bank statement as time goes by.

updating the cash book

Besides the timing differences described above, there may be other differences between the bank columns of the cash book and the bank statement, and *these do need to be entered* in the cash book to bring it up-to-date. For example, the bank might make an automatic standing order payment on behalf of a business – such an item is correctly debited by the bank, and it might be that the bank statement acts as a reminder to the business cashier of the payment: it should then be entered in the cash book.

Examples of items that show in the bank statement and need to be entered in the cash book include:

receipts
- standing order and BACS (Bankers' Automated Clearing Services) receipts credited by the bank, eg payments from debtors (customers)
- bank giro credit (credit transfer) amounts received by the bank, eg payments from debtors (customers)
- dividend amounts received by the bank
- interest credited by the bank

payments

- standing order and direct debit payments

- bank charges and interest

- unpaid cheques debited by the bank (ie cheques from debtors paid in by the business which have 'bounced' and are returned by the bank marked 'refer to drawer')

For each of these items, the cashier needs to check to see if they have been entered in the cash book; if not, they need to be recorded (provided that the bank has not made an error). If the bank has made an error, it must be notified as soon as possible and the incorrect transactions reversed by the bank in its own accounting records.

CASE STUDY

CHECKING THE BANK STATEMENT

situation

The cashier of Severn Trading Company has written up the firm's cash book for the month of February 2001, as follows (the cheque number is shown against payments):

Cash Book

Dr								Cr
Date	Details	Cash	Bank	Date	Details		Cash	Bank
2001		£	£	2001			£	£
1 Feb	Balances b/d	250.75	1,340.50	3 Feb	Appleton Ltd 123456			675.25
7 Feb	A Abbott		208.50	5 Feb	Wages		58.60	
10 Feb	Sales	145.25		12 Feb	Rent 123457			125.00
13 Feb	Sales	278.30		14 Feb	Transfer to bank C		500.00	
14 Feb	Transfer from cash C		500.00	17 Feb	D Smith & Co 123458			421.80
20 Feb	Sales	204.35		24 Feb	Stationery		75.50	
21 Feb	D Richards Ltd		162.30	25 Feb	G Christie 123459			797.55
26 Feb	Sales	353.95		27 Feb	Transfer to bank C		500.00	
27 Feb	Transfer from cash C		500.00		Balances c/d		98.50	954.00
28 Feb	P Paul Ltd		262.30					
		1,232.60	2,973.60				1,232.60	2,973.60
	Balances b/d	98.50	954.00					

The cash balance of £98.50 shown by the cash columns at the month-end has been agreed with the cash held in the firm's cash box. The bank statement for February 2001 has just been received:

National Bank plc

Branch ..Bartown................

TITLE OF ACCOUNT ..Severn Trading Company.......................................

ACCOUNT NUMBER ..67812318..

STATEMENT NUMBER 45

DATE	PARTICULARS	PAYMENTS	RECEIPTS	BALANCE
2001		£	£	£
1 Feb	Balance brought forward			1340.50 CR
8 Feb	Credit		208.50	1549.00 CR
10 Feb	Cheque no. 123456	675.25		873.75 CR
17 Feb	Credit		500.00	1373.75 CR
17 Feb	Cheque no. 123457	125.00		1248.75 CR
24 Reb	Credit		162.30	1411.05 CR
24 Feb	BACS credit: J Jarvis Ltd		100.00	1511.05 CR
26 Feb	Cheque no. 123458	421.80		1089.25 CR
26 Feb	Direct debit: A-Z Finance	150.00		939.25 CR
28 Feb	Credit		500.00	1439.25 CR
28 Feb	Bank charges	10.00		1429.25 CR

solution

Note that the bank statement is prepared from the bank's viewpoint: thus a credit balance shows that the customer is a creditor of the bank, ie the bank owes the balance to the customer. In the customer's own cash book, the bank is shown as a debit balance, ie an asset.

As the month-end balance at bank shown by the cash book, £954.00, is not the same as that shown by the bank statement, £1,429.25, it is necessary to compare individual items in the cash book and on the bank statement for accuracy. The steps are:

1. Tick off the items that appear in both cash book and bank statement.
2. The unticked items on the bank statement are entered into the bank columns of the cash book to bring it up-to-date. These are:
    *   receipt   24 Feb   BACS credit, J Jarvis Limited £100.00
    *   payments   26 Feb   Direct debit, A-Z Finance £150.00
                            28 Feb   Bank Charges, £10.00

    In double-entry book-keeping, the other part of the transaction will need to be recorded in the accounts, eg in J Jarvis Ltd's account in the sales ledger, etc.

3. The cash book is now balanced to find the revised balance:

Dr			Cash Book (bank columns)		Cr
2001		£	2001		
	Balance b/d	954.00	26 Feb	A-Z Finance	150.00
24 Feb	J Jarvis Ltd	100.00	28 Feb	Bank Charges	10.00
			28 Feb	Balance c/d	894.00
		1,054.00			1,054.00
1 Mar	Balance b/d	894.00			

4. The remaining unticked items from the cash book are:

    - receipt 28 Feb – P Paul Limited £262.30

    - payment 24 Feb – G Christie (cheque no 123459) £797.55

    These items are timing differences, which should appear on next month's bank statement. For the time being, they should be noted; if they do not appear on the next month's statement they should be referred to the accounts supervisor for guidance.

dealing with unusual items on bank statements

The following are some of the unusual features that may occur on bank statements. As with other accounting discrepancies and queries, where they cannot be resolved they should be referred to a supervisor for guidance.

out-of-date cheques

These are cheques that are more than six months old. The bank will not pay such cheques, so they can be written back in the cash book, ie debit cash book (and credit the other double-entry account involved).

returned cheques

A cheque received by a business is entered as a receipt in the cash book and then paid into the bank, but it *may be returned* by the drawer's (issuer's) bank to the payee's bank because:

- the drawer (the issuer) has stopped it

- the drawer has no money (the cheque may be returned 'refer to drawer') – ie the cheque has 'bounced'

A cheque returned in this way should be entered in the book-keeping system:

- as a payment in the cash book on the *credit* side

- as a *debit* to the account of the drawer of the cheque in the sales ledger (if it is a credit sale), or sales account if it is a cash sale

On the other hand, if the business itself stops a cheque, the cheque drawn by the business will have been entered as a payment in the cash book (a *credit*). It should now be entered as

- a receipt on the *debit* side

- a *credit to* the account of the payee, most probably in the purchases ledger (if it is a credit purchase)

bank errors

Errors made by the bank can include:

- A cheque debited to the bank account which has not been drawn by the business – look for a cheque number on the bank statement that is different from the current cheque series: care, though, as it could be a cheque from an old cheque book.

- A BACS payment (or other credit) shown on the bank statement for which the business is not the correct recipient. If in doubt, the bank will be able to give further details of the sender of the credit.

- Standing orders and direct debits paid at the wrong time or for the wrong amounts. A copy of all standing order and direct debit mandates sent to the bank should be kept by the business for reference purposes.

When an error is found, it should be queried immediately with the bank. The item and amount should not be entered in the firm's cash book until the issue has been resolved.

bank charges and interest

From time-to-time the bank will debit business customers' accounts with an amount for:

- service charges, ie the cost of operating the bank account
- interest, ie the borrowing cost when the business is overdrawn

Banks usually notify customers in writing before debiting the account.

importance of bank statements

1. It is important to compare the transactions in the bank columns of the cash book with those recorded on the bank statement. In this way, any errors in the cash book or bank statement will be found and can be corrected (or advised to the bank, if the bank statement is wrong).

2. The bank statement is an independent accounting record, therefore it will assist in deterring fraud by providing a means of verifying the cash book balance.

3. By writing the cash book up-to-date, the organisation has an amended figure for the bank balance to be shown in the trial balance (see later in this chapter).

4. Unpresented cheques over six months old – out-of-date cheques – can be identified and written back in the cash book (any cheque dated more than six months' ago will not be paid by the bank).

5. It is good business practice to compare cash book with the bank statement each time a bank statement is received. This should be done as quickly as possible so that any queries – either with the bank statement or in the firm's cash book – can be resolved. Many firms will specify to their accounting staff the timescales for such comparisons – as a guideline, if the bank statement is received weekly, then the comparison should be made within five working days.

BALANCING PETTY CASH BOOK

A petty cash book is balanced by comparing the 'receipts' and the 'total payments' columns – just like other double-entry accounts. Where a petty cash book is operated on the imprest system, a further receipt will be the amount of cash received from the main cashier to restore the imprest amount – this is equal to the total paid out during the week.

The following shows how the petty cash book already seen in Chapter 12 (page 266) is balanced at the end of the week:

		Petty Cash Book							PCB 30	
Receipts	Date	Details	Voucher No	Total Payment		Analysis columns				
					VAT	Postages	Stationery	Travel	Ledger	
£	2001			£	£	£	£	£	£	
50.00	7 Apr	Balance b/d								
	7 Apr	Stationery	47	3.76	0.56		3.20			
	7 Apr	Taxi fare	48	2.82	0.42			2.40		
	8 Apr	Postages	49	0.75		0.75				
	9 Apr	Taxi fare	50	4.70	0.70			4.00		
	9 Apr	J Jones	51	6.00					6.00	
	10 Apr	Stationery	52	3.76	0.56		3.20			
	10 Apr	Postages	53	2.85		2.85				
	11 Apr	Taxi fare	54	6.11	0.91			5.20		
				30.75	3.15	3.60	6.40	11.60	6.00	
30.75	11 Apr	Cash received								
	11 Apr	Balance c/d		50.00						
80.75				80.75						
50.00	11 Apr	Balance b/d								

Note that, here, the imprest amount has been restored at the end of the week and before the petty cash book has been balanced. An alternative method, depending on the policy of the company, is to balance the petty cash book *before* restoring the imprest amount – in the above example, this will give a balance brought down on 11 April of £19.25 (ie £50.00 minus £30.75); the money received from the cashier (£30.75) will then be recorded in the receipts column.

Where a petty cash is not operated on the imprest system, it is balanced at regular intervals by comparing the receipts and total payments columns. Whenever cash is received from the cashier, it is recorded in the receipts column.

As we have already seen in Chapter 12, the petty cashier prepares a posting sheet giving details of the total of each analysis column so that the amounts can then be recorded in the double-entry system by the book-keeper.

RUNNING BALANCE ACCOUNTS

The layout of accounts that we have used has a debit side and a credit side. Whilst this layout is very useful when learning the principles of book-keeping, it is not always appropriate for practical business use. Most 'real-life' accounts have three money columns: debit transactions, credit transactions, and balance. A familiar example of this type of account is a bank statement. With a three-column account, the balance is calculated after each transaction has been entered – hence the name running balance accounts. For handwritten accounts, it can be rather tedious to calculate the balance after each transaction (and a potential source of errors) but, using computer accounting, the calculation is carried out automatically.

The debtor's account of Johnson and Company, used earlier in this chapter, is set out below in 'traditional' format:

Dr			**Johnson and Company**		Cr
2001		£	2001		£
1 Sep	Balance b/d	250	10 Sep	Bank	240
4 Sep	Sales	520	10 Sep	Discount allowed	10
19 Sep	Sales	180	17 Sep	Sales returns	70
			30 Sep	Balance c/d	630
		950			950
1 Oct	Balance b/d	630			

The account does not show the balance after each transaction and, so, has to be balanced at the month-end.

In 'running balance' layout, the account appears as follows:

Johnson and Company		Debit	Credit	Balance
2001		£	£	£
1 Sep	Balance b/d	250		250 Dr
4 Sep	Sales	520		770 Dr
10 Sep	Bank		240	530 Dr
10 Sep	Discount allowed		10	520 Dr
17 Sep	Sales returns		70	450 Dr
19 Sep	Sales	180		630 Dr

With a running balance account, it is necessary to state after each transaction whether the balance is debit (Dr) or credit (Cr). Note that the above account in the books of this business has a debit balance, ie Johnson and Company owes £630 – an asset of the business.

EXTRACTING A TRIAL BALANCE

The book-keeper extracts a trial balance from the accounting records in order to check the arithmetical accuracy of the double-entry book-keeping, ie that the debit entries equal the credit entries.

A trial balance is a list of the balances of every account forming the ledger, distinguishing between those accounts which have debit balances and those which have credit balances.

A trial balance is extracted at regular intervals – often at the end of each month. Now study the example below.

Trial balance of A-Z Suppliers as at 31 January 2001

	Dr	Cr
	£	£
Name of account		
Purchases	7,500	
Sales		16,000
Sales returns	250	
Purchases returns		500
J Brown (debtor)	1,550	
T Sweet (creditor)		900

continued on next page

Rent paid	1,000	
Wages	1,500	
Heating and lighting	1,250	
Office equipment	5,000	
Machinery	7,500	
Stock at 1 Jan 2001	2.500	
Cash	500	
Bank	4,550	
Value Added Tax		1,200
J Williams: loan		7,000
Capital		10,000
Drawings	2,500	
	35,600	35,600

Notes:

- The debit and credit columns have been totalled and are the same amount. Thus the trial balance proves that the accounting records are arithmetically correct. (A trial balance does not prove the complete accuracy of the accounting records – see page 352.)

- The balance for each account listed in the trial balance is the figure brought down after the accounts have been balanced.

- As well as the name of each account, it is quite usual to show in the trial balance the account number. Most accounting systems give numbers to accounts and these can be listed in a separate 'folio' or 'reference' column.

DEBIT AND CREDIT BALANCES – GUIDELINES

Certain accounts always have a debit balance, while others always have a credit balance. You should already know these, but the lists set out below will act as a revision guide, and will also help in your understanding of trial balances.

Debit balances include:

- cash account
- purchases account
- sales returns account (returns in)
- fixed asset accounts, eg premises, motor vehicles, machinery, office equipment, etc
- stock account – the stock valuation at the beginning of the year
- expenses accounts, eg wages, telephone, rent paid, etc

- drawings account
- debtors' accounts (many businesses use a sales ledger control account – see Chapter 17 – the balance of which gives the total of debtors: this balance is entered in the trial balance as 'debtors')

Credit balances include:

- sales account
- purchases returns account (returns out)
- income accounts, eg rent received, commission received, fees received
- capital account
- loan account
- creditors' accounts (many businesses use a purchases ledger control account – see Chapter 17 – the balance of which gives the total of creditors: this balance is entered in the trial balance as 'creditors')

Notes:

- Bank account can be either debit or credit – it will be debit when the business has money in the bank, and credit when it is overdrawn.
- Value Added Tax account can be either debit or credit – it will be debit when VAT is due to the business and credit when the business owes VAT to HM Customs & Excise.

IF THE TRIAL BALANCE DOESN'T BALANCE . . .

If the trial balance fails to balance, ie the two totals are different, there is an error (or errors):

- *either* in the addition of the trial balance
- *and/or* in the double-entry book-keeping

The accounts supervisor needs to be informed if the trial balance does not balance; he or she will give guidance as to what is to be done.

The procedure for finding the error(s) is as follows:

- check the addition of the trial balance
- check that the balance of each account has been correctly entered in the trial balance, and under the correct heading, ie debit or credit
- check that the balance of every account in the ledger has been included in the trial balance
- check the calculation of the balance on each account
- calculate the amount that the trial balance is wrong, and then look in the accounts for a transaction for this amount: if one is found, check that the double-entry book-keeping has been carried out correctly

- halve the amount by which the trial balance is wrong, and look for a transaction for this amount: if it is found, check the double-entry book-keeping
- if the amount by which the trial balance is wrong is divisible by nine, then the error may be a reversal of figures, eg £65 entered as £56, or £45 entered as £54
- if the trial balance is wrong by a round amount, eg £10, £100, £1,000, the error is likely to be in the calculation of the account balances
- if the error(s) is still not found, it is necessary to check the book-keeping transactions since the date of the last trial balance, by going back to the prime documents and primary accounting records

ERRORS NOT SHOWN BY A TRIAL BALANCE

As mentioned earlier, a trial balance does not prove the complete accuracy of the accounting records. There are six types of errors that are not shown by a trial balance.

1. Error of omission

Here a business transaction has been completely omitted from the accounting records, ie both the debit and credit entries have not been made.

2. Reversal of entries

With this error, the debit and credit entries have been made in the accounts but on the wrong side of the two accounts concerned. For example, a cash sale has been entered wrongly as debit sales account, credit cash account. (This should have been entered as a debit to cash account, and a credit to sales account.)

3. Mispost/error of commission

Here, a transaction is entered to the wrong person's account. For example, a sale of goods on credit to A T Hughes has been entered as debit to A J Hughes' account, credit sales account. Double-entry book-keeping has been completed, but when A J Hughes receives a statement of account, he or she will soon complain about being debited with goods not ordered or received.

4. Error of principle

This is when a transaction has been entered in the wrong type of account. For example, the cost of petrol for vehicles has been entered as debit motor vehicles account, credit bank account. The error is that motor vehicles account represents fixed assets, and the transaction should have been debited to the expense account for motor vehicle running expenses.

5. Error of original entry (or transcription)

Here, the correct accounts have been used, and the correct sides: what is wrong is that the amount has been entered incorrectly in both accounts. This could be caused by a 'bad figure' on an invoice or a cheque, or it could be caused by a 'reversal of figures', eg an amount of £45 being entered in both accounts as £54. Note that both debit and credit entries need to be made incorrectly for the trial balance still to balance; if one entry has been made incorrectly and the other is correct, then the error will be shown.

6. Compensating error

This is where two errors cancel each other out. For example, if the balance of purchases account is calculated wrongly at £10 too much, and a similar error has occurred in calculating the balance of sales account, then the two errors will compensate each other, and the trial balance will not show the errors.

Correction of errors is covered fully in Chapter 18.

IMPORTANCE OF THE TRIAL BALANCE

A business will extract a trial balance on a regular basis to check the arithmetic accuracy of the book-keeping. However, the trial balance is also used as the starting point in the production of the financial statements (or final accounts) of a business. These are produced once a year (often more frequently) and comprise:

- profit and loss statement

- balance sheet

The final accounts show the owner(s) how profitable the business has been, what the business owns, and how the business is financed. The preparation of final accounts is an important aspect of accountancy. Final accounts are covered in later NVQ levels. For the moment, we can say that extraction of a trial balance is an important exercise in the business accounts process: it proves the book-keeper's accuracy, and also lists the account balances which form the basis for the final accounts of a business.

CHAPTER SUMMARY

- The traditional 'T' account needs to be balanced at regular intervals – often at the month-end.

- Statements of account received from creditors may need to be reconciled with the balance of creditor accounts; discrepancies are caused by:
  - items in transit
  - payments in the post or banking system
  - purchases returns

- The transactions on a bank statement must be compared with those shown by the bank columns of the cash book.

- When each account in the ledger has been balanced, a trial balance can be extracted.

- A trial balance does not prove the complete accuracy of the accounting records; errors not shown by a trial balance are:
  - error of omission
  - reversal of entries
  - mispost/error of commission
  - error of principle
  - error of original entry
  - compensating error

- The trial balance is used as the starting point for the preparation of a business' financial statements (or final accounts).

KEY TERMS

balance of account	the total of the account to date
timing differences	discrepancies between the bank statement and the cash book that will be corrected over time, such as unpresented cheques and outstanding lodgements
unpresented cheques	cheques drawn, but not yet recorded on the bank statement
outstanding lodgements	amounts paid into the bank, but not yet recorded on the bank statement
running balance accounts	accounts which show the balance after each transaction has been entered; consist of money three columns: debit, credit and balance
trial balance	list of the balances of every account forming the ledger, distinguishing between those accounts which have debit balances and those which have credit balances
error of omission	business transaction completely omitted from the accounting records

reversal of entries	debit and credit entries made on the wrong side of the accounts
mispost/error of commission	transaction entered to the wrong person's account
error of principle	transaction entered in the wrong type of account
error of original entry	wrong amount entered incorrectly in accounts
compensating error	where two errors cancel each other

STUDENT ACTIVITIES

16.1   Which one of the following accounts always has a debit balance?

(a)   capital account

(b)   purchases account

(c)   sales account

(d)   purchases returns account

Answer (a) or (b) or (c) or (d)

16.2   Which one of the following accounts always has a credit balance?

(a)   sales returns account

(b)   premises account

(c)   capital account

(d)   wages account

Answer (a) or (b) or (c) or (d)

16.3   An amount has been entered into the book-keeping system as £65 instead of £56. The error is called:

(a)   compensating error

(b)   mispost

(c)   error of principle

(d)   error of original entry

Answer (a) or (b) or (c) or (d)

16.4 Balance the following accounts at 30 April 2001:

Dr		Sales Account		Cr
2001		£	2001	£
			1 Apr Balance b/d	12,550
			30 Apr Sales Day Book	4,620

Dr		Wages Account		Cr
2001		£	2001	£
1 Apr Balance b/d	3,710			
11 Apr Bank	780			
25 Apr Bank	690			

Dr		Wyvern Traders		Cr
2001		£	2001	£
1 Apr Balance b/d	375		24 Apr Bank	375

Dr		T Johnson		Cr
2001		£	2001	£
15 Apr Bank	240		1 Apr Balance b/d	240
18 Apr Purchases Returns	45		10 Apr Purchases	180
			29 Apr Purchases	215

16.5 The following account appears in your firm's purchases ledger:

Dr		Apple Supplies		Cr
2001		£	2001	£
6 May Bank	780		1 May Balance b/d	800
6 May Discount	20		5 May Purchases	255
12 May Purchases returns	55		26 May Purchases	150
30 May Bank	195			
30 May Discount	5			

During the first week of June, the following statement of account was received from Apple Supplies:

		Dr	Cr	Balance
2001		£	£	£
1 May	Balance b/d			800 Dr
2 May	Invoice 678	255		1,055 Dr
9 May	Payment received		780	
9 May	Discount allowed		20	255 Dr
14 May	Credit note 413		55	200 Dr
23 May	Invoice 721	150		350 Dr

You are to:

- Balance the account of Apple Supplies in your purchases ledger at 31 May 2001

- Reconcile the balance on your purchases ledger account at 31 May 2001 with that shown on the statement

16.6 A firm's bank statement shows a balance of £400. Unpresented cheques total £350; outstanding lodgements total £200. What is the balance at bank shown by the cash book?

(a)   £100

(b)   £200

(c)   £250

(d)   £400

Answer (a) or (b) or (c) or (d)

16.7 The bank columns of Tom Reid's cash book for December 2001 are as follows:

2001	Receipts	£	2001	Payments		£
1 Dec	Balance b/d	280	9 Dec	W Smith	345123	40
12 Dec	P Jones	30	12 Dec	Rent	345124	50
18 Dec	H Homer	72	18 Dec	Wages	345125	85
29 Dec	J Hill	13	19 Dec	B Kay	345126	20
			31 Dec	Balance c/d		200
		395				395

He then received his bank statement which showed the following transactions for December 2001:

BANK STATEMENT		Payments	Receipts	Balance
2001		£	£	£
1 Dec	Balance brought forward			280 CR
12 Dec	Credit		30	310 CR
15 Dec	Cheque no 345123	40		270 CR
17 Dec	Cheque no 345124	50		220 CR
22 Dec	Credit		72	292 CR
23 Dec	Cheque no 345125	85		207 CR

You are to check the items on the bank statement against the items in the cash book and give *two* reasons why the balance in the cash book does not match the closing balance on the bank statement.

16.8 The bank columns of P Gerrard's cash book for January 2001 are as follows:

2001	Receipts	£	2001	Payments		£
1 Jan	Balance b/d	800.50	2 Jan	A Arthur Ltd	001351	100.00
6 Jan	J Baker	495.60	10 Jan	C Curtis	001352	398.50
31 Jan	G Shotton Ltd	335.75	13 Jan	Donald & Co	001353	229.70
			14 Jan	Bryant & Sons	001354	312.00
			23 Jan	P Reid	001355	176.50

He received his bank statement which showed the following transactions for January 2001:

BANK STATEMENT		Payments	Receipts	Balance
2001		£	£	£
1 Jan	Balance brought forward			800.50 CR
6 Jan	Cheque no 001351	100.00		700.50 CR
6 Jan	Credit		495.60	1,196.10 CR
13 Jan	BACS credit: T K Supplies		716.50	1,912.60 CR
20 Jan	Cheque no 001352	398.50		1,514.10 CR
23 Jan	Direct debit: Omni Finance	207.95		1,306.15 CR
24 Jan	Cheque no 001353	229.70		1,076.45 CR

You are to:

(a) check the items on the bank statement against the items in the cash book and update the cash book accordingly; total the cash book and clearly show the balance carried down

(b) give *three* reasons why the balance in the cash book does not match the closing balance on the bank statement

16.9 Andrew Jarvis started in business on 1 April 2001.

During the month he had the following transactions:

2001

1 Apr	Paid £1,000 into business bank account as opening capital
2 Apr	Bought goods for resale, paying by cheque, £255
4 Apr	Paid for advertising by cheque, £60
7 Apr	Sold goods, £195, a cheque being received
8 Apr	Paid rent by cheque, £125
10 Apr	Sold goods, £248, a cheque being received
11 Apr	Drawings £100 by cheque
14 Apr	Bought goods for resale, paying by cheque, £240
16 Apr	Received a loan from J Couchman, £1,000 by cheque
18 Apr	Sold goods, £220, a cheque being received
21 Apr	Bought shop fittings, £1,250, paying by cheque
23 Apr	Bought goods for resale, paying by cheque, £180
24 Apr	Paid for advertising by cheque, £90
25 Apr	Sold goods, £312, a cheque being received
28 Apr	Paid rent by cheque, £125
30 Apr	Drawings £125 by cheque

You are to:

(a)   Record the transactions in his cash book

(b)   Record the transactions in his other double-entry accounts

(c)   Balance all the accounts that have more than one transaction at 30 April 2001

(d)   Draw up a trial balance at 30 April 2001

Notes:

* *day books are not required*

* *Andrew Jarvis is not registered for VAT*

16.10 Produce the trial balance of Jane Greenwell as at 28 February 2001. She has omitted to open a capital account. You are to fill in the missing figure in order to balance the trial balance.

	£
Bank overdraft	1,250
Purchases	850
Cash	48
Sales	1,940
Purchases returns	144
Creditors	1,442
Equipment	2,704
Van	3,200
Stock at 1 Jan 2001	1,210
Sales returns	90
Debtors	1,174
Wages	1,500
Capital	?

16.11 The cashier of the company where you work as an accounts assistant has asked you to balance the cash book and petty cash book at 31 August.

Notes:

- the company has a bank overdraft facility of £2,500

- the petty cash book is kept on the imprest system

- cash is to be withdrawn from the main cash book on 31 August in order to return the imprest amount to £75.00

The cash book and petty cash are as follows:

Dr						Cash Book					Cr
Date	Details	Folio	Discount allowed	Cash	Bank	Date	Details	Folio	Discount received	Cash	Bank
2001			£	£	£	2001			£	£	£
1 Aug	Balances b/d			325	925	7 Aug	Crane & Co		35		845
4 Aug	S Quesne		2		98	12 Aug	Wages			275	
17 Aug	J Ahmed		4	76		14 Aug	T Lewis		15		285
20 Aug	Bank	C		100		20 Aug	Cash	C			100
23 Aug	D Lloyd		3		45	28 Aug	S Ford		5	70	

						Analysis columns			
Receipts	Date	Details	Voucher No	Total Payment	VAT	Postages	Travel	Meals	Office Sundries
£	2001			£	£	£	£	£	£
75.00	1 Aug	Balance b/d							
	4 Aug	Postages	223	7.20		7.20			
	7 Aug	Travel expenses	224	4.50			4.50		
	9 Aug	Postages	225	2.54		2.54			
	12 Aug	Envelopes	226	4.70	0.70				4.00
	14 Aug	Window cleaning	227	7.05	1.05				6.00
	17 Aug	Taxi fare	228	7.52	1.12		6.40		
	21 Aug	Postages	229	8.56		8.56			
	23 Aug	Meals	230	6.35				6.35	
	28 Aug	Envelopes	231	6.58	0.98				5.60

(Petty Cash Book)

You are to:

- restore the imprest amount of petty cash book to £75.00, making appropriate entries in both cash book and petty cash book

- balance the cash book and petty cash book at 31 August 2001 and bring down the balances on 1 September

- explain the meaning of the cash and bank balances brought down in the cash book on 1 September

17 CONTROL ACCOUNTS

this chapter covers . . .

Control accounts are 'master' accounts which record by means of totals the transactions passing through the accounts that they control. In this chapter we will look at:

- the concept of control accounts

- the layout of sales ledger (or debtors) and purchases ledger (creditors) control accounts

- the use of control accounts as an aid to the management of a business

- control accounts and book-keeping

- the use of wages and salaries control account, cash control account and stock control account

NVQ PERFORMANCE CRITERIA COVERED

unit 3: PREPARING LEDGER BALANCES AND AN INITIAL TRIAL BALANCE
element 2
prepare ledger balances and control accounts

- Relevant accounts are totalled

- Control accounts are reconciled with the totals of the balance in the subsidiary ledger, where appropriate

- Authorised adjustments are correctly processed and documented

- Discrepancies arising from the reconciliation of control accounts are either resolved or referred to the appropriate person

- Documentation is stored securely and in line with the organisation's confidentiality requirements

THE CONCEPT OF CONTROL ACCOUNTS

Control accounts are 'master' accounts which control a number of subsidiary accounts. Control accounts work in the following way:

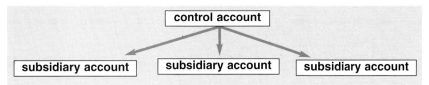

The control account (also known as a *totals account*) is used to record the totals of transactions passing through the subsidiary accounts. In this way, the balance of the control account will always be equal to the total balances of the subsidiary accounts, unless an error has occurred. Two commonly-used control accounts are:

- sales ledger control account (often referred to as the debtors control account) – the total of the debtors

- purchases ledger control account (often referred to as the creditors control account) – the total of the creditors

In the illustration above we have seen how a control account acts as a master account for a number of subsidiary accounts. The principle is that, if the total of the opening balances for subsidiary accounts is known, together with the total of amounts increasing these balances, and the total of amounts decreasing these balances, then the total of the closing balances for the subsidiary accounts can be calculated.

For example:

	£
Total of opening balances	50,000
Add increases	10,000
	60,000
Less decreases	12,000
Total of closing balances	48,000

The total of the closing balances can now be checked against a separate listing of the balances of the subsidiary accounts to ensure that the two figures agree. If they do, it proves that the ledgers within the section are correct (subject to any errors such as misposts and compensating errors). Let us now apply this concept to one of the divisions of the ledger – sales ledger.

The diagram on the next page shows the personal accounts which form the entire sales ledger of a particular business (in practice there would, of

Dr		**Sales Ledger Control Account**			Cr
2001			£	2001	£
1 Jan	Balances b/d		500	31 Jan Bank	443
31 Jan	Sales		700	31 Jan Discount allowed	7
				31 Jan Sales returns	70
				31 Jan Balances c/d	680
			1,200		1,200
1 Feb	Balances b/d		680		

Dr		**A Ackroyd**			Cr
2001			£	2001	£
1 Jan	Balance b/d		100	10 Jan Bank	98
6 Jan	Sales		150	10 Jan Discount allowed	2
				31 Jan Balance c/d	150
			250		250
1 Feb	Balance b/d		150		

Dr		**B Barnes**			Cr
2001			£	2001	£
1 Jan	Balance b/d		200	13 Jan Bank	195
6 Jan	Sales		250	13 Jan Discount allowed	5
				27 Jan Sales returns	50
				31 Jan Balance c/d	200
			450		450
1 Feb	Balance b/d		200		

Dr		**C Cox**			Cr
2001			£	2001	£
1 Jan	Balance b/d		50	20 Jan Bank	50
15 Jan	Sales		200	29 Jan Sales returns	20
				31 Jan Balance c/d	180
			250		250
1 Feb	Balance b/d		180		

Dr		**D Douglas**			Cr
2001			£	2001	£
1 Jan	Balance b/d		150	30 Jan Bank	100
20 Jan	Sales		100	31 Jan Balance c/d	150
			250		250
1 Feb	Balance b/d		150		

course, be more than four accounts involved). The sales ledger control account acts as a totals account, which records totals of the transactions passing through the individual accounts which it controls. Notice that transactions appear in the control account *on the same side* as they appear in the individual accounts. The sales ledger control account can be reconciled with the balances of the individual accounts which it controls (see below). Thus, control accounts act as an aid to locating errors: if the control account and subsidiary accounts agree, then the error is likely to lie elsewhere. In this way the control account acts as an intermediate checking device – proving the arithmetical accuracy of the ledger section.

Normally the whole of a ledger section is controlled by one control account, eg sales ledger control account or purchases ledger control account. However, it is also possible to have a number of separate control accounts for subdivisions of the sales ledger and purchases ledger, eg sales ledger control account A-K, purchases ledger control account S-Z, etc. It is for a business – the user of the accounting system – to decide what is most suitable, taking into account the number of accounts in the sales and purchases ledger, together with the type of book-keeping system – manual or computerised.

From the diagram on the previous page the sales ledger control account and subsidiary accounts will be agreed at the beginning and end of the month, as follows:

Reconciliation of sales ledger control account with debtor balances

	1 January 2001 £	31 January 2001 £
A Ackroyd	100	150
B Barnes	200	200
C Cox	50	180
D Douglas	150	150
Sales ledger control account	500	680

The business will decide how often to reconcile the control account with the subsidiary accounts – weekly, monthly, quarterly or annually. Any discrepancy should be investigated immediately and the error(s) traced.

SALES LEDGER CONTROL ACCOUNT

The set-out of a sales ledger control account (or debtors control account) is shown on the next page. Study the layout carefully and read the text which explains the additional items.

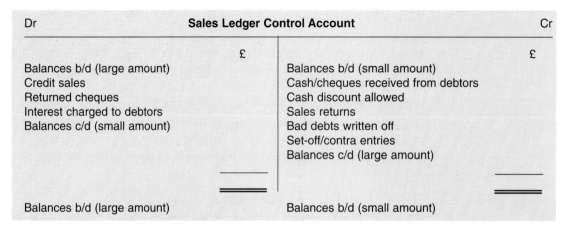

balances b/d

In the layout above there is a figure for balances b/d on both the debit side and the credit side of the control account. The usual balance on a debtor's account is debit and so this will form the large balance on the debit side. However, from time-to-time, it is possible for some debtors to have a credit balance on their accounts. This may come about, for example, because they have paid for goods, and then returned them, or because they have overpaid in error: the business owes them the amount due, ie they have a credit balance for the time being. Such credit balances are always going to be in the minority and so they will be for the smaller amount. Clearly, if there are small credit balances at the beginning of the month, there are likely to be credit balances at the month-end, and these need to be recorded separately as balances carried down – do not 'net off' the two types of balances.

credit sales

Only credit sales – and not cash sales – are entered in the control account because only credit sales are recorded in the debtors' accounts. The total sales of the business may well comprise both credit and cash sales.

returned cheques

If a debtor's cheque is returned unpaid by the bank, ie the cheque has 'bounced', then authorisation for the entries to be made in the book-keeping system must be given by the accounts supervisor. These entries are:

– *debit* debtor's account

– *credit* cash book (bank columns)

As a transaction has been made in a debtor's account, then the amount must also be recorded in the sales ledger control account – on the debit side. Note that the returned cheque is the prime document for the adjustment – like other prime documents it should be stored securely for future reference.

interest charged to debtors

Sometimes a business will charge a debtor for slow payment of an account. The accounting entries, which must be authorised by the supervisor, are:

– *debit* debtor's account

– *credit* interest received account

As a debit transaction has been made in the debtor's account, so a debit entry must be recorded in the control account. The documentation which shows how the interest has been calculated should be stored for future reference.

bad debts written off

The book-keeping entries after a bad debt has been authorised for write off (see Chapter 13) are:

– *debit* bad debts written off account

– *credit* debtor's account

A credit transaction is entered in a debtor's account. This is because the control account 'masters' the sales ledger and so the transaction must also be recorded as a credit transaction in the control account.

set-off/contra entries

See page 370.

PURCHASES LEDGER CONTROL ACCOUNT

The specimen layout for the purchases ledger control account (or creditors control account) is shown below.

The layout is explained on the next page.

Dr		**Purchases Ledger Control Account**		Cr
	£			£
Balances b/d small amount)		Balances b/d (large amount)		
Cash/cheques paid to creditors		Credit purchases		
Cash discount received		Interest charged by creditors		
Purchases returns		Balances c/d (small amount)		
Set-off/contra entries				
Balances c/d (large amount)				
	———			———
	═══			═══
Balances b/d (small amount)		Balances b/d (large amount)		

balances b/d

As with sales ledger control account, it is possible to have balances on both sides of the account. For purchases ledger, containing the accounts of creditors, the large balance b/d is always on the credit side. However, if a creditor has been overpaid, the result may be a small debit balance b/d. It may also be that there are closing balances on both sides of the account at the end of the period. In the balance sheet, any small debit balances should be included with debtors.

credit purchases

Only credit purchases – and not cash purchases – are entered in the control account. However, the total purchases of the business will comprise both credit and cash purchases.

interest charged by creditors

If a creditor charges interest because of slow payment, this must be recorded on both the creditor's account and the control account. The supervisor might well enquire of the creditor why and how the interest has been calculated.

set-off/contra entries

See page 370.

reconciliation of purchases ledger control account

The diagram on the next page shows how a purchases ledger control account acts as a totals account for the creditors of a business. Reconciliation of the balances on the purchases ledger control account and subsidiary accounts is made as follows:

Reconciliation of purchases ledger control account with creditor balances

	1 January 2001	31 January 2001
	£	£
F Francis	100	200
G Gold	200	350
H Harris	300	500
I Ingram	400	900
Purchases ledger control account	1,000	1,950

Any discrepancy should be investigated immediately and the error(s) traced.

Purchases Ledger Control Account

Dr			£	Cr			£
2001				2001			
31 Jan	Purchases returns		150	1 Jan	Balances b/d		1,000
31 Jan	Bank		594	31 Jan	Purchases		1,700
31 Jan	Discount received		6				
31 Jan	Balances c/d		1,950				
			2,700				2,700
				1 Feb	Balances b/d		1,950

F Francis

Dr		£	Cr		£
2001			2001		
17 Jan	Bank	98	1 Jan	Balance b/d	100
17 Jan	Discount received	2	3 Jan	Purchases	200
31 Jan	Balance c/d	200			
		300			300
			1 Feb	Balance b/d	200

G Gold

Dr		£	Cr		£
2001			2001		
15 Jan	Purchases returns	50	1 Jan	Balance b/d	200
28 Jan	Bank	100	9 Jan	Purchases	300
31 Jan	Balance c/d	350			
		500			500
			1 Feb	Balance b/d	350

H Harris

Dr		£	Cr		£
2001			2001		
28 Jan	Purchases returns	100	1 Jan	Balance b/d	300
30 Jan	Bank	200	17 Jan	Purchases	500
31 Jan	Balance c/d	500			
		800			800
			1 Feb	Balance b/d	500

I Ingram

Dr		£	Cr		£
2001			2001		
22 Jan	Bank	196	1 Jan	Balance b/d	400
22 Jan	Discount received	4	27 Jan	Purchases	700
31 Jan	Balance c/d	900			
		1,100			1,100
			1 Feb	Balance b/d	900

SET-OFF/CONTRA ENTRIES

These entries occur when the same person or business has an account in both sales ledger and purchases ledger, ie they are both buying from, and selling to, the business whose accounts we are preparing. For example, M Patel Limited has the following accounts in the sales and purchases ledgers:

SALES (DEBTORS) LEDGER

Dr		A Smith		Cr
		£		£
Balance b/d		200		

PURCHASES (CREDITORS) LEDGER

Dr		A Smith		Cr
		£		£
			Balance b/d	300

From these accounts we can see that:

- A Smith owes M Patel Limited £200 (sales ledger)
- M Patel Limited owes A Smith £300 (purchases ledger)

To save each having to write out a cheque to send to the other, it is possible (with A Smith's agreement) to set-off one account against the other, so that they can settle their net indebtedness with one cheque. The book-keeping entries in M Patel's books will be:

– *debit* A Smith (purchases ledger) £200

– *credit* A Smith (sales ledger) £200

The accounts will now appear as:

SALES (DEBTORS) LEDGER

Dr		A Smith		Cr
		£		£
Balance b/d		200	Set-off purchases ledger	200

PURCHASES (CREDITORS) LEDGER

Dr		A Smith		Cr
	£			£
Set-off purchases ledger	200	Balance b/d		300

The net result is that M Patel Limited owes A Smith £100. The important point to note is that, because transactions have been recorded in the personal accounts, an entry needs to be made in the two control accounts:

– *debit* purchases ledger control account

– *credit* sales ledger control account

Set-off transactions should be appropriately documented and authorised.

SOURCES OF INFORMATION FOR CONTROL ACCOUNTS

Control accounts use totals (remember that their other name is totals accounts) for the week, month, quarter or year – depending on what time period is decided upon by the business. The totals come from a number of sources in the accounting system:

sales ledger (debtors) control account
- total credit sales (including VAT) – from the 'gross' column of the sales day book
- total sales returns (including VAT) – from the 'gross' column of the sales returns day book
- total cash/cheques received from debtors – from the cash book (see Chapter 6)
- total discount allowed – from the discount allowed column of the cash book (see Chapter 6), or from discount allowed account
- bad debts – from the journal, or bad debts written off account

purchases ledger (creditors) control account
- total credit purchases (including VAT) – from the 'gross' column of the purchases day book
- total purchases returns (including VAT) – from the 'gross' column of the purchases returns day book
- total cash/cheques paid to creditors – from the cash book (see Chapter 11)
- total discount received – from the discount received column of the cash book (see Chapter 11), or from discount received account

CONTROL ACCOUNTS AS AN AID TO MANAGEMENT

When the manager of a business needs to know the figure for debtors or creditors – important information for the manager – the balance of the appropriate control account will give the information immediately: there is no need to add up the balances of all the individual debtors' or creditors' accounts. A computer accounting system can print out control accounts at any time. The use of control accounts makes fraud more difficult – particularly in a manual accounting system. If a fraudulent transaction is to be recorded on a personal account, the transaction must also be entered in the control account. As the control account will be either maintained by a supervisor, or checked regularly by the manager, the control accounts add another level of security within the accounting system.

We have already seen in this chapter how control accounts can help in locating errors. Remember, though, that a control account only proves the arithmetical accuracy of the accounts which it controls – there could still be errors, such as misposts and compensating errors, within the ledger section.

CONTROL ACCOUNTS AND BOOK-KEEPING

A business must decide how to use control accounts in its book-keeping system. The commonest way of doing this is to incorporate the control accounts into double-entry book-keeping.

The control accounts therefore form part of the double-entry system in the general (main) ledger: the balances of the sales ledger control account and the purchases ledger control account are recorded in the trial balance as the figures for debtors and creditors respectively. This means that the personal accounts of debtors and creditors are not part of double-entry, but are *subsidiary memorandum accounts* which record how much each debtor owes, and how much is owed to each creditor. From time-to-time, the balances of the memorandum accounts are agreed with the balance of the appropriate control account, and any discrepancies investigated.

The diagrams which follow show how the sales ledger control account and the purchases ledger control account are incorporated into the double-entry book-keeping system (general ledger), with the individual debtors' and creditors' accounts kept in the form of subsidiary memorandum accounts.

When sales ledger and purchases ledger control accounts are in use and journal entries are made (eg for correction of errors – see Chapter 18), transactions involving debtors' and creditors' accounts must be recorded in

- the appropriate control account
- subsidiary memorandum accounts for debtors or creditors

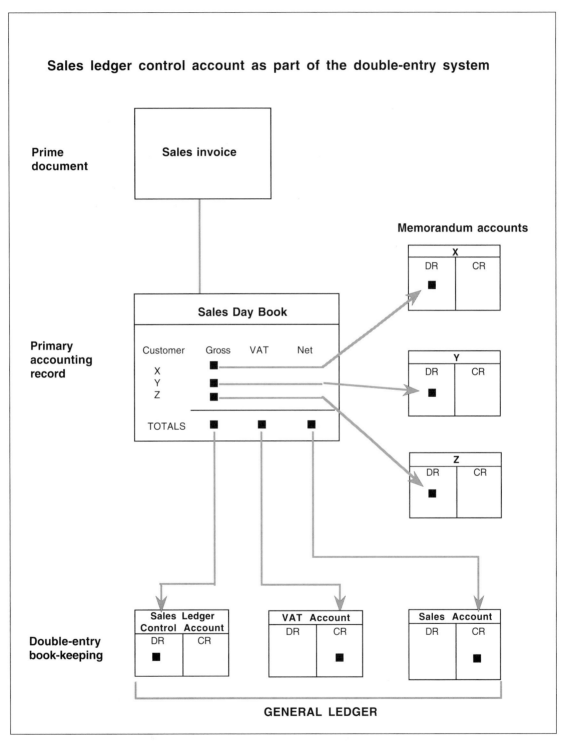

Sales ledger (debtors) control account incorporated into the double-entry book-keeping system; the debtors' accounts are subsidiary memorandum accounts

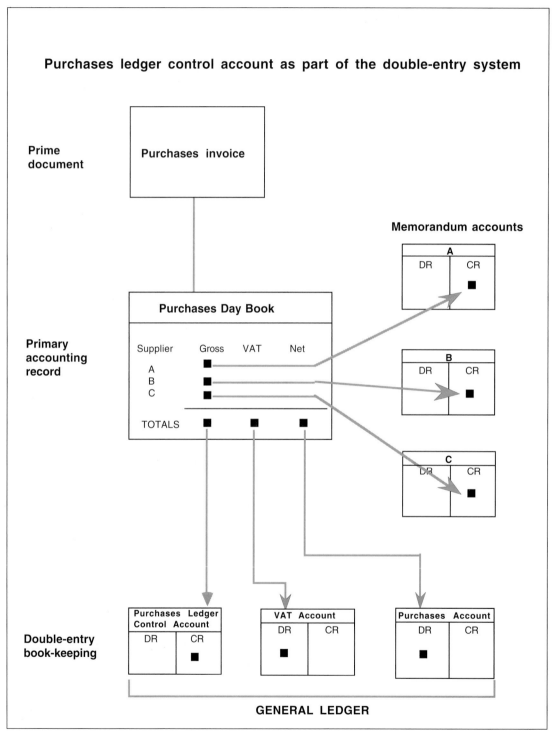

Purchases ledger control account as part of the double-entry system

Prime document

Purchases invoice

Memorandum accounts

Primary accounting record

Purchases Day Book

Supplier	Gross	VAT	Net
A	■		
B	■		
C	■		
TOTALS	■	■	■

A — DR / CR ■

B — DR / CR ■

C — DR / CR ■

Double-entry book-keeping

Purchases Ledger Control Account — DR / CR ■

VAT Account — DR ■ / CR

Purchases Account — DR ■ / CR

GENERAL LEDGER

Purchases ledger (creditors) control account incorporated into the double-entry book-keeping system; the creditors' accounts are subsidiary memorandum accounts.

OTHER EXAMPLES OF CONTROL ACCOUNTS

Sales ledger and purchases ledger control accounts are two commonly-used control accounts, other examples often used in the accounting system are:

• wages and salaries control account

• cash control account

• stock control account

wages and salaries control account

We have already seen in Chapter 10 (pages 224-225) how wages and salaries control account is a master account for the subsidiary accounts which deal with payroll transactions. This is illustrated in the following way:

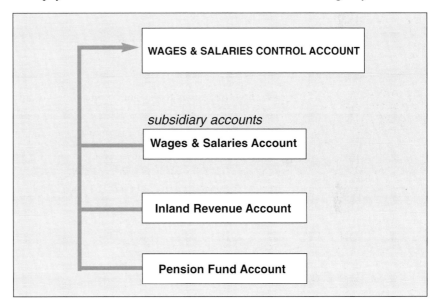

An example of a wages and salaries control account is shown below:

Dr			Wages & Salaries Control Account			Cr
2001			£	2001		£
30 Nov	Bank	3,875		30 Nov Wages & salaries	6,325	
30 Nov	Inland Revenue	1,900				
30 Nov	Pension Fund	550				
		6,325			6,325	

Note: A detailed explanation of the transactions shown in this account is given in the Case Study on pages 225-228.

cash control account

A cash control account is used in conjunction with petty cash book (see Chapter 12), where the control account is the ledger account and the petty cash book is the subsidiary account. This relationship is illustrated in the following way:

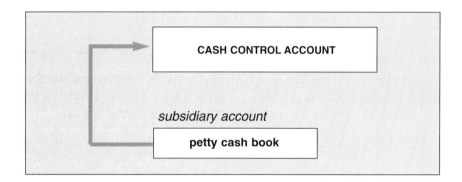

An example of a cash control account is shown below:

Dr		£ p	Cash Control Account		Cr
2001		£ p	2001		£ p
7 Apr	Balance b/d	50.00	11 Apr	Petty cash book	30.75 *
11 Apr	Cash	30.75	11 Apr	Balance c/d	50.00
		80.75			80.75
12 Apr	Balance b/d	50.00			

* The total of the analysis columns for the week (alternatively the total of each analysis column could be shown); please refer to pages 266-268 to see how the amounts from the analysis columns are entered into the double-entry accounts.

In this cash control account a transfer of £30.75 cash from the cash book has restored the petty cash imprest amount to £50.00.

As cash control account is the ledger account for petty cash, it is the balance on this account that is listed on a trial balance. Petty cash book is a subsidiary account, the balance of which should be agreed with the control account at regular intervals. Any discrepancy should be investigated and either resolved, or referred to the accounts supervisor or other appropriate person.

stock control account

As we have seen earlier (pages 280-281) stock account or stock control account is used to record the value of stock that a business holds for resale. As a part of the double-entry system, stock control account acts as the master account for the subsidiary accounts which provide the records of each stock item or stock line held by the business. This relationship is illustrated in the following way:

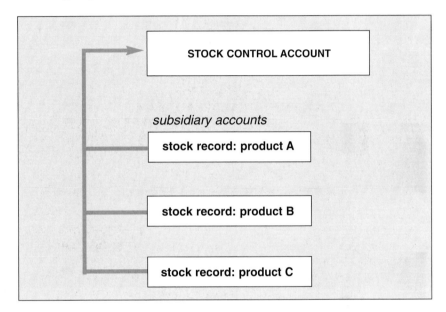

When a business stock takes, a physical count of the stock is carried out; the value of this physical stock is entered into the stock control account which should agree with the stock records held in the subsidiary accounts. Any discrepancy should be investigated and either resolved, or referred to the accounts supervisor or other appropriate person.

CASE STUDY

CASE STUDY: STOCK CONTROL

situation

Golf Sales Limited trades in two types of golf ball: the 'Superspeed' and the 'Titanium'. Each ball is sold in packs of fifteen balls. A stock take was carried out on 31 December 2001 and the physical stocks held were:

			£
'Superspeed'	840 packs at £10 per pack	=	8,400
'Titanium'	525 packs at £15 per pack	=	7,875
			16,275

The total valuation has been entered into the double-entry accounts as follows:

Dr		Stock Control Account		Cr
2001	£	2001		£
31 Dec Trading account 16,275				

The stock records for the two products show the following:

STOCK RECORD

Product Superspeed

Stock units packs of 15 balls

Date	Received	Issued	Balance
2001			
12 Jun	2,000		2,000
5 Jul		500	1,500
9 Aug		1,000	500
28 Sep	1,000		1,500
19 Oct		400	1,100
5 Dec		250	850

STOCK RECORD

Product Titanium

Stock units packs of 15 balls

Date	Received	Issued	Balance
2001			
12 Sep	1,000		1,000
29 Sep		400	600
17 Oct	1,000		1,600
7 Nov		500	1,100
28 Nov		200	900
13 Dec		400	500

solution

A comparison between the physical stock counted at the stock take shows that there is a difference when compared with the stock records. A process of stock reconciliation needs to be carried out so that small discrepancies can be adjusted, and significant discrepancies can be investigated. As the stock records of Golf Sales Limited show small discrepancies these can be corrected by means of a stock adjustment (ADJ) recorded on each stock record, as follows:

SUPERSPEED

Date	Received	Issued	Balance
2001			
31 Dec		ADJ 10	840

TITANIUM

Date	Received	Issued	Balance
2001			
31 Dec	ADJ 25		525

Larger discrepancies will need to be investigated as they could have been caused by:

• an error in the stock record, such as a failure to record a receipt, an issue, or a return of stock

• theft of stock

• damaged stock being disposed of without any record having been made

If discrepancies cannot be resolved, they should be referred to the accounts supervisor or other appropriate person.

Stock taking and the techniques used for valuing stock are covered in detail at level 3 of NVQ in Accounting.

CHAPTER SUMMARY

• Control accounts (or totals accounts) are 'master' accounts, which control a number of subsidiary accounts.

• Two commonly used control accounts are:

– sales ledger (debtors) control account

– purchases ledger (creditors) control account

• Transactions are recorded on the same side of the control account as on the subsidiary accounts.

• Set-off/contra entries occur when one person has an account in both sales and purchases ledger, and it is agreed to set-off one balance against the other to leave a net balance. This usually results in the following control account entries:

– *debit* purchases ledger control account

– *credit* sales ledger control account

• Control accounts are an aid to management:

– they give up-to-date information on the total of debtors or creditors

– by making fraud more difficult

– in helping to locate errors

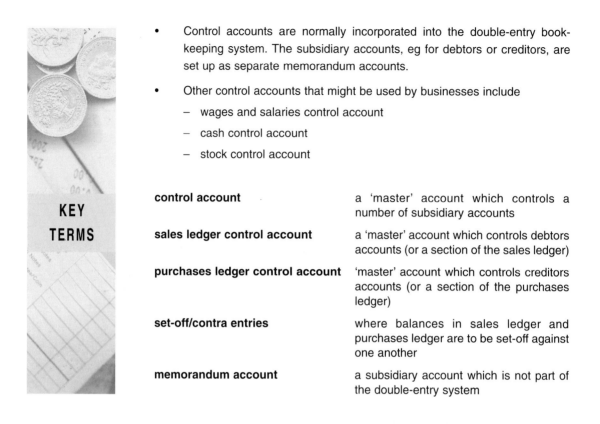

- Control accounts are normally incorporated into the double-entry book-keeping system. The subsidiary accounts, eg for debtors or creditors, are set up as separate memorandum accounts.

- Other control accounts that might be used by businesses include
  - wages and salaries control account
  - cash control account
  - stock control account

control account	a 'master' account which controls a number of subsidiary accounts
sales ledger control account	a 'master' account which controls debtors accounts (or a section of the sales ledger)
purchases ledger control account	'master' account which controls creditors accounts (or a section of the purchases ledger)
set-off/contra entries	where balances in sales ledger and purchases ledger are to be set-off against one another
memorandum account	a subsidiary account which is not part of the double-entry system

KEY TERMS

STUDENT ACTIVITIES

17.1 You have the following information:

- opening creditor balances at start of month   £18,600
- cash/cheques paid to creditors during month   £9,400
- purchases for month   £9,100
- purchases returns for month   £800

What is the figure for closing creditor balances at the end of the month?

(a)   £18,100

(b)   £19,100

(c)   £36,300

(d)   £17,500

Answer (a) or (b) or (c) or (d)

17.2 Which one of the following does not appear in sales ledger (debtors) control account?

(a)   bad debts written off

(b)   discount received

(c)   sales returns

(d)   cash/cheques received from debtors

Answer (a) or (b) or (c) or (d)

17.3 A friend has recently started work as an accounts clerk for a large electrical wholesalers. He asks you the following questions about control accounts:

- "What are the principles of control accounts?"

- "I've heard it said that control accounts help the management of the business. How is this?"

- "In our business we treat the control accounts as being part of the double-entry accounts, with subsidiary memorandum' accounts kept for each debtor and creditor. I thought you told me earlier that debtors and creditors accounts were part of double-entry ..."

Write answers to your friend.

17.4 Prepare a sales ledger (debtors) control account for the month of June 2001 from the following information:

2001		£
1 Jun	Sales ledger balances	17,491
30 Jun	Credit sales for month	42,591
	Sales returns	1,045
	Payments received from debtors	39,024
	Cash discount allowed	593
	Bad debts written off	296

The debtors figure at 30 June is to be entered as the balancing figure.

17.5 Prepare a purchases ledger (creditors) control account for the month of April 2001 from the following information:

2001		£
1 Apr	Purchases ledger balances	14,275
30 Apr	Credit purchases for month	36,592
	Purchases returns	653
	Payments made to creditors	31,074
	Cash discount received	1,048
	Transfer of credit balances to sales ledger	597

The creditors figure at 30 April is to be entered as the balancing figure.

17.6 The sales ledger of Rowcester Traders contains the following accounts on 1 February 2001:

Arrow Valley Retailers, balance £826.40 debit

B Brick (Builders) Limited, balance £59.28 debit

Mereford Manufacturing Company, balance £293.49 debit

Redgrove Restorations, balance £724.86 debit

Wyvern Warehouse Limited, balance £108.40 debit

The following transactions, which have been authorised by the accounts supervisor, took place during February:

3 Feb	Sold goods on credit to Arrow Valley Retailers £338.59, and to Mereford Manufacturing Company £127.48
7 Feb	Redgrove Restorations returned goods £165.38
15 Feb	Received a cheque from Wyvern Warehouse Limited for the balance of the account after deduction of 2.5% cash discount
17 Feb	Sold goods on credit to Redgrove Restorations £394.78, and to Wyvern Warehouse Limited £427.91
20 Feb	Arrow Valley Retailers settled an invoice for £826.40 by cheque after deducting 2.5% cash discount
24 Feb	Mereford Manufacturing Company returned goods £56.29
28 Feb	Transferred the balance of Mereford Manufacturing Company's account to the company's account in the purchases ledger
28 Feb	Wrote off the account of B Brick (Builders) Limited as a bad debt

You are to:

(a) write up the personal accounts in the sales (debtors) ledger of Rowcester Traders for February 2001, balancing them at the end of the month

(b) prepare a sales ledger (debtors) control account for February 2001, balancing it at the end of the month

(c) reconcile the control account balance with the debtors' accounts at 1 February and 28 February 2001.

Note: VAT is to be ignored on all transactions and day books are not required.

17.7 The purchases ledger of Rowcester Traders contains the following accounts on 1 February 2001:

Apple Supplies Limited, balance £1,843.22 credit

Beatty Brothers, £51.47 debit

J Johnson, £675.38 credit

Mereford Manufacturing Company, balance £478.29 credit

Newtown Equipment Limited, balance £684.86 credit

W Wright, balance £987.20 credit

The following transactions, which have been authorised by the accounts supervisor, took place during February:

3 Feb	Bought goods on credit from Apple Supplies Limited, £1,027.98, and from Beatty Brothers £150.68
6 Feb	Paid W Wright a cheque for the balance of her account after deducting 2.5% cash discount
10 Feb	Bought goods on credit from J Johnson £328.22, and from W Wright £476.38
11 Feb	Paid Newtown Equipment Limited a cheque for the balance of the account
14 Feb	Returned goods to Apple Supplies Limited for £157.20
17 Feb	Paid Apple Supplies a cheque for the balance of the account, after deducting 2.5% cash discount
18 Feb	Returned goods to Newtown Equipment Limited for £105.68
24 Feb	Paid J Johnson the amount owing by cheque, after deducting 2.5% cash discount
27 Feb	Bought goods on credit from Apple Supplies Limited £849.36
28 Feb	Transfer of debit balance of £364.68 in the sales ledger to Mereford Manufacturing Company's account in the purchases ledger

You are to:

(a)   write up the personal accounts in the purchases (creditors) ledger of Rowcester Traders for February 2001, balancing them at the end of the month

(b)   prepare a purchases ledger (creditors) control account for February 2001, balancing it at the end of the month

(c)   reconcile the control account balance with the creditors' accounts at 1 February and 28 February 2001

Note: VAT is to be ignored on all transactions and day books are not required.

18 THE JOURNAL AND CORRECTION OF ERRORS

this chapter covers . . .

The journal is the primary accounting record for non-regular transactions, eg correction of errors and other transfers. The journal – like the other day books (or journals) that we have seen – is used to list transactions before they are entered into the double-entry system.

The main uses of the journal are for transactions such as:

- *opening entries*
- *purchase and sale of fixed assets on credit*
- *correction of errors*
- *other transfers*

NVQ PERFORMANCE CRITERIA COVERED

unit 3: PREPARING LEDGER BALANCES AND AN INITIAL TRIAL BALANCE

element 2

prepare ledger balances and control accounts

● *authorised adjustments are correctly processed and documented*

● *documentation is stored securely and in line with the organisation's confidentiality requirements*

USES OF THE JOURNAL

The journal completes the accounting system by providing the primary accounting record for non-regular transactions which are not recorded in any other primary accounting record. The categories of such non-regular transactions include:

- opening entries
- purchase and sale of fixed assets on credit
- correction of errors
- other non-regular transactions or adjustments

The reasons for using a journal are:

- to provide a primary accounting record for non-regular transactions
- to eliminate the need for remembering why non-regular transactions were put through the accounts – the journal acts as a notebook
- to reduce the risk of fraud, by making it difficult for unauthorised transactions to be entered in the accounting system
- to reduce the risk of errors, by listing the transactions that are to be put into the double-entry accounts
- to ensure that entries can be traced back to an authorised prime document, thus providing an audit trail for non-regular transactions; documentation is stored securely for possible future reference

THE JOURNAL – A PRIMARY ACCOUNTING RECORD

The journal is a primary accounting record; it is not, therefore, part of the double-entry book-keeping system. The journal is used to list the transactions that are to be put through the accounts. The accounting system for non-regular transactions is as follows:

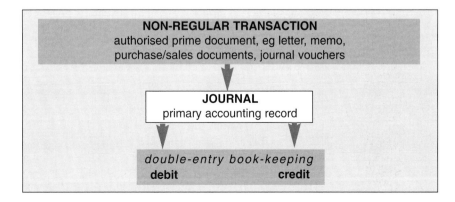

Look at the way the journal is set out with a sample transaction, and then read the notes that follow:

Date	Details	Folio	Dr	Cr
2001			£	£
1 Jul	Bank account	CBR	20,000	
	Capital account	GL		20,000
	Opening capital introduced			

Notes:

- journal entries are prepared from authorised prime documents (which are stored securely for possible future reference)
- the names of the accounts to be debited and credited in the book-keeping system are written in the details column; it is customary to show the debit transaction first
- the money amount of each debit and credit are stated in the appropriate column
- the folio column cross-references to the division of the ledger where each account is found (it can also include an account number)
- a journal entry always balances, ie debit and credit entries are for the same amount or total
- it is usual to include a brief narrative explaining why the transaction is being carried out, and making reference to the prime document whenever possible (in assessments and examinations you should always include a narrative unless specifically told otherwise)
- each journal entry is complete in itself and is ruled off to separate it from the next entry

It is important to note that, when a business uses control accounts (see Chapter 17) which are incorporated into the double-entry accounts, the transactions from the journal involving sales (debtors) ledger and purchases (creditors) ledger must be recorded in the respective control accounts *and* in the memorandum accounts for debtors or creditors.

OPENING ENTRIES

These are the transactions which open the accounts of a new business. For example, a first business transaction is:

1 Jan 2001 Started in business with £10,000 in the bank

This non-regular transaction is entered in the journal as follows:

Date	Details	Folio	Dr	Cr
2001			£	£
1 Jan	Bank account	CBR	10,000	
	Capital account	GL		10,000
	Opening capital introduced			

After the journal entry has been made, the transaction can be recorded in the double-entry accounts.

Here is another opening entries transaction to be recorded in the journal:

1 Feb 2001   Started in business with cash £100, bank £5,000, stock £1,000, machinery £2,500, creditors £850

The journal entry is:

Date	Details	Folio	Dr	Cr
2001			£	£
1 Feb	Cash account	CBR	100	
	Bank account	CBR	5,000	
	Stock account	GL	1,000	
	Machinery account	GL	2,500	
	Creditors accounts	PL		850
	Capital account*	GL		7,750
			8,600	8,600
	Assets and liabilities at the start of business			

* Assets – liabilities = capital

Notes:

- capital is, in this example, the balancing figure, ie assets minus liabilities
- the journal is the primary accounting record for all opening entries, including cash and bank; however the normal primary accounting record for other cash/bank transactions is the cash book
- the amounts for the journal entry will now need to be recorded in the double-entry accounts

PURCHASE AND SALE OF FIXED ASSETS ON CREDIT

The purchase and sale of fixed assets are non-regular business transactions which are recorded in the journal as the primary accounting record. Only *credit* transactions are entered in the journal (because cash/bank transactions are recorded in the cash book as the primary accounting record). However, a business (or an assessment/examination question) may choose to journalise cash entries: strictly, though, this is incorrect as two primary accounting records are being used.

15 Apr 2001   Bought a machine for £1,000 plus VAT (at 17.5%) on credit from Machinery Supplies Limited, purchase order no 2341.

Date	Details	Folio	Dr	Cr
2001			£	£
15 Apr	Machinery account	GL	1,000	
	VAT account	GL	175	
	Machinery Supplies Limited	PL		1,175
			1,175	1,175
	Purchase of machine: order 2341			

20 May 2001   Car sold for £2,500 on credit to Wyvern Motors Limited (no VAT chargeable).

Date	Details	Folio	Dr	Cr
2001			£	£
20 May	Wyvern Motors Limited	SL	2,500	
	Car account	GL		2,500
	Sale of car, registration L201 HAB			

CORRECTION OF ERRORS

In any book-keeping system there is always the possibility of an error. Ways to avoid errors, or ways to reveal them sooner, include:

- division of the accounting function between a number of people, so that no one person is responsible for all aspects of a business transaction

- regular circulation of statements of account to debtors, who will check the transactions on their accounts and advise any discrepancies

- checking of statements of account received from creditors

- extraction of a trial balance at regular intervals

- the checking of bank statements

- checking cash and petty cash balances against cash held

- the use of control accounts

- the use of a dedicated computer accounting program

Despite all of these, errors will still occur from time-to-time and, in this section, we will look at:

- correction of errors not shown by a trial balance
- correction of errors shown by a trial balance, using a suspense account

ERRORS NOT SHOWN BY A TRIAL BALANCE

In Chapter 16 we have already seen that some types of errors in a book-keeping system are not revealed by a trial balance. These are:

- error of omission
- reversal of entries
- mispost/error of commission
- error of principle
- error of original entry (or transcription)
- compensating error

Although these errors are not shown by a trial balance, they are likely to come to light if the procedures suggested in the previous section, above, are followed. For example, a debtor will soon let you know if their account has been debited with goods they did not buy. When an error is found, it needs to be corrected by means of a journal entry which shows the book-keeping entries that have been passed.

We will now look at an example of each of the errors not shown by a trial balance, and will see how it is corrected by means of a journal entry. (A practical hint which may help in correcting errors is to write out the double-entry accounts as they appear with the error; then write in the correcting entries and see if the result has achieved what was intended.) Note that the journal narrative includes document details.

error of omission

Credit sale of goods, £200 plus VAT (at 17.5%) on invoice 4967 to H Jarvis completely omitted from the accounting system; the error is corrected on 12 May 2001

Date	Details	Folio	Dr	Cr
2001			£	£
12 May	N Jarvis	SL	235	
	Sales	GL		200
	VAT	GL		35
			235	235
	Invoice 4967 omitted from the accounts.			

This type of error can happen in a very small business – often where the book-keeping is done by one person. For example, an invoice, when produced, is 'lost' down the back of a filing cabinet. Where a computer accounting system is used, it should be impossible for this error to occur. Also, if documents are numbered serially, then none should be mislaid.

reversal of entries

A payment, on 3 May 2001 by cheque for £50 to a creditor, S Wright, has been debited in the cash book and credited to Wright's account; this is corrected on 12 May 2001

Date	Details	Folio	Dr	Cr
2001			£	£
12 May	S Wright	PL	50	
	Bank	CBP		50
	S Wright	PL	50	
	Bank	CBP		50
			100	100
	Correction of £50 reversal of entries: receipt no 93459			

To correct this type of error it is best to reverse the entries that have been made incorrectly (the first two journal entries), and then to put through the correct entries. Although it will correct the error, it is wrong to debit Wright £100 and credit bank £100. This is because there was never a transaction for this amount – the original transaction was for £50.

As noted earlier, it is often an idea to write out the accounts, complete with the error, and then to write in the correcting entries. As an example, the two accounts involved in this last error are shown with the error made on 3 May, and the corrections made on 12 May indicated by the shading (the opening credit balance of S Wright's account is shown as £50):

Dr			**S Wright**			Cr
2001		£	2001			£
12 May	Bank	50	1 May	Balance b/d		50
12 May	Bank	50	3 May	Bank		50
		100				100

Dr			**Cash Book** (bank columns)			Cr
2001		£	2001			£
3 May	S Wright	50	12 May	S Wright		50
			12 May	S Wright		50

The accounts now show a net debit transaction of £50 on S Wright's account, and a net credit transaction of £50 on bank account, which is how this payment to a creditor should have been recorded in order to clear the balance on the account.

mispost/error of commission

Credit sales of £47 including VAT (at 17.5%) have been debited to the account of J Adams, instead of the account of J Adams Ltd; the error is corrected on 15 May 2001

Date	Details	Folio	Dr	Cr
2001			£	£
15 May	J Adams Ltd	SL	47	
	J Adams	SL		47
	Correction of mispost of invoice 327			

This type of error can be avoided, to some extent, by the use of account numbers, and by persuading the customer to quote the account number or reference on each transaction. All computer accounting systems use numbers/references to identify accounts, but it is still possible to post a transaction to the wrong account.

error of principle

The cost of diesel fuel, £30 (excluding VAT), has been debited to vehicles account; the error is corrected on 20 May 2001

Date	Details	Folio	Dr	Cr
2001			£	£
20 May	Vehicle running expenses account	GL	30	
	Vehicles account	GL		30
	Correction of error: voucher no 647			

This type of error is similar to a mispost except that, instead of the wrong person's account being used, it is the wrong class of account. In the above example, the vehicle running costs must be kept separate from the cost of the asset (the vehicle), otherwise the expense and asset accounts will be incorrect.

error of original entry (or transcription)

Postages of £45 paid by cheque entered in the accounts as £54; the error is corrected on 27 May 2001

Date	Details	Folio	Dr	Cr
2001			£	£
27 May	Bank	CBP	54	
	Postages	GL		54
	Postages	GL	45	
	Bank	CBP		45
			99	99
	Correction of error: postages of £45 entered into the accounts as £54			

This error could have been corrected by debiting bank and crediting postages with £9, being the difference between the two amounts. However, there was no original transaction for this amount, and it is better to reverse the wrong transaction and put through the correct one. A reversal of figures either has a difference of nine (as above), or an amount divisible by nine. An error of original entry can also be a 'bad' figure on a cheque or an invoice, entered wrongly into both accounts.

compensating error

Rates account is overcast (overadded) by £100; sales account is also overcast by the same amount; the error is corrected on 31 May 2001

Date	Details	Folio	Dr	Cr
2001			£	£
31 May	Sales account	GL	100	
	Rates account	GL		100
	Correction of overcast on rates account and sales account			

Here, an account with a debit balance – rates – has been overcast (overadded); this is compensated by an overcast on an account with a credit balance – sales. There are several permutations on this theme, eg two debit balances, one overcast, one undercast; a debit balance undercast, a credit balance undercast.

important notes to remember

We have just looked at several journal entries in connection with the correction of errors. Remember that:

- The journal is the primary accounting record for non-regular transactions. The journal entries must then be recorded in the book-keeping system.
- When a business uses control accounts (see Chapter 17) which are incorporated into the double-entry accounting, the transactions from the journal must be recorded in the sales (debtors) ledger or purchase (creditors) ledger control accounts *and* in the memorandum accounts for debtors or creditors.

TRIAL BALANCE ERRORS: USE OF SUSPENSE ACCOUNT

There are many types of errors which are revealed by a trial balance. Included amongst these are:

- omission of one part of the double-entry transaction
- recording two debits or two credits for a transaction
- recording a different amount for a transaction on the debit side from the credit side
- errors in the calculation of balances (not compensated by other errors)
- error in transferring the balance of an account to the trial balance
- error of addition in the trial balance

When errors are shown, the trial balance is 'balanced' by recording the difference in a suspense account. For example, on 31 December 2001 the trial balance totals are:

	Dr	Cr
	£	£
Trial balance totals	100,000	99,850
Suspense account		150
	100,000	100,000

A suspense account is opened in the general ledger with, in this case, a credit balance of £150:

Dr		Suspense Account		Cr
2001	£	2001		£
		31 Dec	Trial balance difference	150

A detailed examination of the book-keeping system is now made in order to find the errors. As errors are found, they are corrected by means of a journal entry. The journal entries will balance, with one part of the entry being either a debit or credit to suspense account. In this way, the balance on suspense account is eliminated by book-keeping transactions. Using the above suspense account, the following errors are found and corrected on 15 January 2002:

- sales account is undercast by £100
- a payment to a creditor, A Wilson, for £65, has been recorded in the bank as £56
- telephone expenses of £55 have not been entered in the expenses account
- stationery expenses £48 have been debited to both the stationery account and the bank account

These errors are corrected by journal entries shown below. Note that the journal narrative includes details of dates and cheque numbers.

Date	Details	Folio	Dr	Cr
2002			£	£
15 Jan	Suspense account	GL	100	
	Sales account	GL		100
	Undercast on 23 December 2001 now corrected			
15 Jan	Bank account	CBR	56	
	Suspense account	GL		56
	Suspense account	GL	65	
	Bank account	CBP		65
			121	121
	Payment to A Wilson for £65 (cheque no 783726) on			
	30 December 2001 entered in bank as £56 in error			
15 Jan	Telephone expenses account	GL	55	
	Suspense account	GL		55
	Omission of entry in expenses account:			
	paid by cheque no 783734			
15 Jan	Suspense account	GL	48	
	Bank account	CBP		48
	Suspense account	GL	48	
	Bank account	CBP		48
			96	96
	Correction of error: payment by cheque no 783736			
	debited in error to bank account			

After these journal entries have been recorded in the accounts, suspense account appears as:

Dr			Suspense Account		Cr
2002		£	2001		£
15 Jan	Sales	100	31 Dec	Trial balance difference	150
15 Jan	Bank	65	2002		
15 Jan	Bank	48	15 Jan	Bank	56
15 Jan	Bank	48	15 Jan	Telephone expenses	55
		261			261

Thus all the errors have now been found, and suspense account has a nil balance.

OTHER TRANSFERS

Any other non-regular transactions need to be recorded in the journal. Examples of such transactions include:

- bad debts written off
- expenses charged to owner's drawings
- goods for the owner's use

bad debts written off

We have already seen, in Chapter 13, the double-entry book-keeping entries to write off a debtor's account:

– *debit* bad debts written off account

– *debit* Value Added Tax account (if VAT relief is available)

– *credit* debtor's account

15 Dec 2001   *Write off the account of Don's Diner which has a balance of £47, as a bad debt (VAT relief is available)*

The journal entry is:

Date	Details	Folio	Dr	Cr
2001			£	£
15 Dec	Bad debts written off account	GL	40	
	Value Added Tax account	GL	7	
	Don's Diner	SL		47
	Bad debt written off as per memo from accounts supervisor 10/12/01		47	47

expenses charged to the owner's drawings

Sometimes the owner of a business uses business facilities for private use, eg telephone, or car. The owner will agree that part of the expense shall be charged to him or her as drawings, while the other part represents a business expense. The book-keeping entry to record the adjustment is:

– *debit* drawings account

– *credit* expense account, eg telephone

31 Dec 2001   The balance of telephone account is £600; of this, one-quarter is the estimated cost of the owner's private usage

The journal entry to show the transfer of private usage is:

Date	Details	Folio	Dr	Cr
2001			£	£
31 Dec	Drawings account	GL	150	
	Telephone account	GL		150
	Transfer of private use to drawings account			

goods for the owner's use

When the owner of a business takes some of the goods in which the business trades for his or her own use, the double-entry book-keeping is:

– *debit* drawings account

– *credit* purchases account

15 Oct 2001   Owner of the business takes goods for own use, £105

The journal entry is:

Date	Details	Folio	Dr	Cr
2001			£	£
15 Oct	Drawings account	GL	105	
	Purchases account	GL		105
	Goods taken for owner's use			

Note: where a business is VAT-registered, VAT must be accounted for on goods taken by the owner.

CHAPTER SUMMARY

- The journal is used to list non-regular transactions.

- The journal is a primary accounting record – it is not a double-entry account.

- Journal entries are prepared from authorised prime documents, which are stored securely for possible future reference.

- The journal is used for:
  - opening entries
  - purchase and sale of fixed assets on credit
  - correction of errors
  - other transfers

- Correction of errors is always a difficult topic to put into practice: it tests knowledge of book-keeping procedures and it is all too easy to make the error worse than it was in the first place! The secret of dealing with this topic well is to write down – in account format – what has gone wrong. It should then be relatively easy to see what has to be done to put the error right.

- Errors not shown by a trial balance include: error of omission, reversal of entries, mispost/error of commission, error of principle, error of original entry (or transcription), compensating error.

- Errors shown by a trial balance include: omission of one part of the book-keeping transaction, recording two debits/credits for a transaction, recording different amounts in the two accounts, calculating balances incorrectly, transferring wrong balances to the trial balance.

- All errors are non-regular transactions and need to be corrected by means of a journal entry: the book-keeper then records the correcting transactions in the accounts.

- When error(s) are shown by a trial balance, the amount of the error is placed in a suspense account. As the errors are found, journal entries are made which 'clear out' the suspense account.

KEY TERMS

journal	the primary accounting record for non-regular transactions
opening entries	the transactions which open the accounts of a new business
suspense account	account used to place an error shown by the trial balance, pending further investigation
goods for the owner's use	goods taken by the owner of a business for personal use

18.1 Which one of the following will not be recorded in the journal?

(a) credit purchase of a fixed asset

(b) cash sale of goods

(c) write-off of a bad debt

(d) correction of an error not shown by the trial balance

Answer (a) or (b) or (c) or (d)

18.2 Which business transaction goes with which primary accounting record?

business transaction	*primary accounting record*
• credit sale of a fixed asset	• sales day book
• credit purchase of goods from a supplier	• purchases day book
• returned credit purchases to the supplier	• sales returns day book
• customer returns goods sold on credit	• purchases returns day book
• cheque received from a debtor	• journal
• credit sale of goods to a customer	• cash book

18.3 A trial balance fails to agree by £75 and the difference is placed to a suspense account. Later it is found that a credit sale for this amount has not been entered in the sales account. Which one of the following journal entries is correct?

(a) debit suspense account £75; credit sales account £75

(b) debit suspense account £150; credit sales account £150

(c) debit sales account £75; credit suspense account £75

(d) credit sales account £75

Answer (a) or (b) or (c) or (d)

18.4 Henry Lewis is setting up the book-keeping system for his new business, which sells office stationery. He decides to use the following primary accounting records:

• Journal

• Sales Day Book

• Purchases Day Book

• Sales Returns Day Book

• Purchases Returns Day Book

• Cash Book

The following business transactions take place:

(a) He receives an invoice from Temeside Traders for £956 for goods supplied on credit

(b) He issues an invoice to Malvern Models for £176 of goods

(c)   He buys a computer for use in his business for £2,000 on credit from A-Z Computers Limited

(d)   He issues a credit note to Johnson Brothers for £55 of goods

(e)   A debtor, Melanie Fisher, settles the balance of her account, £107, by cheque

(f)   He makes cash sales of £25

(g)   Henry Lewis withdraws cash £100 for his own use

(h)   He pays a creditor, Stationery Supplies Limited, the balance of the account, £298, by cheque

(i)   A debtor, Jim Bowen, with an account balance of £35 is to be written off as a bad debt

(j)   A credit note for £80 is received from a creditor, Ian Johnson

You are to take each business transaction in turn and state:
* the name of the primary accounting record
* the name of the account to be debited
* the name of the account to be credited

Note: VAT is to be ignored.

18.5   The trial balance of Thomas Wilson balanced. However, a number of errors have been found in the book-keeping system:

(a)   Credit sale of £150 to J Rigby has not been entered in the accounts.

(b)   A payment by cheque for £125 to H Price Limited, a creditor, has been recorded in the account of H Prince.

(c)   The cost of a new delivery van, £10,000, has been entered to vehicle expenses account.

(d)   Postages of £55, paid by cheque, have been entered on the wrong sides of both accounts.

(e)   The totals of the purchases day book and the purchases returns day book have been undercast by £100.

(f)   A payment for £89 from L Johnson, a debtor, has been entered in the accounts as £98.

You are to take each error in turn and:

* state the type of error

* show the correcting journal entry

Note: VAT is to be ignored; use today's date for journal entries

18.6   Jeremy Johnson extracts a trial balance from his book-keeping records on 30 September 2001. Unfortunately the trial balance fails to balance and the difference, £19 debit, is placed to a suspense account pending further investigation.

The following errors are later found:

(a)   A cheque payment of £85 for office expenses has been entered in the cash book but no entry has been made in the office expenses account.

(b)   A payment for photocopying of £87 by cheque has been correctly entered in the cash book, but is shown as £78 in the photocopying account.

(c)   The sales returns day book has been overcast by £100.

(d)   Commission received of £25 has been entered twice in the account.

You are to:

* make journal entries to correct the errors

* show the suspense account after the errors have been corrected

Note: VAT is to be ignored.

19 USING THE TRIAL BALANCE

this chapter covers . . .

This chapter links together the primary accounting records (day books), the double-entry accounts system and the trial balance. It shows how the accounting system operates and this is illustrated by means of two fully-worked Case Studies, one for purchases ledger (page 406) and one for sales ledger (page 414).

NVQ PERFORMANCE CRITERIA COVERED

unit 3: PREPARING LEDGER BALANCES AND AN INITIAL TRIAL BALANCE

element 3

draft an initial trial balance

● *information required for the initial trial balance is identified and obtained from the relevant sources*

● *relevant people are asked for advice when the necessary information is not available*

● *the draft initial trial balance is prepared in line with the organisation's policies and procedures*

● *discrepancies are identified in the balancing process and referred to the appropriate person*

THE ACCOUNTING SYSTEM

As we have seen so far, businesses need to record financial transactions for practical reasons:

- they need to quantify transactions such as purchases, sales, expenses
- they need to present the figures in a meaningful way in order to measure the success of the business or organisation

The accounting system can be complex and this chapter seeks to summarise and bring together the key elements that we have studied so far. The process of accounting follows a number of distinct stages which are illustrated in the diagram on the next page.

The rest of this chapter summarises the stages of the accounting system and brings together all that we have seen so far. Included in the chapter are two fully-worked Case Studies which illustrate, firstly, purchases ledger accounting (page 406) and, secondly, sales ledger accounting (page 414); both Case Studies incorporate additional aspects, such as the use of control accounts and journal entries.

PRIME DOCUMENTS

Business transactions generate documents, and we have already studied the key documents in depth in Chapters 2 and 7.

sale and purchase of goods and services

When a business or organisation buys or sells goods or services the seller prepares an invoice stating

- the amount owing
- when it should be paid
- details of the goods sold or service provided

cash sales and credit sales – debtors and creditors

An invoice is prepared by the seller for

- **cash sales** – where payment is immediate, whether in cash, by cheque, by debit card or by credit card (Note that not all cash sales will require an invoice to be prepared by the seller – shops, for instance, normally issue a receipt for the amount paid.)
- **credit sales** – where payment is to be made at a later date (often 30 days later)

the accounting system

PRIME DOCUMENTS

invoices – issued and received

credit notes – issued and received

bank paying-in slips

cheques issued

BACS documents

sources of accounting information

PRIMARY ACCOUNTING RECORDS

day books

journal

cash books (also used in double-entry – see below)

gathering and summarising accounting information

DOUBLE-ENTRY ACCOUNTS

sales ledger – accounts of debtors

purchases ledger – accounts of creditors

general (main) ledger

- 'nominal' accounts for sales, purchases, expenses, capital, loans etc
- 'real' accounts for items, eg fixed assets

cash books

- cash book for cash and bank transactions
- petty cash book

recording the dual aspect of accounting transactions in the ledgers of the accounting system

TRIAL BALANCE

a summary of the balances of all the accounts at the end of the accounting period

arithmetic checking of double-entry book-keeping

FINANCIAL STATEMENTS*

- profit and loss statement

statement measuring profit (or loss) for an accounting period

- balance sheet

statement of assets, liabilities and capital at the end of an accounting period

* the topic of financial statements is covered fully at NVQ levels 3 & 4

A debtor is a person who owes you money when you sell on credit.

A creditor is a person to whom you owe money when you buy on credit.

return of goods – the credit note

If the buyer returns goods which are bought on credit (they may be faulty or incorrect) the seller will prepare a credit note (see page 49 for an example) which is sent to the buyer, reducing the amount of money owed. The credit note, like the invoice, states the money amount and the goods or services to which it relates.

banking transactions

Businesses and organisations, like anyone else with a bank account, need to pay in money, and draw out cash and make payments. Paying-in slips, cheques and BACS transfers are used frequently in business as prime documents for bank account transactions. 'BACS' stands for Bankers Automated Clearing Services which provide electronic transfer of amounts from one bank account to another.

RECORDING OF TRANSACTIONS

Many businesses and organisations issue and receive large quantities of invoices, credit notes and banking documents, and it is useful for them to list these in summary form. These summaries are known as primary accounting records.

The primary accounting records include:

- **sales day book** – a list of sales made, compiled from invoices issued
- **purchases day book** – a list of purchases made, compiled from invoices received
- **sales returns day book** – a list of 'returns in', ie goods returned by customers, compiled from credit notes issued
- **purchases returns day book** – a list of 'returns out', ie goods returned to suppliers, compiled from credit notes received
- **cash book** – the business' record of the cash and bank transactions compiled from receipts, paying-in slips, cheques and BACS documents
- **petty cash book** – a record of low-value purchases, compiled from petty cash vouchers
- **journal** – a record of non-regular transactions, which are not recorded in any other primary accounting record

The primary accounting records provide the information for the double-entry book-keeping system.

DOUBLE-ENTRY ACCOUNTS: THE LEDGER

The basis of the accounting system is the double-entry book-keeping system which is embodied in a series of records known as the ledger. This is divided into a number of separate accounts.

double-entry book-keeping

Double-entry book-keeping involves making two entries in the accounts for each transaction. With a manual accounting system the two entries are made by hand; with a computer accounting system one entry is made on the keyboard, and the computer operator indicates to the machine where the other entry is to be made by means of a code.

accounts

The sources for the entries are the primary accounting records. The ledger into which the entries are made is normally a bound book (in a non-computerised system) divided into separate accounts, eg a separate account for sales, purchases, each type of business expense, each debtor, each creditor, and so on. Each account will be given a specific name, and a number for reference purposes (or input code, with a computer system).

division of the ledger

Because of the large number of accounts involved, the ledger is traditionally divided into a number of sections. These same sections are used in computer accounting systems.

- sales ledger – personal accounts of debtors
- purchases ledger – personal accounts of creditors
- cash books – comprising cash account and bank account, and a petty cash book for low-value purchases. Note that cash books are also primary accounting records
- general (or main) ledger – the remainder of the accounts: nominal accounts, eg sales, purchases, expenses, and real accounts for items owned by the business and organisations

TRIAL BALANCE

The trial balance lists the balances of all the double-entry accounts, distinguishing between those with debit balances and those with credit balances. The total of the debit and credit columns should be equal, which means that the trial balance 'balances'.

A trial balance is prepared or extracted (from the double-entry accounts) at regular intervals – weekly, fortnightly or monthly – depending on the requirements of the business or organisation. One will always be prepared at the end of the financial year, which may vary between businesses and organisations – although 31 December (end of the calendar year) and 30 March (end of the tax year) are popular.

The heading of a trial balance gives the name of the business or organisation whose accounts have been listed and the date it was extracted, eg 'as at 31 December 2001'.

Whilst the trial balance acts as an arithmetic check on the double-entry book-keeping, there can still be a number of errors within the accounts system. As we have seen in Chapter 18, there may be:

- errors not shown by a trial balance
- errors shown by a trial balance

As well as being a check on the book-keeping, the trial balance is a valuable source of information used to help in the preparation of financial statements.

FINANCIAL STATEMENTS

The financial statements (or final accounts) comprise:

- profit and loss statement, which shows the profit (or loss) for an accounting period such as a year
- balance sheet, which lists the assets, liabilities and capital at the end of the accounting period

Financial statements are covered fully at NVQ levels 3 and 4.

CASE STUDIES

To conclude this section of the book and to bring together the book-keeping system, there now follow two fully-worked case studies:

- Case Study 1 (on the next page) focuses on purchases ledger accounting, commencing with the primary accounting records of purchases day book and purchases returns day book, together with some aspects of cash book. The Case Study comprises entry of opening balances into accounts, recording of transactions from the day books and cash book, balancing accounts and transfer of balances (including additional balances) to a trial balance. The debit and credit columns of the trial balance are then totalled and shown to be equal.
- Case Study 2 (on page 414) focuses on sales ledger accounting. As well as

the primary accounting records of sales day book and sales returns day book, it includes aspects of cash book and journal entries. Opening balances are entered into the accounts, transactions are recorded from the day books, cash book and journal, and the accounts are then balanced. The balances are transferred (together with additional balances) to a trial balance, the debit and credit columns of which are totalled and shown to be equal.

The following background information is common to both Case Studies:

You work as an accounts assistant for Wyvern Nurseries. The company runs a garden centre in Wyvern, and buys in plants and other garden and leisure products from suppliers. At its nurseries it grows the 'specialist' range of plants which are also sold to shops and other garden centres in the area. Wyvern Nurseries is registered for VAT.

Your job in the accounts department is principally concerned with purchases and sales ledgers (the subsidiary ledgers) and also with aspects of the general ledger (the main ledger). General ledger contains control accounts, which form part of the double-entry, for purchases and sales ledgers. Individual accounts of creditors and debtors are kept in the subsidiary ledgers in the form of memorandum accounts.

CASE STUDY

PURCHASES LEDGER ACCOUNTING

situation

Today is 1 May 2001 and you are working on the purchases (creditors) ledger and general (main) ledger sections of the accounting system.

Primary accounting records
Day books have been written up by a colleague (the rate of VAT is 17.5%) as follows:

Purchases Day Book						
Date	Details	Invoice No	Gross	VAT	Purchases	Stationery
2001			£	£	£	£
1 May	Garden Supplies Ltd	5439	470	70	400	
1 May	Woodcraft & Co	A471	705	105	600	
1 May	Office Direct	9579	235	35		200
1 May	Pershore Pots	754	329	49	280	
1 May	Pete's Plants	427	188	28	160	
1 May	Garden Supplies Ltd	5459	376	56	320	
	TOTALS		2,303	343	1,760	200

Purchases Returns Day Book						
Date	Details	Credit Note No	Gross	VAT	Purchases returns	Stationery returns
2001			£	£	£	£
1 May	Garden Supplies Ltd	CN194	94	14	80	
1 May	Office Direct	C4571	47	7		40
1 May	Pershore Pots	CN761	141	21	120	
	TOTALS		282	42	200	40

Account balances

The following accounts are relevant and the balances shown are at the start of the day on 1 May 2001:

	£
Creditors:	
Garden Supplies Limited	3,254
Office Direct	729
Pershore Pots	1,068
Pete's Plants	574
Woodcraft & Co	2,784
Other creditors	37,327
Purchases ledger control	45,736
Purchases	325,172
Purchases returns	4,850
Stationery	1,379
Discount received	454
VAT (credit balance)	6,274
Cash	260
Bank (debit balance)	14,170

Include a reconciliation of the balance of purchases ledger control account with the creditors' accounts.

Cash book: payments

Payments made on 1 May 2001 are to be entered into the accounts:

	Total	VAT	Net
	£	£	£
• Pete's Plants (paid by cheque)	354		
• Woodcraft & Co (paid by cheque) (in full settlement of a debt of £1,800)	1,750		
• Stationery (paid in cash)	94	14	80

Trial balance

After writing up the double-entry accounts you are asked to prepare a trial balance at the close of business on 1 May 2001. The following account balances are to be incorporated (there have been no transactions on these accounts on 1 May):

	£
Sales ledger control	82,851
Sales	735,450
Sales returns	6,020
Discount allowed	475
General expenses	73,284
Wages and salaries	119,477
Bank charges	354
Bad debts written off	496
Equipment and vehicles	194,646
Stock at 1 Jan 2001	55,270
Capital	100,000
Drawings	18,910

solution

Tutorial note: the layout of the accounts used in this and the following Case Study is very similar to that often found in Simulations and Assessments.

Purchases ledger

This contains the creditors' accounts and is written up in the following steps:

• enter the opening balances

• enter the amounts from purchases day book (using the gross figure)

• enter the amounts from purchases returns day book (using the gross figure)

• record the amounts of payments from the cash book, including any cash discount received

The accounts are balanced off and the balances carried down to 2 May 2001.

PURCHASES (CREDITORS) LEDGER

Garden Supplies Limited

Date	Details	Amount	Date	Details	Amount
2001		£	2001		£
1 May	Purchases returns	94	1 May	Balance b/d	3,254
1 May	Balance c/d	4,006	1 May	Purchases	470
			1 May	Purchases	376
		4,100			4,100
			2 May	Balance b/d	4,006

Office Direct

Date	Details	Amount	Date	Details	Amount
2001		£	2001		£
1 May	Stationery returns	47	1 May	Balance b/d	729
1 May	Balance c/d	917	1 May	Stationery	235
		964			964
			2 May	Balance b/d	917

Pershore Pots

Date	Details	Amount	Date	Details	Amount
2001		£	2001		£
1 May	Purchases returns	141	1 May	Balance b/d	1,068
1 May	Balance c/d	1,256	1 May	Purchases	329
		1,397			1,397
			2 May	Balance b/d	1,256

Pete's Plants

Date	Details	Amount	Date	Details	Amount
2001		£	2001		£
1 May	Bank	354	1 May	Balance b/d	574
1 May	Balance c/d	408	1 May	Purchases	188
		762			762
			2 May	Balance b/d	408

Woodcraft & Co

Date	Details	Amount	Date	Details	Amount
2001		£	2001		£
1 May	Bank	1,750	1 May	Balance b/d	2,784
1 May	Discount received	50	1 May	Purchases	705
1 May	Balance c/d	1,689			
		3,489			3,489
			2 May	Balance b/d	1,689

Other creditors

Date	Details	Amount	Date	Details	Amount
2001		£	2001		£
1 May	Balances c/d	37,327	1 May	Balances b/d	37,327
			2 May	Balances b/d	37,327

Reconciliation of purchases ledger control account with creditor balances

	1 May 2001	2 May 2001
	£	£
Garden Supplies Limited	3,254	4,006
Office Direct	729	917
Pershore Pots	1,068	1,256
Pete's Plants	574	408
Woodcraft & Co	2,784	1,689
Other creditors	37,327	37,327
Purchases ledger control account (see below)	45,736	45,603

General ledger

General (main) ledger contains all the other accounts of the business, except for cash book (see below). Purchases ledger control account is included in general ledger and records the same transactions as have been entered in the purchases ledger accounts.

Amounts are transferred to general ledger from purchases day book, purchases returns day book and cash book.

GENERAL (MAIN) LEDGER
Purchases Ledger (Creditors) Control Account

Date	Details	Amount	Date	Details	Amount
2001		£	2001		£
1 May	Purchases Returns Day Book	282	1 May	Balances b/d	45,736
1 May	Bank	*2,104	1 May	Purchases Day Book	2,303
1 May	Discount received	50			
1 May	Balances c/d	45,603			
		48,039			48,039
			2 May	Balances b/d	45,603

* £354 + £1,750

Purchases Account

Date	Details	Amount	Date	Details	Amount
2001		£	2001		£
1 May	Balance b/d	325,172	1 May	Balance c/d	326,932
1 May	Purchases Day Book	1,760			
		326,932			326,932
2 May	Balance b/d	326,932			

Purchases Returns Account

Date	Details	Amount	Date	Details	Amount
2001		£	2001		£
1 May	Balance c/d	5,050	1 May	Balance b/d	4,850
			1 May	Purchases Returns Day Book	200
		5,050			5,050
			2 May	Balance b/d	5,050

Stationery Account

Date	Details	Amount	Date	Details	Amount
2001		£	2001		£
1 May	Balance b/d	1,379	1 May	Purchases Returns	
1 May	Purchases Day Book	200		Day Book	*40
1 May	Cash Book	80	2 May	Balance c/d	1,619
		1,659			1,659
2 May	Balance b/d	1,619			

* This returns item could, alternatively, be credited to a stationery returns account

Discount Received Account

Date	Details	Amount	Date	Details	Amount
2001		£	2001		£
1 May	Balance c/d	504	1 May	Balance b/d	454
			1 May	Cash Book	50
		504			504
			2 May	Balance b/d	504

Value Added Tax Account

Date	Details	Amount	Date	Details	Amount
2001		£	2001		£
1 May	Purchases Day Book	343	1 May	Balance b/d	6,274
1 May	Cash Book	14	1 May	Purchases Returns	
1 May	Balance c/d	5,959		Day Book	42
		6,316			6,316
			2 May	Balance b/d	5,959

Tutorial note: only the general ledger accounts with transactions on 1 May have been shown here.

Cash book
Cash book contains both cash and bank account. It performs two functions:

• primary accounting record for cash and bank transactions

• part of the double-entry accounts system

CASH BOOK										
Date	Details	Discount allowed	Cash	Bank	Date	Details	Discount received	Cash	Bank
2001		£	£	£	2001		£	£	£
1 May	Balances b/d		260	14,170	1 May	Pete's Plants			354
					1 May	Woodcraft & Co	50		1,750
					1 May	Stationery		94*	
					1 May	Balances c/d		166	12,066
		–	260	14,170			50	260	14,170
2 May	Balances b/d		166	12,066					

* £80 stationery + £14 VAT

Trial balance

The balance of each account in the double-entry system is listed according to whether it is debit or credit.

Wyvern Nurseries
Trial balance as at 1 May 2001

Name of account	Dr £	Cr £
Purchases ledger control		45,603
Purchases	326,932	
Purchases returns		5,050
Stationery	1,619	
Discount received		504
Value Added Tax		5,959
Cash	166	
Bank	12,066	
Sales ledger control	82,851	
Sales		735,450
Sales returns	6,020	
Discount allowed	475	
General expenses	73,284	
Wales and salaries	119,477	
Bank charges	354	
Bad debts written off	496	
Equipment and vehicles	194,646	
Stock at 1 Jan 2001	55,270	
Capital		100,000
Drawings	18,910	
	892,566	892,566

Tutorial notes to the trial balance:

- debit balances include cash, purchases, sales returns, purchases ledger control, expenses, fixed assets, stock, drawings
- credit balances include sales, purchases returns, sales ledger control, income, capital, loans
- bank account can be either debit or credit – debit when there is money in the bank, credit when overdrawn
- VAT account can be either debit or credit – debit when VAT is due to the business, credit when the business owes money to HM Customs and Excise
- a trial balance which balances is not proof of the complete accuracy of the accounting records

CASE STUDY

SALES LEDGER ACCOUNTING

situation

Today is 2 May 2001 and you are working on the sales (debtors) ledger and general (main) ledger sections of the accounting system.

Primary accounting records

Day books have been written up by a colleague (the rate of VAT is 17.5%) as follows:

Sales Day Book					
Date	Details	Invoice No	Gross	VAT	Net
2001			£	£	£
2 May	Beeching and Sons	SI9075	658	98	560
2 May	The Potting Shed	SI9076	188	28	160
2 May	Beech Ltd	SI9077	282	42	240
2 May	Tranter & Co	SI9078	1,222	182	1,040
2 May	The Potting Shed	SI9079	141	21	120
2 May	Green Fingers Ltd	SI9080	423	63	360
	TOTALS		2,914	434	2,480

Sales Returns Day Book					
Date	Details	Invoice No	Gross	VAT	Net
2001			£	£	£
2 May	Tranter & Co	CN454	141	21	120
2 May	Green Fingers Ltd	CN455	94	14	80
	TOTALS		235	35	200

Cash book

The cash book has been written up and balanced by a colleague as follows:

	CASH BOOK									
Date	Details	Discount allowed	Cash	Bank	Date	Details	Discount received	Cash	Bank
2001		£	£	£	2001		£	£	£
2 May	Balances b/d		166	12,066	2 May	Vehicle purchase*			5,000
2 May	Beech Ltd	50		950	2 May	Bank charges**			28
2 May	Tranter & Co			357	2 May	Drawings		100	
2 May	The Potting Shed			596	2 May	Balances c/d		66	8,941
		50	166	13,969			–	166	13,969
3 May	Balances b/d		66	8,941					

*	the vehicle purchased was a secondhand car – no VAT to reclaim on cars
**	no VAT on bank charges

Journal transactions

The accounts supervisor asks you to make journal entries for the following:

- The sales ledger account balance in the name of AB Garden Services is to be written off as a bad debt, you are told that VAT relief is available on this debt.
- Vehicle insurance of £1,550 has been recorded in the equipment and vehicles account instead of general expenses account.
- A cheque for £275 received on 25 April from a debtor, Beech Limited, has been entered in the account of another debtor, Beeching and Sons, in error (note: there was no discount allowed on this receipt).

Once the journal entries have been checked by the supervisor, they are to be recorded in the double-entry system.

Account balances

The following accounts are relevant and the balances shown are at the start of the day on 2 May 2001:

		£
Debtors:		
	AB Garden Services	47
	Beech Limited	2,341
	Beeching and Sons	847
	Green Fingers Limited	1,236
	The Potting Shed	596
	Tranter & Co	758
	Other debtors	77,026
Sales ledger control		82,851
Sales		735,450
Sales returns		6,020

Discount allowed	475
VAT (credit balance)	5,959
General expenses	73,284
Bank charges	354
Bad debts written off	496
Equipment and vehicles	194,646
Drawings	18,910

Include a reconciliation of the balance of sales ledger control account with the debtors' accounts.

Trial balance

After writing up the double-entry accounts you are asked to prepare a trial balance at the close of business on 2 May 2001. The following balances are to be incorporated (there have been no transactions on these accounts on 2 May):

	£
Purchases ledger control	45,603
Purchases	326,932
Purchases returns	5,050
Stationery	1,619
Discount received	504
Wages and salaries	119,477
Stock at 1 Jan 2001	55,270
Capital	100,000

solution

Journal transactions

The journal entries are as follows:

JOURNAL			
Date	Details	Debit	Credit
2001		£	£
2 May	Bad debts written off account Value Added Tax account AB Garden Services	40 7 47	 47 47
	Bad debt written off on instructions *of the accounts supervisor*		
2 May	General expenses account Equipment and vehicles account *Correction of error of principle on ....*	1,550	 1,550
2 May	Beeching and Sons Beech Limited *Correction of mispost on 25 April*	275	 275

The journal entries are checked by the supervisor and then recorded in the double-entry system.

Sales ledger

This contains the debtors' accounts and is written up in the following steps:

- enter the opening balances
- enter the gross amounts from the sales day book
- enter the gross amounts from the sales returns day book
- record the amounts of receipts from the cash book, including any cash discount allowed
- record the journal entries which relate to sales ledger accounts

The accounts are balanced off and the balances carried down to 3 May 2001.

SALES (DEBTORS) LEDGER

AB Garden Services

Date	Details	Amount	Date	Details	Amount
2001		£	2001		£
2 May	Balance b/d	47	2 May	Bad debts written off	40
			2 May	Value Added Tax	7
		47			47

Beech Limited

Date	Details	Amount	Date	Details	Amount
2001		£	2001		£
2 May	Balance b/d	2,341	2 May	Bank	950
2 May	Sales	282	2 May	Discount allowed	50
			2 May	Beeching and Sons	275
			2 May	Balance c/d	1,348
		2,623			2,623
3 May	Balance b/d	1,348			

Beeching and Sons

Date	Details	Amount	Date	Details	Amount
2001		£	2001		£
2 May	Balance b/d	847	2 May	Balance c/d	1,780
2 May	Sales	658			
2 May	Beech Ltd	275			
		1,780			1,780
3 May	Balance b/d	1,780			

Green Fingers Limited

Date	Details	Amount	Date	Details	Amount
2001		£	2001		£
2 May	Balance b/d	1,236	2 May	Sales returns	94
2 May	Sales	423	2 May	Balance c/d	1,565
		1,659			1,659
3 May	Balance b/d	1,565			

The Potting Shed

Date	Details	Amount	Date	Details	Amount
2001		£	2001		£
2 May	Balance b/d	596	2 May	Bank	596
2 May	Sales	188	2 May	Balance c/d	329
2 May	Sales	141			
		925			925
3 May	Balance b/d	329			

Tranter & Co

Date	Details	Amount	Date	Details	Amount
2001		£	2001		£
2 May	Balance b/d	758	2 May	Sales returns	141
2 May	Sales	1,222	2 May	Bank	357
			2 May	Balance c/d	1,482
		1,980			1,980
3 May	Balance b/d	1,482			

Other Debtors

Date	Details	Amount	Date	Details	Amount
2001		£	2001		£
2 May	Balances b/d	77,026	2 May	Balances c/d	77,026
3 May	Balances b/d	77,026			

Reconciliation of sales ledger control account with debtor balances

	2 May 2001	3 May 2001
	£	£
AB Garden Services	47	–
Beech Limited	2,341	1,348
Beeching and Sons	847	1,780
Green Fingers Limited	1,236	1,565
The Potting Shed	596	329
Tranter & Co	758	1,482
Other debtors	77,026	77,026
Sales ledger control account (see below)	82,851	83,530

General ledger

General (main) ledger contains all the other double-entry accounts, except for cash book (see below). Sales ledger control account is included in general ledger and records the same transactions as have been entered in the sales ledger accounts.

Amounts are transferred to general ledger from sales day book, sales returns day book, the journal and cash book.

GENERAL (MAIN) LEDGER
Sales Ledger (Debtors) Control Account

Date	Details	Amount	Date	Details	Amount
2001		£	2001		£
2 May	Balances b/d	82,851	2 May	Sales Rets Day Book	235
2 May	Sales Day Book	2,914	2 May	Bank	*1,903
			2 May	Discount received	50
			2 May	Bad debt written off	40
			2 May	Value Added Tax	7
			2 May	Balances c/d	83,530
		85,765			85,765
3 May	Balances b/d	83,530			

* £950 + £357 + £596

Sales Account

Date	Details	Amount	Date	Details	Amount
2001		£	2001		£
2 May	Balance c/d	737,930	2 May	Balance b/d	735,450
			2 May	Sales Day Book	2,480
		737,930			737,930
			3 May	Balance b/d	737,930

Sales Returns Account

Date	Details	Amount	Date	Details	Amount
2001		£	2001		£
2 May	Balance b/d	6,020	2 May	Balance c/d	6,220
2 May	Sales Returns Day Book	200			
		6,220			6,220
3 May	Balance b/d	6,220			

Discount Allowed Account

Date	Details	Amount	Date	Details	Amount
2001		£	2001		£
2 May	Balance b/d	475	2 May	Balance c/d	525
2 May	Cash Book	50			
		525			525
3 May	Balance b/d	525			

Value Added Tax Account

Date	Details	Amount	Date	Details	Amount
2001		£	2001		£
2 May	Sales Rets Day Book	35	2 May	Balance b/d	5,959
2 May	AB Garden Services	7	2 May	Sales Day Book	434
2 May	Balance c/d	6,351			
		6,393			6,393
			3 May	Balance b/d	6,351

General Expenses Account

Date	Details	Amount	Date	Details	Amount
2001		£	2001		£
2 May	Balance b/d	73,284	2 May	Balance c/d	74,834
2 May	Equipment and vehicles	1,550			
		74,834			74,834
3 May	Balance b/d	74,834			

Bank Charges Account

Date	Details	Amount	Date	Details	Amount
2001		£	2001		£
2 May	Balance b/d	354	2 May	Balance c/d	382
2 May	Bank	28			
		382			382
3 May	Balance b/d	382			

Debts Written Off Account

Date	Details	Amount	Date	Details	Amount
2001		£	2001		£
2 May	Balance b/d	496	2 May	Balance c/d	536
2 May	AB Garden Services	40			
		536			536
3 May	Balance b/d	536			

Equipment and Vehicles Account

Date	Details	Amount	Date	Details	Amount
2001		£	2001		£
2 May	Balance b/d	194,646	2 May	General expenses	1,550
2 May	Bank	5,000	2 May	Balance c/d	198,096
		199,646			199,646
3 May	Balance b/d	198,096			

Drawings Account

Date	Details	Amount	Date	Details	Amount
2001		£	2001		£
2 May	Balance b/d	18,910	2 May	Balance c/d	19,010
2 May	Cash	100			
		19,010			19,010
3 May	Balance b/d	19,010			

Trial balance

The balance of each account in the double-entry system is listed according to whether it is debit or credit.

Wyvern Nurseries
Trial balance as at 2 May 2001

Name of account	Dr	Cr
Purchases ledger control		45,603
Purchases	326,932	
Purchases returns		5,050
Stationery	1,619	
Discount received		504
Value Added Tax		6,351
Cash	66	
Bank	8,941	
Sales ledger control	83,530	
Sales		737,930
Sales returns	6,220	
Discount allowed	525	
General expenses	74,834	
Wages and salaries	119,477	
Bank charges	382	
Bad debts written off	536	
Equipment and vehicles	198,096	
Stock at 1 Jan 2001	55,270	
Capital		100,000
Drawings	19,010	
	895,438	895,438

Note: A trial balance which balances is not proof of the complete accuracy of the accounting records; errors not shown by a trial balance include:

• error of omission

• reversal of entries

• mispost/error of commission (here a payment from Beech Limited entered in the account of Beeching and Sons)

• error of principle (here vehicle insurance recorded in the equipment and vehicles account)

• error of original entry (or transcription)

• compensating error

**CHAPTER
SUMMARY**

- Businesses record financial transactions in order to
  - quantify transactions
  - present the figures in a meaningful way

- The accounting system follows a number of distinct stages
  - prime documents
  - primary accounting records
  - double-entry book-keeping
  - trial balance
  - financial statements

**KEY
TERMS**

prime documents	sources of accounting information
primary accounting records	day books, journal and cash books where accounting information is gathered and summarised
double-entry book-keeping	recording the dual aspect of accounting transactions in the ledgers of the accounting system
trial balance	arithmetic check of the double-entry book-keeping
financial statements (or final accounts)	comprising profit and loss statement and balance sheet (both of which are covered fully at NVQ levels 3 and 4)

STUDENT ACTIVITIES

The following background information is common to both Student Activities:

You work as an accounts assistant for 'Fashion Traders'. The company buys 'end-of-line' stocks of clothes for men and women in bulk from manufacturers and sells them on to smaller shops and discount stores. Fashion Traders is registered for VAT.

Your job in the accounts department is principally concerned with purchases and sales ledgers (the subsidiary ledgers) and also with aspects of the general ledger (the main ledger). General ledger contains control accounts, which form part of the double-entry, for purchases and sales ledgers. Individual accounts of creditors and debtors are kept in the subsidiary ledgers in the form of memorandum accounts.

19.1 Today is 1 October 2001 and you are working on the purchases (creditors) ledger and general (main) ledger sections of the accounting system.

Transactions

The following transactions have been recorded in the purchases day book, purchases returns day book and the cash book but have not yet been entered into the ledger system. The rate of VAT is 17.5%.

Purchases Day Book						
Date	Details	Invoice No	Gross	VAT	Purchases	Stationery
2001			£	£	£	£
1 Oct	Wyvern Clothes	I 4379	1,457	217	1,240	
1 Oct	Jeans-R-Us Ltd	7629	2,820	420	2,400	
1 Oct	One Stop Office	5438	423	63		360
1 Oct	J & S Manufacturing	3941	1,034	154	880	
1 Oct	Wyvern Clothes	I 4385	1,222	182	1,040	
1 Oct	Dalton & Co	A 3691	1,598	238	1,360	
	TOTALS		8,554	1,274	6,920	360

Purchases Returns Day Book						
Date	Details	Credit Note No	Gross	VAT	Purchases returns	Stationery returns
2001			£	£	£	£
1 Oct	Jeans-R-Us Ltd	C071	141	21	120	
1 Oct	Dalton & Co	CN764	94	14	80	
1 Oct	One-Stop Office	CN342	47	7		40
	TOTALS		282	42	200	40

CASH BOOK									
Date	Details	Discount allowed	Cash	Bank	Date	Details	Discount received	Cash	Bank
2001		£	£	£	2001		£	£	£
1 Oct	Balances b/d		275	2,054	1 Oct	J & S Manufactur	25		775
1 Oct	Bank C		200		1 Oct	Wyvern Clothes	45		1,055
1 Oct	Balance c/d			600	1 Oct	One-Stop Office			624
					1 Oct	Cash C			200
					1 Oct	Balance c/d		475	
		−	475	2,654			70	475	2,654
2 Oct	Balance b/d		475		2 Oct	Balance b/d			600

Balances

The following account balances are available to you at the start of the day on 1 October 2001:

	£
Creditors:	
Dalton & Co	3,076
Jeans-R-Us Limited	2,120
J & S Manufacturing	3,491
One-Stop Office	624
Wyvern Clothes	2,610
Other creditors	78,842
Purchases ledger control	90,763
Purchases	428,494
Purchases returns	8,327
Stationery	3,650
Discount received	841
VAT (credit balance)	8,347
Office equipment	7,750

Journal entries

The following errors have been discovered and will need to be entered in Fashion Traders' journal and double-entry accounts:

- a credit purchase of £420 made on 24 September 2001 from Jeans-R-Us Limited has been recorded in the account of another creditor, Jeans Unlimited (included in other creditors)
- an amount of £1,250 has been recorded in stationery account instead of office equipment account

You are to:

(a) Enter the opening balances listed above into the following accounts:

Dalton & Co
Jeans-R-Us Limited
J & S Manufacturing
One-Stop Office
Wyvern Clothes
Other creditors
Purchases ledger control
Purchases
Purchases returns
Stationery
Discount received
VAT
Office equipment

(b) Using the data from the purchases day book, purchases returns day book and cash book, enter all the transactions into the relevant accounts.

(c) Record the entries in the journal to correct the two errors and then enter the transactions into the relevant accounts.

(d) Balance off all the accounts at the end of the day on 1 October 2001, showing clearly the balances carried down. Include a reconciliation of the balance of the purchases ledger control account with the creditors' accounts.

(e) Prepare a trial balance at the close of business on 1 October 2001 using the balances of the above accounts, cash book, and incorporating the following account balances (on which there have been no transactions on 1 October):

	£
Sales ledger control	130,690
Sales	758,174
Sales returns	12,364
Discount allowed	1,497
General expenses	25,842
Wages and salaries	127,608
Bad debts written off	1,762
Warehouse equipment	85,250
Stock at 1 Jan 2001	165,940
Bank loan	40,000
Capital	115,324
Drawings	28,600

19.2   Today is 2 October 2001 and you are working on the sales (debtors) ledger and general (main) ledger sections of the accounting system.

Transactions

The following transactions have been recorded in the sales day book, sales returns day book and the cash book but have not yet been entered in the ledger system. The rate of VAT is 17.5%.

Sales Day Book					
Date	Details	Invoice No	Gross	VAT	Net
2001			£	£	£
2 Oct	BS Stores Ltd	SI7054	752	112	640
2 Oct	Just Jeans	SI7055	188	28	160
2 Oct	Teme Trading Co	SI7056	329	49	280
2 Oct	BS Stores Ltd	SI7057	376	56	320
2 Oct	Southwick Stores	SI7058	470	70	400
2 Oct	Bentley & Co	SI7059	423	63	360
	TOTALS		2,538	378	2,160

Sales Returns Day Book					
Date	Details	Credit Note No	Gross	VAT	Net
2001			£	£	£
2 Oct	Teme Trading Co	CN761	94	14	80
2 Oct	Just Jeans	CN762	47	7	40
	TOTALS		141	21	120

CASH BOOK									
Date	Details	Discount allowed	Cash	Bank	Date	Details	Discount received	Cash	Bank
2001		£	£	£	2001		£	£	£
Oct	Balance b/d		475		2 Oct	Balance b/d			600
2 Oct	Bentley & Co			420	2 Oct	Wages & salaries			1,250
2 Oct	Just Jeans	10		240	2 Oct	Drawings		310	
2 Oct	BS Stores Ltd	45		1,825	2 Oct	Loan repayment			500
					2 Oct	Balances c/d		165	135
		55	475	2,485			–	475	2,485
3 Oct	Balances b/d		165	135					

Balances

The following account balances are available to you at the start of the day on 2 October 2001:

	£
Debtors:	
Bentley & Co	1,095
BS Stores Limited	1,870
Just Jeans	629
Southwick Stores	145
Teme Trading Co	797
Victoria's Fashions	94
Other debtors	126,060
Sales ledger control	130,690
Sales	758,174
Sales returns	12,364
Discount allowed	1,497
VAT (credit balance)	7,115
Wages and salaries	127,608
Bad debts written off	1,762
Bank loan	40,000
Drawings	28,600

Journal entries

The accounts supervisor asks you to make entries in the journal and the double-entry accounts for the following:

- the sales ledger account balance in the name of Victoria's Fashions is to be written off as a bad debt; you are told that VAT relief is available on this debt

- a cheque for £220 received on 12 September from a debtor, Bentley & Co, has been entered in the account of another debtor, Bentley Stores (included in other debtors), in error; there was no discount allowed on this receipt

You are to:

(a)   Enter the opening balances listed above into the following accounts:
        Bentley & Co
        BS Stores Limited
        Just Jeans
        Southwick Stores
        Teme Trading Co
        Victoria's Fashions
        Other debtors

Sales ledger control

Sales

Sales returns

Discount allowed

VAT

Wages and salaries

Bad debts written off

Bank loan

Drawings

(b)   Using the data from the sales day book, sales returns day book and cash book, enter all the transactions into the relevant accounts.

(c)   Record the entries in the journal for the transactions mentioned by the accounts supervisor and then enter the transactions into the relevant accounts.

(d)   Balance off all the accounts at the end of the day on 2 October 2001, showing clearly the balances carried down. Include a reconciliation of the balance of the sales ledger control account with the debtors' accounts.

(e)   Prepare a trial balance at the close of business on 2 October 2001 using the balances of the above accounts, cash book, and incorporating the following account balances (on which there have been no transactions on 2 October):

	£
Purchases ledger control	96,511
Purchases	435,414
Purchases returns	8,527
Stationery	2,720
Discount received	911
Office equipment	9,000
General expenses	25,842
Warehouse equipment	85,250
Stock at 1 Jan 2001	165,940
Capital	115,324

20 INFORMATION FOR MANAGEMENT CONTROL

this chapter covers . . .

The accounting system is able to provide information to the managers of a business or organisation to help them in decision-making, planning and control. In this chapter we look at:

- the information they need from the accounts system
- the differences between financial accounting and management accounting
- the structure of organisations
- costs (materials, labour and expenses) and income
- cost centres, profit centres and investment centres
- the use of coding for costs and income

NVQ PERFORMANCE CRITERIA COVERED

unit 4: SUPPLYING INFORMATION FOR MANAGEMENT CONTROL

element 1

code and extract information

- appropriate cost centres and elements of costs are recognised
- income and expenditure details are extracted from the relevant sources
- income and expenditure are coded correctly
- any problems in obtaining the necessary information are referred to the appropriate person
- errors are identified and reported to the appropriate person

WHO IS A MANAGER?

Mention the word 'manager' and most people think of stereotypes: male, mid-50s, wears a suit, has his own office with a secretary, not particularly approachable. While this image may have been true thirty or forty years ago, nowadays managers include anybody within the business or organisation who is involved in decision-making, planning and control. (Incidentally the 'man' in manager does not refer to males; instead it comes from the Latin word 'manus' which means 'the hand'.)

Look at the statements below and decide which of these people are managers:

- The managing director of a bank takes the decision to develop e-banking
- The government's health secretary plans to cut hospital waiting lists
- The finance director is controlling the company's spending to ensure that the bank overdraft limit is not exceeded
- The office manager decides to buy a new Xentra photocopier for use in the office
- The accounts supervisor plans to run the computer payroll program next Tuesday
- The accounts assistant controls the petty cash float

The answer is that all of the above are managers because the statements involve decision-making (managing director of the bank, office manager), planning (health secretary, accounts supervisor), and control (finance director, accounts assistant). We can see, therefore, that management is much more broadly-based than the stereotype image portrayed earlier. In fact, we can go further and say that everybody is responsible for something: making decisions, planning what to do and controlling the progress of work.

Clearly there are different levels of management and it is important to recognise that any information for the use of a manager must be tailored to meet the user's needs. For example, the accounts supervisor will wish to know about a bad debt of £50, but this will be of little or no concern to the managing director (who *would* want to know about a bad debt of £50 million!).

Consider these examples and then relate them to the management of the business where you work, or to an organisation that you know:

Decision-making

- higher level: "I have taken the decision to close our factory in Wales"
- intermediate level: "I have decided to buy a new photocopier for the office"
- lower level: "I will pay this petty cash claim"

Planning

- higher level: "We need to start planning the firm's expansion programme"
- intermediate level: "I am planning to increase production of Product Exe next month"
- lower level: "I plan to extract a trial balance first thing tomorrow"

Control

- higher level: "Last month's sales were up by ten per cent"
- intermediate level: "Costs for product Wye were squeezed by five per cent last month"
- lower level: "I have balanced the petty cash book"

The conclusion to be drawn is that we are all managers, but at different levels. For example, within an accounts office, the accounts assistant will be responsible for a different level of management to the supervisor who will, in turn, be responsible for a different level of management to the administration manager.

WHAT INFORMATION DOES A MANAGER NEED?

In order to be able to carry out the functions of decision-making, planning and control, managers need to have relevant management information available to them. Such management information within a business or organisation can take many forms – in this chapter and the next we focus on information available from the accounting records. Such 'known' information is usually the starting point for most management activities.

The Case Study below illustrates how the three themes of management (decision-making, planning and control) relate to the workings of an accounts department. After the Case Study we look in more detail at the accounting information available to management and the purposes to which it is put.

CASE STUDY

MANAGING THE ACCOUNTS DEPARTMENT

situation

You are an accounts assistant at Severnvale Nurseries, a large specialist grower of plants, which supplies garden centres throughout the country. Your experience in the accounts department has been quite varied – you have worked on sales (debtors) ledger, purchases (creditors) ledger, general (main) ledger, cash book and payroll.

Today the accounts supervisor is off work due to illness and the administration manager asks you to take charge of the accounts department which, as well as yourself, consists of two assistants (one of whom is part-time, working mornings only). In the supervisor's in-tray, you find:

- a number of purchases invoices ready to pay (some of which offer cash discount for prompt settlement)
- changes to the weekly payroll – new employees, tax code changes, pay rate alterations; the payroll needs to be processed today to ensure that the pay will be in employees' bank accounts by the end of the week
- a number of sales invoices to process

The company's bank statement has arrived in the post – it is practice to list the differences between it and the cash book on the same day.

The part-time accounts assistant is asking if he should balance the petty cash book and pass it to you for checking – today is the usual day of the week for this to be done.

How will you manage the work of the accounts department?

solution

planning
The first step is to take a few minutes to plan the day's work in order of priority. This would appear to be:

- changes to payroll data to be made
- process the payroll
- take advantage of cash discounts on purchases invoices
- check the terms of payment to see whether other purchases invoices should be paid today
- processing sales invoices

Balancing the petty cash book and comparing the bank statement with the cash book appear to be lower priority and could be left until tomorrow.

decision-making
You brief the two assistants on your plan for the day.

You ask the full-time assistant to enter the changes to the payroll and then to process the payroll, including preparation of cheques and BACS payments, and also to enter the transactions in the double-entry accounts. The accounts assistant has dealt with payroll before.

The part-time assistant, who has limited accounts experience, will process sales invoices by entering them into the sales day book, sales ledger and general ledger.

In the meantime you will go through the purchases invoices in order to identify those that offer a cash discount for prompt settlement – they can be paid by cheque or BACS. The details will then be entered in the cash book and purchases ledger.

control
From time-to-time you check progress on processing the payroll, stressing the need to the accounts assistant to complete the task so that employees will have the pay in their bank accounts by the end of the week. Later on you check the schedule for cheques and BACS payments, together with the entries made in the double-entry accounts. Cheques and the BACS payment schedule have to be signed by an authorised signatory to the company's bank account, so you will need to contact the administration manager to arrange this.

You supervise the work of the part-time assistant and resolve any queries that he may have in processing sales invoices. You check the double-entry transactions and, if time permits, ask the assistant to prepare statements of account to be sent out to debtors: this ensures that customers will pay on time.

From the purchases invoices, you select for payment those that offer a cash discount. You prepare cheques or BACS payments and make the entries in the cash book and purchases ledger. The administration manager will need to arrange for the cheques and the BACS payment schedule to be signed.

You also check other purchases invoices for the terms of payment – some may be due for payment today, having come to the end of their credit term; for others it might be prudent to pay them as the nursery may want to buy further goods from the suppliers in the near future.

You keep control of the accounts department during the day and, if there is time, you will ask for the petty cash book to be balanced (which you can then check) and for the bank statement to be examined for unpresented cheques and outstanding lodgements to see if any items need investigation.

summary

At the end of the day you review progress to see how well your planning, decision-making and control has handled the workload of the department.

With the possibility that the accounts supervisor may not be back to work tomorrow you begin to plan for the next day's work.

ACCOUNTING INFORMATION FOR MANAGERS

The accounting records provide the management of a business or organisation with information to:

- assist with decision-making, for example by giving income from sales, and expenditure costs, of different products or services

- assist with planning, for example by giving details of income and expenditure that can then be estimated for the future

- assist with control, for example by comparing estimates of what was expected to happen with details of what has actually happened

All of these aspects use known information from the accounting records, but some also include estimates of what is likely to happen in the future; such estimates are usually based on what has happened in the past. The accounting records that we have used so far throughout this book are based on actual transactions that have taken place – this type of accounting is referred to as *financial accounting*; taking the actual transactions, looking at them in different ways, and estimating them for the future in order to provide information is referred to as *management accounting*. To use a simple example to illustrate the differences: how much you or a friend *actually* earned last year is financial accounting information; how much you or your friend *expect* to earn next year is management accounting information. In the sections which follow we will look in more detail at the differences between these two types of accounting.

WHAT IS FINANCIAL ACCOUNTING?

Financial accounting is concerned with recording financial transactions that have happened already, and with providing information from the accounting records, for example, in order to prepare VAT returns, and trial balance (the starting point for the preparation of the profit and loss statement and balance sheet – covered at NVQ levels 3 and 4).

The main features of financial accounting are that it:

- records transactions that have happened already
- looks backwards to show what has happened in the past
- is accurate to the nearest penny, with no estimated amounts
- is often a legal requirement to keep accounts (in order to prepare VAT returns, and tax returns for the Inland Revenue showing income and expenditure)
- maintains confidentiality of information (eg payroll details, VAT returns)

CASE STUDY

INFORMATION FROM THE FINANCIAL ACCOUNTS

situation

The accounts supervisor at Severnvale Nurseries (see Case Study page 432) is off work for a second day. Again the administration manager asks you to take charge of the accounts department.

The routine work of the accounts department is going well; you receive two queries from other departments of the business.

MEMORANDUM

To	Accounts Supervisor	Ref	TS 405
From	Tim Smith, Administration Manager	Date	16 May 2001
Subject	Telephone expenses		

Could you please let me have details of the amount spent by the company on telephone expenses last month?

I would appreciate the information as soon as possible. Many thanks.

accounts.dept@severnvalenurseries.co.uk, 16/5/01 10:17 am   **1**

To: accounts.dept

From: Jason.Miles

I need some information as soon as possible for a meeting of sales staff this afternoon. Please let me know amount of sales commission paid last month.

On another matter, I'd like to have last month's sales figure for our range of conservatory plants. Thanks

Jason Miles, Sales Manager

solution

These two requests are examples of how the accounting records can provide management information to other departments of the business. The information is available from the main ledger accounts of telephone expenses, sales commission and sales: conservatory plants (to provide details of sales for each section or product of the business, separate sales accounts need to be established, eg 'sales: conservatory plants'; 'sales: shrubs', etc). Last month's figures can be calculated by comparing the difference between the opening balance at the beginning of the month with the closing balance at the month-end; for example, with telephone expenses:

balance of account at 30 April 2001 .... £7,459 (closing balance)
balance of account at 1 April 2001 .... £6,245 (opening balance)
difference, being amount spent during April 2001 ....£1,214

In providing the information to the administration manager and the sales manager, it is important to note that they will want the total only for the month – they will not be interested in individual amounts (if more detailed information is needed, they will make further enquiries of the accounts department).

The replies to the queries are as follows (using example figures):

MEMORANDUM

To	Tim Smith, Administration Manager	**Ref**	AS 309
From	Acting Accounts Supervisor	**Date**	16 May 2001
Subject	Telephone expenses		

Further to your memo of today, the amount spent on telephone expenses during April 2001 was £1,214.

If I can be of further assistance, please do not hesitate to contact me.

Jason.Miles@severnvalenurseries.co.uk, 16/5/01 11:54 am   **1**
To: Jason.Miles
From: accounts.dept

Further to your e-mail of today, the amounts for April 2001 are as follows:

sales commission paid £2,748

sales of conservatory plants £35,424

If we can be of further assistance, please do not hesitate to contact us.

WHAT IS MANAGEMENT ACCOUNTING?

Management accounting is concerned with looking at actual transactions in different ways from financial accounting. In particular, the costs of each product or service are considered both in the past and the likely costs in the future. In this way, management accounting is able to provide information to help the business or organisation plan for the future.

The main features of management accounting are that it:

- uses accounting information to summarise transactions that have happened already and to make estimates for the future

- looks in detail at the costs – materials, labour and expenses (see below) – and the sales income of products and services

- looks forward to show what is likely to happen in the future

- may use estimates where these are the most useful or suitable form of information

- provides management with reports that are of use in running the business or organisation

- provides management information as frequently as circumstances demand – speed is often vital as information may go out-of-date very quickly

- is not sent to people outside the organisation – it is for internal use

- maintains confidentiality of information (eg payroll details)

HOW THE ORGANISATION IS STRUCTURED

Management information that is available from the accounting records varies according to the structure of the organisation. The diagram on the next page shows how the different types of organisations can be classified between:

- public sector and private sector
- type of industry (note that the term 'industry' includes service providers)

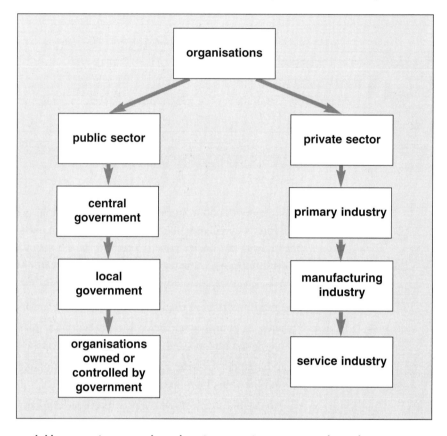

public sector and private sector organisations

Public sector organisations are owned directly or indirectly by central or local government. Examples include the National Health Service and the Post Office.

Private sector organisations are owned by private individuals – as shareholders of a company, owners of partnerships and sole-trader businesses. Examples include well-known names such as Tesco, Marks and Spencer, BT.

types of industry

- primary industries produce the raw materials used by other businesses; examples include oil, gas and agriculture
- manufacturing (secondary) industries manufacture products; examples include the aerospace industry, electronics, pharmaceuticals
- service (tertiary) industries provide services such as transport and tourism

functions within the organisation

The following diagram illustrates the broad functions within most organisations.

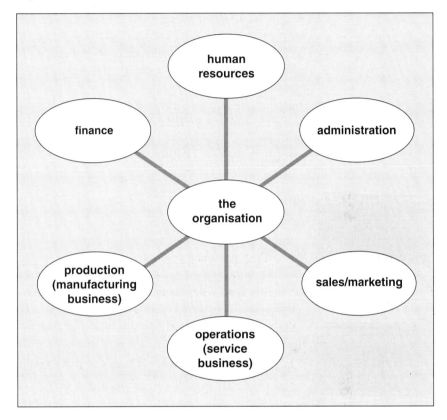

- *finance* – provides financial accounting and management accounting services
- *human resources* – provides the staff to run the business; involved in hiring new staff, laying-off surplus staff, pay and overtime rates, conditions of service
- *administration* – ensures the overall smooth running of the organisation by providing office support
- *sales/marketing* – the promotion and sales of the company's products or services
- *production* – the organisation and operation of the production process in a manufacturing business, including buying materials, incurring labour costs and other expenses and ensuring that production quality and targets are met
- *operations* – the organisation and operation of the provision of services to customers

As businesses grow larger so the functions within the organisation grow more complex. For example, a large manufacturing business may be subdivided into divisions for each product it makes, or even parts of the manufacturing process; a service business may subdivide into different geographical areas. Whatever method is chosen for the organisation of the business will impact on the work of financial accounting and management accounting. In order for the finance department to be able to provide useful management information, systems need to be put in place early on to ensure that information requirements can be met. To give an example, this might mean having separate sales accounts for each main product or service of the business; similarly with the expenditure accounts for costs such as purchases and running costs. In this way the sales income and expenditure for each product or service can be provided readily.

COSTS AND INCOME

Each of the functions of the organisation that we have seen in the previous section incurs costs – eg administration costs, production costs – and some of the functions will generate income, eg from sales of products or services. The accounting system will be able to supply management information about costs and income for each function of the organisation, and answer questions such as:

- what were the sales for products A and B last month?
- what was the payroll cost of the administration department last year?
- what was our income from operations in the last quarter?
- how much did we spend on marketing last year?

In order to provide such information we need to consider the main costs and income and then see how it is analysed to the different functions of the business or organisation.

costs

All businesses and organisations, whether they manufacture products or provide services incur costs – these can be broken down into three elements of cost: materials, labour and expenses.

Materials costs include the cost of:

- raw materials and components bought for use by a manufacturing business
- products bought for resale by a shop or a wholesaler
- service items or consumables, such as stationery, bought for use within a business or organisation

Thus materials range from sheet metal and plastics used in a car factory, computer chips and other components bought in by a computer manufacturer, tins of baked beans and other goods bought in by a supermarket, through to photocopying paper used in a college. It is true to say that all business and organisations incur materials costs.

Labour costs refers to the payroll costs of all employees of the business or organisation. Such costs include:

- wages paid to those who work on the production line of a manufacturing business
- wages and salaries paid to those who work for a manufacturing business but are not directly involved in the production line, eg supervisors, maintenance staff, office staff, sales people
- wages and salaries of those who work in the service industry, eg shops, banks, restaurants, accountants
- public sector wages, eg of central and local government employees

Expenses refers to all other running costs of the business or organisation that cannot be included under the headings of materials and labour. Examples include rent, rates, heating, lighting, telephone, advertising, insurance, and so on.

income

The main source of income for the private sector is from the sale of products or services. There may also be other, smaller, amounts of income, eg interest received on bank balances, rental income if a part of the premises is let to a tenant, government grants and allowances for setting up a new business or buying new technology.

For the public sector, the main sources of income for central and local government are from taxes and rates. Government owned or controlled organisations either receive grants and allowances or, in the case of trading businesses in the public sector, such as the Post Office, receive income from the products and services that they supply.

COST CENTRES

In order to provide management with information from the accounting system the costs – materials, labour and expenses – need to be analysed between the different functions, or sections, within the business or organisation. This is achieved by the use of cost centres.

Cost centres are sections of a business to which costs can be charged.

Thus a cost centre can be any function or section of the organisation. In a manufacturing business it can be an entire factory, a department of a factory, or a particular stage in the production process. In a service industry it can be a shop, or group of shops in an area, a teaching department or a resources centre within a college, a ward or operating theatre in a hospital. Any section of a business can be a cost centre – each of the functions within the organisation that we considered earlier (page 439) would be appropriate cost centres. A manager or supervisor will be responsible for each cost centre and it is this person who will be seeking information from the accounts system.

analysis of costs to different cost centres

Once the cost centres of an organisation have been established it is necessary to ensure that the accounts system is able to give information to the manager of each cost centre. In order to do this, separate accounts are established for each cost centre to cover the main cost headings. For example, labour costs can be split between 'wages and salaries: production', 'wages and salaries: administration', 'wages and salaries: human resources', and so on. By analysing costs in this way the accounts system is able to provide the cost centre manager with information about how much has been spent by, or charged to, the centre over the last month, quarter, half-year, or year. Such information will help the manager to

- plan for the future, eg by using actual costs, will be able to forecast next year's costs
- make decisions, eg by comparing the costs of different products or services, will be helped in deciding whether to increase or decrease output
- control costs, eg by comparing actual costs with budgeted costs (see next chapter), will be able to take steps, where necessary, to reduce costs

Thus the accounts system is able to tell the manager what has happened – at least in terms of financial information.

where does the information come from?

The sources of information to enable the analysis of costs include:
- purchases invoices, for materials and expenses costs
- payroll schedules, for labour costs
- bills and cash receipts, for expenses costs

The amounts of each cost are then analysed to the cost centre which has incurred the cost: the diagram on the next page shows how this process works.

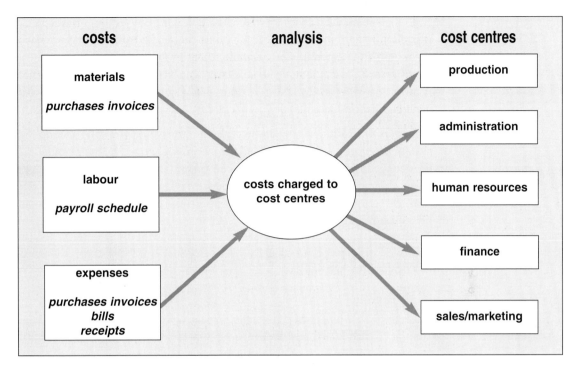

PROFIT CENTRES

For some sections of businesses the cost centre approach of analysing costs is taken to a further level by also analysing sales income to centres. As sales income less costs equals profit, such centres are called profit centres.

Profit centres are sections of a business to which costs can be charged, income can be identified, and profit can be calculated.

From the definition we can see that profit centres have both costs and income. It follows, therefore, that profit centres will be based on sections of the business that make products or services (incur costs) and sell them to customers (receive income from sales). For example, Severnvale Nurseries (see Case Study on page 432) might have conservatory plants as a profit centre as shown in the diagram which follows.

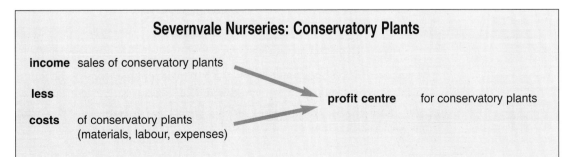

Note that many cost centres provide support services within a business or organisation and, so, cannot become profit centres because they do not have any significant income. For example, the administration department of a business is a cost centre to which costs can be charged, but it does not receive any income. As we have seen profit centres both incur costs and generate income.

Managers of profit centres will be seeking information from the accounting system about the costs incurred and the income generated by their centre. By deducting costs from income they can quantify the profit made and can make comparisons with previous periods (eg last month, last quarter, last year, etc) and also with other profit centres (eg "our profit was higher than yours last month").

INVESTMENT CENTRES

A further development of profit centres is to consider profit in relation to the amount of money invested in the centre. For *investment centres* the profit of the centre is compared with how much money the business has put in to earn that profit.

Investment centres are sections of a business where profit can be compared with the amount of money invested in the centre.

Profit is usually compared with money invested by means of a percentage as shown in the diagram which follows for Severnvale Nurseries.

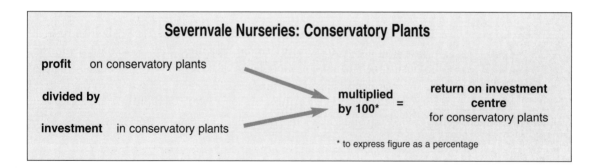

Managers of investment centres will wish to make comparisons of the return on investment for the current period with that of previous periods, and also with the other investment centres of the business, eg "have we done better than last year?", "how do we compare with the other investment centres?"

CASE STUDY

PROVIDING INFORMATION FOR MANAGEMENT

situation

Once again you are standing in for the accounts supervisor at Severnvale Nurseries (see Case Study on page 432).

The managing director, Charlie Rimmack, has telephoned to ask you for accounting information that is needed for this afternoon. Apparently the managers of two sections of the business – the manager for conservatory plants and the manager for shrubs – have been arguing about which one is doing better. Charlie wants information in order to resolve the dispute; she requests details for each section of costs and income for last year, and the amount of money invested in each section at the end of the year. (She says that all figures can be to the nearest £000.)

solution

You go to accounts which have been set up to show costs, income and money invested for each section, and extract the following information for last year:

		Conservatory plants £000s	Shrubs £000s
Costs:	materials	137	151
	labour	93	134
	expenses	45	70
Sales		425	555
Money invested		300	400

In order to help the managing director you decide to present the management information for each section in the following way:

	Conservatory plants £000s	Shrubs £000s
Cost Centre		
Materials	137	151
Labour	93	134
Expenses	45	70
Total	275	355

Here the cost centre for conservatory plants has the lower costs.

Profit Centre		
Income from sales	425	555
less		
Costs (see above)	275	355
Profit	150	200

These figures show that shrubs is the better profit centre.

Investment Centre

Profit (see above)	150	200
Investment	300	400
Expressed as a percentage (multiplied by 100)	50%	50%

Based on last year's figures both sections of the business, as investment centres, are performing as well as each other.

Conclusion

• The information provided by the accounts supervisor is based on figures taken the *financial accounting* records. It is taken from the accounts which record the transactions that have happened already.

• The managing director and the managers of the sections will also be interested in using *management accounting* to provide them with information to help with decision-making, planning and control.

ANALYSIS OF COSTS AND INCOME – CODING

what is coding?

Coding is the means by which costs and income are analysed to centres (cost centres, profit centres or investment centres). A number is written on each prime document received (eg sales invoices, purchases invoices, receipts, etc) to analyse it to a particular centre, and to indicate the type of cost or income represented by the document. The following code, as an example, is used by Severnvale Nurseries (see Case Study on page 432):

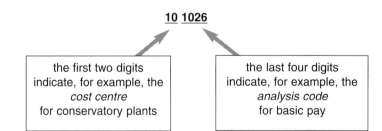

10 1026

the first two digits indicate, for example, the *cost centre* for conservatory plants	the last four digits indicate, for example, the *analysis code* for basic pay

The code 101026 (above) indicates to the book-keeper who is recording items in the accounts that the amount of the prime document is to be debited to 'basic pay – conservatory plants' account. Note that, from the six-digit code used here:

– the first two digits indicate the cost centre

– the last four digits indicate the analysis code

Whilst a six-digit code has been used here, a business can use whatever coding system suits it best – any combination of letters or numbers. For example, Severnvale Nurseries could use letters for the cost centres and numbers for the analysis, so CP 1026 could be used for the conservatory plants (CP) cost centre, with the analysis to basic pay (1026). Whatever system of coding is in use, it must be recorded in the organisation's *procedures manual* (the book that states how all operations within the organisation are to be carried out), so that it can be followed, on a consistent basis, by anybody at any time.

A practical point for the establishment of code numbers is that you would not initially use consecutive numbers but would leave plenty of 'gaps' for future development of the system. For example, a business with three cost centres would not code these as 11, 12 and 13; instead it would be more sensible to use 10, 20 and 30 – leaving plenty of space for any new cost centres.

The analysis codes will group together the three main costs of materials, labour and expenses, and the income items, as shown in the example below.

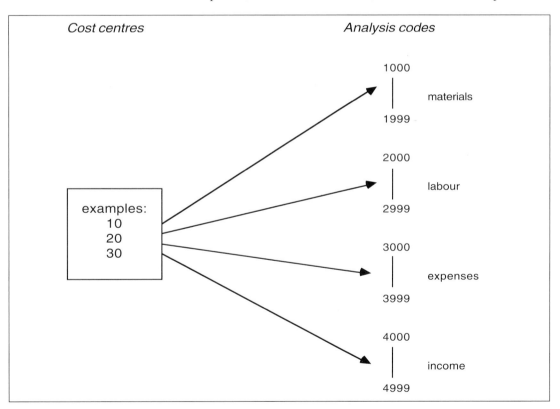

With cost centre numbers in round tens and using a four-digit analysis, the code numbers should not be too difficult to use on a day-to-day basis and will provide the right level of detail. Note that the procedures manual will give the full list of codes and this should be referred to as and when necessary.

Within the accounts department of a business or organisation, it is necessary to code prime documents, both received (purchases invoices, receipts) and issued (copies of sales invoices). The person carrying out such coding – the coding clerk – must work to high standards of accuracy – wrong coding of a document will lead to it being posted to the wrong account in the accounts system, which will lead to incorrect information being supplied to the managers, which could in turn lead to wrong decision-making.

The way in which documents are coded varies from one organisation to another. For some, the code number is written on the document and marked clearly; others use a rubber stamp to provide a layout on which can be indicated the code number and the initials of the person entering the code.

For a coding system to work well:

- codes should provide the correct level of detail, ie cost centre code and analysis code
- coding of documents must be accurate
- code numbers must be complete, ie the full code to be indicated, and not just the cost centre or the analysis code
- coding of documents must be carried out at regular intervals within the timescales required by the organisation

The objective of coding is to provide correct analysis so as to give information from the accounts system to managers. By analysing costs and income to cost (and other) centres we can answer questions such as "how much was the basic pay for my cost centre last month?"; "how much was overtime?".

problems and errors with coding

No administration system within an organisation is completely free of problems and 'fool-proof'. With coding the main problem is in deciding the cost centre and the analysis code to be used – the prime document may not be clear as to which centre has incurred the cost and what type of cost it is. The procedures manual may help but, if not, such items will have to be referred to the supervisor (who may need to make further enquiries).

A further difficulty occurs when a bill is received which relates to more than one cost centre (or even all the cost centres of the organisation). For example, an electricity bill is received for the whole business – how is it to be analysed between the cost centres? The answer here (assuming that no cost centres have their own meters and are billed separately) is to *apportion* the cost over all cost centres to which the bill relates. At its most simple, an equal share could be used – if there were ten cost centres then each would be apportioned one-tenth of the bill. However, some cost centres will have used more electricity than others and an appropriate method of apportionment must be found – this could relate to the number of employees in each centre, or the floor area, or other criteria could be used. The accounts assistant who is coding such costs will need guidance on apportionment either from the procedures manual or the accounts supervisor.

As with much of the work of the accounts department, a high level of confidentiality is needed in coding costs and income. In particular, the managers of cost centres and profit centres may seek to influence the coding process in order to reduce their costs and maximise their income. Thus the query from the accounts department "did your cost centre incur this cost?" will usually produce a negative response from the cost centre manager; by contrast, the question "does this income relate to your profit centre?" will invariably be answered with "yes!" Confidentiality ensures that the accounts department works independently of the other cost (and profit) centres – although some queries may have to be resolved by reference to the centres – and also ensures that management information is accurate.

An error of coding occurs when an incorrect code is applied to a prime document. This will lead to the item being posted to the wrong account in the accounts system. Thus the costs of one cost centre will be overstated whilst those of another will be understated; similarly income will be overstated in one profit centre but will be understated in another.

Incorrect coding means that the accounts system is inaccurate for internal management use within the business or organisation. (External suppliers and buyers of goods and services are unaffected as they will still be paid the amounts due to them, or will receive sales invoices for the correct amounts.) Incorrect management information is being supplied, which could lead to wrong estimates for next year (being based on current-year figures), or to wrong decisions being made.

Accuracy of coding is therefore an important step in the provision of accounts information to managers. It is good practice for some codes – particularly for large amounts – to be double-checked. If wrong codes are found on a regular basis, it would be worthwhile to investigate the coding system to see if it can be simplified.

other discrepancies in documentation

As well as errors of coding, the coding clerk will be on the lookout for discrepancies in documentation. These can include *excessive volumes* and invoices addressed to the *wrong organisation* or be for *fictitious expenses*.

excessive volumes

The coding clerk will also be on the look out for excessive volumes of costs or income. This occurs when the wrong quantity of costs or income is shown on the prime document, and the volume is much greater than the amounts normally seen. Excessive volumes are often caused by a misunderstanding between the buyer and the supplier. For example, you want 30 computer disks for use in the office and fill in a purchase order; the supplier sells disks packed in boxes of 10 and assumes that you mean 30 *boxes* and supplies you with 300 disks!

Clear communication is the best way of avoiding the error of excessive volumes. There should be several checks within the accounts system to avoid the problem, and the coding clerk provides a further line of defence.

wrong organisations

Another error that, in theory, should not slip through the accounts system is where prime documents for costs relate to a different business or organisation. The coding clerk should check carefully that the documents do relate to the organisation, and are not for another business or organisation with a similar name.

fictitious expenses

Another point that the coding clerk can also watch for is where an unscrupulous business sends out invoices for fictitious expenses – for example, to cover the cost of an unwanted entry in a trade directory (which may never be published). Because amounts are small and do not raise suspicions, such invoices are often paid by larger businesses and organisations.

CASE STUDY

CASE STUDY: CODING THE COSTS

situation

Wyvern Royal Infirmary Trust is a National Health Service trust hospital. You are an assistant in the accounts department and today you are working on the purchases (creditors) ledger. For accounting purposes the hospital is divided into a number of cost centres or income centres. The following are the codes for some of the departments which are cost centres:

x-ray department	cost centre code 10
casualty	cost centre code 20
pharmacy	cost centre code 30
physiotherapy	cost centre code 40

The following posting sheet for purchases invoices has been handed to you by the accounts supervisor, Phillippa Farrell, who asks you to complete the coding column for the costs:

WYVERN ROYAL INFIRMARY TRUST

Posting sheet: purchases invoices

Supplier	Department	Description	Amount	Coding
			£	
Zodak Films	x-ray	x-ray film	4,250.57	
Wye Plaster Co	casualty	fine-grade plaster	754.93	
Beech Drugs plc	pharmacy	drugs	2,941.26	
Tyax Sports Ltd	physiotherapy	rowing machines	3,248.36	
Electro Ltd	x-ray	repairs to scanner	1,495.22	
WR Industries plc	casualty	disposable gloves	472.33	
Country Pie Co	kitchen	pies (various)	528.36	
Wyvern Cleaning Co	casualty	cleaning services	2,871.89	
		Check list total	16,562.92	

Prepared by *Ginger Waterman* Date *18 June 2001*

Checked by *Lucinda Luz* Date *19 June 2001*

Coded by _____ Date _____

Posted by _____ Date _____

The accounts supervisor has given you the coding list which includes the following:

cost	code no
cleaning materials	3200
contract cleaning	3225
dressings and plaster	1100
electricity and gas	1350
exercise equipment	1900
laundry contract	3250
mechanical and electrical repairs	3250
medicines and drugs	1500
uniforms and disposables	1600
x-ray film	1125

You are to complete the coding section of the posting sheet as far as you are able. Any items you are not able to code are to be queried by e-mail to the accounts supervisor asking for the appropriate code(s).

solution

Using the cost centre codes and the cost codes, the posting sheet is coded as follows:

WYVERN ROYAL INFIRMARY TRUST

Posting sheet: purchases invoices

Supplier	Department	Description	Amount	Coding
			£	
Zodak Films	x-ray	x-ray film	4,250.57	101125
Wye Plaster Co	casualty	fine-grade plaster	754.93	201100
Beech Drugs plc	pharmacy	drugs	2,941.26	301500
Tyax Sports Ltd	physiotherapy	rowing machines	3,248.36	401900
Electro Ltd	x-ray	repairs to scanner	1,495.22	103250
WR Industries plc	casualty	disposable gloves	472.33	201600
Country Pie Co	kitchen	pies (various)	528.36	
Wyvern Cleaning Co	casualty	cleaning services	2,871.89	203225
		Check list total	16,562.92	

Prepared by   *Ginger Waterman*   Date   *18 June 2001*

Checked by   *Lucinda Luz*   Date   *19 June 2001*

Coded by   _____   Date   _____

Posted by   _____   Date   _____

As you are unable to complete the coding it is important to be able to describe the problem and refer it to the appropriate person. Accordingly, you send the following e-mail to the accounts supervisor, Phillippa Farrell:

Phillippa.Farrell@writ.swest.nhs.uk, 20/6/01 10:32 am
To: Phillippa.Farrell
From: A.Student

I have been coding the purchases invoices but I don't have a cost centre code and cost code for one of the items. The cost centre is the kitchen and the cost code is for pies (presumably the code will be for food). Can you please advise me?

The accounts supervisor replies by e-mail as follows:

A.Student@writ.swest.nhs.uk, 20/6/01 11:44 am
To: A.Student
From: Phillippa.Farrell

Further to your e-mail this morning, the cost centre code for the kitchen is 60; the cost code for food is 3825.

You are now able to complete the posting sheet with the code 603825. You sign as the person coding it, date it, and pass it on for posting to the purchases (creditors) ledger by the data input clerk

CHAPTER SUMMARY

- Managers are those within a business or organisation who are involved in decision-making, planning and control.

- Managers make use of
  - financial accounting to provide reports on past transactions
  - management accounting to provide reports which summarise transactions that have happened in the recent past and to make estimates for the future

- Organisations can be classified between
  - public sector and private sector
  - type of industry (including providers of services)

- The main functions within an organisation include:
  - finance
  - human resources
  - administration
  - sales/marketing
  - production (in a manufacturing business)
  - operations (provision of services to customers)

- The three elements of cost comprise
  - materials, raw materials and components, products bought in for resale, service or consumable items
  - labour, the payroll costs of employees
  - expenses, all other running costs

- Costs are analysed between the different functions or sections of a business or organisation by the use of cost centres.

- Profit centres include an analysis of both costs and income to show the profit (income less costs).

- Investment centres consider profit in relation to the amount of money invested in the centre, and express it as a percentage return on investment.

- Coding is the means by which costs and income are analysed to cost/profit/investment centres.

- Errors in coding and discrepancies in documentation include
  - wrong codes
  - excessive volumes
  - wrong organisations
  - fictitious expenses

KEY TERMS

financial accounting	is concerned with recording financial transactions that have happened already, and with providing information from the accounting records
management accounting	uses accounting information to summarise transactions that have happened in the recent past and to make estimates for the future
costs	comprise materials, labour and expenses
income	the sale of products or services
cost centre	section of a business to which costs can be charged
profit centre	a section of a business to which costs can be charged, income can be identified, and profit can be calculated
investment centre	a section of a business where profit can be compared with the amount of money invested in the centre, and can be expressed as a percentage return on investment
coding	a code number written on prime documents to analyse it a particular cost/profit/investment centre and to indicate the type of cost or income

STUDENT ACTIVITIES

20.1 What are the three main functions of a manager?

20.2 What are the two types of information that the accounting system is able to provide for managers?

20.3 What are the main differences between financial accounting and management accounting?

20.4 "Managers include anybody within the business or organisation who is involved in decision-making, planning and control."

Using your workplace, or an organisation with which you are familiar, give examples of

* the management functions you undertake
* the management functions undertaken by the managing director or chief executive

Show how each management function relates to the areas of decision-making, planning and control.

20.5 You work as an accounts assistant at Surestart Training, an organisation funded by central government. It provides skills training to help young people (aged 16-25) who are unemployed following the closure of a major employer in the area.

On return from holiday, you arrive back at work on Monday to find that the accounts supervisor has been off work due to illness all last week and is not expected back for several days. You are asked by the administration manager to take charge of accounts department. There are two assistants working with you today, one of whom is part-time, working mornings only.

The following tasks are waiting:

*   cash book wasn't written up last week and the bank statement has arrived in the post this morning

*   petty cash book needs to be balanced for last week and the imprest amount restored

*   trainers employed by Surestart Training are due to be paid on Friday; there are pay calculations for hourly-paid trainers to be made, together with changes – new employees, tax code changes, etc – before the payroll can be processed

*   a number of purchases invoices need to be paid – some are due for payment today at the end of the credit period; others offer cash discount for prompt settlement

Show how you will manage the work of the accounts department in relation to the areas of decision-making, planning and control.

20.6 Study the following accounting activities and decide which of them are financial accounting and which are management accounting:

(a)   recording purchases invoices in the creditors' ledger

(b)   listing sales invoices in the sales day book

(c)   using last year's sales figure to estimate next year's sales

(d)   reporting last year's cost of materials

(e)   analysing costs between different cost centres

(f)   calculating the return on investment of an investment centre

20.7 Using your workplace, or an organisation with which you are familiar, give examples of

*   the management accounting information you are asked for

*   the management accounting information your supervisor/manager is asked for

20.8 (a)   Explain the difference between

*   cost centre

*   profit centre

*   investment centre

(b)   Suggest likely cost centres for

*   a school or a college

*   a manufacturing business which makes two product lines

(c)   Give examples of cost centres in your workplace, or an organisation with which you are familiar.

20.9 You work as an accounts assistant at City News and Books, a company which owns a group of shops selling newspapers and magazines, books and stationery. The accounting system has been set up to show costs, income and money invested for each of these three sections of the business: newspapers and magazines, books, stationery.

The finance director has requested details for each section of costs and income for last year, and the amount of money invested in each section at the end of the year. (She says that all figures can be to the nearest £000.)

The accounts supervisor asks you to deal with this request and you go to the accounts and extract the following information for last year:

	Newspapers and magazines	Books	Stationery
	£000s	£000s	£000s
Costs: materials	155	246	122
labour	65	93	58
expenses	27	35	25
Sales	352	544	230
Money invested	420	850	250

The accounts supervisor asks you to present the information for the finance director in the form of a memorandum which shows the costs, profit, and return on investment for each section of the business.

20.10 You are an accounts assistant at Eagle Books, a large publisher of textbooks and novels. The business is split into four divisions: academic textbooks, novels, children's books and sports books. The accounts system is arranged so that each division is a profit centre. There is also a separate cost centre for administration.

An extract from the company's coding manual is as follows:

cost or profit centre number	cost or profit centre name
20	academic textbooks
30	novels
40	children's books
50	sports books
60	administration

analysis code	cost or income
1050	paper
2100	basic pay
2150	overtime
2200	bonus payments

2300	holiday pay
2400	sick pay
3050	authors' royalties
3100	rates
3150	heating and lighting
3200	telephone
3500	building maintenance
3525	computers and equipment maintenance
3550	vehicle running costs
3700	advertising
4050	sales to bookshops
4250	sales to wholesalers

The following prime documents have been received today (amounts are net of VAT, where applicable):

(a)   copy of a sales invoice showing the sale of £14,750 of academic textbooks to Orton Book Wholesalers Limited

(b)   printer's bill of £22,740 for paper for printing sports books

(c)   payroll summary showing overtime of £840 last month in the children's book section

(d)   payment of £1,540 for advertising sports books in the magazine 'Sport Today'

(e)   telephone bill of £1,200 to be split equally between all cost and profit centres

(f)   royalties of £88,245 paid to children's book authors

(g)   copy of sales invoice showing the sale of £1,890 of novels to the Airport Bookshop

You are to code the above transactions using the coding manual extract given.

Your supervisor asks you to provide a summary of the day's costs and income, analysed between materials, labour, expenses, and income. You know that the coding system is split into the following categories:

code numbers	category
1000 – 1999	materials
2000 – 2999	labour
3000 – 3999	expenses
4000 – 4999	income

Reply to your supervisor by means of a memorandum or an e-mail.

21 PRESENTING AND COMPARING MANAGEMENT INFORMATION

this chapter covers . . .

This chapter explains how the information needed by management is collected and presented. This involves:

- establishing exactly what information is needed and who needs it

- appreciating that information can relate to a previous period (eg last year), a corresponding period (eg the same month last year) and a future period (eg forecasts for next year)

- working out any differences between forecast data and actual income and costs

- identifying the correct format in which to present the data (eg e-mail, report, letter) and appreciating that different formats are used depending on who needs the information and how urgent and confidential it is

NVQ PERFORMANCE CRITERIA COVERED

unit 4: SUPPLYING INFORMATION FOR MANAGEMENT CONTROL

element 2

provide comparisons on costs and income

- information requirements are clarified with the appropriate person

- information extracted from a particular source is compared with actual results

- discrepancies are identified

- comparisons are provided to the appropriate person in the required format

- organisational requirements for confidentiality are strictly followed

WHAT INFORMATION DOES THE MANAGER NEED?

what is a manager?

As we saw in the last chapter, the term 'manager' can apply to many different people. A managing director is a manager, so is a supervisor. They are both involved – at different levels of responsibility – in:

- planning what the business does
- making decisions
- controlling business activity

Managers at different levels of the organisation need information so that they can plan, make decisions and run the business more efficiently.

what is management information?

Managers will be interested in financial information for:

- income
- costs

This information comprises:

- a record of transactions that have already taken place and been entered in the accounts of the business – this is part of **financial accounting**
- summaries and analysis of what has happened in the past and estimates of future performance – this is part of **management accounting**

CLARIFYING THE TYPE OF INFORMATION NEEDED

A number of questions need to be asked when gathering data for presenting management information:

1 Who is the **person who needs the information** – is it a supervisor, a departmental manager, or a director?

2 What is the **nature of the information** – does it relate to income (eg sales) or costs (eg wages, expenses)?

3 How is the information to be **presented** – in a standard report form (where you simply have to fill in the figures), an e-mail (quick and brief), a memo, or a letter?

4 How **urgent** is the request? Do you have to give it top priority and do it straightaway, or will later in the week be alright?

5   What **level of detail** is required? Does 'sales for the year' mean the total sales for all products for the year? Does the figure have to be broken down month-by-month and product-by-product?

6   How **accurate** do the figures have to be? The nearest thousand, hundred or an exact figure?

7   How **confidential** is the information? Does it matter if you leave a note of the figures lying around on your desk?

meeting the user's needs

The reason for these questions is that it is important to ensure that you **meet the user's needs** in presenting management information. There is no point in preparing a twenty page memorandum analysing wages figures for different product lines or services on a monthly basis if all the director wanted was the *total* labour cost for this year and last year.

The general principle is that senior managers will want to see information which presents an overview of what is going on so that they can make planning decisions. Departmental managers and supervisors, on the other hand, will be more interested in greater detail so that they can control the day-to-day running of the business. If senior managers want more information they will ask managers and supervisors. Look at the two diagrams which follow. They shows how the finance department provides management information to the two different functions in a business – one relates to income, the other to costs.

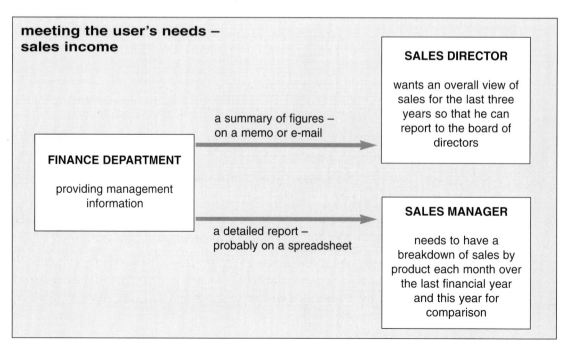

**meeting the user's needs –
sales income**

FINANCE DEPARTMENT

providing management
information

a summary of figures –
on a memo or e-mail

SALES DIRECTOR

wants an overall view of
sales for the last three
years so that he can
report to the board of
directors

a detailed report –
probably on a spreadsheet

SALES MANAGER

needs to have a
breakdown of sales by
product each month over
the last financial year
and this year for
comparison

meeting the user's needs –
production costs

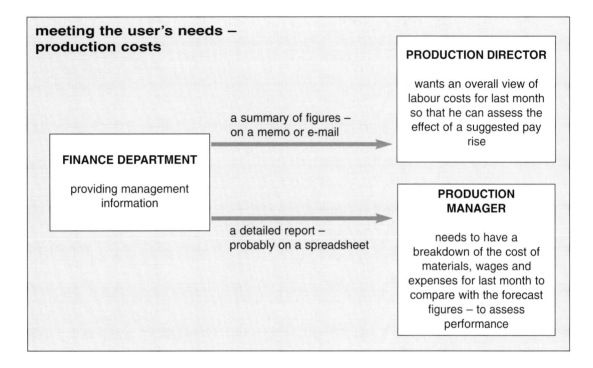

PRODUCTION DIRECTOR

wants an overall view of labour costs for last month so that he can assess the effect of a suggested pay rise

FINANCE DEPARTMENT

providing management information

a summary of figures – on a memo or e-mail

a detailed report – probably on a spreadsheet

PRODUCTION MANAGER

needs to have a breakdown of the cost of materials, wages and expenses for last month to compare with the forecast figures – to assess performance

COMPARING TIME PERIODS

In the Case Study on page 469 we will look at a number of types of management information and the ways in which it is presented. First, however, it is important to appreciate that management information can be compared over different time periods. . .

previous period comparisons

Managers will want to know the answer to questions such as:

"What are the sales for this quarter of the year compared with the figure for the previous quarter?"

"How much overtime was paid to production staff this month compared with last month?"

The data produced will be a **previous period comparison** – a straight comparison between this month or quarter with last month or quarter.

At the end of the financial year the managers are very interested to see how the business has performed over the current year compared with the previous year and are likely to require reports covering sales and costs.

corresponding period comparisons

Another way of comparing financial data is to report on the current period compared with a corresponding period in the past.

For example a gift shop manager may ask on Christmas Eve:

"What are our sales like this month so far compared with the same period last year?"

The manager of a theme park, such as Alton Towers, may ask:

"What income did we get from visitors this weekend, compared with the figure for last weekend?"

He may also ask:

"What income did we get from visitors this weekend, compared with the corresponding weekend last year?"

Corresponding period comparisons are very useful in assessing the performance of a business, particularly if it is a seasonal one, such as a gift shop or a theme park, where previous period comparisons are less useful because the figures can fluctuate considerably from month-to-month.

Look at the data in the table below. You can see that corresponding period comparisons can be made between the two years.

Merrie England Theme Park

Monthly income 2000 - 2001

	Jan £000	Feb £000	Mar £000	April £000	May £000	June £000	July £000	Aug £000	Sept £000	Oct £000	Nov £000	Dec £000	TOTAL £000
2000	130	140	180	250	360	550	760	700	400	140	120	135	3,865
2001	135	140	160	280	410	600	800	720	380	130	125	130	4,010

cumulative comparisons

Another useful method of comparison used by managers is to calculate **cumulative** financial data over corresponding periods. This is very simple: all you have to do is to add each monthly figure to the previous monthly figure as you go through the year. To get the cumulative figure for February 2000 from the above table you add January's and February's figures together (note that they are quoted in £000s), ie £130,000 plus £140,000 = £270,000. To get March's cumulative you add £180,000 (the March figure) to £270,000 = £450,000. The cumulative income table is shown on the next page.

Merrie England Theme Park

Cumulative monthly income 2000 - 2001

	Jan	Feb	Mar	April	May	June	July	Aug	Sept	Oct	Nov	Dec	TOTAL
	£000	£000	£000	£000	£000	£000	£000	£000	£000	£000	£000	£000	£000
2000	130	270	450	700	1,060	1,610	2,370	3,070	3,470	3,610	3,730	3,865	3,865
2001	135	275	435	715	1,125	1,725	2,525	3,245	3,625	3,755	3,880	4,010	4,010

As you can see from the above table, the corresponding periods from the two years can be compared easily. For example, income for the first six months was £1,610,000 in 2000 and £1,725,000 in 2001 (the figures in the table are quoted in £000s).

comparison of forecast data

So far we have compared data from past periods. Management will often require forecasts which can then be compared with what actually happens – for example a sales forecast. The forecast figures may well already be on a table or a spreadsheet file and you will be required to enter the actual figures so that management can see if the business is on target with the forecast or whether sales are better than forecast, or are below target.

The table below shows the sales forecast for a computer company for the first six months of 2001. The forecast figures are in the left-hand column for each month; the actual figures have been entered for the first three months for comparison purposes in the right-hand column under each month.

Helicon Computing Limited

Sales forecast January-June 2001

Jan		Feb		March		April		May		June	
forecast	actual	forecast	actual	forecast	actual	forecast	actual	forecast	actual	forecast	actual
£000	£000	£000	£000	£000	£000	£000	£000	£000	£000	£000	£000
50	**51**	60	**63**	65	**69**	60		65		70	

actual figures entered for management

CASE STUDY

CLARION CARDS LIMITED – EXTRACTING MANAGEMENT INFORMATION

situation

Clarion Cards is a company which manufactures a wide range of greetings cards and calendars. It employs 50 permanent staff at its factory and also takes on temporary employees in the summer.

You work in the Finance Department. One of your jobs is to extract and present financial information for the company management. Your supervisor, Ally Gee, gives you these tasks from time-to-time.

The data for the company's income and costs are shown in the tables on the next page. They are presented as quarterly results (figures for three month periods). They show:

• last year's figures

• this year's forecast figures

• the actual figures for the first two quarters of the year (1 January to 30 June)

The date today is 2 July 2001.

Your supervisor has just received the following memos from the Sales Manager, Bartholomew Simpson and the Production Manager, Ramjit Singh.

Ally has asked you to draft reply memos to go out in his name. He points out that the information is needed by the end of the week and that he will need time to check what you have written.

MEMORANDUM

To Ally Gee, Accounts Supervisor	**Ref** BS101
From B Simpson, Sales Manager	**Date** 29 June 2001
Subject Sales Report	

Please can you supply the following figures by 6 July: I need them for a management meeting.

1. Total sales for the last quarter

2. The sales figure for the corresponding quarter last year

3. The forecast sales figure for the last quarter.

Many thanks.

MEMORANDUM

To   Ally Gee, Accounts Supervisor   **Ref**   RS101

From R Singh, Production Manager   **Date** 28 June 2001

Subject Costs Report

Please can you supply the following figures by 6 July; I have got a management meeting coming up the following week.

1. Total costs for the last quarter.
2. The costs figure for the corresponding quarter last year.
3. The forecast costs figure for the last quarter.

R.S.

QUARTERLY SALES

	Year 2000 Actual £000s	Year 2001 Forecast £000s	Year 2001 Actual £000s
Jan-Mar	150	160	155
Apr-Jun	160	170	165
Jul-Sep	170	180	
Oct-Dec	250	275	

QUARTERLY COSTS

	Year 2000 Actual £000s	Year 2001 Forecast £000s	Year 2001 Actual £000s
Jan-Mar	100	110	105
Apr-Jun	110	120	115
Jul-Sep	180	190	
Oct-Dec	120	125	

Clarion's sales

Most of Clarion's sales are made in the Autumn when the shops stock up with cards and calendars for Christmas, although it receives a steady income throughout the year for its birthday and 'special occasion' cards.

Clarion's costs

Clarions's costs fall into three main categories:

- materials – the cost of paper and card used in the production process
- labour costs – the wages bill
- expenses – all the other costs, such as advertising, insurance, postage, telephone, rent and rates

Clarion is at its busiest in the summer months when it prints its Christmas stock.

solution

You extract the information from the tables of data (shown on the previous page) and prepare the two memos for your supervisor's signature . . .

MEMORANDUM

To   B Simpson, Sales Manager   **Ref**   AG171

From Ally Gee, Accounts Supervisor   **Date**   4 July 2001

Subject Sales Report

Thanks for your memo of 29 June. The figures you requested are:

1.	Total sales for the last quarter (to 30 June)	£165,000
2.	The sales figure for the corresponding quarter last year	£160,000
3.	The forecast sales figure for the last quarter	£170,000

A Gee

MEMORANDUM

To   R Singh, Production Manager   **Ref**   AG172

From Ally Gee, Accounts Supervisor   **Date**   4 July 2001

Subject Costs Report

Thanks for your memo of 29 June. The figures you requested are:

1.	Total costs for the last quarter (to 30 June)	£115,000
2.	The costs figure for the corresponding quarter last year	£110,000
3.	The forecast costs figure for the last quarter	£120,000

A Gee

The memos should be passed to your supervisor for checking and signature. You will need to make sure that he gets them in good time so that he can change anything that needs correcting and so that they can reach the appropriate people by 6 July.

As you will see, the memos are brief, clear and to the point. The information they contain is not particularly sensitive. Ally Gee has not asked you to take care over confidentiality, so you can quite safely put your drafts in his in-tray for checking.

Note also that some of the data relates to a past period – this is part of **financial accounting** and will be taken from the ledger accounts. Some of the information is taken from a forecast – this is part of **management accounting** – which involves looking into the future.

IDENTIFYING DISCREPANCIES (VARIANCES)

Another function of management accounting is the preparation of financial data so that management can compare actual figures with forecast figures. You will be required to draw up or complete a table of figures – possibly on a computer spreadsheet – and to calculate the difference (the discrepancy or 'variance') between the forecast figures and the actual figures.

income forecasts – discrepancies (variances)

Look at the format shown below. It shows the quarterly sales **income** figures for Clarion Cards. This is how the report would appear at the beginning of July 2001 (the date of the Case Study).

CLARION CARDS – QUARTERLY SALES

	Year 2001 Forecast £	Year 2001 Actual £	Discrepancy + or – £
Jan-Mar	160,000	155,000	– 5,000
Apr-Jun	170,000	165,000	– 5,000
Jul-Sep	180,000		
Oct-Dec	275,000		
TOTAL	785,000		

The discrepancy (difference) figure is shown in this column. It is calculated by deducting forecast sales (the left-hand data column) from actual sales (the middle column):

£155,000 – £160,000 = – £5,000
actual – forecast = discrepancy

Note that a minus figure can be shown either with a minus sign, or in brackets:

– £5,000 *or* (£5,000)

A *minus* discrepancy means that actual sales have not been as good as forecast.

A positive discrepancy (a *plus* figure) means that actual sales have been better than forecast.

The actual figures will be filled in at the end of each quarter. The source of the information will be the sales account in the main general ledger.

The forecast figures will have been compiled before the start of the year. They will not form part of the accounts (the financial accounting records), but are a future estimate, made as part of the management accounting process. They are totalled to give an estimate of annual sales.

At the end of the year this total will be compared with the total of the actual sales and the discrepancy for the year will be worked out.

costs forecasts – discrepancies (variances)

The table shown below shows the quarterly **costs** figures for Clarion Cards as it will appear at the beginning of July 2001 (the date of the Case Study). You will see that the format is very similar to the sales forecast. Read the explanations below and note one important difference:

- when you work out the discrepancy between forecast and actual **income** (see previous page) you deduct forecast income from actual income:
  actual – forecast = discrepancy

- when you work out the discrepancy between forecast and actual **costs**, the calculation is different – you deduct actual costs from forecast costs:
  forecast – actual = discrepancy

Study the form and the notes and then read the Case Study which follows.

CLARION CARDS – QUARTERLY COSTS

	Year 2001 Forecast £	Year 2001 Actual £	Discrepancy + or – £
Jan-Mar	110,000	105,000	+ 5,000
Apr-Jun	120,000	115,000	+ 5,000
Jul-Sep	190,000		
Oct-Dec	125,000		
TOTAL	545,000		

The discrepancy (difference) figure is shown in this column. It is calculated by deducting actual costs (the middle data column) from the forecast costs (the left-hand column):

£110,000 – £105,000 = + £5,000
forecast – actual = discrepancy

Note that any minus discrepancy would be shown either with a minus sign, or in brackets: – £5,000 *or* (£5,000)

A *positive* discrepancy (as here) means that costs are lower than forecast – which should please the managers.

A *negative* discrepancy means that costs are higher than forecast – which may be a problem for managers to investigate.

The actual figures will be filled in at the end of each quarter. The source of the information will be the costs accounts in the main general ledger, eg wages, purchases, expenses.

The forecast figures will have been compiled before the start of the year. They will not form part of the accounts (the financial accounting records), but are a future estimate, made as part of the management accounting process. They are totalled to give an estimate of annual costs.

At the end of the year this total will be compared with the total of the actual costs and the discrepancy for the year worked out.

CASE
STUDY

CLARION CARDS LIMITED –
CALCULATING THE DISCREPANCIES

This Case Study is a continuation of the Case Study on page 464.

It is now the last week in December and the end of the financial year for Clarion Cards. It is time for the managers to look at the figures for income and costs. These will be available in the financial accounting records of the business and summarised in the trial balance.

The managers will want to compare the actual figures from the accounts with the forecasts made at the beginning of the year. From this they will be able to tell whether the business has done better – or worse – than expected.

It is your job to work out any discrepancies on the report forms (shown on the previous two pages) and to produce an annual total. The figures for the last two quarters are set out in the tinted table on the right and are shown transferred to the report forms.

CLARION CARDS – QUARTERLY SALES

	Year 2001 Forecast £	Year 2001 Actual £	Discrepancy + or – £
Jan-Mar	160,000	155,000	– 5,000
Apr-Jun	170,000	165,000	– 5,000
Jul-Sep	180,000	185,000	+ 5,000
Oct-Dec	275,000	290,000	+ 15,000
TOTAL	785,000	795,000	+ 10,000

CLARION CARDS QUARTERLY RESULTS

	Jul-Sep £	Oct-Dec £
Sales	185,000	290,000
Costs	195,000	129,000

CLARION CARDS – QUARTERLY COSTS

	Year 2001 Forecast £	Year 2001 Actual £	Discrepancy + or – £
Jan-Mar	110,000	105,000	+ 5,000
Apr-Jun	120,000	115,000	+ 5,000
Jul-Sep	190,000	195,000	– 5,000
Oct-Dec	125,000	129,000	– 4,000
TOTAL	545,000	544,000	+ 1,000

discussion points
What has happened to actual sales and costs for the year? Do you think the managers will be pleased or worried?

dealing with discrepancies (variances)

Dealing with discrepancies (variances) is the job of the managers. Your responsibility is for extracting and presenting the information within the given guidelines and for calculating any discrepancies. As we mentioned earlier, you may use a computer spreadsheet for processing the figures, in which case the discrepancies will be calculated automatically.

Managers will look at the discrepancies and decide whether to investigate the cause. Sometimes nothing can be done – for example the wages bill may have gone up because of an increase in the Minimum Wage, or transport costs may have gone up because of a rise in fuel prices. Sometimes managers will be able to take action – for example cutting down on overtime to reduce the wages bill. These are factors which you will examine in detail in your later studies at NVQ levels 3 and 4. At present you have to concentrate on presenting data – management information – promptly and accurately in the required format.

THE REQUIRED FORMAT

There are a variety of communication formats you may use when compiling management information. Each format is appropriate to different circumstances. Over the next few pages we will look at examples of these formats to illustrate how they are used in practical business situations.

Routine standard reports, like those in the Case Study earlier in this chapter are used regularly to keep managers informed about the performance of the business so that they can make appropriate decisions. These reports will be set out on pre-printed sheets, or templates on a computer spreadsheet. They include:

- the **standard cost report** which summarises the discrepancies between actual and forecast figures for different types of cost: materials, labour and expenses
- the **budgetary control report** which compares actual and forecast figures over a period of time
- **management accounts** which provide managers with information about specific areas of costs or income, for example sales by product or service

The formats commonly used for 'one-off' situations are:

- **memo** or **e-mail** – used to communicate 'one-off' pieces of information
- **note** – used informally to communicate information for managers
- **letter** – often used to communicate information which is confidential

Now study the use of the formats on the next few pages.

STANDARD COST REPORT

A standard cost report summarises the discrepancies between actual and forecast figures for different types of cost. The format below shows the costs for Zenith, a computer manufacturer, in week 2 of June 2001.

The form is pre-printed and each week (or month in some cases) you will fill in the dates and figures which in the text here have a tinted background.

The financial information you need is the actual cost figures for materials, labour and expenses for the product. The rest is a matter of calculation. Study the form carefully and then read the explanations underneath.

STANDARD COST REPORT – ZENITH COMPUTERS

| product | desktop computers | date | 15 06 01 |
| period | week ending 2 June 01 | | |

	forecast cost £000s	actual cost £000s	discrepancy £000s + or −
materials	75	73	+ 2
labour	65	80	− 15
expenses	48	45	+ 3
TOTAL	188	198	−10

this column sets out the types of cost and the total cost for the week; the costs are divided into three categories:
- materials
- labour
- expenses

this column sets out the forecast figures for the types of cost – these figures will already be entered here

you will have to obtain and insert these figures and total them

you will have to calculate the discrepancy figure by deducting the actual cost from the forecast cost

a positive figure has a plus sign and means that costs are lower than forecast

a negative figure has a minus sign and means that costs are higher than forecast

discussion points
What are the managers likely to think about these figures?
How does the report help them to pinpoint any problem?

BUDGETARY CONTROL REPORT

During the course of the year, the managers of a business will want to compare the forecast and actual figures for costs and income so that they can take action if problems arise. A budgetary control report focuses on various areas of the business to compare the forecast and actual figures. These reports may cover departments of the business (cost centres) or types of cost and income.

The budgetary control report shown below looks at the sales performance of Zenith Computers each month. You will have to fill in the figures which in the text here have a tinted background.

SALES BUDGETARY CONTROL REPORT – ZENITH COMPUTERS   date June 2001

	forecast sales (monthly) £000s	forecast sales (cumulative) £000s	actual sales £000s	discrepancy + or – £000s
January	100	100	110	+ 10
February	110	210	115	+ 5
March	110	320	112	+ 2
April	120	440	115	– 5
May	120	560	118	– 2
June	125	685	129	+ 4
July	125	810		
August	130	940		
September	125	1065	sales for the year so far compared	
October	125	1190		
November	140	1330		
December	150	1480		
TOTAL	1480	1480	699	+ 14

this column sets out the forecast sales figures for each month of the year

this column sets out the cumulative forecast sales figures – it shows forecast sales for the year so far

this column sets out the actual sales figures month-by-month

the total at the bottom can be compared with the forecast cumulative total for the year so far

you will have to calculate the discrepancy figure by deducting the forecast sales from the actual sales

a positive figure has a plus sign and means that sales are higher than forecast

MANAGEMENT ACCOUNTS

Managers are likely to need more details from the financial records about aspects of cost or income. You may be asked to provide this information, either on a standard form, or as a 'one off' request made by the manager.

On the next few pages we look at the formats required for 'one-off' situations.

product sales report

You are asked to complete a monthly pre-printed report giving details of sales of individual products.

The example below provides more information about the sales budgetary control report from Zenith Computers shown on the previous page.

The figures you complete are shown with a tinted background. The form may be preprinted, or it may be on a computer spreadsheet file.

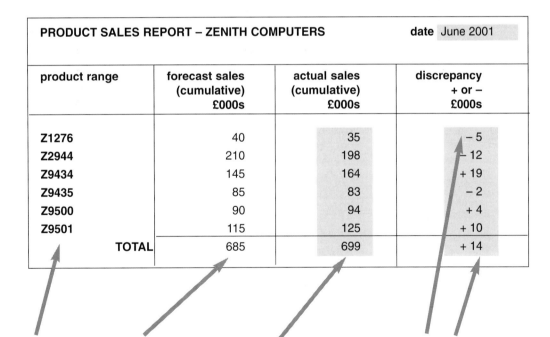

PRODUCT SALES REPORT – ZENITH COMPUTERS   date June 2001

product range	forecast sales (cumulative) £000s	actual sales (cumulative) £000s	discrepancy + or – £000s
Z1276	40	35	– 5
Z2944	210	198	– 12
Z9434	145	164	+ 19
Z9435	85	83	– 2
Z9500	90	94	+ 4
Z9501	115	125	+ 10
TOTAL	685	699	+ 14

product codes for the models of computer produced by Zenith

this column sets out the forecast sales figures for each model

the total at the bottom is the same as the forecast monthly total on the sales budgetary control report

this column sets out the actual sales figures for each model

the total at the bottom is the same as the actual monthly total on the sales budgetary control report

you will have to calculate the discrepancy figure by deducting the forecast sales for each model from the actual sales

a positive figure has a plus sign and means that sales are higher than forecast

FORMATS FOR 'ONE-OFF' REQUESTS FOR INFORMATION

e-mail and memo

These formats can be used for 'one-off' requests for information by managers.

E-mails are used internally if the business has an intranet (a system of computers on-line within the organisation). Memoranda (see page 300) are used as a traditional paper-based means of communication within the business. Both can be used to send confidential information within the organisation, if required. E-mails have the advantage of speed of production and transmission. Also, people also tend to reply to e-mails faster.

The first example below shows how the Production Manager of Zenith Computers is concerned about the labour cost reported for June – it is £15,000 higher than expected (see page 471). He sends an e-mail on the intranet and the Finance Department replies on the same day.

e-mail request

> **Zenith Computers Intranet. John Henson. 18 06 01. 10.32. Re: labour costs.**
>
> To <Ivor Lewinski. Finance.003> from <John Henson. Production.002> 18.06.01.10.32.34. Subject: re: labour costs
>
> Hello Ivor
>
> Please send me a breakdown of the labour costs for June, Week 2. I need information about basic pay, overtime and any bonus payments made. As soon as possible please.
>
> Thanks
>
> Regards
>
> John

e-mail reply

> **Zenith Computers Intranet. Ivor Lewinski. 18 06 01. 14.32. Re: labour costs.**
>
> To <John Henson. Production.002> from<Ivor Lewinski. Finance.003> 18.06.01.16.45.17. Subject: re: labour costs
>
> Hi John
>
> The £80,000 labour costs for June Week 2 comprised £65,100 basic pay and £14,900 overtime. There were no bonus payments.
>
> Regards
>
> Ivor

The same communication could have been done by memorandum, but e-mails have a number of advantages:

- they take less time to write
- they get to their destination more quickly
- they are likely to be answered more quickly
- they are more informal and 'friendly'

This is clearly why e-mails are becoming more popular.

If the request for information shown on the previous page was carried out by memorandum, the request and replies would look like this:

memo request

MEMORANDUM

To   Ivor Lewinski, Finance Department   **Ref**   JH2101

From John Henson, Production Department   **Date** 18 June 2001

Subject Labour Costs, June 2001, Week 2

Please send me a breakdown of the labour costs for June, Week 2.

I urgently need information about basic pay, overtime and any bonus payments made.

Many thanks.

John Henson
Production Department

---

memo reply

MEMORANDUM

To   John Henson, Production Department   **Ref**   IL3411

From Ivor Lewinski, Finance Department   **Date** 21 June 2001

Subject Labour Costs, June 2001, Week 2

Thank you for your memo of 18 June.

The £80,000 labour costs for June Week 2 comprise £65,100 basic pay and £14,900 overtime. There were no bonus payments made in that week.

Ivor Lewinski
Finance Department

---

using notes to supply information

Notes can be used if the information is simple and the request is very urgent. For example, the request for a breakdown of labour costs (see page 475) could have been telephoned through to the Finance Department:

"Please send me a breakdown of the labour costs for June, Week 2. Can you make it urgent? I need the figures by the end of tomorrow."

The Finance Department will then extract the information and write it on a note pad and take it or fax it through to the Production Department. The note will look like this:

---

note to

John Henson   *18 June 2001*

June Week 2 labour costs of £80,000 were made up of:

  £65,100 basic pay

  £14,900 overtime

No bonuses were involved.

Regards
Ivor

---

using letters to supply information

Letters are not often used for requesting and supplying internal management information, they are more commonly used for external communications. They could be used, however, for sending information within a large business which operates from number of sites, although this is more likely to be done by fax, or increasingly, by e-mail.

The one main advantage of letters is that they can be used to send confidential information. A letter addressed to the Finance Manager and marked 'Confidential' should only be opened by that Manager.

An example letter is shown on the next page. Read it through now.

In this case Mr Lewinski can reply either by a letter marked 'Confidential', enclosing all the information on a schedule, or alternatively he could e-mail the information to the MD's private mailbox. As you will appreciate, if this information got into the wrong hands, the company might have serious labour relations problems. Confidentiality here is very important.

Zenith Computers Limited
Unit 17 Westside Industrial Estate
Mereford MR3 5GV
Tel 01908 287422 Fax 01908 287334 E-mail zenith@zenith.co.uk
VAT Reg UK 38771939

Ivor Lewinski
Finance Manager
Zenith Computers Limited

5 July 2001

Dear Mr Lewinski

Labour costs

I am writing on behalf of the Board of Zenith Computers to advise you that the Directors have decided to cut down on the workforce of the company. Labour costs have been increasing at a steady rate over the last two years and in order to make the business more efficient and profitable we need to cut these costs. This will, I am afraid, inevitably mean reducing the workforce by introducing voluntary redundancy and early retirement schemes.

I shall be grateful therefore if you will provide me with the monthly figures over the last twelve month period for the following:

1.   Total labour costs for the company

2.   A break-down of labour costs by Department, including a breakdown into basic pay, overtime and any bonuses

Please appreciate that this information is of a highly sensitive nature and should be kept strictly confidential.

I shall be grateful to receive these figures by the end of this week.

Yours sincerely

R Hutton

R Hutton
Managing Director

---

confidentiality and storage

It is important to realise that information may be confidential. Generally:

- internal management information must not be released to any outside body – particularly competitors!

- some internal management infomration is for restricted circulation; before you undertake a task you must be clear about who can have access and the format you are to use

- management information must be stored carefully so that it is available only to those who should have access to it

CHAPTER SUMMARY

- Managers need information so that they can carry out the management functions of planning, making decisions and controlling the business.

- Managers need financial information relating to costs and to income.

- Some management information is taken from the ledgers which form part of the financial accounting system – they show a record of actual financial transactions which have taken place in the past.

- Some management information is taken from the summaries and budgets which form part of the management accounting system – they estimate future performance.

- Before gathering financial information, a number of questions have to be asked so that the user's needs can be met:
  - who needs the information?
  - what type of information is it?
  - what level of detail is required?
  - what level of accuracy is required?
  - in what format is it to be presented?
  - when does it have to be presented?
  - how confidential is the information?

- Presenting management information involves comparing financial data:
  - the present period with the previous period – this month and last month
  - the corresponding period – this month with the same month last year
  - comparisons with forecasts – this month's actual results against forecast

- Managers will want to know the discrepancies (variances) between actual and forecast figures so that they can take action if they need to.

- Income discrepancies are calculated using the formula
  actual figures minus forecast figures equals discrepancy

- Cost discrepancies are calculated using the formula
  forecast figures minus actual figures equals discrepancy
  Remember that this formula is different for income and costs discrepancies.

- It is important to use the appropriate format when presenting management information. Formats include
  - letter
  - e-mail
  - memo
  - note
  - standard report forms such as a cost report and a budgetary control report

KEY TERMS

manager	a person whose role it is in an organisation to plan, make decisions, and control business activity
management information	financial information relating to the income and costs of the business
financial accounting	accounting records of transactions which have already taken place
management accounting	summaries of what has happened in the past and estimates of future performance
previous period	a comparison of financial data for the present and the last period – eg this month compared with last month
corresponding period	a comparison of financial data for the present period and the same period in the past, eg this June and last June
cumulative data	results from time periods, eg months, added together as the year progresses to produce 'the year so far' figures
forecast data	financial data which is forecast for budgeting purposes
discrepancy	the difference between actual and forecast figures – also known as the variance
income discrepancy	actual figure *minus* forecast figure
cost discrepancy	forecast figure *minus* actual figure
positive discrepancy	in the case of *income* figures a positive discrepancy means that actual income is *higher* than forecast
	in the case of *cost* figures, a positive discrepancy means that actual costs are *lower* than forecast
negative discrepancy	in the case of *income* figures, a negative discrepancy means that actual income is *lower* than forecast
	in the case of *cost* figures a negative discrepancy means that actual costs are *higher* than forecast
standard cost report	a summary of discrepancies between forecast and actual figures, broken down into different types of costs – materials, labour and expenses
budgetary control report	a comparison of actual and forecast figures for costs or income over a period of time
management accounts	reports which provide managers with information about specific aspects of cost or income

STUDENT ACTIVITIES

21.1 Financial accounting aims to provide information for people outside the business. True or false?

21.2 Management accounting aims to provide information for people outside the business. True or false?

21.3 It is important to meet the user's needs when you are gathering information for managers. List five of the points that you will have to bear in mind when requested to provide information.

21.4 The tables set out below show the quarterly sales and costs for Clarion Cards over two years. Study the tables and answer the questions that follow.

QUARTERLY SALES	Year 2000 Actual £000s	Year 2001 Forecast £000s	Year 2001 Actual £000s
Jan-Mar	300	310	320
Apr-Jun	350	370	375
Jul-Sep	380	400	410
Oct-Dec	400	440	450

QUARTERLY COSTS	Year 2000 Actual £000s	Year 2001 Forecast £000s	Year 2001 Actual £000s
Jan-Mar	200	220	225
Apr-Jun	210	240	248
Jul-Sep	230	245	255
Oct-Dec	280	300	320

(a) What is the increase in actual sales between the last quarter of 2001 and the previous quarter?

(b) What is the increase in sales between the last quarter of 2001 and the corresponding quarter in 2000?

(c) What is the difference between actual and forecast sales in the second quarter of 2001?

(d) What is the increase in actual costs between the second quarter of 2001 and the previous quarter?

(e) What is the increase in actual costs between the third quarter of 2001 and the corresponding quarter in 2000?

(f)   What is the difference between actual and forecast costs in the fourth quarter of 2001?

(g)   You receive the following memo:

MEMORANDUM

To   Ally Gee, Accounts Supervisor   **Ref**   BS234

From B Simpson, Sales Manager   **Date**   5 January 2002

Subject Sales and Costs Figures

Please can you supply the following figures as soon as possible

1.   Total sales and costs for 2000

2.   Total sales and costs for 2001

How do the actual sales and costs figures for 2001 vary from the forecast sales and costs for that year?

Total up the actual sales and costs for 2000 and 2001 and draw up a table to present the figures, comparing them with the forecasts. A suggested layout is shown below. Write out a suitable memorandum addressed to B Simpson attaching the table and stating how the actual results differ from the forecasts.

	2000 actual £000s	2001 actual £000s	2001 forecast £000s
Total Sales			
Total Costs			

21.5   You work in the Finance Department of Grampian Plastics and receive the following e-mail from the Sales Manager.

Grampian Plastics Intranet. Iain Mackenzie. 18 01 02. 10.32. Re: Sales figures.

To <Jack Stewart. Finance.002> from<Iain Mackenzie. Sales.001>
18.01.02.10.32.14. Subject: Re: Sales figures.

Jack

Please fax me the monthly figures for last year's export sales. I need the figures for each month and also the cumulative figures month-by-month. Many thanks.

Iain Mackenzie

You look in your records and extract the monthly sales figures for Grampian Plastics for 2001. They are as follows (quoted in £000s):

January £120, February £130, March £125, April £131, May £139, June £141, July £146, August £137, September £139, October £143, November £147, December £135.

Draw up a suitable chart for faxing to the Sales Manager. You are not sure about the format, but your supervisor suggests when you ask her that you run the figures in two vertical columns headed 'Monthly sales' and 'Cumulative sales'.

21.6 Which one of the following formulas shows the calculation for income discrepancies?

A   actual figure *minus* forecast figure

B   actual figure *add* forecast figure

C   forecast figure *minus* actual figure

D   forecast figure *add* actual figure

21.7 Koala Giftware is a business which imports craft products from Australia and sells it to a wide range of UK giftshop outlets. You have just been given the sales and costs figures for the last quarter. They are:

Sales	October-December 2001	£205,000
Costs	October-December 2001	£161,000

You are to complete the sales and costs reports shown below by:

(a)   entering the final quarter's figures in the 'Actual' columns

(b)   totalling the 'Actual' columns

(c)   calculating the discrepancies, adding the plus or minus sign as appropriate

(d)   calculating the total (net) discrepancies in the bottom line of each form

KOALA GIFTWARE – QUARTERLY SALES

	Year 2001 Forecast	Year 2001 Actual	Discrepancy + or –
Jan-Mar	160,000	165,000	
Apr-Jun	170,000	175,000	
Jul-Sep	180,000	182,000	
Oct-Dec	195,000		
TOTAL	705,000		

KOALA GIFTWARE – QUARTERLY COSTS

	Year 2001 Forecast	Year 2001 Actual	Discrepancy + or –
Jan-Mar	110,000	105,000	
Apr-Jun	120,000	115,000	
Jul-Sep	150,000	149,000	
Oct-Dec	165,000		
TOTAL	545,000		

21.8 Tempus Clocks manufactures reproduction antique clocks at its factory in Deddington in Oxfordshire. You have been asked to complete the Standard Cost Report for April 2001. The cost figures you have extracted from the accounts are: materials £34,890; labour £17,560; expenses £19,100. You are to enter the figures on the report and calculate the discrepancies, marking them with a minus or plus sign as appropriate. You are also to total the 'actual' figures and find the net discrepancy and enter the figures on the bottom line.

STANDARD COST REPORT – TEMPUS CLOCKS			
product repro clocks		**date** 01 05 01	
period April 01			
	forecast cost	**actual cost**	**discrepancy** + or −
materials	35,500		
labour	15,800		
expenses	18,500		
TOTAL	69,800		

The following day you receive this note from the Production Manager:

> **Note to** R Hand, Finance Dept   **date** 2 May 2001
>
> Please can you let me know the breakdown of the April labour figure of £17,560? It seems very high and is well above the forecast figure.
> Thanks
> Tom Gilks, Production Manager

You find from your investigations that the April wages bill consists of £14,040 basic pay and £3,520 overtime. The high overtime figure was due to a machine failure which resulted in production staff having to stay on later than normal to meet production targets.

You are to draft a memorandum to Mr Hand, providing the figures and explaining the reason for the discrepancy.

21.9 You work in the Finance Department of a large company and often have to provide financial data to your own boss, and to other Departments. What method of communicating management information would you use in the following cases? Give reasons for your choice of format, stating the level of confidentiality required in each case.

(a)   You are asked by your Sales Director to provide the Area Managers throughout the UK with details of the commission paid to their sales representatives.

(b)   You are asked by your boss for the last month's sales figures for Products A and B.

(c)   You are e-mailed for sales figures by a sales rep who has a laptop connected to the Internet.

ANSWERS TO STUDENT ACTIVITIES

CHAPTER 1: INTRODUCTION TO ACCOUNTING

1.1 (c)

1.2 revenue: (a) (c) (d); capital: (b) (e)

1.3 cash: (a) (b) (d) credit: (c) (e)

1.4 See text, pages 7-8.

1.5 Assets minus liabilities equals capital. See pages 9 - 10. The capital would increase.

1.6 Advantages: speed (and so cheap to use), accuracy, ability to provide information, integrated function. Disadvantages: expensive to install, staff training needed, danger of failure, security risk (on-line hacking), need for back-up systems.

1.7 See text, page 22.

1.8 (a) Jo's pay packet, income tax and national insurance will be incorrect; if Jo does not check the payslip, the error may go undetected.

      (b) The invoice will be incorrect, the customer may exceed the credit limit, the business may lose the customer!

      (c) The bank account may go overdrawn, the business may be charged extra interest and fees, cheques may be 'bounced' resulting in the withdrawal of credit by suppliers.

CHAPTER 2: DOCUMENTS FOR GOODS AND SERVICES SUPPLIED

2.1

(a) delivery note	(b)	returns note	(c)	invoice	
(d) statement	(e)	credit note	(f)	purchase order	

2.2

	total £	discount £	net total £	VAT £	invoice total £
(a)	160.00	32.00	128.00	22.40	150.40
(b)	400.00	80.00	320.00	56.00	376.00
(c)	40.00	none	40.00	7.00	47.00
(d)	8000.00	1600.00	6400.00	1120.00	7520.00

2.3

	net total	discount deducted	total after cash discount	VAT	invoice total*
(a)	128.00	3.20	124.80	21.84	149.84
(b)	320.00	8.00	312.00	54.60	374.60
(c)	40.00	1.00	39.00	6.82	46.82
(d)	6400.00	160.00	6240.00	1092.00	7492.00

*Remember that the VAT is normally added to the total before deduction of cash discount.

2.4   Net monthly = payment of net amount one month after the invoice date.

E & OE = Errors and Omissions Excepted (a supplier has the right to correct an invoice after issue).

Carriage paid = Delivery costs paid to the delivery address (contrast with Ex-Works).

2.5   Examples: Purchase order number, delivery note number, invoice number, stock code, account number, credit note number.
The main importance of coding is for accurate cross referencing.

2.6   The problems are the urgency and the need for accuracy. If the wrong goods are sent the problems will be compounded.

Solutions: telephone or e-mail, and fax a copy of the order pointing out the error.

Best and quickest solution - telephone.

Important point – ask for a replacement corrected order to be sent (marked 'confirmation' to avoid duplication), preferably by fax so that a further check can be made. This is to make sure your position is strong, just in case the customer gets it wrong again! This type of problem can be sorted out at assistant level, but should be reported to the supervisor when he/she returns.

2.7   (a)   Incorrect discount rate applied (10%), wrong addition for total. Goods total should be £76.00, VAT £13.30 and final total £89.30.

(b)   Total before discount should be £250.00. VAT has also been rounded up (should have been rounded down to £35.43). Corrected figures: goods total £225.00 (after deduction of 10% discount), VAT £39.37, final total £264.37.

2.8

	Net amount £	VAT £	Total £
(a)	40.00	7.00	47.00
(b)	34,613.60	6,057.38	40,670.98
(c)	34.03	5.95	39.98
(d)	80.00	14.00	94.00
(e)	0.40	0.07	0.47
(f)	1.03	0.17	1.20

CHAPTER 3: ACCOUNTING FOR CREDIT SALES

3.1   (a)

3.2   (a)

3.3   (a) • The prime documents for credit sales transactions are sales invoices or copy invoices, that have been checked and authorised.

• The details and amounts of the invoices are entered into sales day book. In the money columns of sales day book is recorded:

– gross column, the final total of each invoice

– VAT column, the VAT amount shown on each invoice

– net column, the net ('goods or services total') amount of each invoice

• After sales day book has been written up for the week or month, it is totalled and the information from it is transferred into the double-entry system.

• The book-keeping entries are:

– the amounts from the gross column for each separate transaction are debited to the accounts of the customers in sales (debtors) ledger

– the total of the VAT column is credited to VAT account in the general (main) ledger

– the total of the net column is credited to sales account in the general (main) ledger

    (b) • The prime documents for sales returns transactions are credit notes (or copies of credit notes) issued, that have been checked and authorised.

• The details and amounts of the credit notes are entered into sales returns day book. In the money columns of the sales returns day book is recorded:

– gross column, the final total of each credit note

– VAT column, the VAT amount shown on each credit note

– net column, the net ('goods or services total') amount of each credit note

• After sales returns day book has been written up for the week or month, it is totalled and the information from it is transferred into the double-entry system.

• The book-keeping entries are:

– the amounts from the gross column for each separate transaction are credited to the accounts of the customers in sales (debtors) ledger

– the total of the VAT column is debited to VAT account in the general (main) ledger

– the total of the net column is debited to sales returns account in the general (main) ledger

3.4 (a)

Sales Day Book						SDB 50
Date	Customer	Invoice No	Folio	Gross	VAT	Net
2001				£ p	£ p	£ p
2 Apr	Malvern Stores	4578	SL 110	64.62	9.62	55.00
4 Apr	Pershore Retailers	4579	SL 145	76.37	11.37	65.00
7 Apr	E Grainger	4580	SL 55	32.90	4.90	28.00
10 Apr	P Wilson	4581	SL 172	68.15	10.15	58.00
11 Apr	M Kershaw	4582	SL 90	89.30	13.30	76.00
14 Apr	D Lloyd	4583	SL 95	77.55	11.55	66.00
18 Apr	A Cox	4584	SL 32	38.77	5.77	33.00
22 Apr	Dines Stores	4585	SL 48	119.85	17.85	102.00
24 Apr	Malvern Stores	4586	SL 110	55.22	8.22	47.00
25 Apr	P Wilson	4587	SL 172	41.12	6.12	35.00
29 Apr	A Cox	4588	SL 32	96.35	14.35	82.00
30 Apr	Totals for month			760.20	113.20	647.00

(b)

SALES (DEBTORS) LEDGER

Dr	**Malvern Stores** (account no 110)		Cr
2001		£ p	2001 £ p
2 Apr Sales	SDB 50	64.62	
24 Apr Sales	SDB 50	55.22	

Dr	**Pershore Retailers** (account no 145)		Cr
2001		£ p	2001 £ p
4 Apr Sales	SDB 50	76.37	

Dr	**E Grainger** (account no 55)		Cr
2001		£ p	2001 £ p
7 Apr Sales	SDB 50	32.90	

Dr	**P Wilson** (account no 172)		Cr
2001		£ p	2001 £ p
10 Apr Sales	SDB 50	68.15	
25 Apr Sales	SDB 50	41.12	

Dr	**M Kershaw** (account no 90)		Cr
2001		£ p	2001 £ p
11 Apr Sales	SDB 50	89.30	

Dr		**D Lloyd** (account no 95)			Cr
2001		£ p	2001		£ p
14 Apr Sales	SDB 50	77.55			

Dr		**A Cox** (account no 32)			Cr
2001		£ p	2001		£ p
18 Apr Sales	SDB 50	38.77			
29 Apr Sales	SDB 50	96.35			

Dr		**Dines Stores** (account no 48)			Cr
2001		£ p	2001		£ p
22 Apr Sales	SDB 50	119.85			

GENERAL (MAIN) LEDGER

Dr		**Sales Account** (account no 4001)			Cr
2001		£ p	2001		£ p
			30 Apr Sales Day Book SDB 50		647.00

Dr		**Value Added Tax Account** (account no 2200)			Cr
2001		£ p	2001		£ p
			30 Apr Sales Day Book SDB 50		113.20

3.5 (a)

Sales Returns Day Book						SRDB 8
Date	Customer	Credit Note No	Folio	Gross	VAT	Net
2001				£ p	£ p	£ p
8 Apr	Pershore Retailers	CN 572	SL 145	23.50	3.50	20.00
10 Apr	E Grainger	CN 573	SL 55	32.90	4.90	28.00
16 Apr	D Lloyd	CN 574	SL 95	38.77	5.77	33.00
28 Apr	Malvern Stores	CN 575	SL 110	23.50	3.50	20.00
30 Apr	A Cox	CN 576	SL 32	47.00	7.00	40.00
30 Apr	Totals for month			165.67	24.67	141.00

(b)

SALES LEDGER

Dr			Pershore Retailers (account no 145)				Cr
2001			£ p	2001			£ p
4 Apr	Sales	SDB 50	76.37	8 Apr	Sales Returns	SRDB 8	23.50

Dr			E Grainger (account no 55)				Cr
2001			£ p	2001			£ p
7 Apr	Sales	SDB 50	32.90	10 Apr	Sales Returns	SRDB 8	32.90

Dr			D Lloyd (account no 95)				Cr
2001			£ p	2001			£ p
14 Apr	Sales	SDB 50	77.55	16 Apr	Sales Returns	SRDB 8	38.77

Dr			Malvern Stores (account no 110)				Cr
2001			£ p	2001			£ p
2 Apr	Sales	SDB 50	64.62	28 Apr	Sales Returns	SRDB 8	23.50
24 Apr	Sales	SDB 50	55.22				

Dr			A Cox (account no 32)				Cr
2001			£ p	2001			£ p
18 Apr	Sales	SDB 50	38.77	30 Apr	Sales Returns	SRDB 8	47.00
29 Apr	Sales	SDB 50	96.35				

GENERAL (MAIN) LEDGER

Dr			Sales Returns Account (account no 4010)			Cr
2001			£ p	2001		£ p
30 Apr	Sales Returns Day Book	SRDB 8	141.00			

Dr			Value Added Tax Account (account no 2200)				Cr
2001			£ p	2001			£ p
30 Apr	Sales Returns Day Book	SRDB 8	24.67	30 Apr	Sales Day Book	SDB 50	113.20

CHAPTER 4: RECEIVING AND RECORDING PAYMENTS

4.1

Customer	Change	Notes & coin given in change
1	£1.50	1 x £1 coin, 1 x 50p coin
2	£6.70	1 x £5 note, 1 x £1 coin, 1 x 50p coin, 1 x 20p coin
3	£2.49	2 x £1 coins, 2 x 20p coins, 1 x 5p coin, 2 x 2p coins
4	£3.21	3 x £1 coins, 1 x 20p coin, 1 x 1p coin
5	£0.66	1 x 50p coin, 1 x 10p coin, 1 x 5p coin, 1 x 1p coin
6	£3.78	3 x £1 coins, 1 x 50p coin, 1 x 20p coin, 1 x 5p coin, 1 x 2p coin, 1 x 1p coin
7	£7.24	1 x £5 note, 2 x £1 coins, 1 x 20p coin, 2 x 2p coins
8	£0.58	1 x 50p coin, 1 x 5p coin, 1 x 2p coin, 1 x 1p coin
9	£3.46	3 x £1 coins, 2 x 20p coins, 1 x 5p coin, 1 x 1p coin
10	£1.92	1 x £1 coin, 1 x 50p coin, 2 x 20p coins, 1 x 2p coin

4.2

	£
cash float at start of day	28.71
plus sales made during the day	46.46
equals amount of cash held at end of day	75.17

4.3 (a) 2 x £13.99 = £27.98; 2 x 85p = £1.70; total £29.68 + VAT £5.19 = £34.87

(b) £149.95 + 99p = £150.94; add VAT of £26.41 = £177.35

(c) 2 x £35.99 = £71.98; add VAT of £12.59 = £84.57

4.4 (a) A & S Systems Ltd (G Brown signs as director – an authorised signatory)

(b) Southern Bank PLC

(c) Electron Games Limited

For explanations see page 76.

4.5 A crossed cheque must be paid into a bank account; it cannot be cashed (except by an account holder making a cheque payable to him/herself). A cheque without a crossing – an 'open' cheque – may be cashed by the payee. It is therefore a security risk and is very rare.

4.6 (a) The cheque has to be paid into an account.

(b) The cheque has to be paid in at Barclays Bank, Hanover Square.

(c) The same as (a) – the phrase '& co' no longer has any significance.

(d) The cheque must be paid into the account of the payee.

(e) The same as (d).

(f) The cheque *can* be endorsed over by the payee, but in practice banks will only accept the cheque for the account of the payee – they stand to lose if the cheque has been stolen.

4.7 (a) It should be paid into *Sandra Lobbs* account.

(b) This entitles *anyone* who comes into possession of the cheque to pay it into his/her account.

4.8 See page 77 of text.

4.9 See page 80 of text.

4.10 See pages 82-83 of text.

4.11 (c)

4.12 False

4.13 (b)

4.14 (d)

4.15 See page 86 of text.

4.16 (a) the bank (b) large purchase where cash or near cash is required, eg car purchase, house purchase

4.17 Cheques received through the post, cash sales at the counter.

CHAPTER 5: PAYING INTO THE BANK

5.1 See page 100 of text.

5.2 See page 100 of text.

5.3 False. Debtor

5.4 False. Creditor

5.5 (a) ... mortgagor ... mortgagee

(b) ... bailee ... bailor

(c) agent

5.6 (a) Loan account

(b) Overdraft

(c) Deposit account

5.7 (a) 3 days

(b) 24 hours (or as long as first class post takes)

Yes, the business could obtain same day clearance (the two accounts are at the same branch)

5.8 *'Refer to Drawer, Please Represent'*: the cheque will be put through the bank clearing system again <u>by the bank</u>, so there is nothing the business can do with the cheque. The business will be alerted, however, to a possible bad debt and will review carefully credit given to the customer in question.

'Refer to Drawer': in this case the cheque will be returned to the business which can then make strenuous efforts to recover the money from the customer. This answer is normally very bad news for a supplier as it normally means the buyer is in serious financial difficulties.

5.9 See page 107 of text.

5.10 See page 100 of text.

5.11 (a) credit (b) debit

5.12	Cheques:	£20.00	Cash:	2 x £20 notes	£40.00
		£18.50		5 x £10 notes	£50.00
		£75.25		8 x £5 notes	£40.00
		£68.95		2 x £1 coins	£2.00
		£182.70		6 x 50p coins	£3.00
				4 x 10p coins	£0.40
				2 x 2p coins	£0.04
					£135.44

Total amount of credit: £318.14

5.13 Total of sales vouchers £396.94 less refund voucher £13.50, total of summary £383.44.

CHAPTER 6: CASH BOOK – RECORDING RECEIPTS

6.1 (d)

6.2 *Main responsibilities of the cashier*
- Preparing remittance lists for cheques received in the post
- Recording receipts and payments through the bank and in cash
- Issuing receipts for cash (and sometimes cheques) received
- Making authorised cash payments (except for low-value expenses payments which are paid by the petty cashier)
- Preparing cheques for authorised payments – to be signed by those permitted to sign on behalf of the company
- Paying cash and cheques received into the bank
- Controlling the firm's cash, in a cash till or cash box
- Issuing cash to the petty cashier who operates the firm's petty cash book
- Ensuring that all transactions passing through the cash book are supported by documentary evidence
- Checking the accuracy of the cash and bank balances at regular intervals
- Checking expenses claims and seeking authorisation before making payment
- Liaising with the other accounts staff – accounts clerks and petty cashier

Qualities of a cashier
- Accuracy – in writing up the cash book, in cash handling, and in ensuring that payments are made only against correct documents and appropriate authorisation
- Security – of cash and cheque books, and correct authorisation of payments
- Confidentiality – that all cash/bank transactions, including cash and bank balances, are kept confidential

6.3

Debit			Cash Book: Receipts			CBR 45
Date	Details	Folio	Discount allowed	Cash	Bank	
2001			£	£	£	
1 Aug	Balances b/d			276	4,928	
3 Aug	Wild & Sons Ltd	SL 843			398	
6 Aug	Sales	GL 4001/ 2200		188		
13 Aug	Cash	C			300	
14 Aug	A Lewis Ltd	SL 531	20		1,755	
16 Aug	Sales	GL 4001/ 2200		282		
20 Aug	Harvey & Sons Ltd	SL 467			261	
21 Aug	Bank loan	GL 2210			750	
22 Aug	Sales	GL 4001/ 2200		235	235	
24 Aug	Rent received	GL 4951		100		
29 Aug	Wild & Sons Ltd	SL 843	15		595	
30 Aug	Bank	C		275		
			35	1,356	9,222	

SALES (DEBTORS) LEDGER

Dr		**Wild & Sons Ltd** (account no 843)		Cr
2001	£	2001		£
		3 Aug	Bank	CBR 45	398
		29 Aug	Bank	CBR 45	595
		29 Aug	Discount allowed	GL 6501	15

Dr		**A Lewis Ltd** (account no 531)		Cr
2001	£	2001		£
		14 Aug	Bank	CBR 45	1,755
		14 Aug	Discount allowed	CBR 45	20

s foundation accounting tutorial**

Harvey & Sons Ltd (account no 467)

Dr 2001	£	Cr 2001			£
		20 Aug	Bank	CBR 45	261

GENERAL (MAIN) LEDGER

Discount Allowed Account (account no 6501)

Dr 2001			£	Cr 2001	£
31 Aug	Cash Book	CBR 45	35		

Bank Loan Account (account no 2210)

Dr 2001	£	Cr 2001			£
		21 Aug	Bank	CBR 45	750

Rent Received Account (account no 4951)

Dr 2001	£	Cr 2001			£
		24 Aug	Cash	CBR 45	100

Sales Account (account no 4001)

Dr 2001	£	Cr 2001			£
		6 Aug	Cash	CBR 45	160
		16 Aug	Cash	CBR 45	240
		22 Aug	Cash	CBR 45	200
		22 Aug	Bank	CBR 45	200

Value Added Tax Account (account no 2200)

Dr 2001	£	Cr 2001			£
		6 Aug	Cash	CBR 45	28
		16 Aug	Cash	CBR 45	42
		22 Aug	Cash	CBR 45	35
		22 Aug	Bank	CBR 45	35

6.4

Debit					Cash Book: Receipts				CBR 88
Date	Details	Folio	Discount allowed	VAT	Cash	Bank
2001			£	£	£	£
1 Apr	Balances b/d				85	718
9 Apr	J Bowen	SL 117	5		85	
10 Apr	Sales	GL 4001/2200		70		470
12 Apr	Rent received	GL 4951				250
17 Apr	Sales	GL 4001/2200		14		94
18 Apr	J Burrows	SL 125	25			575
20 Apr	Sales	GL 4001/2200		28	188	
23 Apr	Bank	C			200	
24 Apr	Wilson Ltd	SL 855	10			245
			40	112	558	2,352

SALES (DEBTORS) LEDGER

Dr			**J Bowen** (account no 117)			Cr
2001			£	2001		£
				9 Apr	Cash	CBR 88	85
				9 Apr	Discount allowed	GL 6501	5

Dr			**J Burrows** (account no 125)			Cr
2001			£	2001		£
				18 Apr	Bank	CBR 88	575
				18 Apr	Discount allowed	GL 6501	25

Dr			**Wilson Limited** (account no 855)			Cr
2001			£	2001		£
				24 Apr	Bank	CBR 88	245
				24 Apr	Discount allowed	GL 6501	10

GENERAL (MAIN) LEDGER

Dr			**Discount Allowed Account** (account no 6501)			Cr
2001		£	2001			£
30 Apr	Cash Book	CBR 88	40			

Dr			**Rent Received Account** (account no 4951)			Cr
2001		£	2001			£
			12 Apr	Bank	CBR 88	250

Dr			**Sales Account** (account no 4001)			Cr
2001		£	2001			£
			10 Apr	Bank	CBR 88	400
			17 Apr	Bank	CBR 88	80
			20 Apr	Cash	CBR 88	160

Dr			**Value Added Tax Account** (account no 2200)			Cr
2001		£	2001			£
			30 Apr	Cash Book	CBR 88	112

6.5

Debit					Cash Book: Receipts					CBR 96
Date	Details	Folio	Cash	Bank	Disc allwd	VAT	Sales	Sales ledger	Sundry
2001			£ p	£ p	£ p	£ p	£ p	£ p	£ p
14 May	Balances b/d		205.75	825.30					
14 May	Sales	GL 4001		534.62		79.62	455.00		
14 May	Rent received	GL 4951		255.50					255.50
15 May	Sales	GL 4001	164.50			24.50	140.00		
15 May	T Jarvis	SL 497		155.00	2.50			155.00	
16 May	Loan: T Lewis	GL 2200		500.00					500.00
16 May	Sales	GL 4001		752.00		112.00	640.00		
17 May	Sales	GL 4001	264.37			39.37	225.00		
18 May	Capital	GL 3005		1,000.00					1,000.00
18 May	Wyvern District Cncl	SL 924		560.45	5.00			560.45	
			634.62	4,582.87	7.50	255.49	1,460.00	715.45	1,755.50

SALES (DEBTORS) LEDGER

Dr			**T Jarvis** (account no 497)			Cr
2001		£ p	2001			£ p
			15 May	Bank	CBR 96	155.00
			15 May	Discount allowed	GL 6501	2.50

Dr			**Wyvern District Council** (account no 924)			Cr
2001		£ p	2001			£ p
			18 May	Bank	CBR 96	560.45
			18 May	Discount allowed	GL 6501	5.00

GENERAL (MAIN) LEDGER

Dr			**Capital Account** (account no 3005)			Cr
2001		£ p	2001			£ p
			18 May	Bank	CBR 96	1,000.00

Dr			**Discount Allowed Account** (account no 6501)		Cr
2001		£ p	2001		£ p
18 May Cash Book	CBR 96	7.50			

Dr			**Loan Account: T Lewis** (account no 2220)			Cr
2001		£ p	2001			£ p
			16 May	Bank	CBR 96	500.00

Dr			**Rent Received Account** (account no 4951)			Cr
2001		£ p	2001			£ p
			14 May	Bank	CBR 96	255.50

Dr			**Sales Account** (account no 4001)			Cr
2001		£ p	2001			£ p
			18 May	Cash Book	CBR 96	1,460.00

Dr			Value Added Tax Account (account no 2200)			Cr
2001		£ p	2001			£ p
			18 May	Cash Book	CBR 96	255.49

CHAPTER 7: DOCUMENTS FOR GOODS AND SERVICES RECEIVED

7.1 (a)   purchase order

(b)   delivery note

(c)   goods received note

(d)   remittance advice

(e)   invoice

(f)   returns note

7.2 An unauthorised purchase order cannot be used as the basis for raising an order. The purchase order will have to be returned to the purchaser for signature, or alternatively, if the order is urgent, the purchaser could be contacted and a new order faxed through.

7.3 (d)

7.4 A returns note accompanies any goods returned by the purchaser to the seller; a credit note is issued by the seller when credit has to be given to the purchaser, eg for returned goods. Hence a credit note is usually issued when a returns note is received.

7.5 The buyer would effectively be overcharged. The buyer would request a credit note. Under no circumstances should the invoice be altered.

7.6 The errors are:

(a)   the goods were delivered to the wrong address

(b)   an incorrect customer discount has been applied (10% instead of 15%)

(c)   the wrong goods were sent (product code 4574 instead of 4573)

The total should have been £95 less 15% discount = £80.75 plus VAT of £14.13 = £94.88

The letter should point out these errors and state that the disks are being returned for credit.

CHAPTER 8: ACCOUNTING FOR CREDIT PURCHASES AND PURCHASES RETURNS

8.1   (d)

8.2   (a)   • The prime documents for credit purchases transactions are purchases invoices received from suppliers, that have been checked and authorised.

   • The details and amounts of the invoices are entered into the purchases day book. In the money columns of purchases day book is recorded:

   – gross column, the final total of each invoice

   – VAT column, the VAT amount shown on each invoice

   – net column, the net ('goods or services total') amount of each invoice

   • After purchases day book has been written up for the week or month, it is totalled and the information from it is transferred into the double-entry system.

   • The book-keeping entries are:

   – the amounts from the gross column for each separate transaction are credited to the accounts of the suppliers in purchases (creditors) ledger

   – the total of the VAT column is debited to VAT account in general (main) ledger

   – the total of the net column is debited to purchases account in general (main) ledger

   (b)   • The prime documents for purchases returns transactions are credit notes received from suppliers, that have been checked and authorised.

   • The details and amounts of the credit notes are entered into purchases returns day book. In the money columns of the purchases returns day book is recorded:

   – gross column, the final total of each credit note

   – VAT column, the VAT amount shown on each credit note

   – net column, the net ('goods or services total') amount of each credit note

   • After purchases returns day book has been written up for the week or month, it is totalled and the information from it is transferred into the double-entry system.

   • The book-keeping entries are:

   – the amounts from the gross column for each separate transaction are debited to the accounts of the suppliers in purchases (creditors) ledger

   – the total of the VAT column is credited to VAT account in general (main) ledger

   – the total of the net column is credited to purchases returns account in general (main) ledger

8.3 (a)

		Purchases Day Book					PDB 36
Date	Supplier	Invoice No	Folio	Gross	VAT	Net
2001				£ p	£ p	£ p
2 Apr	Severn Supplies	6789	PL 721	293.75	43.75	250.00
4 Apr	I Johnstone	A241	PL 604	246.75	36.75	210.00
10 Apr	L Murphy	2456	PL 659	217.37	32.37	185.00
15 Apr	Mercia Manufacturing	X457	PL 627	211.50	31.50	180.00
18 Apr	AMC Enterprises	AMC 456	PL 520	405.37	60.37	345.00
24 Apr	S Green	2846	PL 574	464.12	69.12	395.00
30 Apr	Totals for month			1,838.86	273.86	1,565.00

(b)

PURCHASES (CREDITORS) LEDGER

Dr			**Severn Supplies** (account no 721)			Cr
2001		£ p	2001			£ p
			2 Apr	Purchases	PDB 36	293.75

Dr			**I Johnstone** (account no 604)			Cr
2001		£ p	2001			£ p
			4 Apr	Purchases	PDB 36	246.75

Dr			**L Murphy** (account no 659)			Cr
2001		£ p	2001			£ p
			10 Apr	Purchases	PDB 36	217.37

Dr			**Mercia Manufacturing** (account no 627)			Cr
2001		£ p	2001			£ p
			15 Apr	Purchases	PDB 36	211.50

Dr			**AMC Enterprises** (account no 520)			Cr
2001		£ p	2001			£ p
			18 Apr	Purchases	PDB 36	405.37

Dr		**S Green** (account no 574)			Cr
2001		£ p	2001		£ p
			24 Apr Purchases	PDB 36	464.12

GENERAL (MAIN) LEDGER

Dr		**Purchases Account** (account no 5001)		Cr
2001		£ p	2001	£ p
30 Apr	Purchases Day Book PDB 36	1,565.00		

Dr		**Value Added Tax Account** (account no 2200)		Cr
2001		£ p	2001	£ p
30 Apr	Purchases Day Book PDB 36	273.86		

8.4 (a)

	Purchases Returns Day Book					**PRDB 11**
Date	Supplier	Credit Note No	Folio	Gross	VAT	Net
2001				£ p	£ p	£ p
7 Apr	Severn Supplies	CN225	PL 721	58.75	8.75	50.00
14 Apr	L Murphy	X456	PL 659	94.00	14.00	80.00
21 Apr	AMC Enterprises	C3921	PL 520	146.87	21.87	125.00
29 Apr	S Green	CN/SG247	PL 574	79.90	11.90	68.00
30 Apr	Totals for month			379.52	56.52	323.00

(b)

PURCHASES (CREDITORS) LEDGER

Dr		**Severn Supplies** (account no 721)			Cr
2001		£ p	2001		£ p
7 Apr	Purchases Returns PRDB 11	58.75	2 Apr Purchases	PDB 36	293.75

Dr		L Murphy (account no 659)		Cr
2001	£ p	2001		£ p
14 Apr Purchases Returns		10 Apr Purchases	PDB 36	217.37
PRDB 11	94.00			

Dr		AMC Enterprises (account no 520)		Cr
2001	£ p	2001		£ p
21 Apr Purchases Returns		18 Apr Purchases	PDB 36	405.37
PRDB 11 146.87				

Dr		S Green (account no 574)		Cr
2001	£ p	2001		£ p
29 Apr Purchases Returns		24 Apr Purchases	PDB 36	464.12
PRDB 11	79.90			

GENERAL (MAIN) LEDGER

Dr		Purchases Returns Account (account no 5010)		Cr
2001	£ p	2001		£ p
		30 Apr Purchases Returns		
		Day Book PRDB 11		323.00

Dr		Value Added Tax Account (account no 2200)		Cr
2001	£ p	2001		£ p
30 Apr Purchases Day		30 Apr Purchases Returns		
Book PDB 36	273.86	Day Book PRDB 11		56.52

8.5

	Purchases Day Book							PDB 21	
Date	Supplier	Invoice No	Folio	Gross	VAT	Net	Furniture	Carpets
2001				£ p	£ p	£ p	£ p	£ p
2 Apr	T Table Ltd	2790		1,465.81	218.31	1,247.50	1,247.50	
7 Apr	Eastern Imports	8461		936.24	139.44	796.80		796.80
10 Apr	Minster Carpets Ltd	A2431		2,203.40	328.16	1,875.24		1,875.24
14 Apr	Pegasus Ltd	27998		585.30	87.17	498.13	498.13	
16 Apr	United Carpets Ltd	98421		559.55	83.33	476.22		476.22
21 Apr	Gerrard Furniture	47921		977.00	145.51	831.49	831.49	
23 Apr	T Table Ltd	2934		762.45	113.55	648.90	648.90	
28 Apr	Eastern Imports	8991		1,524.33	227.02	1,297.31		1,297.31
30 Apr	Totals for month			9,014.08	1,342.49	7,671.59	3,226.02	4,445.57

CHAPTER 9: MAKING PAYMENTS

9.1   False. No cheque is involved in a BACS payment.

9.2   For security reasons: to prevent fraudulent alterations.

9.3   (d)

9.4   To establish the legal relationship between the bank and the business. The bank has to know *who* can sign cheques, and for what amounts. It also needs specimen signatures so that it can verify written instructions, eg cheque signatures and other payment instructions.

9.5   (a)   See text pages 186 and 189.   (b) Standing order   (c) Direct debit

9.6   (a)   Bank draft   (b) CHAPS

9.7   (a)   He/she doesn't have to rely on carrying his/her own money; or he/she doesn't have to pay!

            (b)   Monitoring of expenditure, or control of expenditure.

9.8   Note that the cash discount is not available – the period has expired. Total £15,255.34.

9.9   Total £4,083.05

9.10   Bank giro completed as below:

9.11   (a)   Standing order completed as shown on the next page.

            (b)   The form will be sent to the National Bank, as they will set up the payments.

            (c)   The standing order will have to be signed by an authorised signatory (or two) within the business. It should also be noted that details of the due payments will be passed to the person in charge of entering up the cash book as the payments will form part of the double-entry book-keeping of the company.

For details of the direct debit – see the next page.

```
┌─────────────────────────────────────────────────────────────┐
│ STANDING ORDER MANDATE                                        │
│                                                               │
│ To _____NATIONAL_____ Bank                                  │
│                                                               │
│ Address __10 CATHEDRAL STREET  MELEFORD  MR1 5DE__            │
│                                                               │
│ PLEASE PAY TO                                                 │
│                                                               │
│ Bank _BARCLAYS_  Branch _EVESHORE_   Sort code │3o 98 15│     │
│                                                               │
│ Beneficiary              Account number  │726 271 61│         │
│                                                               │
│ The sum of │£ 350│  Amount in words THREE HUNDRED AND FIFTY POUNDS │
│                                                               │
│ Date of first payment _15 MAY 2001_  Frequency of payment _MONTHLY_ │
│                                                               │
│ Until _15 APRIL 2002_  Reference __BE/ 6637__                 │
│                                                               │
│ Account to be debited NIMROD DRAINAGE LTD Account number │1203 4875│ │
│                                                               │
│ SIGNATURE(S)  ...........................................     │
│                                                               │
│               ..................................... date...... │
└─────────────────────────────────────────────────────────────┘
```

9.11 (a) Direct debit form completed as shown below.

(b) The form will be sent to Tradesure Insurance, as they will set up the payments.

(c) The direct debit will have to be signed by an authorised signatory (or two) within the business. It should also be noted that details of the due payments are normally advised by the originator of the direct debit (here the insurance company). These will be passed to the person in charge of entering up the cash book as the payments will form part of the double-entry book-keeping of the company.

```
┌──────────────── direct debit instruction ─────────────────┐
│                                                            │
│              Tradesure Insurance Company                   │
│                PO Box 134, Helliford, HL9 6TY              │
│                                                            │
│        Originator's Identification Number  914208          │
│                       03924540234                          │
│ Reference(tobecompletedbyTradesureInsurance)..............  │
│                                                            │
│ Please complete the details and return this form to Tradesure Insurance │
│                                                            │
│ name and address of bank/building society │ Instructions to bank/building society │
│  ──NATIONAL_BANK──────── │ • I instruct you to pay direct debits from my account at │
│  ──10_CATHEDRAL_STREET─── │   the request of Tradesure Insurance Company │
│  ──MELEFORD───────────── │ • The amounts are variable and may be debited on │
│       MR1 5DE            │   various dates │
│ account name            │ • I understand that Tradesure Insurance Company may │
│  NIMROD DRAINAGE LIMITED │   change the amounts and dates only after giving me │
│ account number │ sort code │   prior notice │
│ │1203 4875│ │35.09.75│  │ • I will inform the bank/building society if I wish to │
│                         │   cancel this instruction │
│                         │ • I understand that if any direct debit is paid which │
│                         │   breaks the terms of this instruction, the bank/building │
│                         │   society will make a refund. │
│                         │ signature(s)          │ date │
└──────────────────────────────────────────────────────────┘
```

CHAPTER 10: PAYROLL PAYMENTS

10.1 (a)   gross pay = pay before deductions, net pay = pay after deductions

      (b)   overtime = time worked outside normal hours, shift allowance is paid for normal work in unsocial hours

      (c)   bonus payment extra to normal pay, often based on percentage of sales; piece rate is related to number of items produced

      (d)   time book = signing in book kept on premises; time sheet records hours worked off premises

      (e)   clock card = cardboard card inserted in mechanical clock machine; swipe card = plastic card 'swiped' through electronic reader

10.2 (a) £125; (b) £180; (c) £220; (d) £130; (e) £150

10.3 (a) £210; (b) £240 + £18 = £258; (c) £240 + £72 = £312; (d) £240 + £90 = £330; (e) £234

10.4 (a) £150; (b) £1,247.60; (c) £1,907.60; (d) £2,787.60; (e) £4,767.60; (f) £8,905.60; (g) £16,905.60

10.5 (a) to (d) see chapter text; (e) the entry is likely to be zero because there is no loan to repay; (f) employer's National Insurance Contributions

10.6

employee	employer's contribution (£)	employee's contribution (£)
(a)	0	0
(b)	0	0.30
(c)	1.95	2.40
(d)	20.25	17.40
(e)	69.05	45.90

10.7 Payslips set out as per guide in the chapter.

10.8 Income tax £848.25; National Insurance £997.10; total £1,845.35.

10.9	total	£50	£20	£10	£5	£2	£1	50p	20p	10p	5p	2p	1p
W Rowberry	£211.56	2	5	1			1	1			1		1
M Richardson	£189.74	2	4		1	2		1	1			2	
D Stanbury	£206.83	2	5		1		1	1	1	1		1	1
D Payne	£196.75	2	4	1	1		1	1	1		1		
K Peters	£178.89	2	3	1	1	1	1	1	1	1	1	2	
O Robinson	£183.69	2	4			1	1	1		1	1	2	
number		12	25	3	4	4	5	6	4	3	4	7	2
totals (£)	1167.46	600	500	30	20	8	5	3	0.80	0.30	0.20	0.14	0.02

10.10 (a) BACS – supply of data direct to BACS by employer

(b) automated credit system through the employer's bank (routed via BACS)

(c) cash

10.11 (d)

10.12 (c)

10.13 (a)

10.14 (a) £119,150

(b) £40,510

(c) £71,140

(d)

account	debit (£)		credit (£)	
Wages & Salaries	Wages & Salaries Control	119,150		
Bank			Wages & Salaries Control	71,140
Inland Revenue			Wages & Salaries Control	40,510
Pension Fund			Wages & Salaries Control	7,500
Wages & Salaries Control	Bank	71,140	Wages & Salaries	119,150
	Inland Revenue	40,510		
	Pension Fund	7,500		

10.15 (a) £56,110

(b) £21,105

(c) £2,200

(d) £32,805

(e)

account	debit (£)		credit (£)	
Wages & Salaries	Wages & Salaries Control	56,110		
Bank			Wages & Salaries Control	32,805
Inland Revenue			Wages & Salaries Control	21,105
Pension Fund			Wages & Salaries Control	2,200
Wages & Salaries Control	Bank	32,805	Wages & Salaries	56,110
	Inland Revenue	21,105		
	Pension Fund	2,200		

CHAPTER 11: CASH BOOK– RECORDING PAYMENTS

11.1   (d)

11.2

Credit			Cash Book: Payments			CBP 45
Date	Details	Folio	Discount received	Cash	Bank	
2001			£	£	£	
2 Aug	Purchases	GL 5001/ 2200		94		
5 Aug	T Hall Ltd	PL 451	24		541	
8 Aug	Wages	GL 7750		254		
13 Aug	Bank	C		300		
17 Aug	F Jarvis	PL 510			457	
20 Aug	Drawings	GL 7005		200		
21 Aug	Rent paid	GL 6950			275	
22 Aug	Wages	GL 7750		436		
24 Aug	J Jones	GL 643	33		628	
28 Aug	Purchases	GL 5001/ 2200			235	
28 Aug	Salaries	GL 7750			2,043	
29 Aug	Telephone	GL 6212/ 2200			282	
30 Aug	Office equipment	GL 750/ 2200			705	
31 Aug	Cash	C			275	
			57	1,284	5,441	

PURCHASES (CREDITORS) LEDGER

Dr		**T Hall Limited** (account no 451)		Cr
2001		£	2001	£
5 Aug	Bank CBP 45	541		
5 Aug	Discount received CBP 45	24		

Dr		**F Jarvis** (account no 510)		Cr
2001		£	2001	£
17 Aug	Bank CBP 45	457		

Dr		**J Jones** (account no 643)		Cr
2001		£	2001	£
24 Aug	Bank CBP 45	628		
24 Aug	Discount received CBP 45	33		

GENERAL (MAIN) LEDGER

Dr		**Discount Received Account** (account no 6502)			Cr
2001		£	2001		£
			31 Aug	Cash Book CBP 45	57

Dr			**Drawings Account** (account no 7005)				Cr
2001			£	2001			£
20 Aug	Cash	CBP 45	200				

Dr			**Office Equipment Account** (account no 750)				Cr
2001			£	2001			£
30 Aug	Bank	CBP 45	600				

Dr			**Purchases Account** (account no 5001)				Cr
2001			£	2001			£
2 Aug	Cash	CBP 45	80				
28 Aug	Bank	CBP 45	200				

Dr			**Rent Paid Account** (account no 6950)				Cr
2001			£	2001			£
21 Aug	Bank	CBP 45	275				

Dr			**Telephone Expenses Account** (account no 6212)				Cr
2001			£	2001			£
29 Aug	Bank	CBP 45	240				

Dr			**Value Added Tax Account** (account no 2200)				Cr
2001			£	2001			£
2 Aug	Cash	CBP 45	14				
28 Aug	Bank	CBP 45	35				
29 Aug	Bank	CBP 45	42				
30 Aug	Bank	CBP 45	105				

Dr			**Wages and Salaries Account** (account no 7750)				Cr
2001			£	2001			£
8 Aug	Cash	CBP 45	254				
22 Aug	Cash	CBP 45	436				
28 Aug	Bank	CBP 45	2,043				

11.3

Credit			**Cash Book: Payments**				**CBP 88**
Date	Details	Folio	Discount received	VAT	Cash	Bank	
2001			£	£	£	£	
2 Apr	Purchases	GL 5001/2200		7	47		
3 Apr	Travelling expenses	GL 6330			65		
4 Apr	Telephone	GL 6212/2200		35		235	
6 Apr	ABC Bank: loan	GL 2250				500	
9 Apr	Drawings	GL 7005				600	
13 Apr	M Hughes	PL 498	10			180	
16 Apr	Office stationery	GL 6384/2200		14	94		
17 Apr	Purchases	GL 5001/2200		14	94		
18 Apr	Office equipment	GL 750/2200		70		470	
23 Apr	Cash	C				200	
24 Apr	Wilson Ltd	PL 752	10			245	
25 Apr	Purchases	GL 5001/2200		21		141	
27 Apr	Wages	GL 7750			350		
30 Apr	L Luz	PL 601	20			560	
			40	161	650	3,131	

PURCHASES (CREDITORS) LEDGER

Dr				M Hughes (account no 498)			Cr
2001			£	2001			£
13 Apr	Bank	CBP 88	180				
13 Apr	Discount received	CBP 88	10				

Dr				Wilson Limited (account no 752)			Cr
2001			£	2001			£
24 Apr	Bank	CBP 88	245				
24 Apr	Discount received	CBP 88	10				

Dr				Lucinda Luz (account no 601)			Cr
2001			£	2001			£
30 Apr	Bank	CBP 88	560				
30 Apr	Discount received	CBP 88	20				

GENERAL (MAIN) LEDGER

Dr				Discount Received Account (account no 6502)			Cr
2001			£	2001			£
				30 Apr	Cash Book	CBP 88	40

Dr				Drawings Account (account no 7005)			Cr
2001			£	2001			£
9 Apr	Bank	CBP 88	600				

Dr				Loan Account: ABC Bank (account no 2250)			Cr
2001			£	2001			£
6 Apr	Bank	CBP 88	500				

Dr				Office Equipment Account (account no 750)			Cr
2001			£	2001			£
18 Apr	Bank	CBP 88	400				

Dr				Office Stationery Account (account no 6384)			Cr
2001			£	2001			£
16 Apr	Cash	CBP 88	80				

Dr				Purchases Account (account no 5001)			Cr
2001			£	2001			£
2 Apr	Cash	CBP 88	40				
17 Apr	Cash	CBP 88	80				
25 Apr	Bank	CBP 88	120				

Dr				Telephone Expenses Account (account no 6212)			Cr
2001			£	2001			£
4 Apr	Bank	CBP 88	200				

Dr				Travelling Expenses Account (account no 6330)			Cr
2001			£	2001			£
3 Apr	Cash	CBP 88	65				

Dr   **Value Added Tax Account** (account no 2200)   Cr

2001		£	2001		£
30 Apr	Cash Book	CBP 88	161		

Dr   **Wages and Salaries Account** (account no 7750)   Cr

2001		£	2001		£
27 Apr	Cash	CBP 88	350		

11.4

Credit					Cash Book: Payments					CBP 96
Date	Details	Folio	Cash	Bank	Disc recvd	VAT	Purchases	Purchases ledger	Sundry
2001			£ p	£ p	£ p	£ p	£ p	£ p	£ p
14 May	Purchases	GL 5001/2200		88.94		13.24	75.70		
14 May	Telephone	GL 6212/2200		238.90		35.58			203.32
15 May	Wyvern Finance:loan	GL 2270		250.00					250.00
15 May	Shop rent	GL 6345		255.50					255.50
16 May	Purchases	GL 5001/2200		100.00		14.89	85.11		
16 May	Terry Carpets Ltd	PL 721		363.55	4.65			363.55	
16 May	Stationery	GL 6382/2200	28.20			4.20			24.00
17 May	Drawings	GL 7005	100.00						100.00
17 May	Shop fittings	GL 740/2200		311.37		46.37			265.00
18 May	Longlife Carpets Ltd	PL 624		291.50	4.30			291.50	
18 May	Wages	GL 7750	314.20						314.20
18 May	Trade Supplies	PL 784		145.50	3.50			145.50	
			442.40	2,045.26	12.45	114.28	160.81	800.55	1,412.02

PURCHASES (CREDITORS) LEDGER

Dr   **Terry Carpets Limited** (account no 721)   Cr

2001			£ p	2001		£ p
16 May	Bank	CBP 96	363.55			
16 May	Discount received	CBP 96	4.65			

Dr   **Longlife Carpets Limited** (account no 624)   Cr

2001			£ p	2001		£ p
18 May	Bank	CBP 96	291.50			
18 May	Discount received	CBP 96	4.30			

Dr			Trade Supplies (account no 784)				Cr
2001			£ p	2001			£ p
18 May	Bank	CBP 96	145.50				
18 May	Discount received	CBP 96	3.50				

GENERAL (MAIN) LEDGER

Dr			Discount Received Account (account no 6502)				Cr
2001			£ p	2001			£ p
				18 May	Cash Book	CBP 96	12.45

Dr			Drawings Account (account no 7005)				Cr
2001			£ p	2001			£ p
17 May	Cash	CBP 96	100.00				

Dr			Loan Account: Wyvern Finance (account no 2270)				Cr
2001			£ p	2001			£ p
15 May	Bank	CBP 96	250.00				

Dr			Purchases Account (account no 5001)				Cr
2001			£ p	2001			£ p
18 May	Cash Book	CBP 96	160.81				

Dr			Shop Fittings Account (account no 740)				Cr
2001			£ p	2001			£ p
17 May	Bank	CBP 96	265.00				

Dr			Shop Rent Account (account no 6345)				Cr
2001			£ p	2001			£ p
15 May	Bank	CBP 96	255.50				

Dr			Stationery Account (account no 6382)				Cr
2001			£ p	2001			£ p
16 May	Cash	CBP 96	24.00				

Dr			Telephone Expenses Account (account no 6212)				Cr
2001			£ p	2001			£ p
14 May	Bank	CBP 96	203.32				

Dr			Value Added Tax Account (account no 2200)				Cr
2001			£ p	2001			£ p
18 May	Cash Book	CBP 96	114.28				

Dr			Wages and Salaries Account (account no 7750)				Cr
2001			£ p	2001			£ p
18 May	Cash	CBP 96	314.20				

CHAPTER 12: PETTY CASH BOOK

12.1 (d)

12.2 *Allow:* (a), (b), (f), (g), (h), (j) – all supported by an appropriate receipt being attached to the petty cash voucher.

Refer:

(c) travel to work – not normally a business expense, except for emergency call-outs

(d) donation to charity – subject to authorisation by supervisor

(e) staff tea and coffee – check if it is company policy to pay for this personal expense of the office staff

(i) shelving for the office – this expense is above the authorisation limit of the petty cashier; the item should be referred to the accounts supervisor, who may authorise it for payment through the main cash book.

12.3

petty cash voucher		No. 851
	date *today*	
description		amount (£)
Postage on urgent parcel of spare parts to Evelode Supplies Ltd	4	45
	4	45
VAT		
	4	45
signature *Jayne Smith*		
authorised *A Student*		

Documentation will be a Post Office receipt for £4.45.

petty cash voucher		No. 852
	date *today*	
description		amount (£)
Airmail envelopes	2	00
	2	00
VAT	0	35
	2	35
signature *Tanya Howard*		
authorised *A Student*		

Documentation will be a till receipt from the stationery shop for £2.35.

petty cash voucher		No. 853
	date *today*	
description		amount (£)
Taxi fare re visit to Jasper Ltd	7	32
	7	32
VAT	1	28
	8	60
signature *Josh Delabole*		
authorised *A Student*		

Documentation will be a receipt from the taxi company for £8.60.

12.4

	Expense (excluding VAT)	VAT	Total
	£	£	£
(a)	8.00	1.40	9.40
(b)	4.00	0.70	4.70
(c)	2.00	0.35	2.35
(d)	2.09	0.36	2.45
(e)	4.77	0.83	5.60
(f)	2.96	0.51	3.47
(g)	7.45	1.30	8.75
(h)	0.80	0.14	0.94
(i)	0.85	0.14	0.99
(j)	8.01	1.40	9.41

12.5 **Petty Cash Book** **PCB 42**

Receipts	Date	Details	Voucher No	Total Payment	VAT	Travel	Postages	Stationery	Meals	Misc
£	2001			£	£	£	£	£	£	£
75.00	1 Aug	Balance b/d								
	4 Aug	Taxi fare	39	3.80	0.56	3.24				
	6 Aug	Parcel post	40	2.35			2.35			
	7 Aug	Pencils	41	1.26	0.18			1.08		
	11 Aug	Travel expenses	42	5.46		5.46				
	12 Aug	Window cleaner	43	8.50						8.50
	14 Aug	Envelopes	44	2.45	0.36			2.09		
	18 Aug	Donation	45	5.00						5.00
	19 Aug	Rail fare/meal allow	46	10.60		5.60			5.00	
	20 Aug	Postage	47	0.75			0.75			
	22 Aug	Tape	48	1.50	0.22			1.28		
	25 Aug	Postage	49	0.55			0.55			
	27 Aug	Taxi fare	50	5.40	0.80	4.60				
				47.62	2.12	18.90	3.65	4.45	5.00	13.50

CARR TRADING

Posting sheet: petty cash

account name	account number	debit	credit	reference
		£	£	
VAT	GL	2.12		PCB 42
Travel	GL	18.90		PCB 42
Postages	GL	3.65		PCB 42
Stationery	GL	4.45		PCB 42
Meals	GL	5.00		PCB 42
Miscellaneous	GL	13.50		PCB 42
Cash control	GL		47.62	PCB 42
TOTAL		47.62	47.62	

Prepared by _A Student_ Date _31 August 2001_

Checked by _____ Date _____

Posted by _____ Date _____

12.6   **Petty Cash Book**   **PCB 18**

Receipts	Date	Details	Voucher No	Total Payment	VAT	Postages	Travel	Meals	Sundry Office
£	2001			£	£	£	£	£	£
100.00	2 Jun	Balance b/d							
	2 Jun	Postages	123	6.35		6.35			
	3 Jun	Travel expenses	124	3.25			3.25		
	3 Jun	Postages	125	1.28		1.28			
	4 Jun	Envelopes	126	4.54	0.67				3.87
	4 Jun	Window cleaning	127	5.50	0.81				4.69
	5 Jun	Taxi fare/meals	128	15.41	2.29		3.88	9.24	
	5 Jun	Post/packing	129	11.81	0.48	8.56			2.77
	5 Jun	Taxi fare/meals	130	11.95	1.77		3.83	6.35	
	6 Jun	Pens/envelopes	131	6.35	0.94				5.41
				66.44	6.96	16.19	10.96	15.59	16.74

TYAX SYSTEMS LIMITED

Posting sheet: petty cash

account name	account number	debit	credit	reference
		£	£	
VAT	GL	6.96		PCB 18
Postages	GL	16.19		PCB 18
Travel	GL	10.96		PCB 18
Meals	GL	15.59		PCB 18
Sundry office	GL	16.74		PCB 18
Cash control	GL		66.44	PCB 18
TOTAL		66.44	66.44	

Prepared by _A Student_   Date _6 June 2001_

Checked by _____   Date _____

Posted by _____   Date _____

CHAPTER 13: FURTHER ASPECTS OF DOUBLE-ENTRY ACCOUNTS

13.1   (c)

13.2   (b)

13.3 *Computer*

- The double-entry book-keeping transaction for the purchase of a computer is:
  - *debit* computer account
  - *credit* cash account or bank account

  (This assumes that the computer has been bought as a fixed asset, ie for use in the business, and that it has been paid for either in cash or by cheque.)
- Thus, the computer account records an asset, while cash/bank account has given value.
- The computer, being an asset, is recorded in the accounts by a debit transaction; the method of paying for it is recorded in cash/bank account by a credit transaction.

Capital

- The double-entry book-keeping transaction for the introduction of capital into a business is:
  - *debit* cash account or bank account
  - *credit* capital account

  (This assumes that the capital was in the form of money rather than other assets.)
- Thus, the cash/bank account has gained value, while capital account records a liability to the owner. It is a liability that is unlikely to be repaid immediately as the business would then be unable to operate.

13.4

JAMES ANDERSON

Dr			**Capital Account**			Cr
2001			£	2001		£
				1 Feb	Bank	7,500

Dr			**Computer Account**			Cr
2001			£	2001		£
6 Feb	Bank		2,000			

Dr			**Rent Paid Account**			Cr
2001			£	2001		£
7 Feb	Bank		500			

Dr			**Wages Account**			Cr
2001			£	2001		£
12 Feb	Bank		425			
26 Feb	Bank		380			

Dr			**Bank Loan Account**			Cr
2001			£	2001		£
				14 Feb	Bank	2,500

Dr	Commission Received Account			Cr
2001	£	2001		£
		20 Feb Cash		120

Dr	Drawings Account		Cr
2001	£	2001	£
23 Feb Bank	200		

Dr	Van Account		Cr
2001	£	2001	£
27 Feb Bank	5,000		

Dr	Value Added Tax Account		Cr
2001	£	2001	£
6 Feb Bank (computer)	350	20 Feb Cash (commission	
27 Feb Bank (van)	875	received)	21

13.5

TONY LONG

Debit	Cash Book: Receipts				CBR

Date	Details	Folio	Discount allowed	Cash	Bank
2001			£	£	£
1 May	Capital				6,000
13 May	L Warner: loan				1,000
18 May	Commission received			188	

Credit	Cash Book: Payments				CBP

Date	Details	Folio	Discount received	Cash	Bank
2001			£	£	£
4 May	Machine				2,350
7 May	Office equipiment				2,820
9 May	Rent				350
15 May	Wages				250
21 May	Drawings			85	
29 May	Wages				135

Dr	Capital Account			Cr
2001	£	2001		£
		1 May Bank		6,000

Dr	Machinery Account		Cr
2001	£	2001	£
4 May Bank	2,000		

Dr   **Office Equipment Account**   Cr

2001		£	2001		£
7 May	Bank	2,400			

Dr   **Rent Paid Account**   Cr

2001		£	2001		£
9 May	Bank	350			

Dr   **Lucy Warner: Loan Account**   Cr

2001		£	2001		£
			13 May	Bank	1,000

Dr   **Wages Account**   Cr

2001		£	2001		£
15 May	Bank	250			
29 May	Bank	135			

Dr   **Commission Received Account**   Cr

2001		£	2001		£
			18 May	Cash	160

Dr   **Drawings Account**   Cr

2001		£	2001		£
21 May	Cash	85			

Dr   **Value Added Tax Account**   Cr

2001		£	2001		£
4 May	Bank (machinery)	350	18 May	Cash (commission	
7 May	Bank (office equipment)	420		received)	28

13.6   **JEAN LACEY**

Debit	Cash Book: Receipts				CBR
Date	Details	Folio	Discount allowed	Cash	Bank
2001			£	£	£
1 Aug	Capital				5,000
10 Aug	Commission received			235	
15 Aug	S Orton: loan				1,000
20 Aug	Office fittings				282
24 Aug	Commission received				188

Credit	Cash Book: Payments				CBP
Date	Details	Folio	Discount received	Cash	Bank
2001			£	£	£
3 Aug	Computer				2,115
7 Aug	Rent paid				100
13 Aug	Office fittings				2,350
17 Aug	Drawings			100	
28 Aug	S Orton: loan				150

Dr		Capital Account			Cr
2001		£	2001		£
			1 Aug	Bank	5,000

Dr		Computer Account			Cr
2001		£	2001		£
3 Aug	Bank	1,800			

Dr		Rent Paid Account			Cr
2001		£	2001		£
7 Aug	Bank	100			

Dr		Commission Received Account			Cr
2001		£	2001		£
			10 Aug	Cash	200
			24 Aug	Bank	160

Dr		Office Fittings Account			Cr
2001		£	2001		£
13 Aug	Bank	2,000	20 Aug	Bank	240

Dr		Sally Orton: Loan Account			Cr
2001		£	2001		£
28 Aug	Bank	150	15 Aug	Bank	1,000

Dr		Drawings Account			Cr
2001		£	2001		£
17 Aug	Cash	100			

Dr		Value Added Tax Account			Cr
2001		£	2001		£
3 Aug	Bank (computer)	315	10 Aug	Cash (commission recvd)	35
12 Aug	Bank (office fittings)	350	20 Aug	Bank (office fittings)	42
			24 Aug	Bank (commission recvd)	28

13.7

Date	Details	Folio	Dr	Cr
2001			£	£
29 Nov	Bad debts written off account	GL	80	
	Value Added Tax account	GL	14	
	Dailey Trading Co	SL		94
			94	94
	Bad debt written off as per memo from accounts supervisor dated 29 November 2001			

SALES (DEBTORS) LEDGER

Dr   **Dailey Trading Company** (account no 754)   Cr

2001		£	2001		£
15 Jan	Sales	94	29 Nov	Bad debts written off	80
		—	29 Nov	Value Added Tax	14
		94			94

GENERAL (MAIN) LEDGER

Dr   **Bad Debts Written Off Account**   Cr

2001		£	2001		£
29 Nov	Dailey Trading Co	80			

Dr   **Value Added Tax Account**   Cr

2001		£	2001		£
29 Nov	Dailey Trading Co	14			

CHAPTER 14: COMMUNICATING FOR ACCOUNTING

14.1 The cheque will not be accepted by the bank so it should be returned by post with a request that either a new cheque be issued (best solution) or that the figures changed to £550 and countersigned by the appropriate signatories.

14.2 The e-mail should point out the omissions and ask for a new invoice to be issued as soon as possible. The new net total should be £400, which would then attract cash discount of £10. VAT is charged on the lower amount but the invoice final total does not include the cash discount.

14.3 Fax the invoices through to the customer with a reminder on the fax header sheet that the invoices are now due for payment.

14.4 The memorandum should be correctly headed and addressed. The message should be brief and clear. The memorandum can be signed, although this is not essential. The memorandum should include an 'enc.' (enclosure) marker.

14.5 Examples of chasers are reproduced on pages 303 (mild) and 305 (stronger). The important details to include are invoice amount, number and date (a copy should ideally be enclosed [nb 'enc.' marker]) and terms. The tone should not be too strong – remember that the invoice may even have been lost, or the cheque already be in the post (both common excuses!). The letter should be marked for signature by the Accounts Manager.

14.6 A letter of complaint should be drafted (see page 306). It must contain full details of the problems and ask for a full explanation. The tone should remain polite but firm. Problem (a) would suggest that a refund should be requested and problem (b) that full details should be provided of the interest calculations.

14.7 A letter of apology is required here (see page 307). The error may well be the customer's fault, but on no account should this be suggested in the letter (she is 'a valued customer'). The letter should acknowledge the problem, state what corrective action has been taken and finish on a positive note. The tone should be conciliatory but not 'grovelling' (which sounds insincere). The letter should be correctly addressed and signed off.

CHAPTER 15: BUSINESSES AND THE LAW

15.1 The definition must contain the message that a contract is an agreement that is legally binding and enforceable in a court of law.

15.2 Agreement, bargain, intention to create legal relations. See text on pages 312 to 316.

15.3 (a) Yes. A contract can be oral. A purchase order is just part of the paperwork confirming the agreement.

 (b) Yes. The purchase order and despatch of the goods constitute the agreement, bargain and commercial nature of the transaction.

 (c) No. When the job was done there was no intention to create legal relations or to involve consideration (payment) – it was done as a favour. The £10 followed the job and was just incidental.

 (d) Yes. The fact that the person is a friend is not relevant. There was an agreement, consideration and an intention to create legal relations.

15.4 The cashier is right. The price on the shelf is just an invitation to treat. The price is agreed at the till.

15.5 No. The stipulation that the goods are received by 4 April amounts to a counter-offer to the supplier's terms and does not constitute an acceptance. It would only be a valid contract if the supplier had agreed to the revised terms.

15.6 17 March. The postal rule applies – as long as the letter is correctly addressed stamped and posted.

15.7 He is wrong. He is liable under the Sale of Goods Act which states that goods sold must be of 'satisfactory quality ... fit for the purpose ... as described.' The purchaser is entitled to a replacement or a refund as long as the problem is reported without delay.

15.8 No. The Trades Descriptions Act states that it is illegal to make false statements about goods offered for sale. The chair is advertised as having an adjustable back; if it does not, you are entitled to your money back. You could also report the matter to Trading Standards Department who can pursue the matter.

15.9 False.

15.10 See page 328.

15.11 C

CHAPTER 16: BALANCING ACCOUNTS AND THE TRIAL BALANCE

16.1 (b)

16.2 (c)

16.3 (d)

16.4

Dr			Sales Account			Cr
2001			£	2001		£
30 Apr	Balance c/d		17,170	1 Apr	Balance b/d	12,550
				30 Apr	Sales Day Book	4,620
			17,170			17,170
				1 May	Balance b/d	17,170

Dr			Wages Account			Cr
2001			£	2001		£
1 Apr	Balance b/d		3,710	30 Apr	Balance c/d	5,180
11 Apr	Bank		780			
25 Apr	Bank		690			
			5,180			5,180
1 May	Balance b/d		5,180			

Dr			Wyvern Traders			Cr
2001			£	2001		£
1 Apr	Balance b/d		375	24 Apr	Bank	375

Dr			T Johnson			Cr
2001			£	2001		£
15 Apr	Bank		240	1 Apr	Balance b/d	240
18 Apr	Purchases Returns		45	10 Apr	Purchases	180
30 Apr	Balance c/d		350	29 Apr	Purchases	215
			635			635
				1 May	Balance b/d	350

16.5

Dr			Apple Supplies			Cr
2001			£	2001		£
6 May	Bank		780	1 May	Balance b/d	800
6 May	Discount		20	5 May	Purchases	255
12 May	Purchases returns		55	26 May	Purchases	150
30 May	Bank		195			
30 May	Discount		5			
31 May	Balance c/d		150			
			1,205			1,205
				1 Jun	Balance b/d	150

<table>
<tr><td colspan="3" align="center">**Reconciliation of Apple Supplies' statement of account
as at 31 May 2001**</td></tr>
<tr><td></td><td>£</td><td>£</td></tr>
<tr><td>Balance of account at 31 May 2001</td><td></td><td>150</td></tr>
<tr><td>Add: payment sent on 30 May 2001</td><td>195</td><td></td></tr>
<tr><td>   discount received</td><td><u>5</u></td><td><u>200</u></td></tr>
<tr><td>Balance of statement at 31 May 2001</td><td></td><td><u>350</u></td></tr>
</table>

16.6 (c)

16.7
- lodgement of £13 from J Hill (29 Dec) not on statement
- unpresented cheque of £20 to B Kay (19 Dec) not on statement

16.8 (a)

2001	Receipts		£	2001	Payments		£
1 Jan	Balance b/d		800.50	2 Jan	A Arthur Ltd	001351	100.00
6 Jan	J Baker		495.60	10 Jan	C Curtis	001352	398.50
31 Jan	G Shotton Ltd		335.75	13 Jan	Donald & Co	001353	229.70
13 Jan	TK Supplies	BACS	716.50	14 Jan	Bryant & Sons	001354	312.00
				23 Jan	P Reid	001355	176.50
				23 Jan	Omni Finance	DD	207.95
				31 Jan	Balance c/d		923.70
			2,348.35				2,348.35
1 Feb	Balance b/d		923.70				

(b)
- lodgement of £335.75 from G Shotton Ltd (31 Jan) not on statement
- unpresented cheque of £312.00 to Bryant & Sons (14 Jan) not on statement
- unpresented cheque of £176.50 to P Reid (23 Jan) not on statement

16.9 (a)

Dr					CASH BOOK						Cr
Date	Details	Folio	Discount allowed	Cash	Bank	Date	Details	Folio	Discount received	Cash	Bank
2001			£	£	£	2001			£	£	£
1 Apr	Capital				1,000	2 Apr	Purchases				255
7 Apr	Sales				195	4 Apr	Advertising				60
10 Apr	Sales				248	8 Apr	Rent paid				125
16 Apr	J Couchman: loan				1,000	11 Apr	Drawings				100
18 Apr	Sales				220	14 Apr	Purchases				240
25 Apr	Sales				312	21 Apr	Shop fittings				1,250
						23 Apr	Purchases				180
						24 Apr	Advertising				90
						28 Apr	Rent				125
						30 Apr	Drawings				125
						30 Apr	Balance c/d				425
			–	–	2,975				–	–	2,975
1 May	Balance b/d		–	–	425						

(b) and (c)   **GENERAL (MAIN) LEDGER**

Dr			**Capital Account**		Cr
2001		£	2001		£
			1 Apr	Bank	1,000

Dr			**Purchases Account**		Cr
2001		£	2001		£
2 Apr	Bank	255	30 Apr	Balance c/d	675
14 Apr	Bank	240			
23 Apr	Bank	180			
		675			675
1 May	Balance b/d	675			

Dr			**Advertising Account**		Cr
2001		£	2001		£
4 Apr	Bank	60	30 Apr	Balance c/d	150
24 Apr	Bank	90			
		150			150
1 May	Balance b/d	150			

Dr			**Sales Account**		Cr
2001		£	2001		£
30 Apr	Balance c/d	975	7 Apr	Bank	195
			10 Apr	Bank	248
			18 Apr	Bank	220
			25 Apr	Bank	312
		975			975
			1 May	Balance b/d	975

Dr			**Rent Paid Account**		Cr
2001		£	2001		£
8 Apr	Bank	125	30 Apr	Balance c/d	250
28 Apr	Bank	125			
		250			250
1 May	Balance b/d	250			

Dr			**Drawings Account**		Cr
2001		£	2001		£
11 Apr	Bank	100	30 Apr	Balance c/d	225
30 Apr	Bank	125			
		225			225
1 May	Balance b/d	225			

Dr			**J Couchman: Loan Account**		Cr
2001		£	2001		£
			16 Apr	Bank	1,000

Dr		Shop Fittings Account		Cr	
2001		£	2001		£
21 Apr	Bank	1,250			

(d)

Trial balance of Andrew Jarvis as at 30 April 2001

	Dr	Cr
Name of account	£	£
Bank	425	
Capital		1,000
Purchases	675	
Advertising	150	
Sales		975
Rent paid	250	
Drawings	225	
J Couchman: Loan		1,000
Shop fittings	1,250	
	2,975	2,975

16.10

Trial balance of Jane Greenwell as at 28 February 2001

	Dr	Cr
Name of account	£	£
Bank		1,250
Purchases	850	
Cash	48	
Sales		1,940
Purchases returns		144
Creditors		1,442
Equipment	2,704	
Van	3,200	
Stock at 1 Jan 2001	1,210	
Sales returns	90	
Debtors	1,174	
Wages	1,500	
Capital (missing figure)		6,000
	10,776	10,776

16.11

Dr						CASH BOOK						Cr
Date	Details	Folio	Discount allowed	Cash	Bank	Date	Details	Folio	Discount received	Cash	Bank	
2001			£	£	£	2001			£	£	£	
1 Aug	Balances b/d			325	925	7 Aug	Crane & Co		35		845	
4 Aug	S Quesne		2		98	12 Aug	Wages			275		
17 Aug	J Ahmed		4	76		14 Aug	T Lewis		15		285	
20 Aug	Bank	C		100		20 Aug	Cash	C			100	
23 Aug	D Lloyd		3		45	28 Aug	S Ford		5	70		
31 Aug	Balance c/d				162	31 Aug	Petty cash*			55		
						31 Aug	Balance c/d			101		
			9	501	1,230				55	501	1,230	
1 Sep	Balance b/d			101		1 Sep	Balance b/d				162	

* alternatively a credit to cash control account (see Chapter 17)

				PETTY CASH BOOK						
Receipts	Date	Details	Voucher No	Total Payment	VAT	Analysis columns				
						Postages	Travel	Meals	Office Sundries	
£	2001			£	£	£	£	£	£	
75.00	1 Aug	Balance b/d								
	4 Aug	Postages	223	7.20		7.20				
	7 Aug	Travel expenses	224	4.50			4.50			
	9 Aug	Postages	225	2.54		2.54				
	12 Aug	Envelopes	226	4.70	0.70				4.00	
	14 Aug	Window cleaning	227	7.05	1.05				6.00	
	17 Aug	Taxi fare	228	7.52	1.12		6.40			
	21 Aug	Postages	229	8.56		8.56				
	23 Aug	Meals	230	6.35				6.35		
	28 Aug	Envelopes	231	6.58	0.98				5.60	
				55.00	3.85	18.30	10.90	6.35	15.60	
55.00	31 Aug	Cash received								
	31 Aug	Balance c/d		75.00						
130.00				130.00						
75.00	1 Sep	Balance b/d								

- The cash columns show that there should be £101 of cash held on 1 September in the company's cash till or cash box.
- The bank columns show that the company has a bank overdraft of £162 on 1 September (this is well within the company's bank overdraft facility of £2,500).

CHAPTER 17: CONTROL ACCOUNTS

17.1 (d) **17.2** (b)

17.3 *Principles of control accounts*
- Control accounts are 'master' accounts which control a number of subsidiary accounts.
- Control accounts use total figures:
  - total of opening balances
  - total of amounts increasing the balances
  - total of amounts decreasing the balances

  In this way, the total of the closing balances for the subsidiary accounts can be calculated and then checked against a separate listing of the balances of the subsidiary accounts to ensure that the two figures agree.
- Two commonly used control accounts are:
  - sales ledger control account, the total of the debtors
  - purchases ledger control account, the total of the creditors

Control accounts as an aid to management
- The figures for debtors and creditors are available immediately from the appropriate control account – there is no need to add up the balances of all the individual debtors' or creditors' accounts.
- Control accounts can help in locating errors. The balance of the control account can be checked against the separate listing of balances of the subsidiary accounts to ensure that the two figures agree. However, this only proves the arithmetical accuracy of the control account and subsidiary accounts – there could still be errors, such as misposts and compensating errors, within the ledger section.
- Fraud is made more difficult when control accounts are used – this especially applies to a manual accounting system. The reason for this is that any fraudulent transaction to be recorded on the personal account of a debtor or creditor must also be entered in the control account. As the control account will be either maintained by a supervisor, or checked regularly by the manager, the control accounts add another level of security within the accounting system.

Control accounts and book-keeping
- A business must decide how to use control accounts in its book-keeping system; the commonest way of doing this is to incorporate the control accounts into double-entry book-keeping.
- The control accounts form part of the double-entry system in the general (main) ledger, ie the balances of the sales ledger control account and the purchases ledger control account are recorded in the trial balance as the figures for debtors and creditors respectively.
- The personal accounts of debtors and creditors are not part of double-entry but are kept as subsidiary memorandum accounts which record how much each debtor owes, and how much is owed to each creditor.

- From time-to-time, the balances of the memorandum accounts are agreed with the balance of the appropriate control account.

17.4

Dr		Sales Ledger (Debtors) Control Account			Cr
2001		£	2001		£
1 Jun	Balances b/d	17,491	30 Jun	Sales returns	1,045
30 Jun	Credit sales	42,591	30 Jun	Payments received from debtors	39,024
			30 Jun	Cash discount allowed	593
			30 Jun	Bad debts written off	296
			30 Jun	Balances c/d	19,124
		60,082			60,082
1 Jul	Balances b/d	19,124			

17.5

Dr		Purchases Ledger (Creditors) Control Account			Cr
2001		£	2001		£
30 Apr	Purchases returns	653	1 Apr	Balances b/d	14,275
30 Apr	Payments made to creditors	31,074	30 Apr	Credit purchases	36,592
30 Apr	Cash discount received	1,048			
30 Apr	Set-off	597			
30 Apr	Balances c/d	17,495			
		50,867			50,867
			1 May	Balances b/d	17,495

17.6 (a)

SALES (DEBTORS) LEDGER

Dr		Arrow Valley Retailers			Cr
2001		£ p	2001		£ p
1 Feb	Balance b/d	826.40	20 Feb	Bank	805.74
3 Feb	Sales	338.59	20 Feb	Discount allowed	20.66
			28 Feb	Balance c/d	338.59
		1,164.99			1,164.99
1 Mar	Balance b/d	338.59			

Dr		B Brick (Builders) Limited			Cr
2001		£ p	2001		£ p
1 Feb	Balance b/d	59.28	28 Feb	Bad debts written off	59.28

Dr		Mereford Manufacturing Company			Cr
2001		£ p	2001		£ p
1 Feb	Balance b/d	293.49	24 Feb	Sales returns	56.29
3 Feb	Sales	127.48	28 Feb	Set-off	364.68
		420.97			420.97

Dr		Redgrove Restorations			Cr
2001		£ p	2001		£ p
1 Feb	Balance b/d	724.86	7 Feb	Sales returns	165.38
17 Feb	Sales	394.78	28 Feb	Balance c/d	954.26
		1,119.64			1,119.64
1 Mar	Balance b/d	954.26			

Dr		Wyvern Warehouse Limited			Cr
2001		£ p	2001		£ p
1 Feb	Balance b/d	108.40	15 Feb	Bank	105.69
17 Feb	Sales	427.91	15 Feb	Discount allowed	2.71
			28 Feb	Balance c/d	427.91
		536.31			536.31
1 Mar	Balance b/d	427.91			

(b)

Dr		Sales Ledger (Debtors) Control Account			Cr
2001		£ p	2001		£ p
1 Feb	Balances b/d	2,012.43	28 Feb	Sales returns	221.67
28 Feb	Credit sales	1,288.76	28 Feb	Cheques received from debtors	911.43
			28 Feb	Cash discount allowed	23.37
			28 Feb	Set-off	364.68
			28 Feb	Bad debts written off	59.28
			28 Feb	Balances c/d	1,720.76
		3,301.19			3,301.19
1 Mar	Balances b/d	1,720.76			

(c)   **Reconciliation of sales ledger control account with debtor balances**

	1 February 2001	28 February 2001
	£ p	£ p
Arrow Valley Retailers	826.40	338.59
B Brick (Builders) Limited	59.28	–
Mereford Manufacturing Company	293.49	nil
Redgrove Restorations	724.86	954.26
Wyvern Warehouse Limited	108.40	427.91
Sales ledger control account	2,012.43	1,720.76

17.7

PURCHASES (CREDITORS) LEDGER

(a)   Dr   **Apple Supplies Limited**   Cr

2001		£ p	2001		£ p
14 Feb	Purchases returns	157.20	1 Feb	Balance b/d	1,843.22
17 Feb	Bank	2,646.15	3 Feb	Purchases	1,027.98
17 Feb	Discount received	67.85	27 Feb	Purchases	849.36
28 Feb	Balance c/d	849.36			
		3,720.56			3,720.56
			1 Mar	Balance b/d	849.36

Dr   **Beatty Brothers**   Cr

2001		£ p	2001		£ p
1 Feb	Balance b/d	51.47	3 Feb	Purchases	150.68
28 Feb	Balance c/d	99.21			
		150.68			150.68
			1 Mar	Balance b/d	99.21

Dr   **J Johnson**   Cr

2001		£ p	2001		£ p
24 Feb	Bank	978.51	1 Feb	Balance b/d	675.38
24 Feb	Discount received	25.09	10 Feb	Purchases	328.22
		1,003.60			1,003.60

Dr   **Mereford Manufacturing Company**   Cr

2001		£ p	2001		£ p
28 Feb	Set-off	364.68	1 Feb	Balance b/d	478.29
28 Feb	Balance c/d	113.61			
		478.29			478.29
			1 Mar	Balance b/d	113.61

Dr		Newtown Equipment Limited			Cr
2001		£ p	2001		£ p
11 Feb	Bank	684.86	1 Feb	Balance b/d	684.86
18 Feb	Purchases returns	105.68	28 Feb	Balance c/d	105.68
		790.54			790.54
1 Mar	Balance b/d	105.68			

Dr		W Wright			Cr
2001		£ p	2001		£ p
6 Feb	Bank	962.52	1 Feb	Balance b/d	987.20
6 Feb	Discount received	24.68	10 Feb	Purchases	476.38
28 Feb	Balance c/d	476.38			
		1,463.58			1,463.58
			1 Mar	Balance b/d	476.38

(b)

Dr		Purchases Ledger (Creditors) Control Account			Cr
2001		£ p	2001		£ p
1 Feb	Balance b/d	51.47	1 Feb	Balances b/d	4,668.95
28 Feb	Cheques paid to suppliers	5,272.04	28 Feb	Credit purchases	2,832.62
28 Feb	Cash discount received	117.62	28 Feb	Balance c/d	105.68
28 Feb	Purchases returns	262.88			
28 Feb	Set-off	364.68			
28 Feb	Balances c/d	1,538.56			
		7,607.25			7,607.25
1 Mar	Balance b/d	105.68	1 Mar	Balances b/d	1,538.56

(c) **Reconciliation of purchases ledger control account with creditor balances**

	1 February 2001	*28 February 2001*
	£ p	£ p
Apple Supplies Limited	1,843.22	849.36
Beatty Brothers	*(51.47)	99.21
J Johnson	675.38	nil
Mereford Manufacturing Company	478.29	113.61
Newtown Equipment Limited	684.86	*(105.68)
W Wright	987.20	476.38
Net balances	4,617.48	1,432.88

* debit balances

Purchases ledger control account:

Debit	(51.47)	(105.68)
Credit	4,668.95	1,538.56
Net balance	4,617.48	1,432.88

CHAPTER 18: THE JOURNAL AND CORRECTION OF ERRORS

18.1 (b)

18.2

business transaction	*primary accounting record*
• credit sale of a fixed asset	• journal
• credit purchase of goods from a supplier	• purchases day book
• returned credit purchases to the supplier	• purchases returns day book
• customer returns goods sold on credit	• sales returns day book
• cheque received from a debtor	• cash book
• credit sale of goods to a customer	• sales day book

18.3 (a)

18.4

	primary accounting record	*debit*	*credit*
(a)	purchases day book	purchases account	Temeside Traders
(b)	sales day book	Malvern Models	sales account
(c)	journal	office equipment account	A-Z Computers Ltd
(d)	sales returns day book	sales returns account	Johnson Bros
(e)	cash book	bank account	Melanie Fisher
(f)	cash book	cash account	sales account
(g)	cash book	drawings account	cash account
(h)	cash book	Stationery Supplies Ltd	bank account
(i)	journal	bad debts written off account	J Bowen
(j)	purchases returns day book	I Johnson	purchases returns account

18.5   (a)   *error of omission*

Date	Details	Folio	Dr	Cr
			£	£
today	J Rigby	SL	150	
	Sales	GL		150
	Sales invoice no .... omitted from			
	the accounts			

(b)   *mispost/error of commission*

Date	Details	Folio	Dr	Cr
			£	£
today	H Price Limited	PL	125	
	H Prince	PL		125
	Correction of mispost – cheque no ......:			
	to H Price Limited			

(c)   *error of principle*

Date	Details	Folio	Dr	Cr
			£	£
today	Delivery van	GL	10,000	
	Vehicle expenses	GL		10,000
	Correction of error – vehicle no			
	invoice no			

(d)   *reversal of entries*

Date	Details	Folio	Dr	Cr
			£	£
today	Postages	GL	55	
	Bank	CB		55
	Postages	GL	55	
	Bank	CB		55
			110	110
	Correction of reversal of entries			
	on			

(e)   *compensating error*

Date	Details	Folio	Dr	Cr
			£	£
today	Purchases	GL	100	
	Purchases returns	GL		100
	Correction of under-cast on purchases			
	account and purchases returns account			
	on ....(date).......			

(f)   *error of original entry*

Date	Details	Folio	Dr	Cr
			£	£
today	L Johnson	SL	98	
	Bank	CB		98
	Bank	CB	89	
	L Johnson	SL		89
			187	187
	Correction of error – cheque for £89 received on ....(date)....			

18.6

	Date	Details	Folio	Dr	Cr
				£	£
(a)		Office expenses	GL	85	
		Suspense	GL		85
		Omission of entry in office expenses account – payment made by cheque no .... on ....(date)			
(b)		Suspense	GL	78	
		Photocopying	GL		78
		Photocopying	GL	87	
		Suspense	GL		87
				165	165
		Payment for photocopying £87 (cheque no .... on ....) entered in photocopying account as £78 in error			
(c)		Suspense	GL	100	
		Sales returns	GL		100
		Overcast on ...(date)... now corrected			
(d)		Commission received	GL	25	
		Suspense	GL		25
		Commission received on .... entered twice in commission received account, now corrected			

Dr			**Suspense Account**		Cr
2001			£	2001		£
30 Sep	Trial balance difference	19	(a)	Office expenses	85
(b)	Photocopying	78	(b)	Photocopying	87
(c)	Sales returns	100	(d)	Commission received	25
		197			197

CHAPTER 19: USING THE TRIAL BALANCE

19.1

JOURNAL

Date	Details	Debit	Credit
2001		£	£
1 Oct	Jeans Unlimited	420	
	Jeans-R-Us Limited		420
	Correction of mispost on 24 September		
1 Oct	Office equipment account	1,250	
	Stationery account		1,250
	Correction of error of principle on		

Author's note: the journal entries have been shown first so that all entries from the primary accounting records can be shown in the double-entry accounts.

PURCHASES (CREDITORS) LEDGER

Dalton & Co

Date	Details	Amount	Date	Details	Amount
2001		£	2001		£
1 Oct	Purchases returns	94	1 Oct	Balance b/d	3,076
1 Oct	Balance c/d	4,580	1 Oct	Purchases	1,598
		4,674			4,674
			2 Oct	Balance b/d	4,580

Jeans-R-Us Limited

Date	Details	Amount	Date	Details	Amount
2001		£	2001		£
1 Oct	Purchases returns	141	1 Oct	Balance b/d	2,120
1 Oct	Balance c/d	5,219	1 Oct	Purchases	2,820
			1 Oct	Jeans Unlimited	420
		5,360			5,360
			2 Oct	Balance b/d	5,219

J & S Manufacturing

Date	Details	Amount	Date	Details	Amount
2001		£	2001		£
1 Oct	Bank	775	1 Oct	Balance b/d	3,491
1 Oct	Discount received	25	1 Oct	Purchases	1,034
1 Oct	Balance c/d	3,725			
		4,525			4,525
			2 Oct	Balance b/d	3,725

One-Stop Office

Date	Details	Amount	Date	Details	Amount
2001		£	2001		£
1 Oct	Stationery returns	47	1 Oct	Balance b/d	624
1 Oct	Bank	624	1 Oct	Stationery	423
1 Oct	Balance c/d	376			
		1,047			1,047
			2 Oct	Balance b/d	376

Wyvern Clothes

Date	Details	Amount	Date	Details	Amount
2001		£	2001		£
1 Oct	Bank	1,055	1 Oct	Balance b/d	2,610
1 Oct	Discount received	45	1 Oct	Purchases	1,457
1 Oct	Balance c/d	4,189	1 Oct	Purchases	1,222
		5,289			5,289
			2 Oct	Balance b/d	4,189

Other creditors

Date	Details	Amount	Date	Details	Amount
2001		£	2001		£
1 Oct	Jeans-R-Us Ltd	420	1 Oct	Balances b/d	78,842
1 Oct	Balances c/d	78,422			
		78,842			78,842
			2 Oct	Balances b/d	78,422

Reconciliation of purchases ledger control account with creditor balances

	1 Oct 2001	2 Oct 2001
	£	£
Dalton & Co	3,076	4,580
Jeans-R-Us Limited	2,120	5,219
J & S Manufacturing	3,491	3,725
One-Stop Office	624	376
Wyvern Clothes	2,610	4,189
Other creditors	78,842	78,422
Purchases ledger control account (see below)	90,763	96,511

GENERAL (MAIN) LEDGER
Purchases (Creditors) Ledger Control Account

Date	Details	Amount	Date	Details	Amount
2001		£	2001		£
1 Oct	Purchases Returns Day Book	282	1 Oct	Balances b/d	90,763
1 Oct	Bank	*2,454	1 Oct	Purchases Day Book	8,554
1 Oct	Discount received	70			
1 Oct	Balances c/d	96,511			
		99,317			99,317
			2 Oct	Balances b/d	96,511

* £775 + £1,055 + £624

Purchases Account

Date	Details	Amount	Date	Details	Amount
2001		£	2001		£
1 Oct	Balance b/d	428,494	1 Oct	Balance b/d	435,414
1 Oct	Purchases Day Book	6,920			
		435,414			435,414
2 Oct	Balance b/d	435,414			

Purchases Returns Account

Date	Details	Amount	Date	Details	Amount
2001		£	2001		£
1 Oct	Balance c/d	8,527	1 Oct	Balance b/d	8,327
			1 Oct	Purchases Returns Day Book	200
		8,527			8,527
			2 Oct	Balance b/d	8,527

Stationery Account

Date	Details	Amount	Date	Details	Amount
2001		£	2001		£
1 Oct	Balance b/d	3,650	1 Oct	Purchases Returns Day Book	40
1 Oct	Purchases Day Book	360	1 Oct	Office equipment	1,250
			1 Oct	Balance c/d	2,720
		4,010			4,010
2 Oct	Balance b/d	2,720			

Discount Received Account

Date	Details	Amount	Date	Details	Amount
2001		£	2001		£
1 Oct	Balance c/d	911	1 Oct	Balance b/d	841
			1 Oct	Cash Book	70
		911			911
			2 Oct	Balance b/d	911

Value Added Tax Account

Date	Details	Amount	Date	Details	Amount
2001		£	2001		£
1 Oct	Purchases Day Book	1,274	1 Oct	Balance b/d	8,347
1 Oct	Balance c/d	7,115	1 Oct	Purchases Returns Day Book	42
		8,389			8,389
			2 Oct	Balance b/d	7,115

Office Equipment Account

Date	Details	Amount	Date	Details	Amount
2001		£	2001		£
1 Oct	Balance b/d	7,750	1 Oct	Balance c/d	9,000
1 Oct	Stationery	1,250			
		9,000			9,000
2 Oct	Balance b/d	9,000			

Fashion Traders
Trial balance as at 1 October 2001

Name of account	Dr £	Cr £
Purchases ledger control		96,511
Purchases	435,414	
Purchases returns		8,527
Stationery	2,720	
Discount received		911
Value Added Tax		7,115
Cash	475	
Bank		600
Office equipment	9,000	
Sales ledger control	130,690	
Sales		758,174
Sales returns	12,364	
Discount allowed	1,497	
General expenses	25,842	
Wages and salaries	127,608	
Bad debts written off	1,762	
Warehouse equipment	85,250	
Stock at 1 Jan 2001	165,940	
Bank loan		40,000
Capital		115,324
Drawings	28,600	
	1,027,162	1,027,162

19.2

JOURNAL

Date	Details	Debit	Credit
2001		£	£
2 Oct	Bad debts written off account	80	
	Value Added Tax account	14	
	Victoria's Fashions		94
		94	94
	Bad debt written off on instructions of the accounts supervisor		
2 Oct	Bentley Stores	220	
	Bentley & Co		220
	Correction of mispost on 12 September		

Author's note: the journal entries have been shown first so that all entries from the primary accounting records can be shown in the double-entry accounts.

SALES (DEBTORS) LEDGER
Bentley & Co

Date	Details	Amount	Date	Details	Amount
2001		£	2001		£
2 Oct	Balance b/d	1,095	2 Oct	Bank	420
2 Oct	Sales	423	2 Oct	Bentley Stores	220
			2 Oct	Balance c/d	878
		1,518			1,518
3 Oct	Balance b/d	878			

BS Stores Limited

Date	Details	Amount	Date	Details	Amount
2001		£	2001		£
2 Oct	Balance b/d	1,870	2 Oct	Bank	1,825
2 Oct	Sales	752	2 Oct	Discount allowed	45
2 Oct	Sales	376	2 Oct	Balance c/d	1,128
		2,998			2,998
3 Oct	Balance b/d	1,128			

Just Jeans

Date	Details	Amount	Date	Details	Amount
2001		£	2001		£
2 Oct	Balance b/d	629	2 Oct	Sales returns	47
2 Oct	Sales	188	2 Oct	Bank	240
			2 Oct	Discount allowed	10
			2 Oct	Balance c/d	520
		817			817
3 Oct	Balance b/d	520			

Southwick Stores

Date	Details	Amount	Date	Details	Amount
2001		£	2001		£
2 Oct	Balance b/d	145	2 Oct	Balance c/d	615
2 Oct	Sales	470			
		615			615
3 Oct	Balance b/d	615			

Teme Trading Co

Date	Details	Amount	Date	Details	Amount
2001		£	2001		£
2 Oct	Balance b/d	797	2 Oct	Sales returns	94
2 Oct	Sales	329	2 Oct	Balance c/d	1,032
		1,126			1,126
3 Oct	Balance b/d	1,032			

Victoria's Fashions

Date	Details	Amount	Date	Details	Amount
2001		£	2001		£
2 Oct	Balance b/d	94	2 Oct	Bad debts written off	80
			2 Oct	Value Added Tax	14
		94			94

Other debtors

Date	Details	Amount	Date	Details	Amount
2001		£	2001		£
2 Oct	Balances b/d	126,060	2 Oct	Balances c/d	126,280
2 Oct	Bentley & Co	220			
		126,280			126,280
3 Oct	Balances b/d	126,280			

Reconciliation of sales ledger control account with debtor balances

	2 Oct 2001	3 Oct 2001
	£	£
Bentley & Co	1,095	878
BS Stores Limited	1,870	1,128
Just Jeans	629	520
Southwick Stores	145	615
Teme Trading Co	797	1,032
Victoria's Fashions	94	–
Other debtors	126,060	126,280
Sales ledger control account (see below)	130,690	130,453

GENERAL (MAIN) LEDGER

Sales (Debtors) Ledger Control Account

Date	Details	Amount	Date	Details	Amount
2001		£	2001		£
2 Oct	Balances b/d	130,690	2 Oct	Sales Returns Day Book	141
2 Oct	Sales Day Book	2,538	2 Oct	Bank	*2,485
			2 Oct	Discount received	55
			2 Oct	Bad debt written off	80
			2 Oct	Value Added Tax	14
			2 Oct	Balances c/d	130,453
		133,228			133,228
3 Oct	Balances b/d	130,453			

* £420 + £240 + £1,825

Sales Account

Date	Details	Amount	Date	Details	Amount
2001		£	2001		£
2 Oct	Balance c/d	760,334	2 Oct	Balance b/d	758,174
			2 Oct	Sales Day Book	2,160
		760,334			760,334
			3 Oct	Balance b/d	760,334

Sales Returns Account

Date	Details	Amount	Date	Details	Amount
2001		£	2001		£
2 Oct	Balance b/d	12,364	2 Oct	Balance c/d	12,484
2 Oct	Sales Returns Day Book	120			
		12,484			12,484
3 Oct	Balance b/d	12,484			

Discount Allowed Account

Date	Details	Amount	Date	Details	Amount
2001		£	2001		£
2 Oct	Balance b/d	1,497	2 Oct	Balance c/d	1,552
2 Oct	Cash Book	55			
		1,552			1,552
3 Oct	Balance b/d	1,552			

Value Added Tax Account

Date	Details	Amount	Date	Details	Amount
2001		£	2001		£
2 Oct	Sales Returns Day Book	21	2 Oct	Balance b/d	7,115
2 Oct	Victoria's Fashions	14	2 Oct	Sales Day Book	378
2 Oct	Balance c/d	7,458			
		7,493			7,493
			3 Oct	Balance b/d	7,458

Wages and Salaries Account

Date	Details	Amount	Date	Details	Amount
2001		£	2001		£
2 Oct	Balance b/d	127,608	2 Oct	Balance c/d	128,858
2 Oct	Bank	1,250			
		128,858			128,858
3 Oct	Balance b/d	128,858			

Bad Debts Written Off Account

Date	Details	Amount	Date	Details	Amount
2001		£	2001		£
2 Oct	Balance b/d	1,762	2 Oct	Balance c/d	1,842
2 Oct	Victoria's Fashions	80			
		1,842			1,842
3 Oct	Balance b/d	1,842			

Bank Loan Account

Date	Details	Amount	Date	Details	Amount
2001		£	2001		£
2 Oct	Bank	500	2 Oct	Balance b/d	40,000
2 Oct	Balance c/d	39,500			
		40,000			40,000
			3 Oct	Balance b/d	39,500

Drawings Account

Date	Details	Amount	Date	Details	Amount
2001		£	2001		£
2 Oct	Balance b/d	28,600	2 Oct	Balance c/d	28,910
2 Oct	Cash	310			
		28,910			28,910
3 Oct	Balance b/d	28,910			

Fashion Traders

Trial balance as at 2 October 2001

	Dr	Cr
	£	£
Name of account		
Purchases ledger control		96,511
Purchases	435,414	
Purchases returns		8,527
Stationery	2,720	
Discount received		911
Value Added Tax		7,458
Cash	165	
Bank	135	
Office equipment	9,000	
Sales ledger control	130,453	
Sales		760,334
Sales returns	12,484	
Discount allowed	1,552	
General expenses	25,842	
Wages and salaries	128,858	
Bad debts written off	1,842	
Warehouse equipment	85,250	
Stock at 1 Jan 2001	165,940	
Bank loan		39,500
Capital		115,324
Drawings	28,910	
	1,028,565	1,028,565

CHAPTER 20: INFORMATION FOR MANAGEMENT CONTROL

20.1 • *decision-making* – deciding what action to take, eg production, new products

• *planning* – for the future of the business or organisation

• *control* – comparing actual results with forecasts and seeking reasons for discrepancies

20.2 • *costs* – materials, labour and expenses

• *income* – mainly from the sale of products or services

20.3 *Financial accounting*

• records transactions that have happened already

• looks backwards to show what has happened in the past

• is accurate to the nearest penny, with no estimated amounts

• is often a legal requirement to keep accounts (eg for VAT and Inland Revenue purposes)

• maintains confidentiality of information (eg payroll details, VAT returns, sales figures)

Management accounting

• uses accounting information to summarise transactions that have happened already and to make estimates for the future

• looks in detail at costs – materials, labour and expenses – and income

• looks forward to show what is likely to happen in the future

• may use estimates where these are the most useful or suitable form of information

• provides management with reports that are of use in running the business or organisation

• provides management information as frequently as circumstances demand – speed is often vital as information may go out-of-date very quickly

• is not sent to people outside the organisation – it is for internal use

• maintains confidentiality of information (eg payroll details)

20.4 • A discussion question which focuses on the management functions of decision-making, planning and control.

• The student is likely to undertake tasks such as balancing the petty cash book, reconciling control accounts with subsidiary ledgers, dealing with queries and correcting errors, identifying differences between cash book and bank statement.

• The managing director or chief executive will undertake tasks of a strategic nature, such as deciding whether the business is to expand, which new products are to be developed, reviewing the cost and income figures for last month, monitoring the overall performance of the business or organisation.

20.5 *planning*

The first step is to take a few minutes to plan the day's work in order of priority. This would appear to be:

• changes to payroll data to be made

• process the payroll

• take advantage of cash discounts on purchases invoices

• check the terms of payment to see whether other purchases invoices should be paid today

• write the cash book up-to-date

Comparing the bank statement with cash book and balancing the petty cash book (and restoring the imprest amount) appear to be lower priority.

decision-making

The two accounts assistants are briefed on your plan for the day. You ask the full-time assistant to enter the changes to the payroll and then to process the payroll, including preparation of cheques and BACS payments, and also to enter the transactions in the double-entry accounts.

The part-time assistant is to process payments for those purchases invoices at the end of their credit period.

You will go through the other purchases invoices to identify those that offer a cash discount for prompt settlement – you will take the decision as to whether or not the cash discount is worth taking. The part-time assistant will then process the payments for those that you decide to pay.

control

Progress on processing the payroll needs to be checked from time-to-time – the task needs to be completed so that the employees of Surestart Training can be paid on Friday. Later on you check the schedule for cheques and BACS payments, together with the entries made in the double-entry accounts. Cheques and the BACS payment schedule have to be signed by an authorised signatory to the company's bank account, so you will need to contact the administration manager to arrange this.

You supervise the work of the part-time assistant and resolve any queries in the processing of payments to creditors. You check the double-entry transactions in purchases ledger and cash book together with the cheques or BACS payments. The administration manager will need to arrange for the cheques and the BACS payment schedule to be signed.

If time permits you will ask for the cash book to be written up last week and balanced (which you can then check). You can then examine the bank statement for unpresented cheques and outstanding lodgements. Also, petty cash book can be balanced (which you can check) and the imprest amount can be restored.

summary

At the end of the day you can review progress to see how well your planning, decision-making and control has handled the workload of the accounts department. As the accounts supervisor will not be back for some days, you can plan for the next day's work ...

20.6 (a)   financial accounting

        (b)   financial accounting

        (c)   management accounting

        (d)   financial accounting

        (e)   management accounting (using financial accounting information)

        (f)   management accounting

20.7 • A discussion question which focuses on the different levels of management accounting information.

      • The student is likely to be asked for analysis of costs or income to date, cost centre information, comparisons between actual and estimated figures, estimates for next year of costs for which he or she is responsible.

      • The supervisor/manager is likely to be asked for an analysis of costs and/or income for particular products or services, a comparison of actual costs and/or income with forecasts and the reasons for discrepancies, estimated future costs and/or income for the section of the business or organisation for which the manager is responsible.

20.8 (a) • cost centres – section of a business to which costs can be charged

• profit centre – section of a business to which costs can be charged, income can be identified, and profit can be calculated

• investment centre – section of a business where profit can be compared with the amount of money invested in the centre

(b) • school or college – teaching departments, eg languages, science; also administrative departments, eg human resources, library, educational technology

• manufacturing business – by product, eg product A, product B, or by factory, eg Birmingham, Coventry

(c) A discussion topic which draws on the student's own experience

20.9

MEMORANDUM

To: Finance Director   **Ref:** AS
From: A Student, Accounts Assistant   **Date:** today
Subject: Costs and income for last year

I refer to your request for details of the costs and income for last year of each section of the business. Details are as follows:

	Newspapers and magazines £000s	Books £000s	Stationery £000s
Cost Centre			
• materials	155	246	122
• labour	65	93	58
• expenses	27	35	25
• total	247	374	205
Profit Centre			
Income from sales	352	544	230
less Costs (see above)	247	374	205
Profit	105	170	25
Investment Centre			
Profit (see above)	105	170	25
Investment	420	850	250
Expressed as a percentage	25%	20%	10%

If I can be of further assistance, please do not hesitate to contact me.

20.10 (a)   204250

     (b)   501050

     (c)   402150

     (d)   503700

     (e)   £240 to each centre: 203200, 303200, 403200, 503200, 603200

     (f)   403050

     (g)   304050

MEMORANDUM

To: Supervisor   **Ref:**   AS
From: A Student   **Date:**   today
Subject: Today's costs and income

As requested, I give details of today's costs and income that I have coded:

		£
•	materials (code numbers 1000–1999)	22,740
•	labour (code numbers 2000–2999)	840
•	expenses (code numbers 3000–3999)	90,985
•	income (code numbers 4000–4999)	16,640

Please let me know if I can be of further assistance.

CHAPTER 21: PRESENTING AND COMPARING MANAGEMENT INFORMATION

21.1   True.

21.2   False.

21.3   See text pages 459 to 460.

21.4   (a) £40,000 (b) £50,000 (c) £5,000 (d) £23,000 (e) £25,000 (f) £20,000

(g)

	2000 actual £000s	2001 actual £000s	2001 forecast £000s
Total Sales	1,430	1,555	1,520
Total Costs	920	1,048	1,005

The memo should point out that the difference between actual and forecast figures for 2001 is: Sales £35,000 higher than forecast, Costs £43,000 higher than forecast.

21.5 Monthly sales as per question (suggested left-hand column). Cumulative monthly sales (suggested right-hand column) quoted in £000s:

January £120, February £250, March £375, April £506, May £645, June £786, July £932, August £1,069, September £1,208, October £1,351, November £1,498, December £1,633.

21.6 A

21.7 (b) Sales total £727,000; costs £530,000

(c/d) Sales discrepancies; +£5,000, +£5,000, +£2,000, +£10,000, total +£22,000

Cost discrepancies; +£5,000, +£5,000, +£1,000, +£4,000, total +£15,000

21.8 Discrepancies: materials +£610, labour –£1,760, expenses –£600, total –£1,750. The memo should point out the reason for the labour costs, ie machine failure and added overtime.

21.9 (a) This is highly confidential information which could be communicated by letter, or by e-mail if the managers have restricted access mailboxes.

(b) This is not confidential and could be openly e-mailed or written on a note.

(c) The figures will not be confidential and can readily be e-mailed.

INDEX

also available from Osborne Books for AAT Intermediate . . .

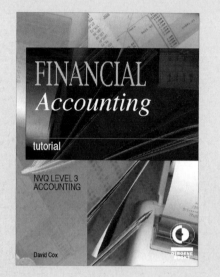

FINANCIAL ACCOUNTING

Tutorial

- easy-to-understand text
- questions and answers

ISBN 1 872962 38 6

FINANCIAL ACCOUNTING

Workbook

- extra questions, assignments and simulations
- Central Assessment practice material

ISBN 1 872962 43 2

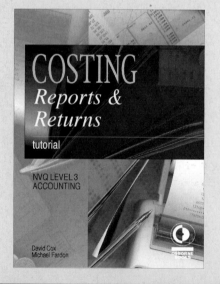

COSTING REPORTS & RETURNS

Tutorial

- two units in one book
- clear explanatory text

ISBN 1 872962 48 3

COSTING REPORTS & RETURNS

Workbook

- extra questions and simulations
- Central Assessment practice material

ISBN 1 872962 53 X

telephone 01905 748071 for details of our mail order service

or shop on-line at www.osbornebooks.co.uk